EXALTED SUBJECTS:
STUDIES IN THE MAKING OF RACE AND NATION IN CANADA

Questions of national identity, indigenous rights, citizenship, and migration have acquired unprecedented relevance in this age of globalization. In *Exalted Subjects,* noted feminist scholar Sunera Thobani examines the meanings and complexities of these questions in a Canadian context. Based in the theoretical traditions of political economy and cultural/post-colonial studies, this book examines how the national subject has been conceptualized in Canada at particular historical junctures, and how state policies and popular practices have exalted certain subjects over others.

Foregrounding the concept of 'race' as a critical relation of power, Thobani examines how processes of racialization contribute to sustaining and replenishing the politics of nation formation and national subjectivity. She challenges the popular notion that the significance of racialized practices in Canada has declined in the post–Second World War period, and traces key continuities and discontinuities in these practices from Confederation into the present. Drawing on historical sociology and discursive analyses, Thobani examines how the state seeks to 'fix' and 'stabilize' its subjects in relation to the nation's 'Others.' A controversial, ground-breaking study, *Exalted Subjects* makes a major contribution to our understanding of the racialized and gendered underpinnings of both nation and subject formation.

SUNERA THOBANI is an assistant professor at the Centre for Research in Women's Studies and Gender Relations at the University of British Columbia and former president of the National Action Committee on the Status of Women.

SUNERA THOBANI

Exalted Subjects

Studies in the Making of Race and Nation in Canada

UNIVERSITY OF TORONTO PRESS
Toronto Buffalo London

© University of Toronto Press Incorporated 2007
Toronto Buffalo London
Printed in Canada

Reprinted 2007, 2009, 2011

ISBN 978-0-8020-9227-4 (cloth)
ISBN 978-0-8020-9454-4 (paper)

Printed on acid-free paper

Library and Archives Canada Cataloguing in Publication

Thobani, Sunera, 1957–
Exalted subjects : studies in the making of race and nation in
Canada / Sunera Thobani.

Includes bibliographical references and index.
ISBN 978-0-8020-9227-4 (bound)
ISBN 978-0-8020-9454-4 (pbk.)

1. Canada – Race relations – Textbooks.   2. Nationalism – Canada –
Textbooks.   3. Canada – Social conditions – Textbooks.   I. Title.

FC104.T54 2007   305.800971   C2006-906616-7

This book has been published with the help of a grant from the Canadian
Federation for the Humanities and Social Sciences, through the Aid to
Scholarly Publications Programme, using funds provided by the Social
Sciences and Humanities Research Council of Canada.

University of Toronto Press acknowledges the financial assistance to its
publishing program of the Canada Council for the Arts and the Ontario
Arts Council.

University of Toronto Press acknowledges the financial support for its
publishing activities of the Government of Canada through the Book
Publishing Industry Development Program (BPIDP).

for my father, who never stood a chance …

Subject: a member of a state other than its ruler, especially one owing allegiance to a monarch or other supreme ruler; under the authority of; under the control or domination of another ruler, country, or government ... a person who is the focus of scientific or medical attention or experiment ... a thinking or feeling entity; the conscious mind; the ego, especially as opposed to anything external to the mind.

Exalted: 1. (of a person or their rank or status) at a high or powerful level: *it had taken her years of infighting to reach her present exalted rank* ... 2. of a noble, elevated or lofty nature: *his exalted hopes of human progress* ... 3. in a state of extreme happiness: *I felt exalted and newly alive.*

Exaltation: 1. a feeling or state of extreme happiness.   2. the action of elevating someone in rank or power.   3. the action of praising someone or something highly.

Oxford Dictionary of English

Contents

x   Contents

Acknowledgments

This book could not have been written without the magnanimous love and resolute support of my family. Sitara has taught me that I could indeed reach for the stars and, with fantastically good fortune, even have one fall into my lap. She has forgiven my every failing and transgression, as has my mother, Roshan. My sisters, Munira and Karima, never far from my heart, have loved me and believed in me even when I have not. Rich Wood, sojourner and deeply kindred spirit, has loved us beyond any expectation I could have had. Without the help of my aunt Laila, I would not have migrated to Canada and, even now, not one day goes by without her praying for my success. This book is as much the achievement of our collective learning and stubborn perseverance as it is of my academic training.

I am deeply indebted to all the women I have worked with in women's movements, as I am to the women who walked before me and paved the path I walk on. I am especially thankful to the women I worked with at NAC, where I learnt some of my most important lessons about the 'Canada' we were trying to transform. Fely Villasin, Winnie Ng, Salome Lucas, Judy Persad, Judy Rebick, Jackie Larkin, Cenen Bagon, Nandita Sharma, Shree Mulay, Fatima Jaffer, Miche Hill, Agnes Huang, Carolyn Wright, Fay Blaney, Terri Brown, Cecilia Diocsin, Amy Go, Avy Go, Lee Lakeman, and Jean Swanson, among many, many others, have taught me so much. Although we have since gone our (often very) separate ways, our struggles together (sometimes even against each other!) have been very important to me.

My deepest thanks also to Sherene Razack, Vanaja Dhruvurajan, Agnes Calliste, Yasmin Jiwani, and Patricia Monture-Angus, for their wonderful comradeship on the Researchers and Academics of Colour for Equity (RACE) Board. I have learned much from their scholarship, which sustains my own. Geeta Sondhi and Shelina Kassam have been a critical part of this sisterhood, they have always been there when I needed them.

I would also like to thank all my colleagues and students at the Centre for Research in Women's Studies and Gender Relations at the University of British Columbia for their support, especially during the very trying period in the aftermath of 9/11 and 'the' speech. Valerie Raoul and Tineke Hellwig, the directors of Women's Studies during that period, demonstrated great courage in their support of me in the face of the very public and high-profile demands for my head (figuratively and literally!). To all the friends and supporters who wrote letters to the university and to newspapers, who phoned radio stations and signed petitions, sent flowers and defended me in a myriad ways, I give my most heartfelt thanks. I am especially grateful to Hanifa Kassam for her kindness at the time, to Zool Suleman and Clayton Ruby for their legal advice, and to the Faculty Association at UBC for their support. A very, very special thank you is also owed to Valerie Raoul and Dawn Currie, the directors of women's studies at UBC when I first moved to the Centre. I owe many thanks to Sneja Gunew and Tineke Hellwig, who were the directors of women's studies while this book was being written. I am grateful also for the UBC Scholar award which allowed me the time to work on this manuscript.

Lakshmi Mudunoori, Mary Velji, Zubeida Rattansi, Noga Gayle, Barbara Binns, Zool Suleman, Mumtaz Ali, Arlene McLaren, Habiba Zaman, Ratna Roy, Larry Mosqueda, Aziz Choudhry, Parin Dossa, Tithi Bhattacharya, Rizwana Jiwa, Yuezhi Zhao, Mandakranta Bose, and Renisa Mawani have all been wonderfully supportive of my work. I am extremely grateful also to Susan Boyd and Dara Culhane for their willingness to share their work with me, and for reading the early drafts of this manuscript. The wonderful dinners and good cheer we have shared have warmed by heart and sustained me in an often alienating academic world. My sincere thanks also to Farah Zeb.

Rich Wood and Munira and Sitara Thobani have patiently and meticulously read drafts of this manuscript in its various stages, pushing me to develop my ideas further and to make this work as comprehensive and accessible as I could. Maureeen McNeil, Inderpal Grewal, and Rudolfo Torres reviewed a couple of the early chapters, and their encouragement for the manuscript's publication helped me to aim higher in reworking it.

Rupa Bagga, Itrath Syed, Almas Zakiuddin, and Cecily Nicholson provided valuable research assistance for this project, I thank them. I am greatly indebted to the two anonymous reviewers of this manuscript, and I bow deeply to the Fates for their supportive readings. Many thanks also to Virgil Duff and Anne Laughlin at the University of Toronto Press, and to Beth McAuley for her copy editing. All errors and shortcomings in this work are, most certainly, my own responsibility.

This book has been written in the hope that the next generation in my family, Sitara, Tariq, Kahlil, Qassim, Nick, and all their cousins, will always have the power to imagine Other-wise, no matter how tempting the seductions of nationality.

Some of the material presented in this book was previously published in various earlier incarnations. I am grateful to the publishers for their kind permission to allow the reprinting of this material:

- S. McIntyre and S. Rodgers, eds., *Diminishing Returns: Inequality and the Canadian Charter of Rights and Freedoms* (Ottawa: LexisNexus, 2006)
- *Race & Class* 42 (July 2000)
- *Canadian Journal of Women and the Law* 12, no. 2 (2000)
- *Atlantis: A Women's Studies Journal* 24, no. 2 (Spring 2000)
- *Canadian Woman Studies/les cahiers de la femme* 19, no. 3 (Fall 1999)
- M. Thappan, ed., *Transnational Migration and the Politics of Identity*, vol. 1 (New Delhi: Sage Publications, 2005)

I came into the world, imbued with the will to find a meaning in things, my spirit filled with the desire to attain to the source of the world, and then I found that I was an object in the midst of other objects.

Sealed into that crushing objecthood, I turned beseechingly to others. Their attention was a liberation, running over my body suddenly abraded into non-being, endowing me once more with an agility that I had thought lost, and by taking me out of the world, restoring me to it. But just as I reached the other side, I stumbled, and the movements, the attitudes, the glances of the other fixed me there, in the sense in which a chemical solution is fixed by a dye. I was indignant; I demanded an explanation. Nothing happened. I burst apart. Now the fragments have been put together again by another self.

Frantz Fanon,
Black Skin, White Masks

We must stand with Guaicaipuro, Paramacone [heroes of Venezuela, probably of Carib origin], and not with the flames that burned them, not with the ropes that bound them, not with the steel that beheaded them, nor with the dogs that devoured them.

José Martí, *Fragmentos*,
quoted in R.F. Retamar,
Caliban and Other Essays

The tradition of all the dead generations weighs like a nightmare on the brain of the living.

Karl Marx, 'The Eighteenth Brumaire of Louis Bonaparte'

INTRODUCTION

Introduction: Of Exaltation

We have inherent strengths as a people of wealth and talent who have forged a community of interests, express a humane set of values, know the struggle to assert and maintain a sense of independence and understand the benefits of working in collegial fashion. In a survey of forty-four countries, with thirty-eight thousand respondents, Canadians showed the highest level of satisfaction with their lives and the general direction of their country. There was not the degree of angst over crime, corruption and the state of public services as in other countries, nor by a long chalk the level of animus against immigration found virtually everywhere else. These characteristics, particularly the latter, translate into real strengths for Canada in pursuing a role in the world.

Canadians are on the road to global citizenship. Increasingly in work, travel, education and in personal and political engagement the world is our precinct, with international trade, finance, technology and business driving much of our global interests. But there is also a political, cultural and even moral dimension to our emerging role in global society ...

Lloyd Axworthy, *Navigating a New World*[1]

Fabrications of Nationhood

The figure of the national subject is a much venerated one, exalted above all others as the embodiment of the quintessential characteristics of the nation and the personification of its values, ethics, and civilizational mores. In the trope of the citizen, this subject is universally deemed the legitimate heir to the rights and entitlements proffered by the state. Even when disparaged as a gendered, sexed or classed sub-ject,[2] and even when recognized to be a subject in the Foucauldian (double) meaning of the word – that is, as *subject* to sovereign power *and* as an individualized and *self-constituting* entity[3] – in its *nationality*, this subject positively commands respect as the locus of state power.

The outsider, on the other hand, cast in the trope of the stranger who 'wants' what nationals have,[4] is a figure of concern.[5] Popularly defined as devoid of the qualities and values of the nation – as being quite alien to these – the stranger provokes anxiety, if not outright hostility. Indeed, the stranger has historically been suspected of embodying the potential for the very negation of nationality within modernity.[6]

There prevails in Canada a master narrative of the nation,[7] which takes as its point of departure the essentially law-abiding character of its enterprising nationals, who are presented (for the most part) as respon-sible citizens, compassionate, caring, and committed to the values of diversity and multiculturalism.[8] Having overcome great adversity in founding the nation, these subjects face numerous challenges from out-siders – 'Indians,' immigrants, and refugees – who threaten their col-lective welfare and prosperity. The nation of citizens has historically imagined itself vulnerable to innumerable such interlopers, compelled to resolutely face down the virulent, chaotic, criminal, and sometimes even deadly menaces posed by them. These outsiders have routinely been depicted as making unreasonable claims upon the nation and its precious finite resources.

In the national imaginary, Indians are presented as making impossi-ble and unending demands for special treatment in their claims to land and state funds and to hunting, fishing, and logging the nation's fast-depleting resources. Immigrants are made responsible for importing 'their' backward cultural practices into the country (dowry, honour kill-ings), along with their diseases (West Nile Virus, Asian Bird Flu, Ebola), their ancient murderous hatreds (the Sikh/Indian, Tamil/Sinhalese conflicts, among others), and their criminal gangs (Colombian drug dealers, Chinese 'snakeheads,' Indo-Canadian gangs). More generous representations of the nation's Others obviously also exist, but on the condition that their distinctive racialized experiences are denied and the political claims arising from such experiences are cheerfully relin-quished in their bid to claim a new hyphenated Canadian identity as beneficiaries of the nation's largesse.

In this book I examine how certain human beings have come to be constituted as Canadian nationals, a relatively new kind of subject, historically speaking. Explicating the technique of the exaltation of this subject as the embodiment of the particular qualities said to character-ize nationality, the following chapters make the case that this technique of power has been central to the processes of modern national forma-tion. In other words, exaltation has been key to the constitution of the national subject as a particular kind of human being, a member of a par-ticular kind of community, and, hence, ontologically and existentially distinct from the strangers to this community.

Benedict Anderson has famously argued that nations are commu-nities of imagination.[9] Tracing the trajectory of Canadian national-formation, in particular, of the constitution of the specific content of Canadian 'nationality' at key historical junctures, this book asks the fol-lowing questions: What do these communities of imagination imagine themselves to be? What specific characteristics does the Canadian nation imagine itself to embody? What were the historical conditions that enabled the emergence and crystallization of these particular quali-ties? What impact have these articulations of national selfhood had on Native peoples, the original inhabitants of the national territory? How were colonizers, settlers, and immigrants, who were the subjects and cit-izens of other states and societies in the first instance, (re)inscribed as Canadians? What disciplinary and regulatory practices enabled the reproduction of this particular kind of human subject?

Western ontologies have long been based in binary constructions with the self being constituted in relation to its excluded Other.[10] Echo-ing the Hegelian dialectic of the self and Other, master narratives of Canadian nationhood define the national's character relationally. The national is law-abiding where the outsider is susceptible to lawlessness; the national is compassionate where the outsider has a tendency to resort to deceit to gain access to valuable resources; the national is toler-ant of cultural diversity where the outsider is intolerant, placing loyalty to ties of kin and clan above all else; and, more recently, the national is supportive of gender equality where the outsider is irremediably patri-archal. Exalted through such narrations, which are inscribed into the juridical order and shape state policies and practices, the national sub-ject is not only existentially but also institutionally and systematically defined in direct relation to the outsider. Such exaltations function as a form of ontological and existential capital that can be claimed by national subjects in their relations with the Indian, the immigrant, and the refugee. The public disavowal of these outsiders' possession of such exalted 'national' qualities is daily evidenced in the sophisticated surveillance techniques, the pervasive border control technologies, and the exclusionary mechanisms deployed against them. The adversarial relationships posited through such discursive moves foreclose the possibilities for coevality, mutuality, and reciprocity.

In its essentials, this master narrative of Canadian nationhood has remained remarkably consistent throughout the (relatively) brief career of the nation. As its mythos recounts the challenges and tribulations the nation has imagined itself to encounter, it also reveals the nation's accounting of who and what it is in the world. Differences between nationals and outsiders are exaggerated, even as the commonalities within these groupings are inflated. National subjects who fail to live up to the exalted qualities are treated as aberrations; their failings as individual and isolated ones. The failings of outsiders, however, are seen as reflective of the inadequacies of their community, of their culture, and, indeed, of their entire 'race.' Conversely, their successes are treated as individual and isolated exceptions.

The categorization of human beings into Canadians, Indians, and immigrants ranks them in terms of their legalistic and sociocultural status. Significantly, it also reflects differences in the quality of the humanity that is said to motivate their actions and forms of behaviour, differences which consequently make them deserving of different claims and entitlements, and which call for different modalities for their management. This book examines how the governance of these subjects/objects has been organized through state policies and popular practices, producing certain subjects as exalted (nationals), others as marked for physical and cultural extinction or utter marginalization (Indians), and yet others for perpetual estrangement or conditional inclusion as supplicants (immigrants, migrants, and refugees).

Despite the many feminist and anti-racist critiques of modern nation formations, surprisingly little attention has been paid to the actual characteristics that are attributed to particular national formations, or to the qualities that are said to distinguish their subjects from Others. I argue that the practices that organize such attributions ought not to be naturalized or individualized. That is to say, they should not be treated as rooted primarily in the character of the individual national subject, with the nation being simply the aggregate of such qualities. Rather than considering such traits as shaped by the innate nature of national subjects in the manner of humanist and liberal traditions, I attribute such characterizations to politicized social processes and trace their interactions with the individualized self-constituting practices of national subjects. In other words, I interrogate and problematize the particular national character traits attributed to the Canadian nation by contesting the notion that they are the inherent aspects of the members of this community, and that some human communities have an excess of certain traits while others suffer a dearth of the same.

Beginning with the recognition that the subjection/subjectification of individuals, communities, and nations takes shape within historically specific contexts and conditions, and that these processes are temporally and spatially defined, I examine the conditions of possibility that enabled Canadians to be inscribed as distinct human subjects with specific national traits at particular historical junctures. I will describe how these characteristics, in being appropriated for subjects-as-nationals, were simultaneously closed off to other human beings who have been spatial and temporal cohabitants. Although the focus of my work is on the constitution of Canadian nationality and its respective forms of alterity, it clearly has relevance for studies of race and national formation within 'modern' societies in general. It has especial relevance to constructions of nationhood in other settler societies, including the United States, Australia, New Zealand, South Africa, and Israel.

Of Exaltation and Commandment

Modernist accounts of the subject as a stable, conscious, unified, and enduring figure, whose actions are shaped primarily by reason, are deeply ingrained within Canadian national mythology. The national subject-as-citizen stands at the centre of Canadian national history. The humanist tradition that permeates such accounts treats human beings as distinct from other species in their capacity to reason, a capacity which is integral to their very nature. Such hegemonic accounts of the modern subject have been strongly contested by a number of theoretical traditions.[11] Rather than being essentially rational, unitary, or stable, human beings – as subjects – are theorized within these traditions as constituted and self-constituting within particular discursive formations. Eschewing the notion that subjects are always already constituted prior to – and outside of – social relations, various philosophers, as well as social and psychoanalytic theorists, have described individuals as subjects-in-process, only partially conscious of their motives and actions and inhabiting multiple subject positions with various intersecting identities and interests. Subjectivity has thus been defined as historically and socially

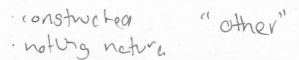
· constructed   " other"
· nothing nature

demonize vs. exalt

subjectivity
modes of power
in-group identify.

8 Introduction

contingent, shaped in and through social relations, as contradictory and fragmentary, inherently unstable and in constant flux.

Many contemporary theorists draw upon Foucault's radical theorization of subjectivity within modernity as shaped by the coming together of knowledge and power within discursive formations.[12] In his studies of the constitution of the human being in the modernist guise of the individuated 'subject,' Foucault named this form of disciplinary power *bio-power*, highlighting its productive and enabling capacities. Bio-power permeates the constituted/self-constituting practices of the subject.[13] Foucault argued that the disciplinary forms of knowledge produced about/by this subject organize the particular 'field of possibilities in which several ways of behaving, several reactions and diverse comportments may be realized,' and that power thus shapes the parameters for subjection/subjectification.[14] Subjectivity, then, cannot be adequately approached without situating it in the context of the discursive power that pervades and moulds it.[15] The 'new' managerial techniques of power Foucault identified 'instill[ed] controlling habits and value-sustaining self images' into subjects, replacing the 'juridico-discursive' form of sovereign power characteristic of the previous monarchal era. With the transition to modernity, technologies of governance changed from the prohibition of particular acts to life-controlling and 'subject-shaping management of action.'[16] That this knowledge/power nexus produces the subject as an effect of power was Foucault's now legendary claim. This nexus constitutes the subject even as it professes to be describing it.

Foucault's theories of discourse, power, and subjectivity have elicited a highly polarized response from feminists. Some have lauded his insights for undermining the traditional rationalist rights-based paradigm, which they define as inherently exclusive, while others have vociferously rejected these insights as irreconcilable with the political project of women's emancipation.[17] Notwithstanding these critiques, Foucault's insights regarding the historical fabrication of the modern subject through deployments of particular political technologies are applicable to my analysis of the deployment of *exaltation* as a technique of power that acculturates the national subject into the isomorphic state-nation-subject triad. While the punitive institutions and technologies examined by Foucault – the prison, the clinic, and the school – integrated disciplinary measures into the body politic, the efficacy of the complementary technique of exaltation, which seduces subjects into reproducing their nationality, has been of no less consequence.

In the case of Canada, the historical exaltation of the national subject has ennobled this subject's humanity and sanctioned the elevation of its rights over and above that of the Aboriginal and the immigrant. The inscription of specific 'national' characteristics into these subjects as elements of their innate humanity elevates such traits from the realm of 'natural' human existence and writes them into the body politic, thereby catapulting them into the sociocultural realm of the national symbolic. Even as exaltation ennobles and elevates the national community, it simultaneously 'naturalizes' these qualities as the essential possessions of the individual subjects who form this community, as being intrinsic to – and reflective of – the superior order of their humanity, arising organically from their natural, individual moral goodness.

The worthiness that exaltation endows onto national subjects does not function at an abstract level. In order to reproduce social relations with some measure of success, such exaltations are concretized and harnessed within a moral economy as very particular qualities and characteristics, recognizably human and self-evidently positively weighted. In this, the technique of power naturalizes itself and appears as guileless, unexceptionally and ordinarily reflecting an ethical polity that is based on the inherently superior qualities of national subjects and not on the repertoire of governance.

The practices that enable exalted characteristics to be writ large onto the political identity of the nation simultaneously enable its individual subjects to constitute their own subjectivity as the embodiment and actualization of such characteristics. The institutionalization of particular 'good' qualities shapes the field of possibilities within which this subject can attempt to unify and stabilize its individual subjectivity *through its* nationality. The process is facilitated by the institutions of the state which recognize these qualities and reflect them back onto the subject as a measure of its own human worthiness. Exaltation thus provides both form and content to an attendant 'structure' of humanity, as it were, which becomes available to these subjects and facilitates their experience of 'belonging' to the community through the recognition and cultivation of such shared nationality.[18]

The endowment of specific characteristics to particular subjects conceals the social relations within which these subjects are enmeshed, fetishizing them instead as the naturalistic originators of these particularly laudable human qualities.[19] Exaltation thus endows ontological coherence and cohesion to the subject *in* its nationality, grounding an abstract humanity into particular governable forms.

In Canadian historiography, exaltation conceals the colonial violence that marks the origin of the national subject, even as it mythologizes and pays obeisance to its national essence. This process remains the necessary condition for the ongoing efficacy of national formation. It also furthers the subject's solidarity with other modern and civilized nation formations that are said to share similar qualities. As a technique of power, exaltation thus politicizes certain human qualities, defining the national community as a whole as possessive of these regardless of the actual attributes of individual members.

Providing concrete form to the national subject's humanity, exaltation furthers national formation such that the subject becomes empowered by its bonds with other subjects constituted as its compatriots and, most importantly, with the state as the aggregate of this community of belonging. Inhabiting exalted national subject positions crystallizes this subject's sense of self and of its belonging in the social world. Further, the fetishization of the national subject as citizen has enabled this subject to experience itself within the liberal fantasy as endowing power to the state, turning reality on its head. Exaltation thus organizes a modality for the subject's bonding with the state and nation. In this way, the technique enables the state to channel the abstract humanity and general 'goodness' of its subjects into socially organized and politically identifiable subject positions, prescribed by, and within, the field of power. Interpellated with very specific characteristics, the national subject becomes enabled to reproduce its sense of goodness in the forms that are legitimately prescribed within a particular national formation, bonding with its compatriots and reproducing the nation's mores and values along with, and as intrinsic to, the subject's own individualized humanity.

Exalted characteristics provide an axis for the grounding of the subject, for 'fixing' its inherently unstable sense of self, offering a national structure to its humanity that promotes cohesion in the face of the fragmentary and highly dissociative aspects of subjectivity. As such, this technique unceasingly adapts itself to the changing priorities and challenges of new historical conditions in order to guard against the erosion of the nationality of subjects. As I will demonstrate in the following chapters, the appropriation of an expanding array of characteristics for exaltation of the Canadian national subject remains ongoing, assuming particular formulations in response to changing global and local circumstances and balance of forces.

Inscribed into state practices, exaltation institutionalizes the differential rights of nationals in relation to their Others, thereby realizing its very tangible and material correspondences and consequences in the social order. As a positive and enabling play of power that institutionalizes valorized characteristics within the state machinery through their association with rights and entitlements, exaltation simultaneously stabilizes state power as collective embodiment (and protector) of such characteristics. The state organizes the rights that nationals come to acquire by treating these as rooted in their own intrinsic worthiness and not in the colonial violence, political, racial, and ethnic dominations, or in the classed and gendered exploitations and resistances that characterize nation formations. The qualities that are said to be shared by nationals bring them directly into the orbit of the state.

As exaltation makes particular subject positions available for appropriation by individual national subjects, the desire to conform to the affirmative meanings of these life-enhancing identifications becomes inculcated in individuals. It gives rise to the desire to belong to the valorized category of humanity, to be seen by others as embodying it, to be able to claim it as one's own property. As national subjects hail each other as possessive of these qualities, they override the 'internal' differences (those of gender, class, region, province, and so on) among themselves in the face of outsiders by expelling and excluding these outsiders as devoid of the very same qualities.

While Foucault's theory of the positive and enabling form of power I have drawn upon is useful in explicating the constitution of the modern subject in its nationality, it is also disquieting for its Eurocentric focus. His concept of bio-power as productive needs to be approached with some caution, particularly so when attention is directed to the nation's outsiders, that is, to those human beings who have been constituted as 'non-western' and 'non-modern' and, therefore, not in possession of the exalted qualities of 'western' nationalities. Then, it becomes apparent that the transition from the juridico-discursive to bio-power described by Foucault is much more complex and problematic, as are the various processes of subject formation within modernity.

Within the global context, Achille Mbembe defines 'commandment' as the absolutist modality of the force relations that govern(ed) the lives of colonized populations. By commandment Mbembe refers to the violence that was intrinsic to the establishment and endurance of colonial sovereignty. It includes the 'combined weakness of, and inflation of, the notion of right: weakness of right in that, in the relations of power and authority, the colonial model was, in both theory and practice, the exact opposite of the liberal model of debate and discussion; inflation of right in that, except when deployed in the form of arbitrariness, and the right of conquest, the very concept of right often stood revealed as a void.'[20] In other words, commandment meant that sovereign violence was 'authority' and 'morality' at the same time. It erased the 'distinction between ends and means,' making the very notion of the 'rights' of the colonized quite expendable.[21]

Mbembe persuasively argues that modernity is characterized by the use of 'multiple concepts of sovereignty' and not a singular form (that of bio-power), and that these different modalities of power are complementary and coterminous. More recently, he has formulated the concept of 'necropolitics' to define the form of sovereign power wherein 'the ultimate expression of sovereignty resides, to a large degree, in the power and the capacity to dictate who may live and who must die.'[22] If multiple forms of sovereignty co-exist within modernity, as Mbembe argues, the processes that shape the subjectivities of the various human beings who are exposed to these different modalities of power can likewise be anticipated to be different.

In the case of Canada, the marking of Native peoples as 'doomed to extinction' is an example of the necropolitics indispensable to the incipient sovereignty. The creation of reserves and, subsequently, the residential school system as the sites for the physical and cultural extinction of these peoples points to the long history of the deployment of necropower in the service of the colonial order and the (re)production of the national subject.

A similar recognition of the deployment of different modalities of power, and of different and coterminous processes of subject-formation, informed Frantz Fanon's earlier analysis of the colonial world. Fanon highlights the dialectic between the psycho-political life of the colonized human being and the socio-economic basis for the (non)recognition of their humanity.[23] Critiquing Hegel's dialectic of the self and the Other, Fanon argues that the alienation of colonized peoples was rooted in the colonial dialectic that shaped the subjectivity of both Black and white 'men.' In other words, the Black man's subjectivity and his alienation were constituted in the racial violence that typified the encounter of the 'native' with modernity and that defined the form of sovereign power imposed upon their lives. Fanon's analysis, drawn upon by Mbembe, refutes the notion of a linear and complete transition from a regime of routine overt violence to bio-power. Instead, it recognizes that the colonized subject/object was formed – and lives – within the soul-destroying brutality that was/is the colonial order.

If violence never leaves the frame in Fanon's account of the process of subjection/subjectification of colonized peoples, neither does his recognition of the relationality of this process. In Fanon's oft-repeated formulation, the Black man's experience of subjectivity was such that, 'not only must the black man be black; he must be black in relation to the white man.'[24] As W.E.B. Du Bois also recognized, the Black man had to contend with a 'double-consciousness,' so that the 'sense of always looking at one's self through the eyes of others, of measuring one's soul by the tape of a world that looks on in amused contempt and pity' remained central to subject-formation.[25] Within this encounter, the question of reciprocity in the balance of power that permeates modernist and liberal ideologies remains no more than a rhetorical gesture. 'What is often called the black soul is a white man's artifact,' Fanon argues.[26] Recognition of this imbalance in force relations – where the colonizing subject had recourse to the violence that upheld his imposition of the non-human status on his Other – was encoded onto the 'bodily schema' of the colonized man. It was 'epidermalized,' so that regardless of what the Black man believed himself to be, or struggled to become, even the young white child could reduce him to a 'phobogenic' object, as Fanon himself experienced.[27]

Exaltation of the Canadian national subject has likewise precluded the possibility of reciprocity, so that even when these subjects were engaged in the murder, enslavement, and torture of Natives, as many were in the founding of the nation, these acts of commandment were constituted/instituted not only as acts in law but also as the very Law of civilization. Viewed as being in the national interest, such acts, as I discuss in chapter 1, were given legal sanction. This sanction was central to the constitution of nationals as 'law-abiding' even in their most murderous actions. While explicitly 'forgotten' within popular Canadian historiography, these moments (and actions) remain implicitly celebrated in the master narrative of nationhood.   public memory

In the foundational moment of Canadian nationhood, the British and French were cast as the true subjects of the colony, while the Indian was expelled as the enemy outsider. Constituted as 'preferred races' within the bureaucratic apparatus of the settler state, the settlement activities of these true subjects accomplished the violent dispossession of Aboriginal populations – a dispossession duly constituted and preserved as 'lawful' to this day. In chapter 1, I examine the methods and strategies by which race as law became central to processes of national formation in which the Christian European as civilized subject was exalted over the heathen Aboriginal, fossilized as essentially primal in nature. This constitution of the national as a juridical subject enabled him/her to indeed become law-abiding in relation to the Indian. The nationalizing of the law-abiding quality ennobled the national while closing it off to Aboriginal peoples (and other populations) who were fantasized in the juridical imaginary as the embodiment of pure lawlessness, regardless of the actual characteristics and practices of particular individuals within these respective communities-in-formation.

The invention of the Indian as a lawless *political* identity was legislated and bureaucratized by the colonial state through the 'legal apartheid' that is the Indian Act.[28] Bonita Lawrence argues that the colonial fantasy embedded in this Act, and the policies designed to accomplish its realization, shape(d) the terrain within which Native identities and subjectivities have been fashioned. Arrogating the power to determine which Native persons were/are Indian, and which were/are to be denied this status, their legal classification into Indian, Metis, half-breed, non-status, and so on by the state established and consolidated a calamitous hierarchy of authenticity among them. Lawrence points out that such legislated codifications disrupted and distorted 'older indigenous ways of identifying the self in relation not only to collective identity, but to the land.'[29] The connection to a land base remains crucial, even if increasingly materially tenuous, to Aboriginal identity and subject formation.

Lawrence also notes that the question of 'authenticity' deeply shapes the state's treatment of Aboriginal peoples. The law demands, as proof of aboriginality, an adherence to a lifestyle supposedly reflective of the 'primordiality' fantasized in the national imaginary in order to even consider the validity of the land claims of Aboriginal peoples; 'Canadian court decisions continue to restrict Aboriginal rights to precontact activities.'[30] Canadian society likewise looks for the 'performance' of such 'authenticity' in order to recognize Native peoples as such. Whether denigrated or pitied as the embodiment of lawlessness and devoid of civilization, whether designated as status or non-status, the figure of the Indian has remained an enduring mark against which national identity is delineated.

In addition to the figure of the Native, there is yet another figure constituted as incommensurable with nationality within the foundational moment of Canadian national formation. This is the figure of the non-European (the non-western) immigrant. As Sara Ahmed observes in her analysis of migration, racialization, and nation-formation, this stranger plays a vital role in how national subjects experience and configure the national community's borders.[31] Fetishized as having 'linguistic and bodily integrity,' Ahmed argues that the figure of the stranger is treated as having an existence prior to its encounter with the national subject. Rejecting the notion of such prior independent existence, she argues instead that it is in the national subject's encounter with the 'stranger,' who is already *known* to be strange, that the stranger is brought into being:

> The figure of the stranger is far from simply being strange; it is a figure that is painfully familiar in that very strange(r)ness. The stranger has already come too close; the stranger is 'in my face.' The stranger then is not simply the one whom we have not yet encountered, but one whom we have already encountered, or already faced. The stranger comes to be faced as a form of recognition: we recognize somebody as a *stranger*, rather than simply failing to recognize them.[32]

Ahmed observes that it is in the subject's encounter with the stranger, in the experience of the proximity of this alien who has come too close, that the subject's sense of being 'at home' in the national space is reiterated. It is in this encounter that the stranger is defined as being out of place, as not belonging. Ahmed also notes that the fetishization of the stranger's 'strangerness' obscures 'the social and material relations which overdetermine their existence.' Revisiting both the Hegelian dialectic of the self and Other, and Althusser's formulation of interpellation/hailing as bringing the subject into being, Ahmed argues that the subject is not only formed in its recognition by the Other, but also by its differentiation among the various others that it encounters. Through this process of differentiation, the 'subject comes to inhabit or dwell in the world.'[33] Furthermore, she argues that whether these (differentiated) strangers are fetishized through forms of exclusion as the site of danger or tolerated as sites of diversity, they nevertheless remain ontologized as strangers. The various dangers that immigrants-as-strangers have been historically said to present to the Canadian nation are examined in the following chapters, and their inclusion in the ideology of multiculturalism is discussed in chapter 4.

Targeted for exclusion from entry into Canada as 'non-preferred races' up to mid-twentieth century and from social and political life when the need for their labour made their presence indispensable to the further development of the national economy, immigrants have acquired a highly qualified inclusion as cultural/social/linguistic strangers since the 1970s. Their earlier exclusion from citizenship gave way to their subsequent integration into its disciplinary regime of (unequal) rights as the demographic pressures of the falling national birthrate, declining European emigration, and the dictates of the global economy made such inclusion inevitable. This qualified inclusion is examined in chapters 3 and 4. Chapters 5 and 6 examine the limits to, and the transformation of, this inclusion in the context of the global economic restructuring of the last decade of the twentieth century and the subsequent 'war on terror' that ushered in the twenty-first.

Much of the recent literature on migration examines the construction of the immigrant as a (racial and cultural) stranger to the nation, a figure that has most often been cast in the trope of the 'suffering' immigrant. The focus has remained mainly on the forms of discrimination and inequalities experienced by migrants in their dislocation, relocation, (lack of) access to citizenship, and integration into receiving countries.[34] Some of this literature seeks to highlight the heterogeneity within these categories, to examine the inequalities among them, and to stress the agency of migrating subjects in their accommodations to, compromises with, and contestations of discriminatory policies and practices.[35] However, the immigrant is a much more complex and ambiguous figure in settler societies like Canada than has generally been suggested. Propelled into the circuit of migration by structural conditions within the global economy, as well as by their desires for economic advancement, migrants have been party to the ongoing colonization of Aboriginal peoples.

Politically and socially located in the liminality between settlers/nationals and the Aboriginal populations marked for physical and/or cultural elimination, these migrants became implicated, whether wittingly or otherwise, in the dispossession of Aboriginal peoples. The more immigrants have sought their own inclusion and access to citizenship, the more invested they have become, with very few exceptions, in supporting the nation's erasure of its originary violence and its fantasies of progress and prosperity. Chapter 2 examines how the collusion of immigrants with an exclusionary white national-building project was to become historically systematized through the institution of citizenship.

Immigrants have thus constituted their subjectivity variously as abject outcasts, humble supplicants, deserving and stubborn claimants, ambitious assistants in the hegemonic Euro-Canadian project, and sometimes even as revolutionary activists. While they have asserted their

identity as a positive one in the face of its denigration by national subjects, they have been much more reticent to challenge the relatively
higher status and opportunities accorded to them vis-à-vis Aboriginal
peoples within the racial hierarchy of the settler society. This observation does not seek to diminish the magnitude of the dehumanization
and exploitation experienced by immigrants, for the effects of such violence have been far too damaging and long lasting to neglect. Nor
should it be read as a suggestion that these immigrants were the authors
of, or even equal partners in, the colonial project.

Colonial practices were developed and defended unabashedly by
European powers, the violence of this process implemented and sanctioned by the force of their states and the cooperation of their willing
populations. Moreover, without the support or protection of the settler
state, or indeed that of the states in their source countries, the immigrants categorized as 'non-preferred races' had precious little room to
manoeuvre in securing their own migrations, relocations, and access to
citizenship. I argue that although the suffering of immigrants cannot be
minimized neither can their participating in (and benefiting from) the
ongoing cultural and material domination of Aboriginal peoples.

In the settler colony-cum-liberal democracy, the status of the immigrant remains ambivalent, fraught within the dynamics of the structural
forces that propel their migration and their subsequent relocation
between indigenous peoples and nationals.[36] Addressing the polyvalent
role of immigrants requires confronting the enormity of the crimes perpetrated against Aboriginal populations, crimes immigrants have often
colluded with. It requires the highlighting of the complex racial hierarchy developed by colonizing powers that introduced and sustained force
relations not only among settlers and Aboriginal peoples but also
among the other racialized groups ranked in the Canadian hierarchy as
lower than whites but higher than Aboriginal peoples. In other words, it
requires examination of the specific roles played by all non-indigenous
populations in the ongoing colonial project, even as the force relations
among these various populations are taken into consideration. Keeping
their sights fixed firmly on gaining equality with nationals, immigrants
have thus far, with few exceptions, ignored the interrogation of their
own positionality with regard to Aboriginal peoples. Most have largely
forsaken the possibilities for building alliances with Aboriginal peoples,
failing to imagine a future of sovereignty for them and what their own
location within such a future might be.

Immigrant identities and the perceptions of their collective interests have been deeply shaped by the state's legal classification of their status as racial outsiders, by their internalization of the racial hierarchy and racisms organized in state policies, by the spatial configurations of the reservation system, and by their (qualified) inclusion in the nation-state's economic and cultural imperialist projects abroad. Relating to Aboriginal peoples largely through the national symbolic, upholding its imagining of the self-determination of Aboriginal peoples to be an impossible political objective, most immigrants continue to articulate their own interests only with regard to the status and interests of nationals.

With their own grasp on citizenship remaining highly tenuous, their claims to membership within the nation and their right to state protection being constantly challenged, immigrants are compelled to protect their hard-won rights against organized attempts to erode these. Nevertheless, transcending the racialization that shapes the national-formation and immigrants' exclusions requires a fundamental challenge to the colonial domination of Aboriginal peoples. This racial domination lies at the very heart of Canadian nationhood, at the core of its identity and its social, juridical, and moral order. It shapes the various modalities of sovereign power. In the absence of a politics that envisions the transcendence of this foundational relation, the anti-racist aspirations of immigrants remain limited at best, and complicitous at worst.

The racial configurations of subject formation within settler societies are thus triangulated: the national remains at the centre of the state's (stated) commitment to enhance national well being; the immigrant receives a tenuous and conditional inclusion; and the Aboriginal continues to be marked for loss of sovereignty. However, given that processes of identity formation are relational, and given that national identity becomes instated in the 'encounters' between national subjects and their various others, the identity of this subject remains inherently and enduringly unstable. It can be realized (fleetingly) only in its ongoing strange encounters with its differentiated others. This identity cannot be stabilized in perpetuity; it cannot be positively fixed once and for all as an identity-for-itself, as an identity-in-itself. In other words, national identity cannot find positive closure. Yet it is just such fixity and impossible stabilization that exaltation, as a political technique, seeks to accomplish.

Constituting Nation, Constituting Race

If the subject is theorized as an effect of power, the nation, as the community of such subjects, cannot be otherwise defined. In its modern

form as the proper domain of state power, and in its function of confer-
ring political legitimacy onto the state, the nation is also an effect of
power. The discourse that structures narratives of Canadian nationhood
reproduces the naturalization of the nation as arising from the common
bonds of shared history, race and ethnicity, values, characteristics, and
aspirations.[37] The Canadian national enterprise is popularized even
now as 'A new people building a new land.'[38] Such racist and romantic
simplicity elides the complex history I examine in this work.

National formations rely heavily on the common-sense conception of
a common identity and interest as being 'immanent in the people' and
of the state as formed by 'the people,' who see their best interests
reflected in its workings.[39] In other words, they rely on a conception
of the nation 'as a deep, horizontal comradeship.'[40] The nation thus
comes to acquire an awareness of itself as an entity – and gains international recognition – as the aggregate of its members and the reflection
of their particular qualities in a corresponding state system. It differentiates itself from (and allies itself with, as is the current situation with the
United States) other nations on the basis of such shared values and
qualities and the common interests they are said to give rise to.

In contrast to the modern doctrine infusing the master narrative
of the nation form as a universalist project, deeply connected to the
Enlightenment ideals of rationality, progress, liberty, and equality, postcolonial theorists such as Partha Chatterjee and Peter Fitzpatrick have
drawn attention to the irrationality of the project. Locating nationalist
thought within the idioms of the Enlightenment, Chatterjee notes that
both are ultimately impossible projects: 'If nationalism expresses itself
in a frenzy of irrational passion, it does so *because* it seeks to represent
itself in the image of the Enlightenment and *fails* to do so. For Enlightenment itself, to assert its sovereignty as the universal ideal, needs its
Other; if it could ever actualize itself in the real world as the truly universal, it would in fact destroy itself.'[41] Chatterjee's point is that the nation
formation has to contend with a central contradiction: the nation pur-
ports to be part of the universalizing project of bourgeois-rational
modernism, marked by its civilizational values, yet it is simultaneously
marked by its own particularities that are based on principles of exclusion and the 'frenzy of irrational passion.' The nation's particularities
are defined against its Others, that is, against those who do not share
these particularities. Hence, the possibility of the realization of the universalizing mission said to be inherent in the project of nation formation, and in the Enlightenment, is rendered ultimately impossible.

Like Chatterjee, Fitzpatrick notes that the nation proclaims itself to be universal,[42] and insists on defining itself as 'the exemplar of universal qualities,' for example, of modernization, democracy, and human rights. Yet the nation also defines itself in relation to that which lies outside itself, which thus lies outside the orbit of the universal. In this, he concurs with Chatterjee, the realization of the nation's universality is made impossible:

> As universal, the nation can have no positive limits and would, without more, lack identity. It can no longer take identity through some mythic sameness with a transcendent model outside itself. Rather, identity and its limits are generated from within, as it were, by constituting the nation as universal in opposition to what is exceptional to its universality. What is 'other' to the universal can only be absolutely, irremediably other. It must exist in a distinct region, quite 'outside' the realm of the universal, and remain as a point of constant opposition to it. This dynamic of identity inevitably results in the 'failure' of the nation as universal. The nation must exclude the other – and so be non-universal – in order to be universal.[43]

Fitzpatrick asserts that a national identity that is formed primarily in relation to that which it excludes remains tied to the excluded, and the excluded Other becomes the nation's 'double.' The Other becomes constituted as both an identity oppositional to that of the nation as well as a threat to the completion of the nation: 'The nation thus remains connected to its double and the possibility of reversion to a savage or barbaric past represented by the double has to be constantly guarded against.'[44] The nation depends on the preservation of its distinctiveness if it is to maintain its self-identity and its coherence. It is this exclusion of the Other that 'renders the nation possible and coherent,' and should this exclusion ever be transcended, the nation itself would cease to exist.[45]

Exaltation delineates the specific human characteristics said to distinguish the nation from others, marking out its unique nationality. As such, it invokes a particular subject position that can be inhabited only by the nation's insiders, or those who seek inclusion – and are allowed to do so – by effacing their difference from this position. The association of precious rights and entitlements with such an identity creates a material stake in protecting these from the encroachments of irresponsible and undeserving Others, and exaltation gives rise to the desire among insiders to defend and protect this valued nationality from the perversions and pollutions of the Other. It creates the desire to limit the Other's access to the much coveted nationality it organizes. In Canada, this exercise of power has provided tangible benefits to the national subject, in the form of proprietorial access to land, citizenship, mobility, employment, social entitlements – in short, to all the accoutrements that the state accords its citizen-subjects. As such, exaltation wins over the national's support for the various disciplinary techniques deployed by the state against outsiders to preserve the coherence of the nation, to preserve this subject's privileged access (even if ultimately illusory) to the state.

The nation's privileges, however, must be carefully regulated to discipline insiders even as outsiders are barred from accessing them equitably. Juxtaposing the shared interests of nationals vis-à-vis outsiders against the conflicting 'internal' interests (classed, gendered, and so on) among them, exaltation subsumes such 'internal' divisions through the structure of humanity that it makes available for all national subjects to claim. Within the boundaries of the nation, 'national' worthiness is certainly not distributed evenly among all subjects. Bourgeois men, for example, are endowed with greater worthiness, and their claim to national resources are deeper and stronger than those of women, the working class, and other such internally devalued groups. Yet even as such groups are denigrated in relation to elite men, exaltation endows worthiness in the form of existential capital to even those in the lowest echelons of the national community, to the most despised genders, and to the poorest classes among them.

This existential capital allows denigrated insiders to affirm their proximity to privileged insiders. It enables denigrated insiders to claim they belong to the same order of humanity as privileged insiders on the basis of their shared nationality. Exaltation enables nationals with even the lowliest 'internal' status to claim civilizational and existentialist *parity* with privileged insiders and civilizational *superiority* in their daily encounters with outsiders. Exaltation is thus crucial to the institutionalization of gendered and other forms of 'internal' divisions within the nation, as it serves to suture the resulting ruptures within the nation, functioning to overcome the forms of 'internal' distinctions and denigrations within the context of a shared 'national' ennoblement. It enhances the social and moral being of all those included within the national enterprise and promotes aspirations of acquiring greater nationality among even the most despised of insiders.

As noted above, Sara Ahmed has argued that it is through the proximity of the stranger who has come too close that the subject experiences itself as being 'at home.' Designating such interactions as 'strange encounters,' Ahmed argues that they are 'impossible to grasp in the present.'[46] Each present encounter encapsulates and 'reopens' past such encounters. In the Canadian context, contemporary encounters between national subjects and Native peoples likewise recap and reopen their past encounters of colonization, genocide, and dispossession, instantiating the past as living present. In the case of the immigrant, contemporary encounters reopen older histories of preferred and non-preferred races, of the internments and racial hatreds expressed in the projects to build Canada as a 'white man's country.'

Despite the most ardent claims of national mythology, the constitution of the nation as Euro-Canadian, that is, as white, was neither a natural nor a predestined inevitability. The shape that this nation has assumed was the outcome of the intense race battles waged – and the race compromises forged – by the state and nation(als) against those whom they sought to eliminate and exclude. It is also the outcome of the continuing efficacy of the contemporary strange encounters that reproduce the force relations that sustain national formation.

Strange encounters between Canadian subjects and immigrants remain pervasive within daily life. 'Vancouver Could See Race Riots: Study Says,' the headline of the *Vancouver Sun* informs its readers;[47] 'Report: Keep Immigrants Out of the Big Three Cities,' advises *The Province*.[48] Both articles refer to a study that claims unless 'major changes' are made to immigration policy, Toronto, Vancouver and other cities could well erupt in race riots. The study identifies a 'feeling' of being 'overwhelmed' as the cause of such potential riots: 'those in major cities – including existing immigrant populations – are feeling overwhelmed.' Too many immigrants concentrated in too few cities, a mixture seemingly certain to result in explosive violence! The implicit assumption is that despite the lack of violence in the nation's values and character, the accumulation of 'strangers' could push nationals to violent extremes. Such mass-mediated encounters reinforce the national anxieties and insecurities so crucial to holding the nation together: 'they' will invade/provoke, 'we' will suffer/lose control.

Concealing the relations of force immanent in the nation's encounters with immigrant others – indeed reversing these relations – the nation is presented in such encounters as the vulnerable entity, and immigrants are depicted as powerful enough to provoke violent explosion. The threat of racial violence in 'our' cities worries, even traumatizes, the nation of subjects.[49] To further underscore the point that it is not the racism of nationals that constructs immigrants as perpetual outsiders that should be alarming, 'existing immigrant populations' are also reported to share the feeling of being 'overwhelmed.' Large numbers of these 'existing immigrant populations' are de jure citizens, indeed, many of them second and third generation Canadian-born. The linking of immigration with race riots, chaos, and violence, and after 9/11, with the 'terrorist threat,' encapsulates and reproduces past encounters in the present moment. Such actual and paranoid encounters remain as crucial to the constitution of the 'sense of nationality' among Canadians as they do to the maintenance of their exalted ontological distance from immigrants. These encounters enact and substantiate the national body politic at the multiple sites of daily life. In the post–9/11 period, the ongoing efficacy of national-formation thus depends upon the success of such processes of 'nationalization,' to borrow a term from Etienne Balibar. Internal differences are subsumed within the context of the larger siege said to have been launched against their shared western identity. Protection of nationals from explosive racial and terrorist violence through the strengthening of state power becomes the solution to the presence of potentially lethal racial strangers.

Stabilizing the Unstable: The State and the Subject

If both subject and nation are inherently unstable – perhaps even impossible – enterprises, the task assumed by the modern state has been to stabilize them, to essentialize them – fix them, as it were – as the subjects/objects of its power. Where Gramsci's concept of 'hegemony' and Althusser's of 'ideological state apparatus' call into question the idea of clear lines of separation between state and civil society, Foucault's concept of bio-power demolishes this distinction entirely by identifying the 'capillary' forms of power permeating social life. After Foucault, no neat division can be drawn between state and civil society, between state power and the individual, between state and the nation: all are inextricably and deeply interpenetrating and constitutive of each other. Through its stabilization of the subject and nation, to the extent that the state is able to do so, it stabilizes itself by reinforcing its domain of power. The reproduction of the state itself thus depends on this ongoing isomorphism of state, nation, and subject.

The concept of 'government,' as defined by Foucault, was far broader, much deeper, and more extensive than the institutional apparatus of the state. Using the term in its sixteenth-century meaning (by which it 'designated the way in which the conduct of individuals or states might be directed'),[50] Foucault argues that government 'designated the disciplinary management of people.'[51] His notion of 'government' certainly includes the institutional mechanisms of the state, but is not restricted to it. Power governs human conduct, and while the state is a key aspect of this governance, force relations are pervasive throughout the social formation, permeating even the most civil, private, and intimate aspects of human life. Having argued that disciplinary regimes of knowledge incorporate the technologies of power that enable the 'pervasive management' of populations, Foucault highlights the active participation of these populations in their governance and the complex role of the state within this regime.[52] Power is exercised, appropriated, contested, and reproduced in daily social life, through the state apparatus certainly, but also through the intimate and interpersonal interactions among the state's subjects/objects of power.

Partha Chatterjee argues that the 'true' form of colonial rule was that of a 'modern regime of power destined to never fulfill its normalizing mission because the premise of its power was the preservation of the alienness of the ruling group.'[53] This 'colonial difference,' Chatterjee writes, was that of race, and the universalization and normalization of disciplinary forms of power could never be realized, given the racialized nature of the colonial project. The impossibility was institutionalized within the state's classification and hierarchical ranking of various sectors of the population, which delineated their differential and unequal access to state power and the rights vouchsafed by the state.[54]

In contrast to the popular notion that the modern state sought only to protect the homogeneity of its nation when it resorted to racial classifications and distinctions, David T. Goldberg has persuasively argued that racialization has been constitutive of the modern state formation, not only of nation formation. Racialized distinctions instituted by the state *produced* homogeneity out of heterogeneous populations: 'Colonialism ... was about managing heterogeneity, dealing with difference through imposition and restriction, regulation and repression.'[55] Demonstrating that 'the *modern* state has always conceived of itself as racially configured,' Goldberg notes that 'race is integral to the emergence, development and transformations (conceptually, philosophically, materially) of the modern nation-state.'[56] State practices remain crucial to the project of constructing 'national' homogeneity out of heterogeneity. They determine access to nationality and its rights and entitlements, and in an especially sophisticated manner given the increase in international migration from the global South into the 'developed' world during the post–Second World War era.

In a similar vein, Michael Omi and Howard Winant argue that the 'racial state' has been central to the organization of the 'racial formation' that is the United States. This state not only intervenes in racial conflicts within society but also, by institutionalizing racial identities within society, is itself the 'preeminent site' of this conflict.[57] The United States, Winant writes, and 'practically every other multiracial society on earth – was a rigid caste society, a virtual race dictatorship, a *herrenvolk* democracy.'[58] The challenges presented by the Civil Rights movement of the 1960s to this racial dictatorship, had the effect of replacing 'racial domination' with 'racial hegemony.'

Likewise, the Canadian state can be accurately characterized as having been an overt racial dictatorship up until the mid-twentieth century, as it organized the governance of Aboriginal populations through the Indian Act and upheld racialized immigration and citizenship legislation to produce a homogeneous and dominant white majority. The outright exclusion of non-preferred races from social and political life gave way after the mid-twentieth century to a liberalization of immigration and citizenship legislation, as I discuss in chapters 2 and 3.

Immigration provided a vital and necessary source of labour, underwriting the nation's prosperity in the post-war era. The welfare state capitalized on the economic contributions of these immigrants, but constituted immigrant families as a burden on the nation-state and subjected them to unequal social entitlements primarily through immigration regulations, key among which were the family sponsorship regulations. However, the increasing proximity of significant numbers of racial strangers in daily life and their demands for inclusion required sustained attention and policy deliberation. In this context, the adoption of multiculturalism as state policy enabled the state to represent itself as having accomplished the transformation from an overt racial settler state to its present liberal-democratic form.[59] While this liberalization enabled the qualified inclusion of immigrants to a historically unprecedented degree, it did so by maintaining their constitution as cultural strangers to the national body.

When the state faltered in its racial commitments – as it sometimes did in relation to the pressures exerted by the demands of economic expansion as well as by the political mobilizations of its denizens – nationals responded by flexing their political muscle to maintain their legally and socially exalted status. Here, it is useful to turn to Chatterjee's tracing of the complicated relationship between state officials,

European subjects, and the colonized Indian populations in the reproduction of the 'colonial difference' during the British Raj. Public service in the state bureaucracy, freedom of speech, and public opinion
were all defined primarily with regard to the European population, and
not the 'natives.'[60] In one particular instance where colonial officials in
Bengal arranged for the translation of a native play in order to familiar-
ize themselves with native opinion, the white population rose 'up in
arms':

> What incensed the planters was the implicit suggestion that the govern-
> ment could treat 'native' public opinion on the same footing as European
> opinion ... This the planters were not prepared to countenance. The only
> civil society that the government could recognize was theirs; colonized sub-
> jects could never be its equal members. Freedom of opinion, which even
> they accepted as an essential element of responsible government, could
> apply only to the organs of this civil society; Indians, needless to add, were
> not fit subjects of responsible government.[61]

Chatterjee's study demonstrates that even as the colonial state actively
structured processes of racialization, legislating and institutionalizing
these, the 'civil' society of colonizing populations played no small role
in the reproduction of such hierarchies, realizing them on the ground,
so to speak.
   As was the case within the Raj, settlers and other European immigrants in Canada mobilized political pressure to protect their exalted
status and rights against those considered to be outsiders and a threat to
their nationality. Spurring on and supporting the state's institutionalization of the 'colonial difference' within its bureaucratic machinery, the
national population was not timid in its agitations to further its own
racial interests and claim sole occupation of the 'nation-space.' It positioned itself as the only 'public' whose opinion was to matter. These subjects reproduced their exalted status, and the force relations invested in
it, through the rituals and practices shaping the daily experience of
racial/national life across the country.
   While the mobilizations of white populations to maintain control of
the national space can be found throughout Canadian history, as Ghassan Hage has discussed in the case of Australia,[62] the restructuring of
the welfare system in the final decade of the twentieth century provides
an excellent example of the mobilizations of nationals and the state in
just such a process of fomenting 'public' opinion that was decidedly hos-

tile to immigrants, as is demonstrated in chapter 5. Increased polarization and economic insecurity accompanied the escalating globalization of the last two decades of the twentieth century in Canada, as was the case in many other countries. The heightened visibility of the corporate agenda driving the state's neo-liberal free-trade policies strengthened public cynicism and undermined the legitimacy of the state. In this climate, the Liberal government of the day launched extensive cross-country public consultations as part of the restructuring of social security and immigration programs. Calling upon 'Canadians' to participate in these, the state provided a national platform for a heightened articulation of the popular anti-immigrant animus discernible in the public sphere since the mid-1980s.

The texts organizing the public consultations constructed immigrants in general, and immigrant women in particular, as an economic burden on the nation, thus helping to crystallize a 'national' consensus in support of limiting their access to citizenship. Whereas the corporate-driven reform of the social security system threatened to deepen the fissures extant within the body politic, the anti-immigrant discourse, sanctioned and further popularized by the consultations, enabled the state to direct animosity towards immigrants and to legitimize itself as the defender of national prosperity against the encroachments of these strangers. The call to Canadians to participate in the reviews elevated their national identity above their other identities (of class and gender, for example) in the face of what were presented as 'foreign' threats unleashed by the forces of globalization. The intensification of race as a relation of power was organized from 'above,' as it were, through these exercises in 'participatory democracy,' which deepened the institutionalization of unequal citizenship rights and strengthened the nation-state relation for the coming century.

Although the Canadian nation-state continues to represent itself on the global stage as a model multicultural society, the 9/11 attacks on the United States exposed the limits of this particular aspect of the nation's self-exaltation. In the era of the global 'war on terror,' the Canadian nation-state is being unabashedly reconstituted as essentially 'western' in nature, its national security and civilizational values (along with those of its American ally) threatened by a fanatical and medieval non-western Other. The crazed non-Christian savage of an earlier era of western expansion has been made to re-enter the global stage with a vengeance. If immigrants and refugees were imagined primarily as a burden on tax-paying Canadians and a drain upon scarce social and economic resources at the end of the twentieth century, the 'Muslim' immigrant and refugee has come to be constructed as a serious threat to the very survival of the west at the dawn of the new millennium.

The discourse of terrorism promoted in/by the media and the specific measures enacted at border crossings exalt the nation as western and racialize the category Muslim, constituting it as the quintessential enemy of the western nation and its allies. Chapter 6 examines how the post–9/11 archetypal image of the Muslim terrorist has become the prototype through which the dark-skinned, bearded, or turbaned male and the dark-skinned, headscarf-wearing woman are framed – and feared – within the nation's imagination. This chapter also examines how the active support of the Canadian nation-state for American Empire-building is profoundly transforming the meanings of Canadian nationality and citizenship.

Predictably enough, the terrorist threat has served up yet another round of public demands and justifications for increased restrictions on immigration and citizenship. Such contemporary constructs of immigrants draw upon countless examples of the strange encounters littered throughout Canadian historiography, giving the contemporary narratives their scaring/staying power.

Racial difference, as a system of hierarchy within the Canadian sociolegal system constitutes the national, the Indian, and the immigrant as different kinds of *legal* beings. In the process, it also constitutes them as different kinds of *human* beings at a symbolic level, ascribing to them different characteristics and values as intrinsic aspects of their (quasi)humanity. These fundamental categories of Canadian nationhood, born in the violence of the colonial encounter, have been institutionalized and sustained by the relations of force still invested in them. It is the relationality among them, sedimented in state practices, that gives these categories their concrete – sometimes explosive, but always political – meanings.

The Canadian, as national subject, has come to experience the state as enabling power, providing it with a much coveted access to citizenship and its valued privileges. While this experience of nationality is tangible in its materiality, it also shapes an exalted subjectivity that facilitates the reproduction of the nation-state relationship. The related and simultaneous primitivization of Aboriginal peoples has been deployed in giving concrete content to the exaltation of nationality. Subjected to commandment in the sense used by Mbembe, the capacity of Aboriginal peoples for sovereignty remains thwarted by the exigencies of this exaltation. Indeed, the future possibilities of Canadian nationhood remain contingent upon the successful destruction of Aboriginal sovereignty, or its effective containment.

In the following pages, I have worked at the interstices of state practices, which define the range of socio-political possibilities, *and* the self-constituting practices of national subjects, within which certain subject positions become mobilized as definitional of the national self. I make the case that underneath the sanitized garb of a postmodern, multiracial, multiethnic 'tolerant' Canada, beats the heart of a stubbornly colonial national-formation, sharing a common imaginary with other white settler societies. *how public memory sustain this imaginary?*

National identity, like the geographical borders of the nation and its regime of citizenship rights, remain contested terrain, for outsiders as well as insiders. Transforming the site of their intended extinction, the reserve, into a site for their cultural survival, Aboriginal peoples continue to challenge (and to accommodate) their domination. Immigrants challenge the practices that mediate their unequal access to citizenship, carving out indelible spaces for themselves in the Chinatowns and Little Indias which sustain their communities across the country. This book has been written in the hope that if the nation(al) has been imagined as an exalted and racialized entity thus far, it is possible – no, it is imperative – to imagine it Other-wise.

LAW

1 Founding a Lawful Nation

The colonial world is a world cut in two. The dividing line, the frontiers are shown by barracks and police stations. In the colonies it is the policeman and the soldier who are the official, instituted go-betweens, the spokesmen of the settler and his rule of oppression ...

The zone where the natives live is not complementary to the zone inhabited by the settlers. The two zones are opposed, but not in the service of a higher unity. Obedient to the rules of pure Aristotelian logic, they both follow the principle of reciprocal exclusivity. No conciliation is possible, for of the two terms, one is superfluous. The settlers' town is a strongly built town, all made of stone and steel. It is a brightly lit town; the streets are covered with asphalt, and the garbage cans swallow all the leavings, unseen, unknown and hardly thought about. The settler's feet are never visible, except perhaps in the sea; but there you're never close enough to them. His feet are protected by strong shoes, although the streets of his town are clean and even, with no holes or stones. The settler's town is a well-fed town, an easygoing town; its belly is always full of good things. The settlers' town is a town of white people, of foreigners.

The town belonging to the colonized people, or at least the native town, the Negro village, the medina, the reservation, is a place of ill fame, peopled by men of evil repute. They are born there, it matters little where or how; they die there, it matters not where, nor how.

Frantz Fanon, *The Wretched of the Earth*[1]

The foundational narrative of Canadian nationhood is a romance of pioneering adventure, of wild lands and savage peoples, of discovery and enterprise, of the overcoming of adversity through sheer perseverance and ingenuity. Europeans discovered an unknown continent and

Europe's intrepid masses came to it: a new people building a new world.[2] Certainly some of these settlers might have been unscrupulous. They may have taken unfair advantage of the natives. But the Indians were lawless heathens and warring tribes, their societies hardly evolved since the dawn of humanity. They were invested in violent rivalries with each other, they lacked the necessary structures for civilized life and were prone to caprice and deceit. The majority of the settlers, immigrants really, were by and large Christian, law-abiding, and industrious, the embodiment of western civilization, goes the story.

More critical accounts of the nation's origins can also occasionally be heard, offering some variations on this national fantasy. It may be allowed that the harm inflicted on Aboriginal populations might have been more extensive than previously understood, that it was sometimes inflicted deliberately. Remorse for this harm might be expressed. Some of the settlers may have acted with intentional cruelty, perhaps even with criminal violence, but they were the exception and their behaviour certainly no worse than could be found among the Indians themselves, or among other societies in past centuries. Such acknowledgments and expressions of remorse are usually rather speedily followed with the assertion that the Indians were too naïve, too unaware of the historical or global forces at work, unable to comprehend fully their own best interests. If they had not resisted the mostly well-intentioned Europeans who settled Canada, if the bad apples among the settlers had been dealt with more sternly by the law, if the Indians had embraced the values of Christian community, of modernity and the rule of law sooner, such tragedies might have been averted. Specific forms of violence or acts of disenfranchisement are also occasionally publicly denounced, but are mediated with reminders that these misbegotten acts were not perceived as such in centuries past, that they should not be judged from the vantage point or the ethos of the present. Contemporary moral judgments should certainly not be applied to the early pioneers and settlers, it is asserted, and certainly not to their descendents who today are the well-meaning citizens of a benevolent liberal democracy that treats its Aboriginal population with a heightened consciousness of their human rights. This community of citizens is vastly more humane than its southern neighbour, the United States.

The originary mythology outlines a rational and coherent explication of how the nation was founded. It describes how the encounter of Europeans with Native peoples during the fur trade led to European settlement and the creation of a new nation (complicated somewhat by negotiations of contending British and French interests), which subsequently made an orderly and largely peaceful transition to a modern, liberal-democratic society. The claim of the lawfulness of the foundations of nationhood (despite some serious excesses), and of national subjects as essentially law-abiding (with some exceptions) is sustained, if not strengthened, by the processes of confession, expressions of profound regret, and celebrations of the constitutional and legislative inclusion of Aboriginal peoples into the embrace of the law.

Radical critiques of Canadian national identity and its self-constituting narratives must contend with the claim that the nation's sovereignty was established, and has been since upheld, under the auspices of the law. The claims that nationals largely abided by the laws of the day, even if it was unfortunate that some laws were discriminatory, that some transgressions went unpunished, and some treaties with Aboriginal peoples went ignored, have to be addressed.[3] For this emergent legality has been indispensable to the sense of national identity that fostered the integration of first the British and French, and subsequently various other Europeans, into the 'imagined' national community as exalted juridical subjects.

In this chapter, I examine such claims to the lawfulness of nationality, highlighting the violence that upholds it. The encounter between the colonizer and the colonized in Canada, as elsewhere, 'was marked by violence and their existence together – that is to say the exploitation of the native by the settler – was carried on by dint of a great array of bayonets and cannons.'[4] In the colonial order, reason and violence did not exist in an oppositional relation, instead, they were both complementary and coterminous: '[C]olonialism provides a site where the banishment of violence through taboo, its opposition to reason, can be subverted. In the colonial project, violence is not opposed to reason; rather, it completes the colonialist logic.'[5] In other words, the reason of conquest required violence, such that the violence of conquest became reasonable. It is therefore imperative to examine the relationship of the violence of colonialism to the law and the transmogrification of this violence into the legalistic structures of the settler society.

In his studied deconstruction of the law, cultural critic Walter Benjamin has unravelled the liberal conception that infuses all western national mythologies, including the Canadian one, of law as an objective, reasoned, and consistent system of rule far beyond the primitive use of brute force. Instead, Benjamin argues that law is integrally and intimately connected to violence and power: 'Lawmaking is power-making, assumption of power, and to that extent an immediate manifestation of violence.'[6] Claiming that neither the making of the law, nor its preservation is feasible in the absence of the violence that enables its exercise, Benjamin writes that 'the function of violence in juridical creation is twofold, in the sense that lawmaking pursues as its end, with violence as its means, *what* is to be established as law, but at the moment of its instatement does not depose violence; rather, at this very point of lawmaking and in the name of power, it specifically establishes as law not an end immune and independent from violence, but one necessarily and intimately bound up with it.'[7]

In a similar vein, Giorgio Agamben draws attention to the arbitrary nature of the law, arbitrary not only in its application but in its very constitution. The notion of sovereignty in western thought relies ultimately upon the sovereign's power over life, and Agamben identifies a central paradox that lies at the heart of sovereignty, that is, 'the fact the sovereign is, at the same time, outside and inside the juridical order.'[8] With the power to decide what is to be included in the law and what is to be excluded from it, the sovereign stands both above and outside the law. Moreover, even after the law has been instituted, the sovereign determines states of exception to the law, determinations that rely on the power of violence to be decisively instituted in moments of 'crisis.' Agamben cautions us against concluding that what is defined as being outside the law is wholly unconnected to it: 'On the contrary, what is excluded in the exception maintains itself in relation to the rule in the form of the rule's suspension. *The rule applies to the exception in no longer applying, in withdrawing from it.* The state of exception is thus not the chaos that precedes order but rather the situation that results from its suspension.'[9] Both Benjamin and Agamben agree that since the preservation of the law depends on the ongoing recourse to violence, the law can never free itself from the violence that is the most significant element of its constituting moment.

The claim of liberal political theory – that the separation of the juridical sphere from the monarchical realm within modern societies ensured greater fairness and equality and fewer infractions of the rule of law – has also been soundly debunked by Foucault, who notes that, 'in political thought and analysis, we still have not cut off the head of the king.' Foucault continues:

> Yet, despite the efforts that were made to disengage the juridical sphere
> from the monarchic institution and to free the political from the juridical,

the representation of power remained caught within this system. Consider the two following examples. Criticism of the eighteenth-century monarchic institution in France was not directed against the juridico-monarchic sphere as such, but was made on behalf of a pure and rigorous juridical system to which all the mechanisms of power could conform, with no excesses or irregularities, as opposed to a monarchy which, notwithstanding its own assertions, continuously overstepped the legal framework and set itself above the laws. Political criticism availed itself, therefore, of all the juridical thinking that had accompanied the development of the monarchy, in order to condemn the latter; but it did not challenge the principle which held that law had to be the very form of power, and that power always had to be exercised in the form of the law. Another type of criticism of political institutions appeared in the nineteenth century, a much more radical criticism in that it was concerned to show not only that real power escaped the rules of jurisprudence, but that the legal system itself was merely a way of exerting violence, of appropriating that violence for the benefit of the few, and of exploiting the dissymmetries and injustices of domination under cover of general law. But this critique of law is still carried out on the assumption that, ideally and by nature, power must be exercised in accordance with a fundamental lawfulness.[10]

Although Foucault did not specifically engage with it, a critique of power and the law that rejected the notion that a 'fundamental lawfulness' could ever be applicable in the colonial situation had been forwarded by Frantz Fanon, the radical theorist of race and decolonization. Valuable as the critiques of law by Foucault, Benjamin, and Agamben remain, none of them specifically address(ed) the establishment of western sovereign power as law in the colonial circumstance. Agamben's Eurocentric focus, like that of many other theorists, does not allow him to recognize that colonialism (which predated his analysis of the concentration camp as the paramount site of exception) has been central to the development of western forms of sovereignty as racialized forms of power through the institution of the law within modernity. Nor does it allow him to recognize that quintessential zone of exception, the reserve, which long proceeded the concentration camp and has endured far longer, indeed, by a number of centuries.

Colonialism created an order based on absolute violence, Fanon argues, an order that relied on the transformation of the 'native' into a 'thing,' an object of exploitation. The colonial encounter gave rise to new species of men, the native and the settler. He also argues that the colonial encounter was structured as a racial one: the violence necessary to bring into being the colonial order fashioned and propagated a racial order. It organized privileges, rights, and entitlements of juridical subjects through a race status actuated as essential and immutable. The native was defined not simply as ignorant of ethics, morals, and values (Christian or other), and native society as not only devoid of such values, but the native, and his/her society, came to be constituted as the very 'negation' of these values, ethics, and morality.[11] The colonial world emerged as a world divided: on the one side, a world of law, privilege, access to wealth, status, and power for the settler; on the other, a world defined *in law* as being 'lawless,' a world of poverty, squalor, and death for the native.

In Canada, sovereign power institutionalized through the law an absolute alterity between different categories of human life, breathing juridical force into the category Canadian while draining it out of the category Indian, solidifying and fixing their identities as different kinds of subjects (and objects) of power. Indians were brought into being as a new category of human life by the 'armed fiction' of the law:[12] the Salish, the Cree, the Mohawk, and the many other indigenous nations preexisted European contact with the 'Americas,' while the Indians did not.

Drawing upon Fanon's work, Achille Mbembe argues that colonial sovereignty relies on very 'particular' kinds of violence: the founding violence of conquest; the legitimating violence of transforming conquest into moral authority; and the ordinary and banal violence necessary for the maintenance of colonial sovereignty.

> Colonial sovereignty only existed in areas where these three forms of violence were deployed, forming a seamless web. This violence was of a very particular sort, immediately tangible, and it gave the natives a clear notion of themselves in proportion to the power that they had lost. Its distinctive feature was to act as both authority and morality; it could do so for two reasons. First, it eliminated all distinction between ends and means; depending on circumstances, this sovereign violence was its own end and came with its own 'instructions for use.' Second, it introduced virtually infinite permutations between what was just and what unjust, between right and not-right. Thus, in regard to colonial sovereignty, right was on *one* side. And it was seized in the very act of occurring. In face of it, there could only be 'wrong' and infraction. Anything that did not recognize this violence as authority, that contested its protocols, was savage and outlaw.[13]

Claims of sovereign legality in Canada, as in the case of the African societies that are the subject of Mbembe's inquiries, rest historically upon one elemental 'truth': Europe was lawful, Indians were not. European powers claimed sovereignty over the Americas through the power of *their* law, pronouncing as lawless, anarchic, and even despotic the conditions of existence in the 'savage' worlds that Europe was discovering. Conquest resulted in the establishment of European sovereignty over the colonial world, and this violence, this power of the sovereign, became constituted in law as racial power, as racial violence. As a juridical subject, the Canadian national was conceived of this violence. The suppression of Native peoples, and of their socio-political orders, remains the necessary condition of Canadian sovereignty, as it does for the exaltation of the national as law-abiding subject.

Giorgio Agamben has described an intriguing concept, that of 'homo sacer,' used by the ancient Romans to refer to a category of persons defined as 'sacred,' persons who could be killed with impunity yet could not be sacrificed.[14] The violence wrought upon this enigmatic figure, Agamben tells us, 'is classifiable neither as sacrifice, nor as homicide, neither as the execution of a condemnation to death nor as sacrilege.'[15] Agamben explains that the Greeks distinguished between two main forms of life: 'zoë,' the form of bare life that was believed to be the 'form of living common to all living beings,' including animals; and 'bios,' the 'form of living proper to an individual or a group,' that included 'political' life.[16]

The concepts of zoe and homo sacer help shed greater light on the law's treatment of Aboriginal peoples. Emptied of their politico-human status by the legal regimes of colonizers, the indigenous peoples of the Americas became consigned to a liminality between zoë and homo sacer. Having been officially declared by the sovereign to be primitive life, devoid of the civilized, politico-legalistic form defining human life as European life, they could be destroyed with impunity. And although indigenous peoples were declared as doomed to extinction for the 'sin-crime' of indigeneity, they were also simultaneously valorized as sacred in the western imagination. In their modern incarnation as savages, they were construed as remnants of a past golden age of humanity, of an earlier, purer stage of natural human life, now said to have vanished from Europe. Indigenous peoples became the embodiment of humanity's childhood, its innocence, lost to Europeans with the development of modernity. Said to live outside the purview of both human and divine

(Christian) law as savages and heathens, indigenous peoples became constituted in the European imaginary as the fossilized reminders of a lost age when human beings lived in complete harmony with, and as a part of, nature. Indigenous peoples became the quintessential homo sacer of modernity, who, although sacred in the sense described by Agamben, could be, indeed had to be, destroyed on the altar of progress. Reducing them to bare life allowed for demonizing them *and* making them sacred after the fact. Indigeneity became a form of life that had to be honoured, if only nostalgically, even as it was condemned to extinction.

The Canadian nation and its subjects are sustained through such originary violence, both ontological and epistemological, with this violence having become instituted and regulated through the law. Against this perspective, it might be argued that although the early colonizers did indeed seize control of the land and define Aboriginal peoples as lawless, Canadian law has since recognized (however reluctantly and however meagrely) the principle of pre-existing, inherent Aboriginal rights and title to the land. It might be claimed that the state has (however belatedly) recognized the principle of Aboriginal self-government, as well as the necessity for negotiations with, and acquisition of the consent of, Aboriginal nations in its legal determinations of their land claims.

It might even be argued that First Nations are restored to their rightful historical status in the concept of the 'three founding nations' that today constitutes Canadian-ness for the more progressive sectors of the nation.[17] However, the very concept of Aboriginal rights, of Aboriginal title, presupposes the existence of a sovereign power, alien and external to First Nations, with the power to determine the nature, the form, and, most importantly, the extent of the rights of Aboriginal peoples.[18] This is a colonial relation, albeit a more benign one than that of centuries past. As for the three founding nations concept, its amnesiac suppression of the violence of the encounter among these three nations, its reduction of the heterogeneity of indigenous societies to a monolithic Aboriginal nation, is unconscionable.

Making Canadians

The whites told only one side. Told it to please themselves. Told much that is not true. Only his own best deeds, only the worst deeds of the Indians, has the white man told.

Yellow Wolf, Nez Perce (1877), quoted in Ronald Wright, *Stolen Continents*[19]

Few things are so dangerous as believing one's own lies.

Ronald Wright, *Stolen Continents*[20]

European claims to colonial territories rested upon variations of the following themes: indigenous peoples were not fully human; they were not Christian; they were not civilized; they had not evolved; they were doomed to extinction by history and progress; they had no recognizable legal systems or concepts of property rights and were thus lawless; and they did not cultivate their lands. In the particular case of Canada, British and French sovereignty over Aboriginal peoples and their lands was legitimized ideologically through claims to Christian and European civilizational superiority, and legally through the assertion of sovereignty by the colonizing powers, who sometimes negotiated treaties with some indigenous nations. The British Crown's assertion of sovereignty was deemed sufficient to erase Aboriginal title to ancestral lands within the legal systems of the Empire, as was to be the case subsequently within the legal regime of the Canadian state.[21] Thus elevated, British law came to subjugate and supplant the pre-existing Indigenous politico-adjudicative processes and orders. The historical exaltation of the Canadian as lawful, and the denigration of the Indian as essentially lawless became an inevitable consequence.

Mbembe identifies the mode of governance in the colony as 'commandment,' characterized by an arbitrariness and unconditionality that made the native an object of power and 'the prototype of the animal.'[22] If the rule of law in the colonies was of Europe, by the European, for the benefit of the European, commandment was the absolute principle imposed upon the Indian. Mbembe has identified colonial sovereignty as imposed and sustained by three particular kinds of violence. As discussed above, the first was the foundational violence by which the right of conquest was asserted and territory mapped out for the exercise of power, enabling the sovereign to create itself as the singular power within its borders. The second was a legitimating violence, transforming the initial violence into 'authorizing authority.' The third was the violence necessary for the maintenance of domination, for ensuring its permanence, manifesting itself in 'banal' and 'ordinary' situations.[23] Violence became both 'authority' and 'morality.'[24]

As has been well documented, the founding of the Canadian nation-state was predicated upon the disruption of Aboriginal societies, and the imposition of Europe's legal regimes onto them.[25] With Aboriginal

societies being defined as lawless, their socio-political systems and practices became constructed as 'customary' and 'traditional' rituals not
worthy of modernity. All three forms of violence identified by Mbembe
can be found to have shaped this Canadian experience.

Founding Violence

The founding of the Canadian nation clearly did not take place in isolation from the larger conquest of the Americas where Europeans, as
Christians, claimed the sanction of a divine sovereign in their conquest
of the peoples they designated heathens. The coming of Europe to the
Americas has been described as turning the world upside down for
indigenous peoples.[26] The genocidal violence of this inaugural moment
of the integration of indigenous economies within colonial empires has
also been well documented.[27] European powers, including Spain, Britain, and France, were successful in destroying or subjugating the self-
determination of numerous indigenous societies, despite the intense
resistance they encountered. The brutality of the Spanish and Portuguese might have been different in scale and style from those of the
British and French, but it is important to bear in mind that all contributed to the colonization of the Americas: the violence of each colonizing power sustained the larger colonial process, and the settlement of
Canada was of apiece with this larger historical phenomenon. In this situation of utter commandment, the 'rights' of Europeans included the
right to kill heathens, and it was a power exercised throughout the
Americas.

Moreover, the British and French conquests and assertions of sovereignty over indigenous lands and peoples were steeped in the same
claims of religious, racial, and cultural superiority as were those of the
other Europeans. Henry the VII charged John Cabot with crossing the
Atlantic 'to conquer, occupy and possess' the lands of 'heathens and
infidels.'[28] Nor did the British and French shy away from using similar
forms of violence as had the Spanish and the Portuguese: wars were
waged against indigenous societies; bounties were offered for scalping
Indians in Nova Scotia in the 1700s;[29] poisoned food and blankets con-
taminated with smallpox were used to decimate indigenous populations; starvation, coercion, trickery, and deception were used to compel
Native peoples to negotiate treaties and to gain sexual access to the
women.[30] French and British occupation of indigenous lands, the dis-
placement of Indians from the land onto small reserves in favour of

settlers from Europe, maintained a historical continuity with the earlier waves of genocidal violence throughout the Americas.[31] Bonita Lawrence has noted that Canadian authorities often used threats of resorting to the forms of military violence used by the American authorities in their attempts to control and pacify Native peoples in Canada.[32] To claim a peaceful and orderly founding of a nation by Europeans anywhere on this continent, innocent and unconnected to this orgiastic violence, as does Canadian national mythology, is clearly an exercise in absurdity.

Authorizing Authority

The imposition of European legal regimes within the Americas was a complicated affair, systematized over a number of centuries by various colonizing powers with their own interests. A number of scholars have observed that the importation of European sovereignty into the Americas was based upon a number of myths and fictions: first, the myth of European 'discovery' of the Americas;[33] second, the religio-legalistic concept of terra nullius, which legitimated the fiction that the continent was 'empty of people' before the arrival of Europeans; and third, of terra incognita, which allowed European sovereigns to 'claim underlying title to unknown lands.'[34] The self-endowed right of discovery of European powers was translated into their right of ownership of such discovered territories.[35] This right of discovery, and the internationalization and subsequent secularization of European law, were the most pertinent factors in legitimizing the subjugation of Aboriginal peoples, of turning the violence of conquest into authorizing authority. All three factors were deeply intertwined, sustaining and shaping their co-development.

European sovereigns understood that the question of the legality of colonial rule was to play a critical role in the maintenance of colonial relations, as well as in legitimizing their own claims of sovereignty over these lands against those of other European powers who coveted the same.[36] Their respective religious and secularist intellectuals debated whether it was the absence of Christian religion or of civilized law in colonized societies, or the racial inferiority of colonized peoples that justified their conquest. The right of these sovereigns' ownership was upheld in the state structures and legal regimes developed within Europe. It was granted the sanction of their churches and of their leading political intellectuals, some of whom overtly justified the genocide of conquered peoples while others justified the legal pronouncements of territorial ownership. Significantly, these Europeans also insisted that they conquered inferior peoples without blood on their hands.[37]

The imposition of European legal systems at the international level was accomplished as this law was simultaneously being transformed from Christian (divine) law into secular law. Widely identified as symbolizing the modernization of European societies, secular law is presented as a solution to the obscurantism and prejudices of the pre-modern era. It is not insignificant, however, that in its new secular form, the modern legal system was much better equipped to reproduce colonial racial hierarchies. Colonized peoples were being converted to Christianity in large numbers across European empires, with the consequence that they acquired formal status as co-religionists of Europeans. This new religious status presented challenges to the legitimacy of their continued domination under divine law as heathens, and the transition to secular law was extremely useful in overcoming these challenges. Thus, the changing social relations within the colonies were a significant consideration driving the secularization of European law.

It is important to note that in the name of Christianity, the conquest of indigenous peoples could be – indeed was – justified because of their heathen status, which was equated with their race status. With the transition to secular law, religious identity was no longer primarily equated with racial identity: racial heirarchies could now be preserved and enhanced even among co-religionists. Secular law enabled colonial hierarchies to be justified on the basis of scientific theories of race and on the basis of the cultural practices and rituals of colonized populations. Categorization of their status as savage, as well as determinations regarding the stage of their evolution, became central to the question of whether indigenous peoples could be understood to be properly sovereign.

European powers constituted themselves as law-upholding entities at the international level by forging a secular law that was to enable, and sustain, their racial domination of colonized peoples. The uncivilized were cast in international law 'as incapable of self-determination,' and European imperialism proceeded on the presumption of Europeans that 'civilized nations were not bound by rules in the treatment of such people.'[38] The nations of Europe thus claimed the mantle of legality and sovereignty for themselves while imposing illegality and destroying the sovereignty of others. Whereas the religious structure of medieval law had previously exalted Christians above all others, secular law, embodying the shared racial identities and interests of European nation(al)s, became the law of imperial power. Law became the rule of race.

As was the case with other European powers, the British also initially considered the Christianizing of pagans as rationale enough for their colonial ventures. Claims about their Christian superiority were deeply fused with their claims to cultural superiority in their relations with Indians, and bringing these heathens under Canadian stewardship was justified in religious terms as late as the 1880s: 'Let us have Christianity and civilization to leaven the masses of heathenism and paganism among the Indian tribes; let us have a wise and paternal government faithfully carrying out the provisions of our treaties ... They (Native people) are wards of Canada, let us do our duty by them,' urged Alexander Morris (1880), who 'arranged' some of the earlier treaties.[39]

Anthony Anghie has challenged the contention that the development of international law was simply the extension of European law to the territories discovered by Europe. Instead, he has argued, it was the imperative of colonization that led to the reinvention of medieval European laws into a system of international imperial governance. Anghie examines the work of Francisco de Vitoria, the Spanish theologian, who is credited with developing the primitive origins of modern international law in the sixteenth century. He points out that the question of sovereignty and the colonial relationship was the central theme of this work: '[I]nternational law, such as it existed in Vitoria's time, did not *precede* and thereby effortlessly resolve the problem of Spanish-Indian relations; rather, international law was created out of the unique issues generated by the encounter between cultures.'[40]

Dismissing papal authority and divine law, Vitoria forwarded a secular system of human and natural law that he claimed was applicable to both the Spanish and Indians. Although Vitoria granted Indians the power to reason, he argued that their cultural difference and personality led them to violate and resist this natural law, thereby compelling the Spaniards to protect themselves against such violations. Vitoria's lectures are significant, Anghie tells us, because although he recognized the Indians as being governed by their own coherent political systems, he used this recognition to justify Spanish conquest by holding the Indians responsible for impeding and resisting the imposition of the natural law that allowed Spaniards to 'travel' and 'sojourn' where they pleased. The Indians violated this law in resisting the incursions of the Spaniards, and thereby invited just and legally sanctioned retaliation.[41] Anghie thus summarizes his analysis of Vitoria's work:

The problem of cultural difference plays a crucial role in structuring Vitoria's work – his notions of personality, *jus gentium*, and, indeed, sovereignty itself. Vitoria's jurisprudence can be seen to consist of three primary elements connected with this problem. First, a difference is postulated between the Indians and the Spanish, rendered primarily in terms of the different social practices and customs of each society. Second, Vitoria formulates a means of bridging this difference, through his system of *jus gentium* and his characterization of the Indian as possessing universal reason and therefore capable of comprehending and being bound by the universal law of *jus gentium*. Third, the Indian, possessing universal reason and yet backward, barbaric and uncivilized, is subject to sanctions because of his failure to comply with universal standards. It is precisely what denotes the Indian as different – customs, practices, rituals – that justifies the disciplinary measures of war, directed toward effacing Indian identity and replacing it with the universal identity of the Spanish. These sanctions are administered by the sovereign Spanish on the nonsovereign Indians.[42]

Anghie's analysis of the secularization and internationalization of law that Vitoria's work enabled finds that it pivoted on the widespread and widely accepted notion of indigeneity as an 'inferior' condition.

In her examination of the relationship among law, culture, and power that enabled the British – and subsequently Canadian – states to acquire title to indigenous lands in British Columbia, anthropologist Dara Culhane traces Canadian law to British common law. This law emerged in the fifth-century Anglo-Saxon invasion and was furthered with the Norman conquest of 1066, which introduced a 'centralized state and church, and the arbitrary power of the king.'[43] While the British sovereign's claim of 'underlying title to all land' was rooted in the concept of the 'hovering' sovereign,[44] the Crown's claim to title over foreign lands was rooted in the 1608 *Calvin's Case*, which legitimized the colonization of Ireland on the basis of the inferiority of these peoples' cultural development, that is, on the basis that they were 'not-Christian enough.'[45] Culhane notes that as a result, British laws determining that country's relationship with colonized peoples had already been established by the time it colonized Canada. These rules were based on the concept of terra nulluis, applicable in the discovery of uninhabited lands; and the doctrine of conquest, applicable in situations where indigenous peoples inhabited the land. In the first instance, British law became the law of these uninhabited lands. But, as Culhane notes, 'already inhabited nations were simply legally *deemed to be uninhabited* if the people were not

Christian, not agricultural, not commercial, not 'sufficiently evolved' or simply in the way,' as was the case in the province of British Columbia.[46]

The Royal Proclamation, signed by King George in 1763, remains at the heart of the question of Aboriginal status and entitlement.[47] In this, the Crown proclaimed that indigenous peoples were under the protection of the British Crown and prohibited Indian lands from being settled or developed without their consent, or without that of the Crown.[48] Among other considerations, the Proclamation sought to protect the monopoly of the Crown, which had to contend with maintaining British alliances with various Aboriginal peoples in its rivalry with the French and the Americans. The growing encroachment of European settlers who attempted to purchase land directly from Native peoples was also of major concern. Prohibiting the acquisition and settlement of territories that were not covered by treaties without the consent of the Crown, the Proclamation 'differentiated' Indian title from non-Indian title in   a number of significant ways: it recognized the existence of Indian nations and the need to negotiate with them; it defined Indian title as collective, not individual, reducing this title to 'use rights'; it stipulated Indian title could only be transferred to the Crown; it recognized a 'fiduciary duty' of the state to Indians, and a duty to protect them; and it required Indian lands to be surrendered only with community consent.[49] The Proclamation reflected the conflicting interests among the various strata of colonial powers wrestling with each other within the parameters of the Empire, that is, British control versus that of settler elites, federal control versus that of provincial governments.[50]

The alien British regime was to allow the Native no rights, no entitlements, no claims to legality, except those which the sovereign decided to bestow in the interests of preserving and maintaining the colonial order. The laws imposed by the British overrode and sought to negate the social relations within Native societies, declared to have never properly existed. The varied social systems and structures of governance among different indigenous societies,[51] – some matrilineal and matrifocal, others a combination of matrilineal and patrilineal systems,[52] most based on women's active participation in politics, economic activity and decision-making[53] were declared non-existent. As the sovereign used its authority to organize a settlement that would not contest, but further, its monopolistic hold on power, enabling settlers to migrate and gain access to the land by constituting them as juridical subjects, it simply annihilated the juridical existence of Native peoples, placing them outside the parameters of the law unless it determined otherwise. Whereas the acquisition of approximately half of the nation's territory was justified through some process of treaty-making, the other half was possessed through the alien Crown's assertion of its sovereignty.

Maintaining Sovereignty

Our understanding of law is not represented within the structure of the Canadian legal system ... We, as individuals, did not participate in the process whereby the legal system was formed. We did not participate in the process of agreeing to the assumptions and values reflected in that system. Further, we have been excluded as Peoples in participating in the formation of that system. More importantly, First Nations Peoples have never consented to the application of the Canadian legal system to any aspect of our lives.   •

Patricia Monture-Angus, *Thunder in My Soul*[54]

The maintenance of colonial sovereignty at the level of daily life depended upon the ability of nationals to wrest and hold control over the land and its resources, as it did upon the law's institutionalization of the claims of these settlers against those of the Indian. It also depended upon the relegation of Native peoples to the zones of exclusion organized by the reserve system and the enduring politico-ideological construction of the Indian body as a site of exception to the law.[55] As scholars have noted, early legislation defining Indian-ness was centrally connected to the appropriation of Native people's lands and to the conditions of their banishment to reserve lands.[56] Legislation first defining Indian-ness was passed in 1850. It determined Native peoples' access to reserve lands and was followed by the Gradual Enfranchisement Act in 1869, which gave the superintendent of Indian Affairs the power to determine access to Indian lands. The British North America Act (1867) was the legal instrument that created the Canadian nation, and soon after Confederation, the various legislations and policies governing Native peoples were consolidated into the Indian Act (1876), which organized the governance of Native peoples separately from that of nationals. The Indian Act, as racialized and gendered a piece of legislation as one might encounter anywhere under the auspices of the empire, has been aptly described as representing the 'Euro-Canadian government's apartheid system'[57] and the 'bureaucratized hatred' of Native peoples.[58]

Creating a framework for the governance of Indians on the basis that they needed protection and could be civilized through assimilation, the Act defined which Native peoples were to be eligible for Indian status and which were to be denied such status. The Act made the status and rights of Native women within their communities directly dependent upon their relationships with men: Native women and their children would lose status upon marriage to non-status men.[59] Consequently, the Act organized Indian status in a manner that had 'nothing to do with whether the person was actually of Indian ancestry,' it was driven primarily by the goal of eliminating Native populations.[60]

Colonial administration of the zones of exception, the reserves, was subsequently organized through the imposition of band councils, which barred the participation of women in the (truncated) political process, ensuring that resources available to communities would be channelled largely through the men. Gendered inequalities became deeply institutionalized as a result.[61] The legislation institutionalizing band councils into a 'municipal-style elected system ... bypassed the national or tribal governments recognized in the Royal Proclamation' and 'bypass[ed] the power of the confederacies' created by Native peoples.[62] It fragmented First Nations into smaller band groupings, 'foster[ing] loyalties at the level of the local community, at the expense of the broader national affinities arising from a common language, culture, spirituality and historical experience.'[63] The band system weakened the political power of Native nations by furthering and institutionalizing divisions within them.[64]

The political disempowerment of Native women in the treaty making process, as well as through the Indian Act, was critical to the project of making Aboriginal peoples' lands available to settlers. Bonita Lawrence argues that in Haudenosaunee society, 'female-led clans held the collective land base for all of the nations of the confederacy' and that 'clans organized along the female line frequently controlled land inheritance.'[65] The disempowerment of these women was key to the privatization of indigenous lands, she concludes. The women 'saw holding on to the land base as the only way in which the social fabric of the society to nurture the next generation would survive at all.' They 'strenuously resisted' losing the land. The racial gendering of the Indian Act thus specifically targeted Native women and their children for loss of status, a loss crucial to reducing the numbers of Native populations. The women who lost their status, and their children, were 'bled' off from their nations, further undermining these nations' bargaining power, as well as their ability to reproduce their socio-cultural heritage.[66]

The Act provides interesting insights into the contradictory manner in which the state constructed definitions of 'race.' While Aboriginal peoples were to be distinguished on the basis of their race and designated as Indians, the women's 'race' was to be lost upon marriage to non-status men. Their race was to be determined by their relationship to men, particularly through marriage. The Act thus created a severe disjuncture in the lived experiences of these women: while they could lose their Indian status, the loss of this status would not end their racialization in daily life. As the Native women who fought against this inequality – ultimately forcing the Act's amendment – demonstrated, the women did not stop 'being' raced upon the loss of official status.[67] Lawrence discusses how deep and far-reaching the effects of the Indian Act have been on Native populations. Defining it as 'much more than a body of laws that for over a century has controlled every aspect of status Indian life,' she argues that it 'provides a conceptual framework that has organized contemporary First Nations life in ways that have been almost entirely naturalized, and that governs ways of thinking about Native identity.'[68]

Along with its assertion of title over indigenous lands, the state commanded that Indians exist officially only in the infantilized capacity of wards, prohibiting their existence as juridical subjects.[69] As was the case with the deployment of the concept of terra nullius to claim European legal entitlement over territories emptied of Aboriginal presence, a corresponding humanitas nullius was deployed through the Act to empty Native peoples of their human status. The development of the reserve system created zones of exception in the sense described by Agamben.[70] Marked for physical and cultural extinction by the sovereign, the application of the law to these peoples was suspended while unprecedented powers over their lives and deaths were concentrated in the hands of the Indian agents.

Mohawk legal scholar Patricia Monture-Angus argues that the most basic right of a people is that of naming themselves: 'Not being in control of the process of naming, that is, defining who you are, serves as one of the most express examples of silencing that I can think of.'[71] The category Indian certainly attests to the historical misrecognition of geography by European explorers,[72] but it also encodes the ongoing epistemic and ontological violence that upholds the colonial encounter.[73] Through the category Indian, the colonial state sought to empty Aboriginal peoples of their historical consciousness, their being-for-themselves, and attacked their power to name themselves. It erased the many differences between various Aboriginal nations, dehumanizing them while it homogenized them.[74] Expressing what Ward Churchill has so aptly termed the 'fantasies of the master race,' this renaming of Aboriginal peoples was intrinsic to the process of remaking them in the image that Europeans had of them.[75] The sustained attempts to wipe out their spiritual, cultural, and political practices, including the pot-latch, the Sun Dance, and various other spiritual-political ceremonies, were committed to the same objective.[76]

Claiming an insidious power that went deeper than control over phys-ical life or death, the sovereign asserted its right to prescribe the kind of life, and the form of spiritual expression – that is, the relation to the sacred – that was to be henceforth permissible for the dominated peo-ples. Through the Indian Act, the state took upon itself the power to determine which Aboriginal women and men were to be given Indian status and which were to be pushed towards psycho-spiritual annihila-tion through the loss of such status.[77] While the criteria for determining Indian status have fluctuated historically – from bloodlines, skin colour, adoption, marriage to residency, lifestyle, reputation and character – the power to determine these criteria was always claimed by the state.[78] As numerous scholars have pointed out, consultation with Native com-munities was considered utterly unnecessary in any of these matters.[79]

Euro-Canadians, with the power of law behind them, built themselves a new world and made themselves into a new people. The Indian Act was as much about enhancing the domain of nationals as it was about controlling Aboriginal peoples. Constructing the nation as white re-quired Europeans to come forth and multiply as Canadians, and to this end, the state endowed them with the rights to enter the country, to set-tle the stolen land, to live and work on it. The state upheld the legality of the national's ownership and the Aboriginal's dispossession of the land, and herein is rooted the proprietary relationship among law, state, Aboriginals, and nation(als), racialized in all its permutations. The national subject came to know itself as a lawful subject, an exalted mem-ber of the nation. It experienced its humanity as being of a different order than that of the Indian. This subject's humanity could be instanti-ated and tangibly experienced in its access to land and other resources, in its juridical relation with the apparatus of the burgeoning state that allowed its very presence on the land. With an evolving sense of national identity, possessed of the right to be present on the land, to own it, to work it, to travel across its length and breadth, the national subject con-stituted itself as such in the knowledge that although the Indian might be of the land, he/she was not worthy of it, had no legitimate, or respectable claim to it. The white national subject, however, was worthy of the land, this worthiness being decreed by the very law of the land. Such exaltation entitled the successful national to claim the right to territory, to mobility, and in the process, to experience itself as a juridical, hence fully human, subject.

Canadian legal history demonstrates how these social relations and processes of subjection were organized, contested, and upheld. In her study of the history of the law during the first half of the twentieth century, Constance Backhouse has found racial distinctions to be 'widely' upheld:

> Collectively, these legal documents illustrate that the legal system has been profoundly implicated in Canada's racist past. Legislative and judicial sources provide substantial evidence to document the central role of the Canadian legal system in the establishment and enforcement of racial inequality. Legislators and judges working in combination nipped, kneaded, and squeezed artificial classifications into rigid, congealed, definitions of race in Canadian law. They jointly erected hierarchies of racial grouping and delineated segregated boundaries based on race. In their hands, the law functioned as a systemic instrument of oppression against racialized communities. When the individuals and groups who bore the brunt of racism sought to turn the tables and call upon the legal system for redress, the registers typically failed in their quest ... It is essential to recognize that racism is located in the systems and structures that girded the legal system of Canada's past ... The roots of racialization run far deeper than individualized, intentional activities. Racism resonates through institutions, intellectual theory, popular culture, and law.[80]

Among the cases discussed by Backhouse are the following. In *King v. Phelps* (1823), the Six Nations claimed that they were an independent people with title to their land and were not subject to British law. The Crown argued this claim was 'absurd' and the judge ruled in favour of the Crown. Likewise, in *Shelden v. Ramsay* (1852), the judge ruled the Six Nations did not have title over their land. In 1921, the Ontario Supreme Court heard the case *Sero v. Gault*, in which a Mohawk woman, Eliza Sero, had her fishing net confiscated by a fishery inspector, Thomas Gault, who deemed the fishing to be illegal as she did not possess a fishing license.[81]

Backhouse tells us that while cases of such fishing violations were most frequently treated as criminal prosecutions, in this instance, the lawsuit was actually brought by Sero herself, who claimed that the fishery inspector had no jurisdiction over the Tyendinaga Mohawk Territory where her net was used. She argued that provincial laws had no jurisdiction over her as she was a member of an independent Kanienkehaka Mohawk nation, not a 'subject of the King,' and claimed damages from Thomas Gault for the value of her net. Her (white) lawyer claimed the Mohawk were an 'independent' people, and the Six Nations of Grand River intervened in the case, with their lawyer (also white) arguing that self-government of these nations was their most fundamental right. The judge ruled against Eliza Sero's claim.

Canadian legal history, littered with such decisions, reveals the law's recognition that European settlement was irreconcilable with Aboriginal control over the land. Backhouse also tells us that the Six Nations 'never wavered' in their claims to title over their lands, and that First Nations never acquiesced to the extension of the jurisdiction of Canadian courts to themselves. However, the judicial elite repeatedly held otherwise. The words of Judge Riddell (who was described as an 'ardent imperialist' of his time) in the *Phelps* decision perhaps best sums up the sentiment prevailing among them:

> The solicitor-general took the ground, which has ever since been held good law, that the Indians are bound by the common law and have no rights higher than those of other people ... In the United States there has been from time to time question as to the legal status of Indians and Indian land; in Ontario there never has been any doubt that all the land, Indian or otherwise, is the king's, and that Indians are subject in the same way as others. There are no troublesome subtleties in Canadian law.[82]

The decision made a disingenuous use of the claim that Indians had the same rights as non-Aboriginals in order to neutralize their claim to their ancestral territory.

In the case of the province of British Columbia, Native peoples did not enter into treaties with either the British or Canadian states, they were not conquered by military force, nor did they sell their land. Culhane explains the legal basis used by the provincial government for its acquisition of the territory:

> Since 1871, when British Columbia joined Canadian Confederation, all successive governments of that province had taken the position that no

Aboriginal rights recognizable by 'civilized law' existed prior to Britain declaring sovereignty over the territory. And even if these rights had existed, the Province of British Columbia's argument continued, the simple act of assertion of sovereignty by a European power over those lands was sufficient to extinguish any pre-existing Aboriginal title and rights. Legally, the Province of B.C. told First Nations, you do not exist. This position provided the rationale for provincial governments' consistent refusals, until 1990, to participate in any discussions or negotiations with federal government and Aboriginal representatives on Aboriginal title and rights issues.[83]

Legal cases regarding Aboriginal title were not allowed to be taken to court in the province until the 1960s, despite the lobbying of Aboriginal peoples for a century. And then, the province would hold steadfast to this legal position until almost the end of the twentieth century.[84] Culhane points out that a multitude of barriers were put up when the Allied Tribes of British Columbia sought to bring their claims to court. Arguing that the British had broken their own laws in asserting sovereignty over the province, the First Nations representatives who argued the case were deemed 'too assimilated and not representative' of the Indians for having acquired education.[85] The First Nations leaders who argued an Aboriginal perspective in 'broken English' were deemed too savage to know what they were talking about. The documents that revealed that the federal and provincial governments were aware of this claim at the time the province joined the federation were 'lost.' A ban was imposed on raising funds for land claim cases, and when it was finally lifted (1951) and First Nations initiated litigation, the prevailing view was that these nations were inventing their stories because 'no one had heard these claims before.'[86] Culhane notes that when the laws did not work in favour of the settlers and their legal regime, they simply broke these laws and then prohibited any legal channel for redress by First Nations.[87]

A number of scholars have found that the legal system was 'implicated' in the country's racist past. The key point, however, is not that the law was discriminatory and that racism can be found in its rulings. It is that the Canadian legal system *is* a regime of racial power. The law upheld the rights of nationals over those of Aboriginal peoples time and time again, and in this process, it extended its own legitimacy as the sole 'authorizing authority' within the settler colony. It institutionalized the violence of the dispossession of Aboriginal peoples in their daily encounters with Canadians. Parliament's criminalization in 1927 of Aboriginal peoples who raised money for litigation for their claims to sovereignty without the written consent of the Department of Indian Affairs can certainly be described as racist.[88] However, the very coming into being of a Parliament that claimed the authority to act in this manner, the existence of such a sovereign authority *in the context of the ongoing colonization of Aboriginal peoples,* reflects the deeply racialized nature of this sovereign power, its politics, and its laws.

Contemporary claims to lawfulness by national subjects remain rooted in this relationship of race to law. For law has entrenched the constitution of the Aboriginal as lawless: Aboriginal claims to land, their claim to human status, were literally outside the parameters of this law. The eminent Judge Riddell opined on the reason for this in a law journal in 1929, writing that Aboriginal peoples had 'savage appetites' and 'little conception of government by law.'[89] The judge was voicing a long-held opinion within the legal tradition shaped, and shared, by European powers. To them, 'Amerindians' were 'like beasts in the woods' because of their alleged nomadic lifestyle.[90]

Becoming Canadian

Nation-building was steeped as much in the epistemic ejection of Aboriginal peoples from the category human as it was in the dispossession of Aboriginal peoples from their lands. The Indian is a simulation whose experiences are cast primarily in settler narratives of absence and victimry, Vizenor has observed. 'The absence of natives as an *indian* presence is a simulation that serves the spurious histories of dominance,' he argues.[91] If the Indian is a simulation, no less of a simulation is the Canadian who was being concurrently constituted as an active presence in national narratives of heroism and endurance. European settlers, in transforming themselves into Canadians, were constituting themselves into a different kind of subject, metamorphosing into nationals.

While the colonial state instituted itself as the sole authority, colonizers and settlers enacted and realized this authority on the ground. The sovereign upheld its claim to colonial territories and enabled its subjects to assert their individual claims to these lands. As mentioned earlier, the Royal Proclamation sought to curtail settlers from engaging in direct purchases of land from Native peoples. The settlers, subject to the laws of the sovereign, were nevertheless allowed privileges and rights in accomplishing the eradication of Aboriginal sovereignty. Indeed, many were recruited and encouraged to settle the colonies as the sons and daughters of the Empire, as the bringers of Christian salvation and civilization, as adventurers and pioneers with the right to acquire the wealth and resources that awaited them and their acumen. For the most, they responded by constituting themselves as the only civil society, the only public whose opinions counted, the only subjects whose rights had to be protected.

As I have argued above, violence in this context was more than the individual caprice of unscrupulous settlers, it was the necessary condition for the preservation of the colonial order. The successful colonizing power was the one which emerged triumphant in the efficacy of its violence; the adroit national was the one who was able to actualize this sovereignty on the ground as he cleared, settled, and laid claim to the land; as he hunted down Indians or drove them away; as he hounded them out of fishing, hunting, logging, and otherwise harvesting the lands he brought under his control.

Divided as they were by class, gender, ethnicity, even by regional and provincial interests, it was most clearly in their common interest in the subjugation of Native peoples that settlers forged a common cause, a cause at the heart of reconstituting themselves as Canadians. Their active participation in, and tacit approval of, the dispossession of Aboriginal peoples enabled various European colonizers and settlers to fashion their relationships as nationals with one another, and with their state.

In his study of the making of the reserve system in British Columbia, Cole Harris notes that settlers 'took it for granted that the land awaited them.' While debates raged about the conditions under which they could gain access to the land, 'with rare exceptions, the proposition that almost all provincial land was unsettled and unused – or used slightly in ways that deserved to be replaced by more intensive, modern land uses – was not debated,' he relates. Settlers widely believed that Indians were too primitive to have proprietorship of the land.[92] They fancied themselves entering a wilderness, a paradise ripe for the plucking. And pluck they did. As the imagined nation became actualized through recourse to the law, and as Native peoples were forced onto reserves, some settlers undertook the project with an easy conscience, others with trepidation.[93] 'Colonialism spoke with many voices, and was often deeply troubled about its own contradictions, while tending to override them with its own sheer power and momentum,' Harris reminds his readers.[94] Despite the trepidations, the enticements of reproducing the racial hierarchy proved too strong to resist.

In an interesting gesture, Harris dedicates his book to one Gilbert Malcolm Sproat, 'a colonizer who eventually listened' and who represents for Harris the 'troubled' colonist. Having purchased land from the Crown, Sproat set out in 1860 to establish a logging camp and sawmill on Vancouver Island. Upon finding a Nuu-chah-nulth (whom Sproat called the Aht) camp on the land, and upon being informed by their chief that the land was theirs, Sproat paid again for the land. This time he paid the Nuu-chah-nulth directly the value of some twenty pounds, stipulating that they depart by the next day. When they did not, Sproat persisted: 'Only ... when he brought up his ships armed with cannon, and the Aht "saw that resistance would be inexpedient," did they begin to remove themselves.'[95]

Harris recognizes, as Sproat himself obviously did, that violence was law, and with the cannons in the hands of the whites, the law was white. Sproat informed the chiefs that King George had ordered them to sell the land because they were not 'using' it. Europeans would 'buy' the land 'at a fair price,' he assured them. Here, what constituted the proper use of the land was to be determined by the British sovereign, fairness was to be determined by settlers, and property rights were to be upheld by British (canonical?) law. Walter Benjamin has argued that violence lies at the heart of the contract, and this interaction of Sproat's graphically bears out his claim.

Sproat was apparently conflicted about whether he had the right to buy the land, troubled that it was only 'under the fear of loaded cannon pointed towards the village' that the chief had been induced to sell it.[96] Sproat's men suffered no such doubts. They argued with him that the land was not being put to civilized use. They also argued that if they could not have access to such lands, colonialism could not proceed. Harris reports that Sproat himself remained troubled about whether this argument 'constituted the basis of a right.' Nevertheless, he, too, 'took European civilization and Aht savagery for granted and shared his workmen's views that the land was unused.' Although Sproat felt strongly that Europeans had a responsibility to treat the 'natives' fairly, he recognized full well that settlers would take what they could. He asserted bluntly, 'this, without discussion, we on the west coast of Vancouver Island were all prepared to do.'[97]

The need to maintain a clear conscience might have given pause to the more troubled among the settlers, but it does not seem to have affected their appetite for settlement. Sproat's actions, as well as those of the European men who abandoned Aboriginal wives and children in the transition from the fur trade to settlement, reveal the ways in which these men reconstituted themselves, how they actualized their 'difference' as subjects of a superior order.[98] The replacement of indigenous geographies with settler 'roads, fields, villages and towns' proceeded in British Columbia, Harris relates. The colonial state and the various organizations supporting British emigration within the empire encouraged (sometimes compelled) many Europeans to migrate. Those with wealth acquired proprietorial rights to the land while the less well-off became integrated into the national market economy and benefited from the state's protection of their rights against those of Native peoples.

Nationals actively participated in their own self-exaltation, and also engaged collectively in the phantasmagoric project of inventing the Indian. This imaginary Indian, a 'white man's fantasy' was constituted as their savage Other by nationals.[99] Defined as doomed by history and civilization (not Europeans) for extinction, Aboriginal peoples became romanticized, when not outright despised, in the narratives that nationals developed. Their passing was mourned by the more humane among them, their existence sentimentalized.[100] Aboriginals were constituted either as ignoble savages, as Emma Laroque has argued, and thus requiring forceful subjugation, or as noble savages, hence requiring a more benevolent stewardship. Both constructs argued the case for the inevitability and desirability of colonial rule.

Reproducing the law's denial of the Aboriginal's right to exist as juridical subjects, nationals actively erased or distorted their presence in the social imaginary, as well as in their narrations of the historical record. Such erasures allowed for their emergence as the only legitimate heirs to the nation's resources. Such erasures and self-exaltations were reproduced in the following manner: 'An entire vocabulary is tainted with prejudice and condescension: whites are soldiers, Indians are warriors; whites live in towns, Indians in villages; whites have kings and generals, Indians have chiefs; whites have states, Indians have tribes. Indians have ghost dances, whites have eschatology.'[101] In such narratives, the national subject experienced and reproduced its own humanity, its civilized status and legal entitlement in direct relation to the non-human, non-civilized, disentitled status of the Indian. So, for an interesting example, one Mary E. Inderwick, living in Alberta, wrote to her family of her loneliness in 1884. Reporting that the she lived twenty-two miles from the nearest 'woman,' she referred to the 'squaw' who was 'the nominal wife of a white man near us.'[102] This Aboriginal woman, like her own maid, did not count. The category woman was inapplicable to these women among whom the lonely Inderwick lived.

It should not be surprising, therefore, that the land featured large in the cultural and emotional topography of the nation. The land bewitched the nation's venerated artists and deeply shaped their experience of their nationality; it came to be defined as more present than the actual presence of Aboriginal peoples in the national imaginary. 'Canadian national identity is deeply rooted in the notion of Canada as a vast northern wilderness, the possession of which makes Canadians unique and "pure" of character,' points out Bonita Lawrence.[103] The 'idea of a national population being "moulded" by the "challenge" of the land' is also deeply embedded within national institutions, including the Canadian Museum of Civilization.[104]

If the young nation assumed the role of protagonist in nationalist narratives, the land was made to assume that of the antagonist. Tales of pristine rivers and virgin mountains (tempting settlers to penetrate ever deeper), of harsh winters and wild forests (then angrily punishing them for this feat) abound in the national imaginary, as do the stories of individual perseverance and triumph over nature.[105] The forces of nature that shape the land are represented as also shaping the national character, cultivating a pioneering spirit and a noble perseverance in these subjects. When the presence of actual Aboriginal peoples was given some recognition, the peoples themselves were featured as savage and wild. Daniel Francis describes the reaction of the poet, Charles Mair, upon his encounter with the Native peoples with whom he was to enter into treaty negotiations:

> Instead of paint and feathers, the scalp-lock, the breech-clout, and the buffalo robe ... there presented itself a body of respectable-looking men, as well dressed and evidently quite as independent in their feelings as any like number of average pioneers in the East ... One was prepared, in this wild region of forest, to behold some savage types of men; indeed, I craved to renew the vanished scenes of old. But, alas! one beheld, instead, men with well-washed unpainted faces, and combed and common hair; men in suits of ordinary store-clothes, and some even with 'boiled' if not laundered shirts. One felt disappointed, even defrauded. It was not what was expected, what we believed we had a right to expect, after so much waggoning and tracking and drenching and river turmoil and trouble.[106]

Francis likens Mair's response to his own more recent experience when, upon visiting a museum in Alberta, he became aware that the Indians who worked there did not look like those he 'knew' from school texts and films. Searching for the source of these images, Francis argues that European (and Canadian) artists had an enormous influence in their fabrications of the imaginary Indian.[107] It was through such works of art, widely displayed in museums and published in books (including school textbooks), that Canadians and other Europeans constructed their knowledge about who and what Indians were really like.

From the paintings of the Group of Seven to the novels of Margaret Atwood, and to the iconic image of Prime Minister Pierre Trudeau in a buckskin jacket canoeing on a lake (featured on the cover of his memoirs), this relationship of real Canadians to the land, emptied of Aboriginal peoples except as symbolized in relics, features prominently in the artistic and mythic representations of their nationality.[108] As they celebrated their mythologized relationship to the land, colonial violence was faded into insignificance.[109] As protagonists, white nationals battled with the largely empty land, with the forces of nature, transformed now into an adversary whose harsh brutality had to be tamed in the unfolding plot of civilized settlement. The relationship of the settler was constituted as primarily to the land, emptied of Aboriginal life as human life. Aboriginal peoples were disappeared into nature, faded into the landscape, made indistinguishable from it. And if they were made to appear, as they did in some instances, they appeared only to 'enhance the romanticism of the scenery.'[110] As part of nature, of the landscape, the question of their sovereign right to proprietorship over the land became quite inconceivable in such narratives.

The fantasy of unsullied origins allowed the innocence of the land to be claimed by the national subject as its own, and the brutality and savagery of colonial violence to instead be projected onto the land itself, and onto the savage who was part of this landscape. If the concept of terra nullius allowed for the 'worlding of the world' by colonizers, by which Spivak refers to 'the assumption that when the colonizers come to a world, they encounter it as uninscribed earth upon which they write their inscriptions'[111] – then this mythologized relationship of the national to the land allowed for a simultaneous inscription of the narrative of a pristine human innocence into the national self. In this strange reversal, the land became 'worlded' with an angry, hostile, and active presence and power, and the national self with the innocence of the wilderness, persevering only for the sake of human progress.

Euro-Canadians imagined themselves as fully human in their relation to the dispossessed Indians, and their experience of this racial-ized humanity was very tangible. In concrete terms, this humanity could be accessed in their ordinary lives on the lands they worked and in the property they owned. It was actualized in their mobility and in the places where they could work, in the kind of work they could do, the level of income they could earn. Their dress, their language, their manners, all marked out their human status vis-à-vis the Indian. Mah-mood Mamdani cautions us against thinking of law as only 'individuat-ing and disaggregating classes.' He tells us that law also 'collates' and creates 'group identities': 'Legally inscribed and legally enforced, these identities shape our relationship to the state and to one another through the state.'[112] The legality of European presence on the land, coupled with the illegality of Aboriginal claims, became literally em-bodied in the whites living and working in the towns, cities, farms and villages.

Most certainly some (perhaps many) nationals were sensitive to, and sympathetic with, the claims of Aboriginal peoples to the land and its resources. Individuals like Sproat, as well as the white lawyers who repre-sented the Six Nations in the cases examined by Backhouse, advocated publicly on behalf of Aboriginal peoples, no doubt at considerable pro-fessional and personal cost to themselves. They clearly desired a more equitable relationship between Aboriginal peoples and the nation, and attempted to make the juridical order more just. However, no historical record of settlers and nationals who submitted their claims to land to Aboriginal adjudication has yet been found. The presence of a signifi-cant number of nationals who were prepared to recognize the sover-eignty of Aboriginal laws on the land they claimed as theirs, who were willing to submit themselves to these Aboriginal legal and adjudica-tive processes and who challenged the imposition of European legal regimes on Aboriginal societies remains yet to be discovered.[113] The sovereign institutionalized the subjugation of Aboriginal peoples, and the nation's subjects, exalted in law, were the beneficiaries of this pro-cess *as members of a superior race*, albeit to differing degrees based on class, gender, ethnicity, and other social relations.

Land, with all its resources, is the basis for a successful nation–state relationship, and colonial land policies enabled the state to expand its activities and institutional base even as it expanded its population base. Racialization became systematized and incorporated into the emerging market economy, and the insistence on the rule of law which enabled all this remains key to the self-presentation/preservation of Canadian sovereignty, as it does to the self-constituting practices of national subjects.

The oft-repeated insistence on the essentially law-abiding nature of nationals points to a recognition, subjugated but nonetheless present, of the questionable legitimacy of the claims to superiority over Aboriginal peoples, as well as a recognition, however desperately denied, of the horrific violence wreaked upon them. The institution of the law made it possible for colonialists and settlers to rationalize and thus conceal this violence, to systematize it in the interest of the reproduction of the nation-state. It allows nationals, even today, to accommodate themselves to it.

As for Aboriginal peoples, their defiant claims of their sovereignty have remained unshaken in the five centuries since Columbus landed in the Americas:

> Court hearings, jurisdiction, judges sitting in the courtrooms, making decisions that formulate or change our lives [...] And the people who are making these decisions don't even know who we are ... The rights of the Houdenosaunee do not come from any treaty. They do not come from any court decision or law. The rights of the Houdenosaunee came long before your people came here. We have not changed ... It must be set down today, solid, as it was three, four thousand years ago, that we are the landowners. This house is ours. This must be set down, so that my grandchildren's grandchildren will be safe, that they will be able to conduct the ceremonies of our people. They will still be able to sing their songs and speak their language. And they will still be able to teach you people about peace, harmony and living together.[114]

The zones of exclusion mapped out by the sovereign, marking out the actual sites for the extinction of Aboriginal peoples, have been transformed by the resistance of these peoples into the sites of their survival and renewal, into the sites of the reproduction of their socio-cultural practices.

Settlers entered into a relationship with the colonial state, participating in the dispossession of Aboriginal peoples, and in this process, transformed themselves into nationals. Some did so with much violence and zeal, others attempted to do so more humanely and with some trepidation. Some believed necessary the annihilation of entire Aboriginal communities, others sought to extend them some measure of legal protection. Most seemed to have agreed that the rule of law should be upheld, and almost all seemed to have agreed that the Law was White.

Lest it be concluded that the discursive practices examined above belong to a past long since transcended, it should be noted that the 'imaginary Indian' continues to carry potent legal currency in the present. In his now infamous comments, Mr Justice Allan McEachern of the Supreme Court of British Columbia opined as follows in the Gitskan-West'suwet'en land claim case in 1991: 'The plaintiffs' ancestors had no written language, no horses or wheeled vehicles, slavery and star-vation was not uncommon, wars with neighbouring peoples were com-mon, and there is no doubt, to quote Hobbs [*sic*], that aboriginal life in the territory was, at best, "nasty, brutish and short."'[115] As Lawrence points out: 'Native people who are revealed as transgressing the bound-aries of so-called authenticity through their modernity can be dismissed as fakes, or severely restricted in their abilities to develop their commu-nities in contemporary ways.'[116] The judge is certainly not alone in sub-scribing to such views, Aboriginal peoples are routinely subjected to the test of 'authenticity.'

The legal absurdity that Aboriginal lands were empty, that the sover-eignty of the Crown could accomplish the extinguishment of Aboriginal claims to self-determination, continues to shape the law's interactions with Aboriginal peoples. Canadian courts have now, of course, sanc-tioned the notion that that 'Aboriginal rights pre-existed European arrival and are inherent: recognized, and not created, by British sover-eign'; that these rights are 'unique'; that governments must consult with Aboriginal peoples before issuing logging and mining rights to corpora-tions;[117] and that Aboriginal consent is required in the surrender of their title. Yet the goal of extinguishing these rights remains at the heart of the law's recognition of these rights: 'The final goals that courts and governments have shared – the desired outcome of litigation, as well as land claims and treaty negotiations – is the extinguishment of Aborigi-nal title, absolutely and forever; and the confirmation of the singular sovereignty of Crown title, absolutely and forever.'[118]

The entire discourse of Aboriginal title presupposes a sovereign alien to Aboriginal peoples who nevertheless has the power and authority to determine the extent of this title. Even if every single case regarding Aboriginal title from this day forth is ruled in favour of Aboriginal claim-ants, this cannot erase the reality that it is Canadian law, European law, that remains the authorizing authority deciding on the fate of Aboriginal nations. This is a colonial relationship, it is a relationship of racial domination. In the absence of a negation of this colonial relation, Aboriginal peoples can only be included within the jurisdiction of this law, albeit on a more benign basis and with greater authority than has been the case in the past. Transforming itself in accommodation to Aboriginal sovereignty remains the real task and test of Canadian justice.

CITIZENSHIP

2 Nationals, Citizens, and Others

It is not enough to call it a question of cheap labour; it is not enough to raise the question of colour, race or creed. To be a Canadian citizen, at the beginning of the twentieth century, is no small thing. The men who built up this country, who hewed homes out of the forest, were men of first class, A1 stock, and the responsibility they left us is great. The sentiment expressed in the proud phrase, *Civic Romanus sum*, becomes the citizen of Canada as well as it became the citizen of Rome. A race of men who cannot appreciate our mode of life, our mode of education, all that goes to make up Canadian citizenship, are not fit immigrants of this country. On the broad grounds of Canadian citizenship I attack this question.

A Member of Parliament (1906), quoted in Peter Ward, *White Canada Forever*[1]

One of the great advantages of being Canadian is that it's so easy. The anthem isn't all that hard, maple syrup tastes good, and the Constitution and laws of the land are, for the most part, sensible.

The lack of a national mythic identity actually makes it easier for migrants from more deeply rooted cultures to integrate into the national fabric.

But if immigrants are going to shun the political process, or even fail to vote, then the bedrock of those few principles we do prize above all – liberal democracy under the rule of law – could be imperiled.

John Ibbitson, 'Canada's Immigrant Challenge' (2005)[2]

The Rights of Citizens

Noting that the 'control of migration – of immigration as well as emigration – is crucial to state sovereignty,' feminist philosopher and political theorist Seyla Benhabib tackles the contentious issues of international human rights, national sovereignty and citizenship (that is, membership within a political community), as well as the challenges presented to these by global migrations in her recent Seeley Lectures at Cambridge University.[3] Drawing upon Immanuel Kant's notion of 'cosmopolitan right' and Hannah Arendt's reflections on statelessness and the individual's 'right to have rights,' Benhabib argues that a profound contradiction is to be found between the paradigm of universal human rights and the rights of sovereign democratic societies to shape the boundaries that define their respective political communities.

Kant's conception of cosmopolitan right addressed the vexing question of the moral and legal relations of individuals who cross borders to the states whose jurisdiction they enter. Benhabib reads Kant's concept of this right as defining 'a novel domain situated between the law of specific polities on one hand and customary international law on the other hand.'[4] Cosmopolitan right extends 'a right of temporary sojourn' to foreigners, a right which arises from 'a special contract of beneficence' that accrues to all human beings 'by virtue of their common possession ... of the surface of the earth,' so long as the recognition of this right does no harm to the receiving society.[5] Benhabib argues that such a right should also include permanent residency, not just temporary sojourn, under specific circumstances. This right should be grounded in a recognition of the universality of human rights and not in the 'beneficence' of receiving societies, as Kant would have it.

The question of statelessness was a key concern for Hannah Arendt in the wake of the devastating consequences of the imposition of this condition upon Jews and other minorities in Europe with the rise of fascism, and Benhabib is especially attentive to this concern. For Arendt, totalitarianism's 'disregard for human life and the eventual treatment of human beings as "superfluous" entities began ... when millions of human beings were rendered "stateless" and denied the "right to have rights."'[6] Although Arendt criticized the 'weaknesses' of the nation-state system and highlighted the moral obligation that endows all individuals with the 'right to have rights,' she remained 'sceptical' about 'all ideals of a world government.'[7] Benhabib argues that because the condition of statelessness abrogates all human rights, it is too serious an issue to be treated as only a question of sovereign privilege.

For her part, Benhabib makes a case for the principles of 'moral universalism' and 'cosmopolitan federalism' to uphold the recognition of the 'rights of others.'[8] Arguing that citizenship and the granting of the right of permanent residence 'ought not to be viewed as unilateral acts

of self-determination' since access to this status has serious consequences for 'other entities in the world community,' she advocates 'just
membership' and 'just distribution' as a way out of the conundrum of
reconciling universal human rights with the principle of sovereignty.
The 'others' whose rights are the particular concern of Benhabib's
deliberations are variously defined as 'aliens,' 'strangers,' 'immigrants,'
'asylum seekers,' and 'refugees.' Benhabib identifies a paradox in this
situation where citizens with rights decide upon the extent of the rights
to be granted to others, pointing out that this paradox 'can never be
completely eliminated.' Despite this being the case, she argues that the
impact of these decisions can – and should – be mitigated: 'We can render the distinctions between 'citizens' and 'aliens,' 'us' and 'them,'
fluid and negotiable through democratic iterations.'[9] The notion that
moral and ethical obligations are owed by the community of citizens to
these Others permeates Benhabib's reasoning, as does a commitment
to the 'cosmopolitan solidarity which increasingly brings all human
beings, by virtue of their humanity alone, under the net of universal
rights.'[10]

I begin my examination of Canadian citizenship in this chapter with a
discussion of Benhabib's work because questions of ethical and responsible citizenship are among her key concerns, as is the relationship
between the sovereignty of liberal-democratic societies and international law. Citizenship has, of course, long served as the signifier par
excellence of membership in the nation-state and is much valorized in
master narratives of nationhood, including that of the Canadian nation.
This institution is universally accepted as reflecting the height of the
evolution of the human being as a modern political subject, with clearly
delineated rights and entitlements.[11] The claims of nationals to a legitimate and unassailable membership within the political community are
rooted in their historical access to this institution. For previously
excluded groups, these claims are also cherished as the result of their
struggles to make the institution more inclusive. Benhabib's conceptualization of the community of citizens whose right it is to decide on their
own fate, as well as that of the Others who aspire to share their status, is
based on just such a definition of the institution. Canadians routinely
describe their citizenship, immigration, and refugee policies as the most
humanitarian and compassionate in the world. These claims shape their
sense of collective pride and national identity.

In this chapter, I want to trouble Benhabib's deliberations on a number of counts. Notwithstanding her commitment to 'democratic itera-

tions,' her conceptualization of citizenship is based largely on an 'internal' discussion within the political community, with strangers being cast largely as supplicants dependent on the responsibly exercised largesse of nationals. Rather than examining citizenship from the perspectives of those denied this status, such as indigenous peoples, it is largely the experience of those included within this institution that remains at the centre of her conceptualization of the institution. The experiences of Others with whom Benhabib is concerned are not at the centre of the conceptual schema, and all she can offer them is an invitation to participate in 'democratic iterations' with enfranchised, and hence, powerful communities of citizens.[12] My point is that numerous Aboriginal, critical race, and third world theorists of decolonization have pointed to the racialized nature of the rights-based regime of citizenship. They have made a strong case for a radical restructuring of the geopolitical order in order to transform the vast inequalities in this order. Benhabib, however, forecloses this possibility with immodest haste.

Benhabib's easy assumption that the Others who cross borders are always supplicants requires interrogation. For although she acknowledges interdependence among societies within the global economy, she dismisses the possibility of a radical restructuring of this interdependence by declaring it both impossible and undesirable. Agreeing with the 'liberal cosmopolitan vision that in a world of radical, and not merely accidental and transitory, interdependencies among peoples, our distributive obligations go well beyond the natural duty of assistance,' she confesses she is 'made uncomfortable by the imposition of a global redistributive principle to create economic justice among peoples, unless and until the compatibility of such a principle with democratic self-governance is examined.'[13] Whose self-governance, one might well ask? That of the powerful communities of enfranchised citizens? Or that of their disenfranchised and powerless Others? Propelled into the circuits of migration at its lowest echelons, these Others are increasingly drawn from the ranks of 'the wretched of the earth,' to use Fanon's term.

The desirability of implementing the principle of global economic justice is here trumped by a defence of the principle of the sovereignty of enfranchised citizens. Benhabib explains that, because determining the 'aggregate responsibilities' which arise from global interdependence is too difficult a task to measure or judge precisely, a program of radical global redistribution 'is a fallacy of misplaced concreteness.'

Instead, she says, 'setting general global goals, upon which democratic consensus can be generated, is more desirable.'[14] Hence, the recognition that the obligations of citizens to Others arise not only from moral and ethical considerations but also from economic and material exploitation is declared too disquieting and complicated a problem to resolve.

The reality that the prosperity and living standards of citizens in the hypercapitalist world are directly and concretely underwritten by the land, labour, and resources of dispossessed Others is referred to, and then conveniently put aside. Relations between citizens and their Others – which were forged in the labyrinth of the global market economy, binding slave and master, colonizer and colonized, developed and underdeveloped, North and South together in a vice that has not loosened much in the current phase of globalization – are treated as largely irrelevant to the questions at hand. These relations cannot be characterized as anything other than appropriation, dispossession, and exploitation. Such observations, however, are not used to support demands that the rights of the dispossessed supersede those of the possessors.

While in theory any human being could potentially become an 'immigrant' and an outsider, those who actually present themselves as such at the borders of hypercapitalist countries are very particular kinds of persons. The aliens who present themselves at Britain's borders, for example, come mainly from its ex-colonies, including India and Pakistan. This flow of human beings has been defined as the 'direct result of the history of colonialism and imperialism of the previous centuries.'[15] In the case of France, the Algerians against whom the borders have to be guarded are hardly strangers, having been subject to French rule during its reign as a colonial power.[16] As for the United States, the borders are patrolled most zealously against Mexicans, whose refusal to recognize the absoluteness of this border is based in the American appropriation of a significant portion of their country's rich land mass.

Likewise, the aliens who present themselves at the Canadian borders today come from countries that are among the most coveted sites for the operations of Canadian corporations. Many of these countries are also the destinations of the high-flying trade missions led by a dizzying array of prime ministers and trade ministers. It might well be asked, then, what makes a Chinese woman, who sews a shirt in a Chinese factory that sells for three dollars on the streets of Vancouver, a stranger when she presents herself at the Canadian border as a migrant? Is not the relationship between the nation of consuming citizens and this woman – and with the countless others like her whose lives are spent making the products that clothe, feed, nurture, and sustain them – an intimate one?

Although Benhabib's call for a more ethical and internationally accountable recognition of the rights of Others is to be lauded, her formulation of the problem renders invisible the reality that this 'problem' is today, as it has been at least for the previous five centuries, mainly a problem of race. It is the racialization of persons-on-the-move that is central to their ontologization as aliens by exalted citizens, who claim inalienable rights for themselves while helping to destroy those of Others. The crisis of immigration into the west is a racial crisis, for it threatens the erosion of white supremacy by the potential enfranchisement of aliens. In the modern era, with the brief periods of exception for Jews, the Irish and Eastern Europeans, white populations have generally been able to travel as and where they please.[17]

The meaning of the status of the sojourner, or the degree of hospitality extended to all persons-on-the-move, cannot be equated. For example, while seasonal migrant workers from Mexico are deemed a perennial problem in the United States, and domestic workers are regulated through live-in requirements in Canada, corporate and trade executives, finance and development experts, among others, cross borders with ease and frequency. The latter are courted by the most lucrative employment contracts, tax exemptions, and housing and living allowances, all of which characterize the lives of expatriates in the countries of the global South. Indeed, a whole system of international institutions promoting trade and development has been organized, including the International Monetary Fund, the World Bank, and the World Trade Organization, to facilitate precisely their right to global travel and cosmopolitan hospitality as they make the planet the site of their entrepreneurial ventures.

For those who want to 'help' the developing world, a corresponding global network of non-governmental agencies has also been organized to facilitate the expression of their humanitarian impulses. That almost all of these white (and increasingly, multicultural subjects living in the west) persons-on-the-move choose to maintain their citizenship in the hypercapitalist world should not surprise us, so utterly devoid of value is the citizenship of the previously colonized world where they make their livelihoods, help the needy, and have their holiday fun. To facilitate the travel of western tourists to the most fashionable vacation sites, for another example, local communities are displaced; their land, water, and other resources appropriated to build and service the hotels and

resorts in which tourists expend their leisure time. The crisis of migration today, as in the past, is thus largely a problem of controlling
persons-of-colour-on-the-move, of regulating those who refuse to
remain where they belong.

Benhabib too readily accepts the principle that self-governing political communities of citizens in powerful countries should have the right
to decide on the fate of relatively powerless Others. Her reluctance to
challenge the power relations between citizens and their Others, I
believe, forecloses the possibility of ethical relations between them. Who
will decide what is ethical? What is moral? Will it be the powerful communities of enfranchised citizens? Benhabib's answer is a resounding
yes. Power as ethics. This is inevitable, Benhabib tells us. Perhaps so. But
the kindest observation one can make about such a state of affairs is that
this is the way the world works today, that this is realpolitik, this is how
power expresses and organizes itself. To drape this state of affairs with
the mantle of ethics or morality empties these values of meaningful content. The principle she accepts has been challenged by the civil rights
and anti-racist movements of the twentieth century, and the lessons of
these movements should be applied to non-citizens. Surely at the very
least an examination is required of how communities of citizens have
come to acquire such power over the lives of others? Ultimately, Benhabib's vision is one which enhances the power of the powerful, albeit
with a desire to have them use such power responsibly, in an enlightened manner, as it were. It is a vision that helps foster a sense of the
inevitability of current conditions for the future.

Citizenship in a Settler Society

The limitations of Benhabib's naturalized assumptions of citizenship
entitlement and alien incursions are perhaps nowhere as obvious as in
the case of settler societies-cum-liberal democracies such as Canada.[18]
In this case, the political community of citizens is a community based
in the legal negation of Aboriginal sovereignty, with Aboriginal peoples today among the strangers and aliens who seek to defend their
rights from the incursions of citizens. All manner of philosophical
niceties advanced by nationals-as-citizens to define their relationship to
Others, such as the right of hospitality or the moral obligation that is
owed the Other for sharing a humanity increasingly being treated as
an abstraction, fall apart in the face of actual encounters with the
stranger. These are rarely, if ever, mediated by such philosophical

subtleties, but always tainted by the hostile and mundane exigencies of power.

In the case of Canada, all non-Aboriginal populations have historically become nationals or Others through processes of migration. However, the unequal conditions organizing these migrations have been such that different rights have been allowed these populations and their descendents. The question of migration and citizenship are thus deeply entwined in national formation, with immigration policies organizing access to formal citizenship. The conditions of migration have thus been of signal importance in Canadian history, for nationals as well as immigrants.

The central contradiction of Canadian citizenship, deeply rooted in its earliest stages of development, is that the citizenship rights of settlers, nationals, and immigrants remain based in the institution of white supremacy. Citizenship originated in the dispossession of Aboriginal peoples and was denied for almost a century to most people of colour or, if allowed, only erratically and as matters of exception. Here, the category citizen did not emerge through some internal process within a natural community, with regretable consequences for outsiders. Citizenship emerged as integral to the very processes that transformed insiders (Aboriginal peoples) into aliens in their own territories, while simultaneously transforming outsiders (colonizers, settlers, migrants) into exalted insiders (Canadian citizens). The category citizen, born from the genocidal violence of colonization, exists in a dialectical relation with its Other, the Indian, for whom the emergence of this citizenship was deadly, not emancipatory.

The institution of citizenship was key to the processes of settlement, economic development, and nation-building. It organized and normalized colonial dispossession through the granting of individual rights of domicile and land ownership to nationals, even as it gave concrete meaning to the category Indian, primarily as lack, including the lack of 'the right to have rights.' Settlement, access to land, mobility, and the development of the market economy all relied upon this extension of civil and political rights to settlers. With these rights invested in the institution of citizenship, the institution itself became inseparable from the forced internal migrations of Aboriginal peoples onto reserves and the destruction of their communities as sovereign entities.

Access to formal citizenship for all non-Aboriginal populations was organized through migration or by birth within national borders. If a major condition for the founding of the nation-state was the acquisition of national territory, no less important was the recruitment of a national population, for which the state turned primarily to European source countries.[19] Immigration policy became central to the process of generating a national population and regulating its access to resources. From Confederation until the 1960s and 1970s, immigration and naturalization legislation distinguished first British and French, and later, other Europeans, as 'preferred races' for integration into the nation.[20] This exaltation positioned Europeans as the 'true' subjects of the nation. For over a century after Confederation, the state therefore organized and solidified white racial identity as *political* (citizen) identity. The nation's racial identity, as well as its legal citizenship, thus became fused as white.[21]

The western scientific theories of white racial superiority popular during this period, and instituted in state practices, saturated the hallowed institution of citizenship. It is ironic that even as the nation was imagined to be a homogenous entity in its foundational moment, free of the contaminating influence of the Native cultures that preceded it and of the polluting presence of Black and Asian peoples, the specific legislations enacted by the state demonstrate elite recognition that this was not indeed the case. The Indian Act and the various immigration and citizenship legislation attest to the presence of various Others, even as they simultaneously testify to the commitment to expel them from nationality. In the introduction, I discussed Goldberg's assertion that the modern racial state constructed racial homogeneity out of heterogeneity, an assertion that is certainly upheld by the Canadian experience.

Citizenship was instituted in a triangulated formation: the Aboriginal, marked for physical and cultural extinction, deserving of citizenship only upon abdication of indigeneity; the 'preferred race' settler and future national, exalted as worthy of citizenship *and* membership in the nation; and the 'non-preferred race' immigrant, marked as stranger and sojourner, an unwelcome intruder whose lack of Christian faith, inherent deviant tendencies, and unchecked fecundity all threatened the nation's survival. These foundational horizons were institutionalized in the burgeoning apparatus of the settler state and its expanding geographical domain, as well as in the inscription of whiteness as embodiment of legitimate and responsible citizenship.

Relatively disenfranchised groups among national subjects, including women and the working class, challenged state and elite power to increase their own access to citizenship. Unevenly endowed as their rights were, however, these groups made common cause with the elite and the state in curtailing the access of non-European populations to the same rights. Here, another aspect of citizenship becomes evident: citizenship serves as a status that mobilizes national subjects, classed and gendered as they may be themselves, in defense of the institution against the claims of those designated as undeserving outsiders.

The unequal conditions under which respective phases of migration into Canada have been organized have had long-lasting consequences for access to citizenship. Non-preferred races were no longer overtly designated as such after the 1960s, and they acquired increased access to citizenship. However, their de facto unequal rights have been maintained through their ideological designation as immigrants, newcomers, new Canadians, and visible minorities, even after they acquire de jure status as citizens. The category immigrant undermines the very notion of the nation as a homogenous entity, as well as of the nation as a non-racial entity.[22] It reveals the heterogeneous nature of the population by drawing attention to the presence of racial Others within the nation's psychosocial and physical space. However, the racialized category immigrant also paradoxically helps sustain the myth of the nation as homogenous, by constructing as perpetual strangers those to whom the category is assigned, even when they are second or third generation Canadian-born citizens, as is the case with the contemporary use of the term 'immigrant communities.'

As racially excluded immigrants sought to expand the institution of citizenship to accommodate their own demands for inclusion, they left largely unchallenged the role of this institution in the dispossession of Aboriginal peoples. The extension of citizenship rights to these racialized immigrants thus resulted in their qualified integration into the political community, but at the cost of fostering their complicity in the colonial domination of Aboriginal peoples.

An examination of the institution of Canadian citizenship reveals that if the domination of the emerging settler society by Europeans was not divinely ordained, it certainly was not historically inevitable either. Colonization and the opening of the country to mass immigration attracted not only Europeans but also other colonized and enslaved populations, including Black and Asian migrants, many of them fleeing the ravages of slavery, economic underdevelopment, poverty, and political upheaval. These populations also sought improved life prospects for themselves and their families within the new nation. The potential certainly existed for their emergence as a significant sector of the nation's swelling population. Asians in particular, with their geographical proximity to the Pacific Rim, and Blacks, with their northbound migrations to escape the brutality of the slave economy of the southern United States, carried the historical potential to make the emerging social order a very different kind of entity. However, the racial policies of the state and the racial preoccupations of the white population destroyed this possibility, which would have rendered more difficult, if not entirely impossible, the consolidation of Euro-Canadian hegemony. State support for white nationals, prominent among which was their access to citizenship, gave them the decisive edge in their conflicts with non-preferred races. This support enabled them to emerge as the dominant majority with control over the emerging socio-economic and political institutions.

The increased migrations of those previously designated non-preferred races after the liberalization of immigration and citizenship legislation in the 1970s meant the nation once again faced the spectre of non-whites emerging as a significant demographic and cultural force, with their growing economic and political power eclipsing the white domination of national institutions. These fears have not diminished with time. The notion that the liberalization of immigration and citizenship legislation since the 1970s somehow brought to an end the historical racialization of the nation will be contested in the following sections.

Citizenship Rights and Rites

Although citizenship was of concern to the ancient Greeks, the advent of modernity brought about a profound reconceptualization of the human subject and its relation to sovereign power. Cast in the modern figure of the citizen, the status of this subject became inextricably linked with the individualist and rationalist ethos, as well as with the notions of equality, fairness, and just treatment at the heart of liberal political theory. Although citizenship is a complex and deeply contested construct, it has been enthusiastically welcomed as an emancipatory measure by those included within its orbit, and desperately struggled for by those excluded from its entitlements.

The British sociologist T.H. Marshall, highlighted what he defined as citizenship's inherently egalitarian impulse: 'Citizenship is a status bestowed on those who are full members of a community. All who possess the status are equal with respect to the rights and duties with which the status is endowed.'[23] Marshall argued that in the historical march towards 'progress,' the general trend of citizenship in modern societies

was to include previously excluded groups (beyond propertied bourgeois males to include women and the working class) and to broaden
the rights it encapsulated (from civil to political and then, social rights).
Marshall predicted that the political equality instituted in the status of
citizen would help counter the economic inequalities generated within
the class structure of the economy.

Critics of Marshall's theory have pointed out that it does not recognize gender inequalities, nor does it acknowledge the reality that the
extension of rights to previously excluded groups has been the outcome
of the political struggles of these groups and not some benevolent
impulse inherent to the institution itself.[24] Marshall's theory has also
been critiqued for its conceptualization of the economic and political
spheres as functioning independently from each other.[25]

For their part, feminists have argued that the liberal concept of the
citizen is deeply masculinist, hiding the sexual contract that underpins
the social contract of citizens within a common brotherhood.[26] They
have pointed out that while citizenship is located within the public
sphere, it is in the private sphere that male domination of women is
organized. This domination subsequently shapes women's rights within
the public sphere.

Most critics of Marshall tend to focus on the reformist project of citizenship, on the content of its rights and entitlements, and on the forms
of exclusion of particular groups. Useful as these critiques are, the popular practices of national subjects as they articulate and give concrete
meaning to their status as citizens also require attention. Citizenship has
had a profound impact on the self-constituting practices of these subjects, who have come to conceive of their humanity largely within the
context of this paradigm.

The status of citizen exalts the national subject as an equal among its
compatriots, thus upholding the chimera of its equality despite its experience of deeply entrenched socio-economic inequalities. It also enables
the shaping of individual subjectivity in a manner that underscores this
mythic equality, however unrealized this equality might remain in practice. The hailing of the subject-as-citizen enables it to experience itself as
beyond the whims and mercies of a tyrannical sovereign, safe from arbitrary infractions. Instead, this subject experiences itself as the anchor of
an enlightened sovereign power and, hence, as an *empowered* subject
itself. The wide array of 'social customs' and 'conventional acts' through
which these individuals enact and realize their citizenship as *empowered
subjects* are therefore as relevant as the legal rights incorporated within

the status.[27] In this section, I characterize these practices as rituals and rites, which sustain the citizenship of nationals in their daily encounters with each other, and with outsiders.

Rituals and rites are most often associated with the realm of the sacred, but a number of social theorists have made a convincing case that ritual, and in particular the 'interaction ritual,' remains the 'basic social event.'[28] Rituals lie at the heart of social life, sustaining social bonds among members of the community through their repeated performance. Among the rituals and rites of citizenship can be included the affective recitations of national anthems; the raising of flags; the public pledges and oaths of allegiance to the sovereign; and the celebrations of national holidays and the parades, plays, firework displays, street parties, family dinners, and so on, that mark these. The political practices associated with elections, referendums, voting, and so on, are also ritualistic enactments of citizenship. Such rituals and rites are clearly integral to producing the forms of affiliation that are central to civic integration; they become the sites where members of the collective perform their own belonging and recognize that of their compatriots.

The rites and rituals of citizenship, however, can – and do – assume other more overtly malevolent expressions. Among the rites that have also inducted individuals into the national political communities in North America are the ritualized forms of 'national' violence, such as the lynching of Black men in the southern United States, the painting of swastikas on synagogues and the 'Paki-bashing' by ultranationalists; the raping of women in situations of war and conflict; the burning of crosses; the pulling off of Muslim women's headscarves; the organized riots and mob violence enacted upon the bodies of Chinese and other aliens. Such rites also include the highly ritualized erasures of the presence of minorities in national historiography and the markers of national accomplishments, as well as the more banal liturgies recited against their presence (why don't they speak English? do they have to wear turbans? why do they have to live in such large families? their clothes and houses smell; they are too noisy; their religions and customs are strange; their marriages are arranged and their costumes gaudy; and so on). The exclusion of racial minorities from housing, employment, access to loans, the repeated questioning about where they are really from, the repeated insistence that they provide documents to prove their legality add to the repertoire of these bonding rituals among nationals.

Such banal practices tend to be treated as isolated, unrelated, and based largely in individual ignorance and certainly not meant to offend.

This sort of approach hides their highly repetitive and ritualized occurrence, as well as the widespread social tolerance – if not explicit sanction – they enjoy. It hides how consistent they have remained throughout the history of the Canadian nation, as well as their continuity as they are passed on from generation to generation. Identifying these practices as rites of citizenship directs attention to their important function in reinforcing notions of legitimate belonging, in reinforcing the incontestability of the citizenship of nationals as they enact their insider status. Rites have symbolic value as well as concrete outcomes, and they signify the limits of the acceptable. Most importantly, they demonstrate who has power and who is prohibited from exercising such power. In examining these rites, one gets a glimpse of how nationals craft their own superiority above all others, how the exalted status they lay claim to is given substantive shape. In the following discussion, I argue that it is in attending to both the *rights* and *rites* of citizenship that an understanding of the full meaning and power of the institution in the lives of social subjects can be grasped.

Making Canadian Citizens

No nation, no man, has a right to take possession of a choice bit of God's earth, to exclude the foreigner from its territory, that it may live more comfortably and be a little more at peace. But if to this particular nation there has been given the development of a certain path of God's earth for universal purposes; if the world, in the great march of centuries, is going to be richer for the development of a certain national character, built up by a larger type of manhood here, then for the world's sake, for the sake of every nation that would pour in upon it that which would disturb that development, we have a right to stand guard over it. We are to develop here in America a type of national character, we believe, for which the world is to be richer always. It may be the last great experiment for God's wandering humanity upon earth. We have a right to stand guard over the conditions of that experiment, letting nothing interfere with it, drawing into it the richness that is to come by the entrance of many men from many nations, and they in sympathy with our constitution and laws ...

We, in Canada, have certain more or less clearly defined ideals of national well being. These ideals must never be lost sight of. Non-ideal elements there must be, but they should be capable of assimilation. Essentially non-assimilable elements are clearly detrimental to our highest national development, and hence should be vigorously excluded.[29]

The colonizing migrations of European settlers created overseas populations to govern and develop colonies in the interests of European powers,
and were intended to be a permanent affair in white settler societies.[30]
Immigration policies across the British Empire were intimately linked to
this imperial goal:[31] 'All the British colonies of settlement – Canada, Australia, New Zealand and South Africa – were from the first deeply committed to the dream of becoming outposts of the "British race." The only
settlers to be encouraged to sail to the new lands were British-born denizens of the home islands who shared the ethnic roots and world view of
the colonies' white populations.'[32] The migration projects of the British
Empire established racial hierarchies within its vast domain, also shaping
the pattern of migration into Canada. After Confederation, the Dominion undertook the aggressive recruitment of high-quality immigrants
from Britain and, when necessary, from other European countries.

The development of Canada as a self-governing territory, with its own
political institutions and population base, was built upon its close ties to
Britain and its privileged white status.[33] The political autonomy that the
new state acquired through the British North America Act (1867)
enabled it to further consolidate colonial relations and expand west-
wards. As power passed into the hands of 'businessmen-cum-elected
members of the British-Canadian ruling class' and a smaller 'French
elite,'[34] the state set out to eliminate 'culturally distinct populations of
"Indians" through their forced assimilation'[35] and to build a nation
based on British institutions and social systems. Until almost the mid-
twentieth century, the actual legal status of 'Canadians' was that of British subjects with domicile in Canada; immigration and naturalization
legislation organized access to this legal status.[36] The creation of a distinct Canadian citizenship was to wait until 1947, when the first Citizenship Act was legislated.

During this period, Aboriginal peoples were relegated to an infantilized status as wards of the state under the Indian Act, subjected to the
racialized 'coercive tutelage' of the nation-state that assumed the 'form
of arbitrary restraint or guardianship exercised by one power over
another.'[37] All aspects of Aboriginal people's lives were controlled,
including where they could reside, where they could travel, and what
work they could do.[38] With settlement eroding the economic base of
Aboriginal societies, it consequently undermined the power of Aboriginal nations to determine their political systems, the conditions and
forms of membership within their political communities, and the attendant forms of social relations.[39]

The extension of citizenship to Aboriginal communities was tied to the goal of encouraging private ownership of land by Aboriginal peoples as individuals. It sought to destroy their collective ownership of these lands, hence making them available to Europeans.[40] Access to citizenship rights was thus extended to Aboriginal peoples upon their renunciation of Indian status and their adoption of the civilized institutions of private property, wage labour, and the money economy.[41] This assimilationist goal, which emphasized individual identity (and rights) above familial and community ones, presented a no-win situation for Aboriginal peoples. They had to choose between remaining wards of the state by refusing to assimilate and encountering the full force of the nation's racism by accepting assimilation. Moreover, Native women were barred from participation in the colonial forms of governance imposed upon their societies, including the band council system, which eroded the political power they had previously enjoyed.[42]

Citizenship, as the quintessential hallmark of liberal democracy, was thus racialized from its very importation into the country; Aboriginal peoples were granted no democratic space or extension of rights and entitlements within the national political institutions that came to govern their lives.[43] Indigenous forms of sociopolitical systems, their organization of the rights, entitlements, obligations, and responsibilities which bound the members of these communities together, were simply deemed non-existent and irrelevant by the state. These systems of relations were denigrated as 'customary' and 'traditional' (that is, pre-modern) and, therefore, destined to die out. Although many of these systems were much more egalitarian, the constitution of Aboriginal peoples as lawless and uncivilized precluded the recognition of these customary and traditional rights as legal and political rights. These rights still continue to be treated as simply religious and cultural. The subordination of Aboriginal systems of rights by the colonial state was coterminous with, and necessary to, the development of citizenship rights for nationals. Canadian citizenship, therefore, represented an assault on Native peoples, a drive towards their cultural and political elimination; it articulated relations not only between citizens and their state but also between citizens and Aboriginal peoples as Indians and, hence, as non-citizens.

Settlers were recruited with offers of 'free land and easy wealth as inducements,' as well as with other forms of social and financial supports.[44] Certainly not all emigrants from Britain and France had access to such incentives, their class, gender, and sexuality gave rise to inequal-

ᵒ

ities in such access. However, their classification as preferred races and, hence, as *future citizens*, provided them with significant opportunities for land ownership and upward socio-economic mobility. Britain was experiencing the unprecedented upheavals of the Industrial Revolution, and its elites were particularly keen to export the unemployed, the poor, and the criminal to the colonies, which often provoked the ire of settlers who resented the arrival of these lower orders.[45] They were, however, rarely met with the bitter hostility and angry political opposition accorded the arrival of non-European migrants.

Although patriarchal and capitalist values shaped the settler state's recruitment of high-quality settlers, their exaltation as *preferred races*, including the women and working classes among them, juxtaposed their gendered and classed inequalities within a shared racial/national interest. In other words, while conflicting gender and class interests within these communities were reproduced subsequent to their migration, their integration into the nation as preferred races suppressed these material divisions within the framework of an otherwise – and equally material – shared racial interest in the new social order. For these settlers and immigrants, claiming and preserving their racial identity brought tangible rewards.

A number of scholars have noted that in the early phase of nation-building, the settler state was faced with balancing two contending goals, that of maintaining the whiteness of the nation while also ensuring a supply of labour adequate to the task of economic development.[46] These scholars have argued that state policy sought to balance these two goals. Nation-building initially elevated British and French settlers over other Europeans, but the exigencies of settling the country soon required the immigration of other Europeans, as well as non-Europeans.

In addition to the role of state policy, however, it is important to note that white supremacy had to be established on the ground across the country. It had to be constantly defended and reproduced at the level of daily life. This assertion of racial supremacy throughout the social order, and its ongoing maintenance, was the outcome of repeated conflict between the British and French, as well as between all Europeans and the non-Europeans allowed entry into the country most reluctantly. Cycles of racial conflict, and racial accommodation, occurred within the dynamic and changing milieu of the emerging settler society, in which social norms, values, and political structures were in their early stages. These various populations experienced numerous false starts and unexpected successes. The politico-symbolic borders of the nation were thus in flux, changing and shifting to include European ethnicities other than British and French during the course of the twentieth century. However, they did not shift so far as to include Asian and Black, or any other non-white migrant group.

Benedict Anderson's formulation of the nation as shaped by elites in the form of 'official nationalism,' as well as by the 'popular nationalism' of other classes, is pertinent to the experience of Canadian nation-building.[47] The 'official nationalism' of the state, expressed most strongly in the Indian Act and the immigration and citizenship policies, interacted with the 'popular nationalism' of its white subjects, who actively enacted the dispossession of Native peoples on the ground, as they did the exclusion of 'non-preferred' races from equal access to land, mobility, and employment. The popular racism these subjects articulated forged a common interest among them *as nationals* through their exclusion of outsiders. White hegemony was thus established on the ground and defended by nationals who gave concrete meaning to a collective sense of selfhood. They staked the legitimacy of their claims to rights on an explicitly racial basis, in contrast to the illegitimate and intolerable claims of racial outsiders.

The active participation of British and French women in nation-building has been found to have been of vital importance: 'the appearance of white women was coterminous with white settlement and brought both a sharp rise in racist sentiment and heightened class-consciousness within fur-trade society.'[48] With European women coming into the country for permanent settlement, the segregation of Native peoples could be accomplished more effectively. Many European men who had previously engaged in intimate relations with Native women abandoned them and their children.[49] As settlement proceeded, the boundaries of the nation became ideologically delineated most strongly in relation to Native women.[50]

During the nineteenth and early twentieth centuries, the organizations established by Canadian women largely shared the goal of Canadian men to 'Keep Canada White.' These women's concerns about the quality of the race and the nation shaped their advocacy for the extension of citizenship rights to white women,[51] such that even as they confronted their gendered inequalities, most did so in the name of furthering the national interest by stressing the importance of women to family and nation. The class status of many feminist activists meant that they had close ties to men of the ruling elite.[52] When they established national organizations, such as the National Council of Women, they carved out a significant space for themselves in the new order: 'This Council is to bring us in touch with other parts of the Dominion, and we shall be the "Foremothers" of a great nation.'[53]

Trades unions were likewise extremely hostile to the presence of non-preferred races, whom they defined as taking jobs away from white workers.[54] By constructing Asian workers as an economic threat to their own well-being, white workers could mobilize campaigns against their immigration and employment; their trades unions used such campaigns to strengthen and consolidate their own membership base and political muscle, particularly in provinces like British Columbia.[55]

Lisa Lowe has noted that Orientalist constructs abounded within American national culture during this period, and that they were central to the denial of citizenship rights to Asian immigrants until the mid-twentieth century. Canadians likewise drew upon these constructs, fashioned by Europeans in their encounters with the Orient, to interpret their own strange encounters with Asian migrants in North America. In an interesting study of anti-Asian racism in British Columbia (from the mid-nineteenth to the mid-twentieth century), Peter Ward has analysed how the white citizens of the province remained committed to the preservation of their racial identity. With few exceptions, politicians, writers, media commentators, clergy, and trade unionists mobilized for this political goal at the provincial and federal levels. Having relegated Aboriginal populations to the margins, Ward points out that the target for the white population's racist and nativist sentiments were the Asians, 'a dynamic, growing segment in west coast society.'[56]

Ward's study demonstrates how vigorously the white segment of the population identified itself in racial terms, how stubbornly it constructed its interests as national interests, and how aggressively it fought to maintain the exaltation of its racial identity as *the* national identity. In the national imaginary, Asians were constructed as filthy, immoral, lazy, diseased, and cunning, inassimilable and corrupting of the white community.[57] Deemed unworthy of citizenship, their lawlessness was seen as amply demonstrated in their lying, thieving, drug-dealing, gambling, and prostitution – practices which were all attributed to them as essential aspects of their character:

> The Chinese were considered a grave source of lawlessness in other ways as well. According to popular belief, they had a penchant for petty theft as well as serious crime. In the eyes of their critics, the Chinese could be trusted only when watched. They reputedly escaped punishment for most

of their crimes. A frequent explanation for this was that the Chinese shared a universal disregard for truth. As one observer noted, they considered the 'adherence to truth ... An admission of weakness.' Instead they placed a much higher value on 'duplicity' and 'capacity to deceive,' for their morality permitted 'whatever contributes to immediate success in the object they desire to obtain.' Because of their guile, their offences went unreported and their testimony in court could not be trusted. Furthermore, through secret societies, the Chinese systematically conspired to commit and conceal crimes. These societies allegedly controlled Chinatown's opium dens and gambling halls and also extorted money from their countrymen. 'Tong' wars among them erupted on occasion. To outside observers the Chinese secret society often seemed an insidious device to evade the law with impunity. It was a further sign of the depths of Chinese depravity.[58]

Fears were propagated in the media that the presence of Asians kept other whites away from the province, thwarting the expansion of the economy and thereby harming the interests of all upstanding citizens. On the question of citizenship, the view was widespread among the white population that inferior races were much too debased for inclusion.

As they imposed such representations onto the unwanted migrants, these subjects exalted themselves as clean, orderly, lawful, healthy, and civilized, and hence worthy of citizenship. The successful imposition of such constructs reinforced their beliefs that Asian migrants were essentially intruders, while they themselves belonged. Most nationals publicly performed the rites and rituals of citizenship to promote the emerging racial hierarchy and to enhance their access to political and economic power through the disenfranchisement of Others. Among such rites were the routine harassment of migrants; the active petitioning of provincial and federal governments to curb Asian and Black immigration; organized forays into Asian neighbourhoods and attacks on Asians; the burning down of their camps, homes, and shops; boycotts of the businesses of whites who employed Asians; and the segregation of non-white children from their own in order to pass their racial privileges onto subsequent generations.[59]

Freda Hawkins has assessed the resistance among Canadians to the immigration of non-preferred races during the first half of the twentieth century:

Undisputed ownership of these territories of continental size was felt to be confirmed forever, not only by the fact of possession, but by the hardships and dangers endured by the early explorers and settlers ... The idea that other peoples, who had taken no part in these pioneering efforts, might simply arrive in large numbers to exploit important local resources, or to take advantage of these earlier settlement efforts, was anathema.[60]

The myth of national descent described by Hawkins – which, incidentally, is still upheld today – presupposes and attributes to previous generations the same 'national' motives and interests as subsequent generations, who are defined as having a direct link with the early colonizers as their rightful (and righteous) heirs. The direct relation established between 'early explorers and settlers' and today's upstanding and responsible citizens becomes comprehensible only within the context of the continuity of their shared racial identity. Narrations of such a mythological line of descent enables subsequent generations of Canadians to define themselves as repositories and preservers of the national inheritance, even as they make invisible the colonial violence which in actuality brought far more 'hardships' and 'dangers' to Native peoples than it did to the 'early explorers and settlers.' The widespread race hatred expressed by the 'pioneers' who actively campaigned to prohibit the migration of Black and Asian immigrants, while they themselves were taking possession of the land, presented far more hardships and dangers to these migrants.

The myth of benign national origins and responsible citizenship that holds sway over the master narrative of nationality renders invisible the ritualized hatred organized towards non-whites, mythologizing nationals instead as adventurous pioneers and explorers who settled North America and who acted to exclude others only to defend their nation against the provocations of aggressive invaders. The myth also makes invisible the contributions of non-preferred races to the development of the national economy, contributions which many scholars have found to have been absolutely vital to the development of the nation's economy.[61] Despite the recruitment of many such undesired migrants as cheap labour by employers, the prevailing ideology of the period fantasized nefarious motives and imagined Asians as plotting to swamp and invade their society,[62] fantasies which are routinely expressed to this day.

As noted above, the legal status of Canadians until the mid-twentieth century was that British and French subjects. The first Canadian Citizenship Act was legislated after the end of the Second World War. The Act recognized the country's historical ties to Britain and the Commonwealth. It also reflected a 'growing sense of a separate Canadian national identity,' and sought to foster a 'greater sense of national unity' in the post-war period.[63] The dismantling of the British Empire (and those of other European powers) underway during this period no doubt exerted its own pressures, making somewhat urgent the necessity for the development of an independent Canadian political identity.

The Citizenship Act created three classes of citizens: natural born, naturalized, and those granted citizenship by virtue of a certificate of citizenship.[64] It also specified particular grounds, including disloyalty and treason, for the revocation of citizenship and the deportation of certain classes of citizens.[65] The deportation clause, however, was not applicable to natural-born citizens, whose citizenship thus became defined as unconditional and irrevocable. Although some Members of Parliament pointed out that natural-born citizens were also likely to commit treason, Paul Martin Sr., instrumental in the development of the Act, rejected all attempts to remove the exemption on Canadian-born citizens on the basis that such a move would render them stateless.[66]

The first Citizenship Act thus distinguished between classes of citizens even *after* they acquired this legal status, ensuring that citizenship status was not to be unconditional for all citizens. As discussed earlier, Arendt discussed how grave were the dangers of denying particular individuals the 'right to have rights,' and the seriousness of the consequences of the imposition of a condition of statelessness upon them. The new Citizenship Act maintained this right of the state to impose a condition of statelessness upon immigrant citizens, thus allowing their immigrant status to permeate their citizenship even after they became naturalized, distinguishing them from the real citizens whose status could not be revoked. In institutionalizing the deportation clause, the new Citizenship Act allowed the use of this clause to curtail the access of specific groups to full citizenship, such as the right to political activism and access to public assistance, as Barbara Roberts found in her study.[67]

On the eve of the introduction of the Act (1946), 80 per cent of the population was of British and French ancestry.[68] While not all of them would have been natural-born citizens, the unconditional citizenship granted to this category would privilege those among them who were Canadian-born, as well as all their descendents. Excluded from this deep belonging were the citizens-come-lately, the immigrant-cum-citizens, who were to be treated with suspicion, even if they demonstrated complete loyalty to the state.

The Act allowed independent access to citizenship for Canadian women, stipulating they would not lose this status upon marriage to a non-citizen. This was in stark contrast to the political treatment of Aboriginal women who *lost* their Indian status (and political membership in their community) upon marriage to non-Aboriginal men. The Act also allowed non-citizen women to become eligible for citizenship through marriage to a Canadian citizen and, in this way, extended these women's access to citizenship. However, given the racialized immigration policies and the rampant fears of miscegenation that marked the period, few women of the non-preferred races would have been able to benefit from this increased access to citizenship.

Section 10 of the Act allowed the minister of immigration to grant certificates of citizenship, and also stipulated (unequal) eligibility criteria on the basis of linguistic proficiency. For applicants fluent in either English or French, the period of domicile required was five years. For applicants who spoke neither of these languages, domicile was defined as a period of twenty years. Then, as now, non-European working-class immigrants, particularly women, would have been the least likely to have fluency in these languages. As non-preferred races, these immigrants already encountered significant barriers to enter and reside in the country. Now, the Act stipulated that they were required to meet the longest residency requirement for citizenship eligibility.

Prime Minister MacKenzie King thus paid tribute to the Canadians who had made Canadian citizenship possible: 'The vision and courage of men and women have transformed our country, almost within living memory, from small and virtually unknown regions of forest and farm into one of the great industrial nations of the world.'[69] His comments ignored the reality that 'our' country had been built on the lands of Aboriginal peoples, instead declaring the country as having been among the 'virtually unknown regions' of the world. The creation of modern citizenship by this Act thus reinforced and consolidated the white settler ideology and deepened the institutionalization of colonial relations.

The Citizenship Act also helped to bridge the divisions among the different European ethnicities in the country. Paul Martin Sr. noted this objective when introducing the Act: 'No matter where we come from or what our origins, French, English, Scandinavian, Scottish, Ukrainian, Irish or whatever else, one thing at least we can all be, and that is Canadians.' Notable by its absence was any reference to Canadians of non-European ancestry. If there were any doubts that the Act would transform the racialized character of the nation, MacKenzie King put them to rest less than one month after the Act was tabled:

With regard to the selection of immigrants ... I wish to make it quite clear that Canada is perfectly within her rights in selecting persons who we regard as desirable future citizens. It is not a 'fundamental human right' of any alien to enter Canada. It is a privilege. It is a matter of domestic policy.

There will, I am sure, be general agreement with the view that the people of Canada do not wish, as a result of mass migration, to make a fundamental alteration in the character of our population. Large-scale migration from the Orient would change the fundamental composition of the Canadian population.[70]

Racialized immigration policies regulating access to formal citizenship were to remain in effect for close to three decades following the introduction of the Act.

Contesting Nationality?

Although the earliest arrival of Black and Asian migrants can be traced to the pre-Confederation period, the racism they encountered in the national commitment to 'Keep Canada White' greatly curtailed this migration.[71] Even when their labour was recognized as necessary for economic development, these migrants were reviled and cast in the figure of the inassimilable and degenerate stranger. Constructed as neither co-religionists nor co-civilizationists, their categorization as non-preferred races constituted them as unworthy of citizenship and minimized the value of their labour.

As was the case in other settler societies, like the United States,[72] racial classifications were legislated in Canada to restrict the immigration of non-preferred races: the Chinese Immigration Act of 1885, the Exclusion Act of 1923, the Continuous Passage Requirement of 1908, various head taxes, and the institutionalization of race in the 1910 Immigration Act were among some of the more notorious pieces of legislation.[73] Migrants from Africa, Asia, and the Caribbean – a part of the British Empire in which they had the status of British subjects – were denied the same mobility rights as white subjects through such policies.[74] Even when these migrants managed to enter the country, racialized legal exclusions applied to them whether *they were naturalized citizens or not*, as they did to their descendents, whether *they were Canadian-born or not*.[75]

As discussed above, immigration and nationalization legislation enacted from Confederation until the mid-twentieth century secured the emergence of the white population as a majority.[76] During this period, it was entirely feasible that the non-preferred races might well have emerged as 'market-dominant minorities,' with economic control of the various sectors within which they were engaged.[77] Instead, as the exclusionary policies were implemented, the numbers of these populations actually declined. From exclusionary state policies to their everyday denigrations within the public sphere, the figure of these migrants instead became crystallized as quintessential latecomers. The diversity of languages, cultures, ethnicities, and historical experiences and consciousness among migrants from Africa, Asia, Latin America, and the Caribbean, in short, the entire world outside Europe, was conflated in the essentialized and homogenized demographic category non-preferred race imposed upon them. This classification was to later become translated into a similarly homogenized category, that of the immigrant.

David T. Goldberg has argued that state imposition of racial distinctions among populations created homogenized nations out of heterogeneous populations, rather than the reverse. The granting of Canadian citizenship rights along racial lines created a social order based on just such a commitment to create a national homogeneity. The treatment of Black settlers and Chinese migrants serve as useful examples of how this political erasure of the heterogeneity of the population was attempted.

Black settlers, among the earliest undesired communities to migrate to Canada, were subjected to treatment that was in contrast to that of whites.[78] Despite being considered as political allies in defending British interests against American expansion, Black settlers were given access to land on the basis of a 'license of occupation,' and not on the basis of ownership.[79] The refusal to grant them ownership, in tandem with the other racist practices discussed above, sent a clear message to this community: 'American negroes were not welcome and were not encouraged to come; and, although no law was passed to exclude them, careful administrative procedures ensured that their applications would be rejected.'[80] Although most Black people in the United States were 'too poor and disadvantaged to contemplate migration,' some did come to the Prairies during the nineteenth century. But without 'the necessary reinforcements,' their numbers did not increase.[81] In fact, they actually declined.[82]

The building of the railway, a central plank in the National Economic Policy, was indispensable to the settlement of the western provinces and to the expansion of the national market economy. Chinese (and later

South Asian) men were recruited to build this, and so critical was the labour they provided that without it, the building of the railways would have been 'indefinitely postponed.'[83] After the project was completed, however, the Chinese migrants were defined as a threat to society and 'virtually every evil was blamed upon them.'[84]

The subsequent Chinese Immigration Act of 1885 imposed a head tax on Chinese immigrants to curtail their entry.[85] The Exclusion Act in 1923 sought to prevent all Chinese immigration, with the consequence that less than fifty Chinese immigrants were permitted to enter the country between 1923 and 1947.[86] Similar legislation was also enacted to curtail South Asian and Japanese immigration, among them the Continuous Passage requirement introduced in 1908.[87] In the year after its introduction, only six South Asian immigrants entered the country; in the year prior to its introduction, these immigrants had numbered 2,500.[88] The 1910 Immigration Act legislated prohibitions on the grounds of race and became the 'principal instrument' for the 'Keep Canada White' policies. This Act remained in effect for the next fifty years,[89] during which time immigration from Europe was actively solicited. In the first decade of the twentieth century, immigration accounted for 44 per cent of the growth in the population.[90] The restrictions on non-white immigration ensured that the majority of this growth remained white.

The policies promoting European immigration were gendered, tailored to meet the special campaigns that recruited women. The policies restricting non-European immigration were also gendered, with women being particularly defined for exclusion: if white women were to be the 'mothers' of the nation, non-white women were said to herald its doom. Few women from China and South Asia were allowed to immigrate prior to the 1960s. Single Black women were allowed entry as domestic workers, but only on the condition that their families not accompany them.[91] As will be discussed more fully in the next chapter, women of the non-preferred races were constituted as morally degenerate, sexually depraved, and endowed with a fecundity more animalistic than human. Keeping them out of the country was considered a special priority of immigration policies.

Yet, despite the intense discrimination these migrants encountered, they persisted in their attempts to enter the country. They used legal means when they could and resorted to extra-legal means when compelled to do so. They mobilized their budding communities against racist policies in Canada and within the British Empire; they lobbied for family reunification and for the right of illegal immigrants to remain in the country.[92] They also organized to gain access to Canadian citizenship.

The early religious and social organizations these immigrants established formed vital networks of support to sustain their communities. These organizations provided financial assistance to arriving migrants and assisted them in securing employment and housing. Those who were employed provided support for the sick and the unemployed. In the process, these immigrants faltered sometimes, yet often prospered and strengthened the presence of the communities they established.[93] Some, however, could not withstand the intense racism they encountered and returned to their countries of origin.

Non-preferred races came from various classes, including farmers, peasants and workers, merchants, small business owners, and entrepreneurs. They pooled resources and bought businesses and farms, despite these activities sparking vehement resistance from whites. Asian workers in British Columbia, for example, soon stood on the 'middle rung in the province's labour hierarchy.'[94] The economic competition they presented to white domination of the economy was real enough, and the white population responded by calling for an end to further Asian immigration, as well as the eviction of those already settled. The most far-reaching of these efforts resulted in the evacuation of Japanese-Canadians from British Columbia during the Second World War.

Although largely cast in the trope of the 'suffering' stranger subjected to intense political and socio-economic discrimination and inequalities, these migrants also actively carved out economic opportunities and financial successes for themselves. They struggled for their 'right to have rights,' to borrow from Arendt. Citizenship status was equated with full human status, with civilized status, and with recognition of the individual as a valuable member of the political community whose interests were to be protected by the state, at least in theory. People of colour understood full well the power invested in this institution and sought access to that power, contesting the racialized identity of the nation, both materially and symbolically. Excluded from citizenship and constituted as despised and inferior races in the national symbolic, for them citizenship was not only a means to gain legal rights but also a means to destroy such racialized constructs by gaining recognition of their common humanity. Unfortunately, however, migrants challenged only their exclusion from citizenship, not the institution itself.

Even when these migrants did acquire it, their citizenship remained a tenuous affair. The experience of Japanese-Canadians provides the definitive example, illustrating the ever-present threat to racial minorities of a state of exception to their precarious access to equality in the regime of citizenship. Japanese-Canadians were given greater access to immigration than other Asians as a result of Canadian state support for the alliance between the British and Japanese states.[95] However, their relatively greater access to citizenship did not protect them from becoming defined as an enemy race and having their citizenship suspended in a moment defined as a national crisis.[96] The internment of this community, and the suspension of their rights, separated families and destroyed an economically vibrant community. The suspension was to remain in effect for seven years, as their racial identity was deemed more significant than their citizen status or their remarkable contributions to the nation's economy.

The role of white citizens in mobilizing for the eviction and internment of Japanese-Canadians was critical and has been defined as 'spontaneous' and 'widespread.'[97] In the virulent eruption of this racism, state and nation worked in concert to contain a racial enemy within the citizenry, as they had done before. The internment was still in effect at the time of the introduction of the first Citizenship Act, and it was referred to by Members of Parliament from British Columbia who asked for reassurance that the Act's introduction would not allow Japanese-Canadians to return to the province. Reassuring them it would not, Paul Martin Sr. agreed to an amendment upholding the Order in Council for the internment.[98] Neither the state nor the majority of the population seem to have considered necessary any pretence that the Citizenship Act was intended to establish, or would have the effect of establishing, equality in the treatment of all citizens.

The internment of Japanese-Canadians had been preceded by decades of popular political mobilizing against their access to fishing licences, their ownership of land, and their access to employment and educational opportunities. The internment and dispersal of this community played no small role in ensuring white domination of the fisheries in the province, as well as the other industries in which Japanese-Canadians had presented serious challenges to white domination. The racialization of their citizenship helped consolidate the economic domination of white nationals at a time when both state and national formation were still in a state of flux, when the form and character of the national state was yet to be crystallized.

Although victims themselves of European domination and colonizing processes in their countries of origin, non-preferred races were to contribute to the marginalization of Aboriginal populations as they sought greater inclusion in the colonial society, oblivious – or even hostile – to Aboriginal presence. These migrants made the modality of their own exclusion the site of their struggles for inclusion. In the process, they contributed to the further development of the settler society and of its economy and its social institutions, thereby strengthening the colonial project. In the assertions of their agency – which included practices of resistances, of accommodations and compromises, sometimes even of compradorship – the unwelcome strangers also became unwitting accomplices to the exploitation of Aboriginal peoples.

Many of the immigrants who became party to the marginalization of Aboriginal peoples had themselves been coerced into migration, whether under conditions of enslavement, as was the case with Black migrants, or under conditions of indentureship, as was the case with many Chinese and South Asian migrants. Then as now, it would be difficult to draw too fine a distinction between coerced and 'voluntary' migration. It is thus not so much the form of their migration as it is the forms of agency they were to assert in Canada that give rise to the following concerns. Can a citizenship based on the destruction of the sovereignty of Native peoples ever be expanded without deepening this colonial relation? Can those previously excluded from citizenship ever be included without becoming complicit to this Aboriginal dispossession? Can a citizenship conceived in, and maintained by, a genocidal violence leave untainted any group which comes to be included in its orbit, no matter how severe the forms of their own previous exclusions or how tenuous their subsequent inclusion?

The extent to which these migrants exercised 'choice' in seeking inclusion in citizenship, and the other courses of action that were practicable for them, are clearly matters for debate and outside the scope of my discussion. Caught between the Scylla of a devastating disenfranchisement that threatened their survival in the country and the Charybdis of a colonialist citizenship regime that made them complicit in the nation's domination of Aboriginal peoples, they mobilized for enfranchisement and the expansion of citizenship rights to include their particular claims. Their pursuit of citizenship reflects their recognition of the marginal presence and diminishing power of Aboriginal peoples, as it does their recognition that the chances of improving their own status lay in their seeking greater parity with nationals. Ironically enough, their attempt to include themselves into citizenship created a democratic space that was in many ways a condemnation of the race-based regime of citizenship rights. The egalitarian aspects of expanding citizenship were thus created by excluded populations, not by the state, nor by those included in the regime of citizenship, who sought to protect this hallowed institution from the encroachments of undeserving Others.

The unwelcome migrants, much like the welcome Europeans, related to Native peoples through the national symbolic. Many of them would have been familiar in their countries of origin with the western cultural construct of the Red Indian as an impediment to modernity and economic progress, given that this construct was pervasive throughout European colonies. Many of them would also have been familiar with a similar construction of indigenous peoples in their own societies. Inculcated with such popular cultural constructs of the racial hierarchies promulgated by western powers and their own national elites, these migrants claimed their relatively higher status than Aboriginal peoples within this hierarchy in Canada. With few exceptions, the migrants internalized these constructs, and many have continued to reproduce them since.

The political struggles that migrant populations waged to gain equal access to citizenship, and to economic and social institutions, focused their attention more intently on the forms of power and the institutions serving the interests of nationals. The relocation of Native communities onto reserves furthered the geographical contiguity of these migrants with white nationals and further distanced them from Native communities. Consequently, the more these migrants sought proximity to nationals, the more they furthered their own social and political distance from Native communities. Their descendents, many oblivious to their own histories of racialized exclusions, are all the more readily amenable to reproducing this distance.

The Indian Act, immigration policies, the provisions of the Citizenship Act, and the treatment of Japanese-Canadians as enemies of the nation on the basis of their race demonstrate the very deep and integral connections between law, citizenship, and nationality in the constitution of the real national subject as one with an incontestable right to citizenship.

Liberalizing Citizenship

Canadian society underwent significant transformation in the 1960s and 1970s, a period of liberalization that brought about shifts in the organization of processes of racialization. Among the key policy changes during this period were the elimination of overtly racial classifications in immigration policies, increased access to Canadian citizenship for previously excluded groups, and the adoption of state multiculturalism. Aboriginal peoples also acquired greater access to education and the courts, as well as to the franchise. Many of the restrictions on their mobility were also removed. In this section, I focus on some of the most significant changes to immigration and citizenship policies.

The Immigration Regulations of 1962 emphasized the labour market needs of the country. The point system introduced in 1967 reflected this and focused on the education, profession, occupation, language, and skill levels of prospective immigrants, as well as on their family ties to Canada.[99] Popularly defined as instituting a non-discriminatory immigration program, the point system was subsequently entrenched in the Immigration Act, 1976–77.[100] Immigration for permanent settlement became organized mainly through the independent and family immigrant classes, as well as through the refugee protection program.[101]

Citizenship legislation was also revised during this period and the 'preferential treatment' of British subjects was removed.[102] Inequalities in the residency requirements for citizenship eligibility (twenty years for residents who did not speak English or French) were also removed.[103] These changes greatly expanded access to citizenship for all immigrants admitted for permanent settlement, including those previously designated non-preferred races. Effectively ending the official 'Keep Canada White' policies of an earlier era, these changes became widely defined as reflecting a period of innovation.[104] Subsequently, the Canadian immigration program has come to be defined as among the most humanitarian and compassionate in the world. These liberalized immigration policies, the source of considerable national pride, have come to sustain contemporary exaltations of Canadian nationality as the most generous and humane in the world.

The result of the changes to immigration and citizenship policies have been significant. Whereas 90 per cent of all immigrants prior to 1961 were European-born, they came to represent only 25 per cent between 1981 and 1991, during which six out of the ten largest source countries were in Asia.[105] A number of scholars have pointed out that while the point system made a commitment in principle to end race and sex discrimination, it did not do so in effect. First, resources for immigrant recruitment and processing are allocated unequally, favouring developed countries over developing ones. Second, immigration officers have discretionary powers to allocate points to applicants for their personal suitability and independent status. The allocation of these points reflect the biases of the officers, who have disproportionately favoured male applicants as independents over female applicants.

The liberalization of immigration policy undoubtedly reflected a growing awareness among nationals of the damaging effects of overt racial distinctions in state policy. But with Aboriginal populations having been decimated and displaced onto reserves, immigration was the primary source of population growth. The increased presence of immigrants in the country became an unavoidable necessity, as was the case in the other hypercapitalist countries also experiencing labour shortages. As a result of the pressures on Canada to present itself as the destination of choice for immigration, and of the political organizing of migrants for access to citizenship, the liberalization of citizenship became unavoidable. I will return to the Immigration Act and the point system in the next two chapters. Here, I wish to highlight three aspects of the changes to immigration and citizenship legislation that maintained the earlier racialized constructs of nation, nationals, and citizenship.

In the absence of a just resolution to the challenge of Aboriginal sovereignty, Canadian citizenship remained rooted within the colonial dynamic and continued to be a means to further the cultural and political elimination of Aboriginality. The drive to extend citizenship to Aboriginal peoples remained tied to the objective of 'bleeding' them off from their nations, and to regulate their integration into the Canadian mainstream, primarily as individuals with no special claims arising from their historical relationship to the land. In other words, citizenship remained the 'final solution' to the Indian problem no less so in the present than was the case in the past.[106]

Further, the deployment of citizenship to confer an (abstract) 'equality' on all subjects, including Aboriginal peoples, enabled it to construct Aboriginal peoples in the national imagination as ingrates who demanded preferential treatment and special rights, over and above what was a fair entitlement of all other citizens. In their rejection of assimilation into the mainstream, Aboriginal people were all the more readily constructed as demanding more than their fair share, and hence, as discriminating *against* Canadian citizens, placing them at a disadvantage.[107] More sympathetic nationals have come to regard Aboriginal peoples' conflictual relationship to citizenship as mainly a conflict between their ethnic and cultural identity on the one hand, and their civic and political identity on the other. In other words, they approach

Aboriginal struggles as primarily cultural and ethnic, and not as political struggles.

This reading of the situation allows such nationals to dissociate the cultural (and spiritual) practices of Aboriginal peoples from their political demands for sovereignty. The former can be accommodated, even celebrated, without significant political and economic transformation, while the latter, which demands a fundamental transformation of nationality, can be ignored. Aboriginal struggles for sovereignty are clearly tied not only to their ethnic, spiritual and cultural identity, but also to their self-determination, and hence to their political and civic identities as sovereign peoples. The separation of the two enables nationals to fancy themselves as supportive of Aboriginal rights even as they reproduce the colonial hierarchy.

Increased access to de jure citizenship for non-Canadian-born individuals continued to be organized primarily through the unequal conditions of their immigration after the liberalization, as had been the case previously. The unequal conditions of entry for the family class, for example, which required a sponsor to undertake financial responsibility for their dependents, denied these dependents equal entitlements to social programs even after they acquired legal citizenship.

The immigration policies that regulated the entry of domestic workers trapped them into a near-complete dependency on their employers by the stipulation that they live-in at their place of employment for a period of two years. Although recognized as workers in immigration policy, the treatment of domestic workers in this policy was quite unlike that of the independent class, which regulated the entry of other categories of workers but made no such stipulation for their entry into the country. The regulation of temporary workers, on the other hand, prohibited their subsequent access to citizenship. The unequal conditions that organized migration continued to organize a multitiered citizenship, which has become instituted through the specific regulations of the immigration program.

Sponsorship regulations, for example, denied sponsored immigrants and their families equal access to the social rights of citizenship. Whereas those immigrants who did not speak English and French were required to prove residency for twenty years before they could acquire citizenship and its social entitlements prior to the liberalization of these policies, the liberalized sponsorship regulations stipulated unequal access to social entitlements for *all* sponsored immigrants for the duration of their sponsorship, even after their acquisition of citizenship

(which has required shorter residency periods than the sponsorship regulation). These regulations have had particularly serious consequences
for immigrant women, as will be discussed in the next chapter.

Liberalized citizenship maintained the earlier distinctions between
Canadian-born and naturalized citizens, reproducing the unconditionality of the citizenship of the former and the conditionality of the citizenship of the latter. The state's ability to deport foreign-born citizens
was preserved, these citizens were to remain vulnerable to the potential
imposition of the condition of statelessness. The unconditional 'right to
have rights' for non-Canadian-born citizens is yet to be achieved.

The role of citizenship in institutionalizing the dispossession of
Aboriginal peoples' resources, the inequalities sponsorship regulations
organize within the body politic, and the maintenance of the deportation clause contribute to the enduring symbolic attachment of citizenship to whiteness. Despite these serious limitations, the liberalization
of citizenship has enabled representations of the nation-state as being a
liberal democracy in essence rather than a colonial settler society.
Indeed, the removal of overt racial preferences has led to a greater exaltation of the white status of nationals. It has granted greater legitimacy
to the nation-state's definition of itself as a civic, not racial entity, committed to the modernist project of human progress. As a consequence
of the continuities in the historical racialization of the category of citizen, and of the multitiered structure of citizenship, the institution itself
remains obstinately racialized so that it refers not simply to a political
identity but also to a white identity reinscribed as a political one. Racial
identity (white, officially British and French) is repeatedly reinscribed as
the authentic and trustworthy marker of citizenship in daily life. Nationality and citizenship coexist in an overlapping manner, so that some citizens can claim nationality while others are denied such claims, even
when they share the legal status of citizenship.

The symbolic association of citizenship with whiteness can be regularly witnessed in seemingly innocent rites, such as routine questioning
of immigrants about where they are really from; in the not so innocent
exhortation to immigrants to go back to where they came from; and in
the 'reasonable' demand that they produce identity papers and proof of
residence when they attempt to access health, education, and social services. Such rites of citizenship, even when couched in the form of polite
requests to prove legality, reflect the common-sense knowledge shared
among nationals that strangers need to prove their legality before they
should be allowed to access their rights. The expansion of citizenship to

include people of colour has undoubtedly brought about significant changes in their status and rights, an important one being the right of family reunification. However, citizenship has failed to be the panacea many had dreamed it to be.

A. Sivanandan, the director of the Institute of Race Relations in Britain, has noted that Black people in Britain wear their 'passport' on their 'faces.'[108] Immigration and citizenship legislation regulate the presence of people of colour in most western countries such that even when they have legal status as citizens, they are nevertheless also defined as not belonging to the nation.[109] The result, as Ahmad and Husband point out, is that 'citizenship is not merely a legal status; it is a vehicle for nationalism and a focus for defining national identity.'[110] The political practices of the Canadian nation-state have likewise stamped the citizenship of people of colour on our faces, so that our right to cross borders and to make claims to social entitlements are met with greater suspicion and vigilance. As in Britain, Sweden, Germany, and the United States, the social rights of citizenship structure the exclusion of people of colour as foreigners by granting them unequal access to social entitlements.[111] Such exclusion is certainly no aberration, it is inherent in citizenship as a mechanism for the political induction of real citizens into nationality.

Moreover, before the events of 11 September 2001, the London bombings of 7 July 2005, and the global effects of the U.S.-led 'war on terror,' Canadians might well have considered the processes of outright exclusion from citizenship, such as those experienced by Japanese-Canadians, as isolated and aberrant, a shameful moment in the nation's past which is best relegated to the historical archives. In the wake of these events, however, it is clear that these familiar (and tested) processes can be applied to Muslims or any other non-preferred group, resulting in the suspension of their citizenship rights and in their being presented as a threat to the nation in moments of crisis.

Canadian citizenship was integrative and inclusive for European immigrants until well into the twentieth century. It organized their membership in the nation and gave them formal legal rights and entitlements. As such, citizenship was an institution that expanded their political participation and enhanced their exalted status as modern subjects. Yet, simultaneously, it also became an exclusionary mechanism, producing Indians and immigrants as racial strangers. During the eighteenth, nineteenth, and twentieth centuries, argues T.H. Marshall, capitalist societies were developing 'good societies' in which the institution of citizenship evolved to organize civil, political, and social rights. Citizenship symbolized the drive towards greater equality in the historical 'march of progress.'[112] Benhabib, for her part, also furthers such an understanding of citizenship, naturalizing the right of citizens to have rights, and presenting as equally natural their inclination to protect these from the encroachments of outsiders. Contrary to such formulations, Canadian citizenship emerged with the clear intention to produce racial divisions among the populations within the territorial bounds of the nation-state, divisions which remain significant to this day and which continue the project of all racial states to produce national/racial homogeneity in the face of actual heterogeneity.

COMPASSION

3 The Welfare of Nationals

Undeniably, the 'social safety net' we built over the past several decades helped make Canada one of the world's most successful countries, rich in prosperity and opportunity. Programs such as unemployment insurance, social assistance and social services, child benefits, universal pensions and a national network of widely accessible colleges and universities have made our nation a beacon of civilized values. Those values of compassion, ensuring the basic necessities of food and shelter for all, and sharing opportunity are at the heart of the social security system we've inherited.

Human Resources Development Canada, Agenda: Jobs and Growth[1]

The post-war development of the welfare state in most of the hypercapitalist world, including Canada, has been generally defined as a watershed. Marking a turn away from the social Darwinist ethos of the laissez-faire system towards a more humane and compassionate capitalism, the welfare state has been defined by the ideals of collective social responsibility for all citizens within the polity, including the most vulnerable among them.[2] Modernist narratives of national progress received a significant boost with the extension of the institution of citizenship to encapsulate social rights, in addition to civil and political ones. As T.H. Marshall rightly predicted, the inclusion of social entitlements in the institution of citizenship strengthened the social bonds within the community of citizens. This state form drew an equation between the welfare of Canadians and their families with that of the nation and, as such, defined the well-being of nationals as being among the highest of the state's priorities.

Critical scholars of the welfare state have pointed out that rather than doing away with the socio-economic inequalities of class and gender, the welfare state further institutionalized and deepened these.[3] According to their critiques, the transition to the welfare system became necessary in order to stabilize an economic system inherently prone to periods of economic recession, and to contain the political challenges presented to the status quo by labour and women's movements. The expansion of citizenship to include social entitlements resulted in the welfare state's stabilization of the consumption levels and patterns indispensable to the ongoing accumulation of capital. It also satisfied the demands of working-class and feminist movements, which had been greatly emboldened by their sacrifices in support of national war efforts during the two world wars as well as by their recent enfranchisement. The development of social entitlements enhanced the legitimacy of the state as representing the interests of all members of society, not just the privileged elite. Where laissez-faire capitalism had introduced the cash nexus and eroded the bonds of community life, the welfare state mitigated this erosion by 'recreating community-like conditions' that furthered the 'social integration' of the working class into bourgeois society.[4] In short, the welfare state increased the legitimacy of the state, stabilized the capitalist system, and weakened class solidarity among the proletariat.

Feminist scholars have drawn particular attention to the gendered nature of the welfare state. The development of this state form institutionalized the sexual division of labour, giving rise to the 'public patriarchy' of the welfare state in addition to the 'private patriarchy' of the family.[5] Further, Linda Gordon and Nancy Fraser have identified distinct 'male' and 'female' tracks within social programs: the first includes contributory social insurance programs that 'replace wages temporarily or permanently lost through illness, injury, unemployment, or retirement'; and the second includes means-tested public assistance programs. On the one hand, male workers have disproportionately greater access to the programs of the first track, given its association with full-time employment. Women, on the other hand, tend to rely more on the second track, which is organized on the basis of need, not contributions, and which provides access through income testing. Defining women primarily as wives and mothers with a weak attachment to the labour market, these programs support the maintenance of the wage system with the adult male worker at its centre. Over time, the means-tested social assistance programs came to be largely stigmatized as 'welfare,' and, during the last two decades of the twentieth century, more as charity than as entitlement.[6]

These theorists conclude in the main that the transition to the welfare state transformed the debate about and the processes organizing the distribution of material goods, leaving intact the underlying social relations of class and gender. Few among them have sought to examine the impact of the welfare state on processes of racialization and national formation. Most have left unquestioned the organization of access to social programs through the institution of citizenship, contributing to the normalization of this institution as the ideal modality for the state's relation with its subjects.

In this chapter, I argue that as the welfare state constituted itself as 'compassionate' and 'caring,' it exalted national subjects as possessive of the same qualities. Deepening both the value and legitimacy of nationality, the social programs of the welfare state institutionalized the human worthiness of its nationals as compassionate and, hence, as deserving of the greater entitlements of the social safety net. The new moral economy of care enabled nationals to claim these human characteristics as their own (politicized) traits in their self-consisting practices. Foregrounding the relationship between race and nation, I examine how the welfare state's appropriation of the characteristic of compassion made it emblematic of Canadian national identity, thus endowing political currency on this characteristic as possessed by nationals, but not by their Others. Committed to ensuring the welfare of all Canadians and their families (in principle, even if not always in practice), the social safety net was defined as a 'sacred trust' of the nation and reflecting its ethic of care. It has been key in organizing the social solidarity of nationals and the expulsion of strangers in the post-war period. Social citizenship exalted Canadians and their families as deserving subjects, worthy of the entitlements they could claim as a right, indeed, as a virtue of their very character, which was said to both give rise to, and be re-flected in, these programs.[7]

I also argue that the organization of access to social programs through the institution of citizenship meant that the historical racialization of Canadian citizenship discussed in the previous chapters infused the development of social entitlements. Institutionalized through the bureaucratic machinery of the public sector, and the 'caring' professions, the social safety net provided vital supports to nationals while binding them in racialized relations of obligation and reciprocity. The technical machinery of care thus provided Canadians with the vital socio-economic supports and services that are the subject of many of the studies of the welfare state. In other words, the welfare system reinforced citizenship as the mechanism organizing the racial hierarchy of the settler society.

The welfare state's valorization of the feminized characteristic of compassion emphasized this gendered aspect of the nation-state. Where the laissez-faire settler state had emphasized the masculinized aspects of the national subject as discoverer, conqueror, pioneer, and settler, the welfare state emphasized the feminized aspects of both state and nationals by constituting them as compassionate and caring. The valorization of feminized qualities was to have great significance in the relations of nationals as benefactors with their Others. The transition to the welfare state thus signalled a major shift in the role Canadian women were to play in the public sphere and in the contribution of femininity to the national symbolic. I argue that the emphasis on the feminized aspects of state and nation has deeply influenced the organization of gender relations among the various populations within the social order.

With the constitution of Canadian men and women as compassionate and caring citizens, their families likewise became constructed as modern and committed to egalitarian relations, notwithstanding their gendered, heterosexist, and classed complexities. As large numbers of the nation's women gained employment in the public sector and housewives were given access to income support programs, the claims of subscription to egalitarian gender relations within the family could be sustained with greater credibility. This claim to gender equality as an aspect of nationality was defined in direct relation to the gendered 'deficiencies' that came to be attributed to the nation's Others.

The welfare state's extension of its machinery of care to the Canadian family exalted it as the site of (re)production of the nation and its values. In contrast, Native and immigrant families were defined as threatening the nation's welfare. Aboriginal families had been marked for systematic destruction through the residential school system, which was maintained by the welfare state until the 1960s. Introduced in both the United States and Canada after the 'Indian wars' of the nineteenth century, this system devastated Native families as children were forcefully removed from their families and communities. Driven by a policy designed to 'Kill the Indian' and 'Save the Man,' the preservation of the residential school system for decades after the development of the welfare state meant that the cultural and political extinction of Aboriginal peoples as self-determining nations was integrated as an objective of this state form.[8] During the 1960s, the apprehension of Aboriginal children for placement in residential schools gave way to their apprehension by the child protection services of the welfare bureaucracy for adoption and placement in foster families, almost all of which were non-Aboriginal. The nation's extension of the ethic of compassion to Aboriginal populations maintained the constitution of Aboriginality as a threat to Aboriginal children. The child protection services thus maintained the construction of Aboriginal mothers as deficient, now capitalizing on the devastating impact of the residential school system on Aboriginal families to further legitimize such apprehension. In the welfarist national imaginary, Native families were deficient; Native mothers deviant and a menace to their own children; and the nation the caring benefactor of these children.

As for immigrant families, the overtly racialized immigration and citizenship legislation, which distinguished between preferred and non-preferred races, remained in effect until the 1960s and 1970s, during which period the social programs of the welfare state were greatly expanded. As discussed in chapter 2, women of the non-preferred races were marked for particular exclusion from the nation, their sexuality and fertility defined as a specific threat to the nation's purity. The liberalization of immigration and citizenship legislation in the 1960s and 1970s drew upon these earlier constructs, constituting immigrant women primarily as family members of immigrant men and their economic dependents. They were thus the financial responsibility of their sponsors, not of the nation. The immigration regulations for the family class, under which the immigration of these women was largely regulated, placed specific restrictions on these families' access to social entitlements and, hence, to their de facto citizenship. These practices have had an inordinate role in the construction of immigrant women as dependents of immigrant men, as exceptionally family and tradition bound, and the passive objects of hyperpatriarchal immigrant communities.

The extension of the citizenship rights of nationals to include access to the social safety net has been material and tangible, enhancing their economic security and social value. This extension of rights has also profoundly shaped their sense of individual moral worthiness. In contrast, the Native family has remained marked for cultural extinction. The immigrant family has been subjected to increased regulation and enhanced patriarchal control through the figure of the sponsor. This family was now constituted as hyperpatriarchal at best, and pathologically dysfunctional at worst. If the welfare state strengthened the sense of entitlement of nationals and deepened the social bonds among them, it simultaneously magnified the sense of disentitlement and expulsion from the national community for those whom it excluded. The welfare state has never been quite as compassionate or as universal as has generally been presumed.

Race, Nation, and Welfare

In her study of social policy in the United States, Linda Gordon has made the persuasive case that these policies were informed by the experience of the white social reformers – women and men – who developed them. As a result, social policies came to incorporate a white vision of welfare. By not challenging the racial domination that was so central to the organization of American society, these policies instead helped to reproduce it. Black women reformers, however, developed a significantly different vision of welfare in the programs they established in their communities. These women identified the racial domination of their communities as a key factor with which they had to contend. As Gordon puts it, 'Race issues were poverty issues, and women's issues were race issues.'[9] She argues that Black feminists confronted their racial domination and defined its elimination as central to the welfare of their communities.

Gordon's insights are useful in highlighting the similarly distinct visions of welfare that emerged from the experiences of Canadian nationals, Aboriginal peoples, and immigrant communities. While the former developed a vision that enhanced white supremacy as national supremacy, the latter two recognized that ending the respective forms of the racial domination of their communities lay at the heart of their welfare. In the case of Aboriginal peoples, their efforts to preserve families and communities, religio-political traditions, and cultural practices, and their claims to sovereignty and title to land was integrally connected to their welfare. Political self-determination was inseparable from their collective social welfare. The loss of their lands and the imposition of Indian status upon them were the most significant factors in eroding their welfare.[10] For immigrants, the question of family reunification, the removal of racial barriers in immigration policies, and their unequal access to citizenship were centrally connected to their welfare and security.

Although ignored in much of the writing on the Canadian welfare state, the question of race has been of central importance to its development. The preservation of the 'quality' of the nation was an important objective in the transition to the welfare state in most hypercapitalist countries, including Canada. The blueprint for the welfare state developed by Keynesian economic policies and Lord Beveridge's social policies in Britain were to shape welfare regimes in most of the hypercapitalist world.[11] The development of social programs in that country had as much to do with the state's global ambitions of maintaining its hegemony over its rapidly disintegrating empire as it did with liberal ideals of expanding citizenship rights on the home front. Liberalism was being compelled to redefine itself at the national level by the increasing poverty and destitution that threatened to pull apart the national social fabric; by the demands of the newly enfranchised masses; and by the electoral challenges posed by the growing support for socialist and social-democratic political parties. In North America, these national concerns were also prevalent. Moreover, the economic upheavals of the Great Depression of the 1930s, and the two world wars, helped the new liberalism to garner the support of North American ruling elites – liberals and conservatives alike – who came to accept the inevitability of greater state intervention in the economy if the capitalist system was to survive and if its volatile economic cycles were to be stabilized.[12] The international front was no less a cause of concern for North American elites.

In Britain, the declining birth rate and the deteriorating health of the population would clearly have profound consequences for maintaining that country's international competitiveness, particularly in the face of the serious challenges – both military and economic – presented by the various national independence movements and post-colonial states. The intense rivalry among various European and North American countries that sought to enhance their own power within the changing geopolitical order exacerbated this concern.[13] The two world wars had underscored the critical necessity for maintaining healthy 'national' populations that could be drafted into service for the protection of national interests.[14] Recognizing their citizens as indispensable to securing their international interests, ruling elites in the hypercapitalist world applied the doctrine of the survival of the fittest to national, as well as individual, success: 'No nation could hope to survive in the coming struggle for existence, taught this new doctrine, unless it improved its racial stock physically and mentally and breached those deep cleavages within its body politic which set one class apart from the other.'[15]

The carnage of the two world wars and the devastation wreaked by fascism had also forced a recognition of the horrors of the 'scientific' doctrines of racial superiority in the hypercapitalist world. Similarly, the growing power of national independence movements had heightened the sensibility in Europe about the horrors of colonial rule. These move-ments were forcing the dismantling of the British and other European empires, as well as a renegotiation of the geopolitical order.

The modernist impulse said to inspire the development of western civilization had also imploded from within the heart of Europe with the rise of fascism, exposing the violence at the heart of Europe's claims to moral, racial, and civilizational superiority. It is surely no coincidence that in this climate the welfare state's emphasis on compassion and 'care' as the characteristic of its nationals emerged. The welfare state's characterization of the nation-state as shaped by the ethic of compas-sion, which was to be the basis for their social solidarity, became an important means by which a claim to western civilizational and moral superiority could be reconstituted.

In tandem with the redefinition of liberalism from above, as it were, trade union and feminist activism from below had gained increased sup-port and momentum, as mentioned earlier. Having made valuable con-tributions to their national war efforts, both movements demanded major reforms for a redistribution of wealth at the end of the Second Warld War, lending their newly acquired political rights in support of the new (left) political parties.[16] The pragmatism of ruling elites who sought to deradicalize and contain these movements helped consolidate the general social consensus in favour of the welfare state.[17] The ex-pansion of citizenship to include social rights would ensure collective provision of basic needs. It would also allow social solidarity to be strengthened and the market economy to be stabilized.[18] Social integra-tion, or more appropriately social control, which was a major function of the bourgeois state, required such maintenance of order and contain-ment of social conflict at home and the strengthening of its imperial prowess abroad. And with its pro-natalist social policies designed to sup-port women's role as mothers of the 'imperial nation,' the welfare state equated support for the 'family' with support for the 'nation.'[19] The development of the social safety net thus did not seek to challenge the racialization of the nation-state relationship within the international order. Rather, its framers sought the opposite, that is, a strengthening of the powers of their respective races as nations through improvements to the welfare of the nation's families.[20]

A number of scholars have noted the very intimate relationship between the family, as the core institution of nation-formation, and colonialist discourses, which were committed to preserving racial purity during the nineteenth and early twentieth centuries.[21] The family was conceptualized as the preeminent site for the socialization of future citizens, with women being assigned a central role in the symbolic and material reproduction of the family, and through this, of the race and nation. Patricia Hill Collins has identified six specific aspects of the traditional nuclear family ideal that articulate with processes of nation-formation and its attendant structures of racial hierarchies. She argues that the family unit:

1 naturalizes hierarchical relations among its members, and in the process, socializes them into naturalizing other social hierarchies
2 links notions of 'home' and privatized space with notions of racial and national space
3 reinforces beliefs in 'blood ties' as 'naturally' binding its members together while 'naturally' separating races and nations
4 promotes ideas of obligations and responsibilities by virtue of 'natural' bonds, ideas which then translate into 'natural' obligations and responsibilities towards race and nation, and not towards outsiders
5 enables the transfer of wealth and property through the generations, reproducing class inequalities along with racial, gendered and national ones, and
6 enables the regulation of the population through family planning measures, legitimating eugenicist practices.[22]

The traditional heterosexual nuclear family ideal thus operates as a 'fundamental principle of social organization,' with the family constituting 'primary sites of belonging to various groups: to the family as an assumed biological entity; to geographically identifiable, racially segregated neighborhoods conceptualized as imagined families; to so-called racial families codified in science and law; and to the U.S. nation-state conceptualized as a national family.'[23]

Hill Collins's insights provide an interesting way to approach the traditional nuclear, middle-class family ideal that lies at the heart of Canadian national formation, an ideal which was incorporated into the welfare machinery. The valorization of this ideal as the *national* ideal meant that the experiences of Aboriginal women, and of women of colour, with/in the family were to be markedly different, as a number of anti-racist scholars have found.[24]

National Welfare

Most studies of the Canadian welfare state trace its beginnings to the social legislation introduced in the late nineteenth and early twentieth

centuries. Alvin Finkel, for example, makes the case that social legislation in Canada was 'minimal' prior to the 1930s. The rapid increase in
welfare legislation after the Second World War led to the development
of the welfare state, with its myriad programs being expanded through
the following decades and into the 1970s.[25] Although Jane Ursel also
notes that the growth of the national welfare system occurred largely in
the post-war years, she begins her study of Canadian public policies in
an earlier period and identifies three major phases.

The first phase takes place between 1884 and 1913, when the crisis of
the wage labour system gave rise to increasing poverty. This situation
resulted in the beginning of state intervention in welfare. Legislation
was initially developed to protect working families, including the 1884
Factories Act, the 1885 Wages Act, and the 1888 Shops Act. These were
related specifically to child custody issues and women's property rights.
During the second phase, 1919 to 1939, the state actively supported private welfare institutions and introduced labour legislation to support
the wage system. Legislation included the 1914 Employment Agencies
Act, the 1915 Workmen's Compensation Insurance Act, the Minimum
Wages Acts, as well as Maintenance Acts for women and children. In the
third phase, 1940 to 1968, the state developed a national welfare system
that socialized the costs of the reproduction of families through federal
welfare legislation.[26]

As had been the case in Britain, momentum for the reform of the
laissez-faire system had escalated as a result of two major developments.
The enfranchisement of the working class and women (racial minorities
in both categories were enfranchised later than whites) was one such
development. The second was the formation of the Cooperative Commonwealth Federation (the precursor to today's New Democratic Party)
in the 1930s, which quickly became a significant electoral force representing the interests of farmers and workers. Elite support for social programs during the period 1930 to 1945, including from within the
leadership of the Conservative Party, stemmed from the recognition
'that repression alone might not be sufficient to preserve the existing
system against the threat of socialism.'[27] The social consensus shared by
both labour and capital for state provision of income support programs
to citizens thus crystallized in a class compromise. These social programs provided valuable income security to working-class families, but
also had the effect of deepening their integration into bourgeois rule.[28]

Like the demands for reforms made by the trade union movement,
white women's organizations also lobbied for social policies to help mit-

igate women's inequality.[29] Feminists argued that women's poverty was
directly related to their domestic responsibilities within the family and
their consequent economic dependence on men.[30] The feminists supported the creation of social programs to provide income assistance to
women, and few among them questioned women's role in the sphere of
reproduction. Popularly referred to as 'maternal feminists,' these first-
wave feminists stressed the important role of women as mothers in
ensuring the well-being of families and, most importantly, of children.
Equating the well-being of the family with the well-being of the nation,
they argued for the provision of social supports for women to help them
fulfill their responsibilities to both:[31] 'Motherhood, and their role in
defending the home front, had earned women the vote; in the post-war
period, it would be their activities in the home that would test their met-
tle as citizens.'[32]

In her examination of Canadian public policy over the period of a
century, Ursel has argued that these policies were developed to support
the reproduction of the patriarchal nuclear family by socializing the
costs of its reproduction.[33] Whereas under laissez-faire capitalism these
costs were privatized by making families responsible for their own reproduction, the state socialized the provision of income support and services to families under welfare capitalism. Further, the economic expansion of the post-war period created increased demand for women's
labour outside the home. Social programs that provided income support to families enabled employers to access this labour at a lower cost.
Public policy thus met the needs of both capital and families, and kept
intact the sexual division of labour.[34]

A more critical reading of the Canadian experience, however, charts a
somewhat different trajectory for state provision of social support to its
nationals. As discussed in chapter 2, concerns regarding the 'quality' of
the 'race,' and its equation with the quality of the nation, were rife
under British rule. They remained equally prominent after Confederation.[35] Scholars have documented the various forms of socio-economic
'assistance' provided by the British state, and later by the Canadian
state, to entice the immigration and settlement of preferred races into
the colony from the eighteenth to the twentieth centuries. These early
supports were considered vital by the state to building a nation and
included such prosaic measures as subsidized transportation for emigrants through 'assisted' passages; the provision of lodgings, employment counselling, and job contacts for new arrivals; cash grants and
plots of land for settlement; and provision of training in farming meth-

ods and other new technologies.[36] These forms of assistance were certainly not treated as entitlements, nor were they provided on the scale (and in the range) of the extensive social programs of the welfare state. Nevertheless, it is in these early forms of support that the precursors of the social programs can be found. It is notable that such supports were provided to *prospective* nationals and *future* citizens on an overtly racial basis.

The provision of specific forms of support to white women as 'daughters' of the Empire and 'mothers' of the nation was considered especially important. Their participation in the reproduction of British social and familial mores within the settler colonies was understood to be indispensable. In recognition of this, Women's Emigration Societies were formed to organize the migration of middle- and working-class women to British colonies, including Canada, during the years 1862 to 1962. Such societies gained the support of the colonial states for their various undertakings, and working closely with government officials, they organized passages and lodgings for women and found them employment as governesses, teachers, and domestic workers. They also helped cultivate the expectation that the women would marry European settlers in the colonies, and hence build the population base of the settler societies.[37]

Similarly, government officials periodically organized direct recruitment of such women for emigration.[38] These state-sponsored (and sometimes state-organized) forms of assistance long predated the pro-family legislation of the welfare state. While these forms of support certainly cannot be equated with the social safety net, they cannot be ignored either. They were crucial in constituting state discourses regarding the importance of state support for the nation's families, the importance of these families to nation-building, and the relation between the quality of these families and the quality of the nation. The welfare state drew upon these discourses and institutionalized them in its subsequent organization of access to social programs through the mechanism of citizenship.

The European women who migrated to Canada experienced improvement in their socio-economic status, notwithstanding the gendered forms of participation in nation-building available to them upon arrival. To many of them, '[e]migration offered a resolution to domestic tensions which poverty, legality, and convention made otherwise unresolvable.'[39] The labour of these women (waged and unwaged) played a crucial role in national formation. No less crucial was the development of their social identity, and that of their families, as civilizing pioneers who were building a new society. The various forms of economic and social supports available to them, which were linked to immigration priorities, nurtured the development of this identity.

If the state institutionalized the family ideal in immigration and settlement policies, white women actively participated in various ways to realize this ideal and, in doing so, constituted themselves as nationals.[40] The ideal was valorized by maternal feminists and other social reformers, as well as by national subjects in general, as they turned it into a prime site for the reproduction of the imperial hierarchies that defined Aboriginal communities and non-preferred races as unworthy of similar support. The nationality acquired by white women increased their stake in the preservation of this status, and of the white family, through moral reform for 'social purity.'[41] Most were heavily invested in the imperial project and defined themselves as members of a superior race and nation. Like their male counterparts, they viewed the sexuality and fecundity of immigrant women as a threat to the nation. They rarely supported the demands of Black and Asian migrants for family reunification, and when they did offer some support for such demands, it was based more in their fears of miscegenation than in any positive regard for the equal treatment of migrant women.[42] Indeed, many women reformers defined the containment of immigrant women's sexuality and fecundity as a vital national interest, and claimed a space for themselves at the helm of the efforts to contain such threats to their nationality.

The political and social mobilization of nationals for development of social programs to enhance the welfare of Canadian families was rooted in their concern for white families. Ironically, as contemporary feminist critics have noted, the social programs of the welfare state incorporated and further institutionalized gender and class divisions, most particularly in maintaining the sexual division of labour.[43] Despite such consequences, the welfare state provided nationals, both women and men, with a 'floor on the standard of living,' signifying the responsibility the state was willing to assume for their well-being. Access to social programs enhanced their sense of entitlement as citizens.[44]

Feminists have found that social programs offered women 'a measure of economic insulation against total dependence on men' and promoted a 'feeling of entitlement,' which empowered them and fuelled their further claims to full citizenship.[45] The welfare state enhanced women's economic advancement both through the provision of social services to them and their families and through developing employment opportunities for them within the growing public sector. The employment of large numbers of Canadian women in the public sector aided their constitution as (relatively) independent *economic* agents, making valuable contributions to the nation·and entitled to the same rights and benefits as men. This situation contributed in no small measure to the constitution of western societies as more committed to the ideals of gender equality than the 'traditional' non-western communities within their midst.

As Evans and Wekerle have observed, the welfare state encapsulates much more than tangible social services and programs. Its policies and programs also 'redistribute status, rights and life opportunities.'[46] Gordon has also discussed the importance of the 'feeling of entitlement' women experienced through their access to social programs. This 'feeling of entitlement,' and its symbolic and material inclusion of women in nationhood, would be immensely inflated in these women's encounters with racialized Others. As I discuss below, such strange encounters constituted excluded Others as individually unworthy of entitlements and their families as deficient. Moreover, social citizenship deepened the meaning of 'belonging' to the national community, strenthening the historically entrenched commitment of national subjects to protect it from the encroachments of undeserving Others.

The Welfare of Aboriginal Peoples

Out of a hundred that have passed through our hands scarcely have we civilized one. We find docility and intelligence in them, but when we are least expecting it they climb over our enclosure and go run the woods with their relatives, where they find more pleasure than in all the amenities of our French houses. Savage nature is made that way; they cannot be constrained and if they are, they become melancholy, and their melancholy makes them sick. Besides, the Savages love their children extraordinarily and when they know that they are sad they will do everything to get them back.

Ursuline Mother de l'Incarnation, quoted in Suzanne Fournier
and Ernie Crey, *Stolen from Our Embrace*[47]

If the Canadian family was exalted as the bedrock of the nation, and its reproduction was articulated to the social programs of the welfare state, the Aboriginal family was constituted as a threat to national advancement. This constitution of Aboriginal families and communities as a hindrance to the modernizing project can be traced to the earliest stages of state and national formation.[48] Colonizers and settlers considered inevitable the disintegration of these communities in the historical march of progress, and the physical elimination or cultural assimilation of these peoples the only practical options. This consideration was, of course, driven by the desire of nationals to gain control over lands: if the physical destruction of Aboriginal peoples was impossible to accomplish, for whatever reasons, their cultural extinction became official state policy in both the United States and Canada until well into the 1960s and 1970s.

Lawrence has argued that this goal of reducing Aboriginal populations, thereby weakening their political claims, shaped the 'policies of removal' designed to 'bleed off' Aboriginal peoples from their communities.[49] She notes that women were particular targets of these policies, which placed a high priority on the loss of Indian status for women and their children. Such bleeding off also included the classification of mixed-race Native children as not 'real' Indians and delegitimized their Aboriginal identity. At the end of the 'Indian wars' (1890s), which drastically reduced the Aboriginal population of North America to '5 percent or less of its pre-contact total,' both the United States and Canada devised the residential school system to 'digest' the survivors.[50] In Canada, there was little doubt regarding the purpose of this institution: 'to be rid of the Indian question. That is [the] whole point. Our objective is to continue until there is not a single Indian in Canada that has not been absorbed into the body politic, and there is no Indian problem.'[51] Ward Churchill has pointed out that five generations of Aboriginal peoples went though this system, which replaced the earlier policies of physical extermination with those of cultural extinction. This system was widely considered by nationals to be the more humanitarian option for 'saving' Indians.

The residential school system institutionalized the idea that Aboriginal families were incommensurable with the national ideal and that the 'welfare' of Aboriginal children was in conflict with that of their families and communities, including that of their mothers. From 1846 to 1984, this system removed the children from their families, placing them in the state supported schools run by many Christian organizations. There, the children were to be civilized out of their Aboriginal identity and indigenous ways of life.[52] At a time when the European family was considered a 'haven in a heartless world,' and prime importance was placed on educating European women to become good modern mothers, the removal of Aboriginal children was widely sanctioned as a means to destroy Aboriginality.[53] Aboriginal women were already 'wilded' in the settler imagination of the nineteenth century as sexual 'savages,' and civilizing their children was deemed possible only if they were removed from these women's care.[54] The destruction of Aboriginal women's agency was thus 'a major factor' in the development of residential schools.[55] As Patricia Monture-Angus and other Aboriginal scholars have noted, 'removing children from their homes weakens the entire community' and 'removing children from their culture and placing them in a foreign culture is an act of genocide.'[56]

The Royal Commission on Aboriginal Peoples has described these schools as 'internment camps for Indian children.'[57] Tens of thousands of children – from the earliest age possible – were interned in these schools modelled on penal institutions.[58] The adoption of Christian names, values, and morals by the children and the inculcation of the work ethic and respect for private property were defined as their means of salvation. Punished severely for speaking indigenous languages, for attempting to preserve familial relationships with other children – including with their siblings – and for maintaining their traditional and cultural practices, generations of these children were left to fend for themselves, far from their families, to survive as best they could.[59] Although ostensibly taken to be 'educated,' these children were put to work in the schools where their labour contributed to their own upkeep, as well as that of their wardens.[60]

Housed in unsanitary conditions, many of the children were malnourished and overworked and were denied medical care even when sick and dying. Approximately half perished in these schools between 1867 and 1912, noted Duncan Campbell Smith, and the Bryce report found that approximately 42 per cent died annually on average.[61] George Manuel, a Native leader, remembers the effects of the harsh disciplinary practices considered necessary by the guardians of these children: 'Learning to see and hear only what the priests and brothers wanted you to see and hear, even the people we loved came to look ugly.'[62]

Many of the children were subjected to widespread physical and sexual assault by their guardians.[63] The power of these guardians over their young wards was sanctioned and upheld by the state and the religious organizations, even after knowledge of the abuse was discovered and documented.[64] Churchill argues that the harshness of the regime imposed upon the children intensified when the children sought to resist the violence. He states that some of these measures – which

included corporal punishment and forcing children to eat their own
vomit – were tantamount to torture, and that the very institution was
founded on violence. Consequently, the step from physical violence to
sexual violence was a small, even if a psychologically convoluted one.

The claim that the residential school system intended to save Aboriginal children granted it a legitimacy that continues to be upheld even
now by the institutions that perpetrated this violence. By placing the
blame solely on individual perpetrators when recognition of the extent
of the abuse cannot be avoided, the systemic nature of the violence can
be denied.[65] Indeed, so deep was the historical investment in the representation of the nation-state as being engaged in a humanitarian and
compassionate civilizing project that public knowledge about the extent
of the abuse, documented by government officials and reported by the
media for over half a century, did not prevent its ongoing recurrence.[66]
Abusers were simply transferred to other institutions upon discovery,
government studies were suppressed, and the residential system was preserved.[67]

In sharp contrast to this treatment of Aboriginal children, the dependence of Canadian children upon their parents, and especially upon
their mothers, was treated as necessary and crucial to the children's
development and emotional well-being. The responsibility for raising
well-disciplined children who would be the citizens of the 'modern, scientific age' was defined by child-rearing experts and other professionals
as too serious a task to be left in the hands of individual mothers. These
experts, however, refused to countenance any direct intervention in the
family that bypassed parents, denouncing the very idea as a form of 'bol-
shevism.'[68] Instead, Euro-Canadian women, as mothers of the nation,
were subjected to 'heightened public scrutiny,' their homes were
'invaded' by 'experts' who argued that '[w]e are only now discovering
that Empires and States are built up of babies.'[69] Invested in the
national project, these women are reported to have welcomed such
assistance. Education and other services were to be funnelled to the
family through the mothers, and experts advocated for such support as
vital to the well-being of the family.

Aboriginal mothers, however, were treated altogether differently.
Aboriginal mothers (and fathers) who sought to keep their children
within their families and communities were met with a barrage of legal
barriers, as well as extra-legal forms of coercion. Food rations were with-
held from communities that resisted the apprehension of their children, and chiefs who refused to turn over the children were deposed.[70]

Family members and community elders fought in vain to halt the removal of their children. The successive generations of children placed in residential schools were forced to live with the deep racial denigration of their communities by their teachers and guardians. They were taught hatred and disrespect for their own identity, family, and culture:

> Residential Schools implemented a well-established technology that targeted the spirits, minds, feelings, and bodies of its wards. Its goal was not so much to create as to destroy; its product was designed, as far as possible, to be something not quite a person: something that would offer no intellectual or spiritual challenge to its oppressors, that might provide some limited service to its 'masters' (should the 'masters' desire it), and that would learn its place on the margins of Canadian society.[71]

The utter degradation of the children instituted within the residential school system and its attempt to turn them into 'something not quite a person' was occurring within the same period, and in the same 'national' space, as was the development of the compassionate and caring welfare system.

The removal of Aboriginal children continued until the 1960s and 1970s, when the residential school system was replaced by the child protection system, which apprehended Aboriginal children in disproportionately high numbers.[72] The alcoholism, violence, sexual abuse, suicide, and other social problems that were the direct legacy of the residential schools were subsequently used by the child welfare system to legitimize its apprehension of Aboriginal children.

Characterized as an 'agent of colonialization,' the Canadian child welfare system was marked by three distinct features: the 'lack of decision-making power' of Aboriginal communities over this system; the 'devaluation' of Aboriginal child-rearing practices; and the subordination of Aboriginal communities to non-Aboriginal communities.[73] Marlee Kline notes that the child welfare system further 'naturalized' the removal of Aboriginal children, and that central to the system's legitimation was the ideological construct of Aboriginal women as 'bad mothers' who were a danger to their own children. The 'dominant ideology of motherhood,' which still prevails in Canadian society, albeit to a lesser degree than was the case in the mid-twentieth century, defined motherhood as the highest ambition of women:[74] 'A "good" mother is always available to her children, she spends time with them, guides, supports, encourages and corrects as well as loving and caring for them physically. She is also responsible for the cleanliness of their home environment ... A "good" mother is unselfish, she puts her children's needs before her own.'[75]

As discussed earlier, experts argued in the mid-twentieth century that 'good' mothering did not come naturally to women and that they had to be educated to become good mothers. Indeed, the Canadian state invested quite heavily in infant and child welfare programs. Katherine Arnup has documented the ways in which women were 'educated' into motherhood: 'Through films, radio talks, lectures, clinics, and home visits by public health nurses, and through the production of pamphlets and booklets at a staggering rate, experts sought to teach mothers the skills of scientific motherhood.' She has noted that such education was 'not forced upon women; on the contrary, they actively sought it.'[76] Such educational projects exalted Canadian mothers.

No such investments were expended on Native women. Colonial stereotypes of these women, ubiquitous in a society which had for generations already depicted them as sexually promiscuous and morally deficient, lent support to the apprehension of their children. Communal living and extended family structures within Native communities were defined as promoting immorality and primitivity, and their child-rearing practices were condemned in the exaltation of the middle-class, nuclear Canadian family as the national norm.[77] The poverty and violence that shaped Aboriginal women's lives and that severely limited their ability to provide for their children were rendered invisible by the dominant 'ideology of motherhood,' which pathologized the women.[78]

Many Aboriginal women were themselves survivors of the residential school system, and the systemic discrimination they lived with made them among the poorest and most highly exploited group of women in the country.[79] Their lack of access to adequate housing, employment, and health-care services and their exposure to routinized violence were used to justify the removal of their children. The residential school system was ideologically based on the construction of Aboriginality as primitivity, and thus as irremediable lack. The child welfare system, for its part, pathologized individual Aboriginal mothers and their families as deficient, further enhancing personalized definitions of this lack.[80]

Where the residential school system had placed children in large institutions, child protection services placed them in the privatized care of foster and adoptive families, most of them non-Aboriginal. Siblings were often separated from each other and placed with different families: 'In the foster and adoptive care system, aboriginal children typically vanished with scarcely a trace, the vast majority of them placed until they were adults in non-aboriginal homes where their cultural identity, their legal Indian status, their knowledge of their own First Nation and even their birth names were erased, often forever.'[81] Many of the children were also sent for adoption during the 1960s and 1970s to the United States, Australia, and other countries.[82] Like the children placed within the residential school system, many of the children apprehended by child protection services are also known to have experienced physical and sexual abuse, and to have been put to work for their new 'families.'

The federal government provided funds to the provincial governments for every child apprehended, thus deepening the stake of the provinces in the numbers of Aboriginal children taken into 'care.'[83] Aboriginal activists note that such funds were used to create employment for social workers, as 'reserves provided a ready-made industry' for their activities:[84]

'Big, shiny American cars would come onto the reserve, followed by the social worker's car,' says Maggie Blacksmith, now a Dakota Ojibway Child and Family Services social worker who herself lost a son to the Manitoba government. 'When they left, there'd be a little Indian child sitting in the back of the American car, bawling their eyes out. The social worker always had a piece of paper saying it was legal. We know the social worker was paid but we'd have known right away if any parents got money, because we lived so closely together and we were all so poor, money would have been conspicuous. If parents tried to keep their kids, the social worker called the Mountie.'[85]

Monture-Angus has made a direct link between the removal of these children and their subsequent high levels of incarceration in the criminal justice system. This 'vicious cycle of abuse,' she argues, demonstrates the link between 'family breakdown and delinquency.'[86] And as the documents prepared for the Indian affairs minister in 2005 demonstrate, the apprehension of Aboriginal children has remained unabated into the twenty-first century.[87] This continued denigration of Aboriginal families, and of Aboriginal women as mothers in particular, feeds the culturally supremacist exaltation of Canadian mothers and families.

The welfare state's provision of social services and other forms of income assistance to Canadian families sought to help preserve the family unit (except for the very poor and low-income single mothers). It thus promoted the social and symbolic value attached to these families.

The child-rearing practices of middle-class Canadian mothers and fathers were made normative by the welfare system, the positive recognition of their worthiness enhanced by social benefits. No such considerations informed the welfare system's interactions with Aboriginal families. In their case, warfare and welfare were clearly not oppositional systems. Indeed, welfare became the extension of warfare, and the manner of waging this war further exalted the nationals on its front lines as compassionate and caring.

The Gender of Caring

The development of the public sector created a tremendous expansion of employment opportunities for Canadian women, especially in the 'caring professions' of social work, health care, and education. The ethic and labour of caring has long been associated with women and femininity.[88] Feminists have drawn attention to the gender segmentation within the labour market that resulted in high numbers of women being employed in these caring occupations of the public sector.[89] Although significant inequalities in remuneration and work conditions structured women's participation in the labour force, the expansion of the public sector nevertheless enabled white women's mass entry into paid work. The public sector provided them with access to the valuable job benefits of full-time work, thus mitigating their economic dependence on men and their families.

Most of the women employed in the public sector and in the field of social welfare were white until the liberalization of public policy in the 1960s and 1970s, which improved women of colour's access to education and their access to employment in the caring professions. In the case of Britain, Gail Lewis has found that social work as a field of employment was only opened to Black women in the 1980s.[90] In Canada, it was well into the 1970s that women of colour made inroads into the public sector, and even then, they tended to be concentrated in the lower rungs because of the gender *and* race segmentation in the labour market.[91] Aboriginal women, of course, remained marginalized within the education system and in the labour market.

While the working conditions and material benefits of employment in the caring professions have received some attention, the impact of such employment on the self-constituting practices of the large numbers of white women who were thus employed has received less attention. Women's employment in this sector was strongly tied to their emergence as political agents within reformist social movements; 'Anglo-Canadian women, working as nurses, social workers, and teachers, were often in the vanguard' of child welfare movements.[92] Carol Baines, Patricia Evans, and Sheila Neysmith make the general observation that '[t]he most common reason young women enter the human service professions is a desire to help others and serve society, and indeed nursing, social work, and teaching have recognized the importance of a commitment to an ethic of care in recruiting members to their professions.'[93] The few studies that have paid attention to how caring work affects practitioners demonstrate that the work these women perform deeply shapes their sense of self as caring and compassionate professionals.

Moreover, these women's sense of self is deeply connected to their understanding of the depth of the dependence of their clientele upon their work, as Arnup astutely notes. She argues that the ongoing role of 'experts' – as such – relies upon this dependence: 'If experts succeeded in raising parents' self-confidence to the level of self-sufficiency, they might in fact render themselves obsolete.'[94] Women working in the 'caring' professions thus experience their work as socially necessary and *valuable*, and as contributing to the creation of better living conditions for the children they are charged with helping.

In an interesting study of white women psychotherapists, Kerstin Roger argues that these women gained 'elite status' through the 'professionalization of helping activities in the early twentieth century.' She argues that the 'professional use of empathy became a regulatory device for social relations of difference,' and this work enabled the women to reproduce their own superiority as caring white subjects.[95] Interviewing women with backgrounds in nursing, social work, and Christian missionary work, Roger found that they became 'invested with kindness and innocence' through their helping work with clients (both white and non-white). She observed that the 'quality of the acts of empathy is situated within the fantasies and desires that the psychotherapist has for herself, for her social identity and for her professional relationships.'[96] These studies suggest that working in the caring professions has a profound influence on the self-constituting practices of the white women who work in them.

In her study of pre-service teachers in a province with a significant Aboriginal population, Carol Schick found that her interview subjects remained committed to preserving their white privilege within the elite space of the university in which they were situated. Even while participating in a (required) cross-cultural course, which Shick anticipated might well challenge such privilege, these subjects performed their whiteness as normative and innocent, assertively claiming their place as the 'rightful occupants' of the white-dominated university space. In one particularly revealing interview, a participant who was supportive of Aboriginal issues nevertheless expressed anxiety about 'where she fit in,' raising her concern that the relatively recent practice of hiring Aboriginal teachers might have negative consequences on her own employment prospects.[97] The possibility that Aboriginal professionals might occupy positions as service-deliverers, rather than simply as consumers and clients, was experienced by her as a personalized sense of loss with regard to her future employment. Significantly, this possibility destabilized this participant's sense of belonging and entitlement because she worried about where she might 'fit in.'

Caring for the Other

The welfare state has been popularly represented both domestically and internationally as a 'compassionate' one, and the professions it promotes as caring. The studies discussed above, limited as they are in size and scope, demonstrate that the practitioners of such 'compassion' imbibe this characterization into the fashioning of their own subjectivity. In the child-protection services, for example, this work of protecting Aboriginal children would surely have had an even greater impact on the securing of these professionals' personal identities as upholding the civilized values of a civilized society. After all, Aboriginal children are defined as particularly vulnerable, and their protection and care defined as an especially laudable responsibility.

With the power to determine which Aboriginal children were 'at risk' and how and when to intervene in their exercise of this power, child protection professionals could have been in little doubt about the level of control they had over Aboriginal families and communities. This power, based on their access to nationality and its devastating consequences for Native populations, became concealed in the characterization of their work as an expression of their innate human(e) sensibilities. Such caring was rooted in the cultural values and norms of white supremacy. No level of recourse to the good intentions of such reformist professionals can erase the recognition that their work furthered the goal of digesting and reforming Aboriginality, imposing the nation's racial values onto Aboriginal mothers and their children.

A 'condescending pity for the plight of young Native children and a concern for the moral effects of "the mingling of the races" on the Caucasian population' characterized the discursive framing of early child welfare policy. Those involved in child-saving work reproduced the race, class and gender norms of the period, and expected gratitude and subservience from the children and adolescents they saved.[98] Social workers 'felt little harm could befall an aboriginal child rescued from poverty and placed with a nice, middle-class white family.'[99] Whether motivated by the desire to help or to control these families, the exercise of power invested in the work of the caring professions reinscribed the superiority of national values, as it did the professional's own access to nationality. It elevated their own cultural (as professional) judgments above the emotional bonds, cultural practices, and material interests of Aboriginal mothers, their children, and families. Many of these professionals might have had great sympathy for Aboriginal families. Their work was undoubtedly emotionally demanding, and they had access to far fewer resources than they deemed necessary to do their work effectively. But with every exercise of the power invested in them by the welfare state, they reinforced the nation's (and their own) exaltation and deepened the powerlessness of Aboriginal families.

The different experts, from priests and nuns to Indian agents and social workers, who vied to extend their own form of human(e) control over Aboriginal children and families, expanded the nation's sense of cultural and racial superiority. As discussed earlier in this chapter, Linda Gordon has argued that social policies in the United States were shaped by the racial experiences and visions of the white reformers who developed them. In this, they implicitly reproduced white racial domination. Robert Lieberman agrees that the development of the welfare state preserved racial rule in American society, and he adds that this has severely diminished the prospects for cross-class and cross-race political alliances.[100] A similar situation can be found in the development of the residential school system and, subsequently, in the child welfare system in Canada. Both systems reproduced the colonial objective of destroying Aboriginal communities through regulating Aboriginal families and their identities. Both systems thwarted cross-racial political alliances with other sectors of the population as they simultaneously strengthened the bonds among nationals who saw themselves as compassionate subjects, and among nationals and the welfare state which the nationals defined as upholding their 'sacred trust.'

It can likewise be anticipated that the non-Aboriginal families that accepted Aboriginal children also experienced the enhancement of their own sense of cultural and moral superiority. The moral capital they accumulated in their designation as worthy of providing care for the children, unlike the children's own birth families and communities, surely contributed to their exaltation. The financial compensation such families received from the state for taking in Native children has been identified by a number of Aboriginal adoptees as a major consideration for their foster families. But even when the financial interest might have been a minor factor, the enormous rewards accruing to these families in a moral economy of exchange was not insignificant. Constituted as caring and compassionate in the face of moral degeneracy and cultural deficiency, the power of these families over Aboriginal children was near complete. If they chose to, they could rename the children and deny them access to their cultural heritage and linguistic background.

It is difficult to imagine how these families could have escaped seeing themselves as superior for wanting to protect the children from their 'dysfunctional' families and 'doomed' communities. These widely shared representations of their national identity as compassionate would be irremediably shaken should nationals ever seek to come to terms with the following question posed by an Aboriginal elder:

> Where are our artisans, our weavers, our fishermen, medicine people, dancers, shamans, sculptors and hunters? For thirty years, generations of our children, the very future of our communities, have been taken away from us. Will they come home as our leaders knowing the power and tradition of their people? Or will they come home broken and in pain, not knowing who they are, looking for the family that died of a broken heart?[101]

This elder clearly recognized the warlike impulse of the nation's compassion.

Racial Citizenship, Racial Entitlements

Until the mid-twentieth century, white social reformers regarded the non-British European immigrant family with considerable anxiety and reformist zeal. Attributing all manner of social problems to these families, reformers committed themselves to modernizing them into a North American ideal; that is, the patriarchal, nuclear, middle-class model that was to be the norm.[102] Defining their objective as helping this immigrant family 'adjust' and integrate into Canadian culture and society, reformers sought to restrain what they defined as the overly dominant power of the husbands whom they counselled to develop 'companionate' and more 'egalitarian' relationships with their wives.[103] Across the spectrum of the social welfare network, priority was placed upon teaching 'Canadian ways' to these families.[104] Providing much more to non-British European families than just direct services, social service agencies promoted fellowship and familiarity with the dominant values of the society. They provided valuable opportunities to socialize with other Canadians in order to help build a general sense of belonging. In short, these agencies sought to Canadianize the new European arrivals through the numerous services and social activities they organized.[105] Their work was informed by their belief in these families' cultural inferiority in comparison with the British and their need for re-education.

During this period, immigration policies sought to regulate the 'right' to family life along race and class lines; white immigrants were encouraged to bring and build families in the service of national (re)production, while all non-white immigrants were restricted from migrating with their families. Non-preferred race families were defined as having the potential to overwhelm the whiteness of the nation, and they were thus marked for exclusion except in a few circumstances. Chinese and South Asian merchants were allowed to bring family members, who were exempted from paying the head tax. But working-class immigrants from these communities were prohibited from bringing their families into the country.[106] These men were denied the right to family life, as they were either not allowed to bring family members or were unable to pay the head tax to do so.[107] Many Chinese men, as is well known, lived out their lives in Canada as 'married bachelors' because their wives and children were forced to remain in China. Immigration policies had specific gendered and classed consequences for family life until well after the mid-twentieth century.[108]

When Asian women were allowed to immigrate, they were able to do so primarily as a result of their relationship to male relatives, not in their own right as independent and economically productive subjects.[109] The exceptions to this were the Black and Asian women who were allowed to enter as domestic workers. Women of the non-preferred races, classified as 'immigrant women' in a later era, personified the boundaries against which national purity had to be protected. Colonial concerns regarding racial purity and middle class morality constituted these women as particularly threatening. As Enakshi Dua has found, 'women of colour were racially gendered as posing a threat to the racialized nation as they could not reproduce a white population, allowed for the possibility of interracial sexuality, and challenged, by their presence within the nation-state, the very racialized moral order that the white nuclear family was to protect.'[110]

Dua has examined a particularly significant public debate (in the 1910–15 period) on the question of whether 'Hindoo' women should be allowed to join their husbands in Canada. Prohibitions on their entry arose mainly from concerns that their presence would encourage other Indians to migrate to Canada, that they 'would facilitate the emergence of ethnic communities' in a country committed to preserving its white identity, and that their fertility would be a danger to preserving the whiteness of the nation.[111]

Dua discusses the paradox in which those who opposed the women's immigration did so in the name of preserving the whiteness of the nation, while those who supported it also shared this goal. The latter supported such immigration in order to minimize the risks of miscegenation and from a patriarchal concern that husbands not be separated from their wives. Having defined white women primarily as 'mothers of the nation' (that is, in relation to their reproductive capacities), it is no surprise that Asian women were likewise viewed primarily with regard to their reproductive capacities. Dua describes how the public debate raised the question of these women's immigration only in their capacity as wives of immigrant men and not in the capacity of their independent right to mobility. The presence of the women was thus imagined by nationals as permissible only in the context of their role as wives and family members, not in any other capacity. When the immigration of these women was finally permitted, it was organized so that it enhanced the role of South Asian men as patriarchs. However, to view the struggles of these men and women for family reunification in such circumstances only in terms of the family as the pre-eminent site of women's oppression, as many second-wave feminists have done, is short-sighted indeed.

A number of critical race theorists have argued that the family is a complex institution for racialized minorities. While certainly a site for the control of women and children, the family is also a site of refuge from the racism that permeates socio-economic life.[112] Where Canadian state practices sought to deny family life to non-preferred races for over a century, the struggles of these migrants for family reunification was, among other things, a challenge to their racialization as belonging to an inferior order of humanity, undeserving of family life.

Although the racialized and gendered immigration policies that were in place until the mid-twentieth century sought to prohibit the immigration of non-white women, they were unable to entirely halt it. Women (and men) of the non-preferred races found numerous ways to enter the country. However, when the women were successful in doing so, they found themselves few in number and, hence, in disproportionately male-dominated migrant communities.[113] Legal prohibitions ensured that they found few other women on whose support they could rely. These systemic conditions had the effect of increasing the women's dependence upon men, both within the family and within the community.

Constituted primarily as dependents in the national imaginary, their sexuality and fertility defined as a potent threat if not properly controlled and channeled, immigrant women were made to embody the line of demarcation against which 'national' interests had to be defended. Adding insult to such injury, the women also came to be defined as 'naturally' and 'culturally' more family and tradition bound, amenable to greater patriarchal control by men in their families and communities than were Canadian women. The Orientalist constructs rife in Canadian society masked the gendered and racialized effect of immigration policies. Instead, they routinely inscribed immigrant women as passive and highly subservient and their communities as inherently patriarchal as a result of their 'backward' cultures and traditions.

The efforts of undesired immigrants to subvert the racialized and gendered adverse effects of immigration and citizenship legislation were central to the strategies they developed to improve their own welfare and social security, along with that of their communities. Such efforts were committed to reclaiming their full humanity in the face of their racialized disenfranchisements.[114] While the extent of the provision of social welfare to these immigrants prior to the 1960s and 1970s has received little scholarly attention, the historical record does demonstrate that they relied primarily on the collectively funded community networks and socio-religious and educational organizations they established. Survival hinged upon the resources they pooled to provide financial assistance, housing, and other forms of support to one another.[115] Although small in numbers, women's contributions to these activities were critical for their families and communities. Women were also actively engaged in the political campaigns organized for family reunification, as well as those contesting other forms of racialized exclusions.[116] While more research is required to help develop a clearer historical picture of the myriad welfare services organized within these communities, it is clear that political challenges to their racial domination was central to the welfare services they developed for and by themselves.

For over three decades in the post-war period, a period that was critical for the expansion of the social safety net and the welfare ideology that constituted citizens as worthy of social entitlements, state policies restricted the access of these unwelcome immigrants to full citizenship. Franca Iacovetta has found that immigrants 'potentially had access to a fairly wide network of services associated with the postwar welfare state' after 1945. As she explains:

> Notwithstanding their shortcomings, the immigrants benefited from a national system of unemployment insurance, mothers' allowances, and improvements in health, welfare and workers' compensation schemes. They could also tap the more traditional forms of aid offered by charitable agencies, churches and volunteer groups that had long served immigrant and working-class families. In Toronto, middle-class women's organizations, such as the Young Women's Christian Association (YWCA), the Women's Christian Temperance Union (WCTU), and the Toronto Junior League, organized clothing and food drives and baby clinics, hosted child-rearing lectures, and dispatched volunteers to meet women arriving by train to Union Station. Both nationally and locally, the Imperial Order Daughters of the Empire (IODE) was involved in citizenship work, educating immigrants in Canadian government and encouraging them to become naturalized citizens. Many local branches regularly 'adopted' needy families, who were then supplied with emergency funds and had their house bills paid. Toronto's settlement houses acted as job placement centres and offered English classes and recreational activities. So, too, did Catholic, Jewish, and Protestant organizations, some new ones also emerged at this time. Through their referral services, all of these groups were in frequent contact with government departments, including the local offices of the National Employment Service (NES), the Immigration Branch, and the provincial Department of Public Welfare. Clients were also referred to hospitals, family court, and a host of family and child-protection agencies, that, as in the case of the Children's Aid Society, were semi-autonomous but nevertheless an integral part of the apparatus of the welfare state.[117]

The use of racial classification for organizing access to formal and substantive citizenship meant that most of the immigrants who had access to the services described above were of European descent. The development of welfare provisions drew upon a discursive frame that defined non-white families as highly undesirable, and the women of these families particularly so.

The Welfare of Immigrants

The post-war expansion of key social programs, including health care, education, and social assistance, made Canadian women and children the 'particular beneficiaries of this expanded safety net.'[118] The same could not be said of immigrant women or their children. Immigrant women continued to be constructed primarily as family dependents of their individual sponsors by the liberalized immigration program institutionalized by the Immigration Act, 1976-77. The status of future nationals, deserving of equal access to social citizenship, evaded immigrant women even after the introduction of the race-neutral point system. Surely, it needs to be noted that this liberalization of immigration and citizenship occurred in the same moment that marks the beginning of the end of the 'universality' of the welfare system. As Janine Brodie notes in her study of citizenship, 'Canadians were told that it was "essential to the unity of the country" to show a "greater willingness to sacrifice ... to take less so that others may have enough"' in speeches from the throne by 1977.[119] The others who were said to deserve more, as the universality of social programs was eroded, certainly did not include immigrants. By the time the point system was institutionalized, the 'retreat' of the nation's expanded social safety net was already being set in motion.

As discussed in chapter 2, the point system introduced in 1962, and modified and entrenched in the Immigration Act, 1976–77, organized immigration into two main categories: the independent class and the family class.[120] Defined as a class designed to meet labour-market needs, and hence as making an economic contribution to the nation, the independent class was organized through the allocation of points for the applicant's level of education, occupation, and work experience. The family class was defined as allowing the immigration of family dependents, whose presence was of benefit to individual sponsors and whose domicile was to be financially supported by these sponsors. Family reunification was framed primarily as a measure to help ease the resettlement of the sponsor. The organization of immigration into these categories, and the specification of unequal conditions of entry for each, effectively gendered immigration.

The ideological context of the independent class, including its nomenclature, organized it as a masculinized category. In western patriarchal terms, men are defined as independent economic agents, as heads of households in their own right *as men*,[121] whereas women are largely defined as their family and economic dependents.[122] The point system integrated these deeply patriarchal constructs, constituting male immigrants as productive. In contrast, it feminized the family class and rendered invisible the economic contributions of those it defined as 'dependents.'[123] The very naming of this category underscored its feminization.

Not surprisingly, studies have found that immigration officers were more likely to process the applications of women under the family class, even when they applied under the independent class. Men, however, were more likely to be processed under the independent class as heads of households.[124] This situation ranked the value of immigrants by virtue of their economic and financial contributions to the nation. It denied immigrant women independent access to domicile and concealed their economic contributions. It also undermined their autonomy and independent access to citizenship by deepening their dependence on sponsors.

The sponsorship regulations for the family class stipulated that sponsors had to assume financial responsibility for 'dependents' for periods of up to ten years:[125]

> The practice of sponsorship reflects the view that while family reunification is desirable on social grounds, integration related matters are the responsibility of the family and costs are not to be borne by the state. Sponsors agree to provide or assist with lodgings and to provide food, clothing, incidental living needs, and counseling to the sponsored immigrant(s) during the specified period of settlement. They also agree to provide financial assistance so that the sponsored immigrant(s) shall not require financial maintenance support from federal or provincial assistance programs described in the regulations pertaining to the 1976 Immigration Act (schedule VI of the current regulations). Thus, sponsorship is viewed by the federal and provincial governments as a commitment that the designated immigrants will not require economic assistance.[126]

The sponsorship regulations remained in effect for a decade, long after the period of domicile (three to five years) required for citizenship eligibility. The Immigration Act also allowed immigration officers to restrict the entry of persons who might become public charges and to revoke landed status in cases where immigrants had failed to support themselves.[127] These regulations have had far-reaching consequences for women.

The sponsorship regulations also drew upon the earlier construct of immigrant women as possessing a fecundity that could prove costly to the nation, and therefore maintained the privatization of some of the costs of reproducing the immigrant family. The regulations reinforced the notion that immigrant families remained 'foreign,' even after being accepted for permanent residence in the country and even after they acquired de jure citizenship. They formalized the fact that the welfare of these families did not constitute a national responsibility, unlike that of 'real' Canadian families.

In cases where sponsored immigrants attempted to access social assistance programs, they encountered numerous obstacles stemming both from this status and from the lack of clarity among social service providers about the level of access to which they were entitled.[128] Such claims were met with demands of proof of a complete breakdown of the sponsorship relation, which many claimants feared would make them potentially subject to deportation.[129] In the cases where sponsored immigrant women were allowed access to social assistance programs, it was largely at the discretion of the particular provincial and municipal jurisdictions to which they made the claims.[130]

While the prohibitions on the access of sponsored immigrants to social assistance programs (including housing and old-age security) have deepened their status as non-deserving, lesser citizens, sponsorship regulations have also organized unequal entitlements for sponsors. Like their dependents, sponsors have also been prohibited from making claims to social assistance programs in order to qualify as sponsors, even if they have been legally entitled to such claims.[131] Access to social citizenship for immigrant families continued to be regulated through the sponsorship regulations of the immigration system.[132]

Although the sponsorship agreement required sponsors to provide financial support to their dependents, many studies demonstrate that immigrant women had higher labour-force participation rates than Canadian-born women and that they found employment fairly quickly after their arrival.[133] However, their classification as dependents – and not workers headed for the labour market – meant that their access to language and job-training programs was restricted.[134] Because immigrant men experienced considerable discrimination within the economy, the dependence of immigrant families on male wages alone was more limited than that of Canadian families.

The ideological construct of the immigrant male as hyperpatriarchal was greatly buttressed by the sponsorship regulations. As head of the household, the immigrant man was held solely responsible for his family, and his control over its members was enhanced by his power as a sponsor. The regulations thus created the conditions for a shift in power relations within the family after migration. Restricted access to social assistance, and to social housing in particular, reinforced sponsored women's economic dependence on men and increased their vulnerability to violence within the family.[135]

Moreover, while sponsorship regulations exempted sponsored women from access to key social security programs, they did not exempt them from paying the taxes that funded these programs. The underlying principle of the welfare state – that citizens, as tax payers, have a legitimate right to access the programs collectively funded by these taxes – was not extended to these women. The taxes they paid amounted to yet another economic contribution to the welfare of the nation which they could not access; indeed, Canadian members had far greater access to these programs.[136] Immigrant women and their families have been integrated only too well into the national economy, but in a manner that has furthered their socio-political exclusion and economic exploitation, limited their access to citizenship, and maintained their difference from Canadian women and their families.

When family reunification became a core part of the point system, the immigrant family attracted greater scrutiny and regulation. Racialized constructs of arranged and fraudulent marriages (popularly dubbed 'marriages of convenience') proliferated within Canadian society. Concerns that immigrants took unfair advantage of the nation's generous social programs, to the extent of engaging in bogus marriages, created a situation where the legitimacy of these marriages, and of the family relations of immigrants, had to be proved to immigration officers. The various tests devised to assess this legitimacy routinely intruded upon the personal and intimate lives of immigrants. Whereas the informal common-law marriages of Canadians were increasingly being granted legality, the legality of immigrant marriages required a plethora of documentation before they were (often, not always) recognized.

The development of the family class brought the entire immigrant family under increased state regulation, with immigration policies defining which family relationships were to be recognized and who within these relationships would be allowed entry. Sponsorship criteria valorized the heterosexual nuclear family form as the norm, in contrast to the extended family form which was the norm in many other parts of the world.[137] An element of instability was also introduced into these families, with family members being left behind in the country of origin, sometimes for very long periods, while their applications were being processed.[138] Often, these family members found that their status and role had changed significantly upon reunification with their families.

Sponsorship regulations have played no small role in the popular construction of immigrant families as overly patriarchal and of immigrant women as family bound, dependent on their families and cultural communities. The Canadian woman was exalted as a deserving social and political citizen in her own right and her economic opportunities and social value were enhanced by the expansion of the public sector, but the reverse was true for immigrant women.

While sponsorship increased immigrant women's dependence upon their sponsors, it also increased their dependence on their families as sites of refuge from racism within Canadian society. The state's organization of immigration thus reinforced this conflictual relationship: on the one hand, patriarchal structures were strengthened as a direct result of state policy; on the other hand, these families often became the only sites of support against the racism these women encountered. Black feminists have pointed to the similarly complex relationship of Black women to the family in the United States[139] and of Black and Asian women in Britain.[140] The racialization of the nation, of its citizenship and its social entitlements within the welfare state, gave rise to a similar experience for immigrant women in Canada.

Welfare in a Settler Society

After the 1960s and 1970s, Canadian women's increased socio-economic opportunities, as well as the visibility of the second-wave mainstream women's movement, changed the construct of the Canadian male as patriarch with sole authority and control over the family. Many Canadian women claimed an independent status for themselves as citizens in their own right, bringing about a major shift in the traditional nuclear family and its gendered relations.[141] During the same period, however, the sponsorship regulations of a liberalized immigration program reinforced the traditional family ideal for immigrant families, increasing the distance between the modern and egalitarian Canadian family and the ultrapatriarchal immigrant family. The reality that immigrant women participated in paid work in disproportionate measure did not dislodge their image as passive dependents. Nor did immigrant men's support for immigrant women's greater participation in the labour market and increased access to citizenship, education, and professional training dislodge their image as hyperpatriarchal.

Even when immigrants – as citizens – have acquired de jure entitlement to social programs, the racism and classism intrinsic to the caring professions hollows out their entitlements.[142] The overt and subtle 'blame-the victim' approaches of many social workers towards people of colour continue to pathologize them within the network of social services.[143] According to Usha George, even when immigrants have equal entitlement to social programs, the racism that remains 'rampant' within social work disadvantages them.[144] She cites the absence of appropriate services, the prejudices of many social service providers, and the lack of attention paid to structural inequalities within society as evidence of this racism.

The racialization that constructs immigrants as less worthy of citizenship means that all people of colour are likewise perceived as outsiders, regardless of whether they are born in Canada or whether they have citizenship status. Even though Canadian-born women of colour have de jure entitlement to social programs, their racialization associates them with an ideological immigrant status and they, too, are defined as deserving of lesser entitlement. Although the actual legal status of Canadian-born women of colour is different from that of women of colour with immigrant status (de jure), both are routinely perceived simply as immigrant women.

Access to social programs as an integral right of citizenship came to be accepted as natural and normal in the welfare era. Such access could certainly have been organized along different principles, and with different eligibility criteria, had there been a commitment to ensure that this access became truly universal. Instead, the organization of social entitlements through the political institution of citizenship meant that the Canadian welfare state incorporated racialized constructs of the nation and its real citizens into the social policies organizing these entitlements. This organization of social entitlements strengthened the institution of citizenship as the key mechanism regulating membership in the nation and access to its resources.

The transition from the laissez-faire state to the welfare state reproduced the political and social constitution of citizens as white, whose needs were institutionalized in social programs. The basis of the relationship between the welfare state and its nationals remained rooted within their shared racial status, now characterized as arising from their shared quality of compassion. This compassion reinforced the perceived reciprocity among white citizens and maintained a profound tension among nationals, immigrants, and Aboriginals. The organization of welfare has been such that Canadians experienced social rights as a progressive measure. In this, they experienced the benevolent face of the state, which assumed some measure of responsibility – however limited – for their welfare and that of their families. These citizens gained a stake in preserving access to social programs for nationals, the benefits of which assumed very concrete and tangible forms. Linda Gordon has stressed the importance of the 'feeling of entitlement' for women which the welfare system created, even as she points out that this system 'solidified' the inequalities inherent in citizenship.[145] The value of this feeling of entitlement enabled the sedimentation of the Canadian national character as compassionate.

The welfare state's treatment of Aboriginal peoples revealed it to be obstinately colonial, effecting not only the dispossession of their lands but also of their children and families. Simultaneously, people of colour encountered this state as one that racialized them upon entry into the country and foreclosed their equal access to citizenship rights. It cast aspersions on their family structures and on the legitimacy of their family relations. People of colour encountered the welfare state as a state actively hostile, or at best, indifferent to their social well-being. The welfare state in Canada has certainly solidified a shared feeling of entitlement among nationals. It also has solidified the racialized bonds between the state, nation, and the real citizen.

DIVERSITY

4 Multiculturalism and the Liberalizing Nation

Cultural diversity throughout the world is being eroded by the impact of industrial technology, mass communications and urbanization. Many writers have discussed this as the creation of a mass society – in which mass produced culture and entertainment and large impersonal institutions threaten to denature and depersonalize man [*sic*]. One of man's [*sic*] basic needs is a sense of belonging, and a good deal of contemporary social unrest – in all age groups – exists because this need has not been met. Ethnic groups are certainly not the only way in which this need for belonging can be met, but they have been an important one in Canadian society. Ethnic pluralism can help us overcome or prevent the homogenization and depersonalization of mass society. Vibrant ethnic groups can give Canadians of the second, third, and subsequent generations a feeling that they are connected with tradition and with human experience in various parts of the world and different periods of time.

Prime Minister Trudeau, quoted in 'The Federal Response'[1]

I was responsible at the same time for my body, for my race, for my ancestors. I subjected myself to an objective examination. I discovered my blackness, my ethnic characteristics; and I was battered down by tom-toms, cannibalism, intellectual deficiency, fetishism, racial defects, slave-ships, and above all else, above all: 'Sho' good eatin.'

Frantz Fanon, *Black Skin, White Masks*[2]

Respect for diversity and cultural pluralism became emblematic of the Canadian national character with the adoption of multiculturalism as state policy during the tenure of the flamboyant and immensely popular prime minister Pierre Elliott Trudeau. The liberalization of immigration policy and citizenship in the 1960s and 1970s that has been discussed in previous chapters was transforming the pattern of immigration into the country. As immigration from the South overtook that from European source countries, the resulting demographic shift compelled a significant – and perhaps irreversible – transformation of the nation's characterization of itself. The adoption of multiculturalism enabled the nation's self-presentation on the global stage as urbane, cosmopolitan, and at the cutting edge of promoting racial and ethnic tolerance among western nations. This redefinition of national identity was said to signify the nation-state's commitment to valuing cultural diversity. The policy is considered even now by its official proponents as 'one of our finest achievements.'[3] It is lauded for having 'helped bring us international recognition and opportunity.'[4]

Increased confrontations between French and English Canada, resulting from francophone demands for greater autonomy from the federal state, and the growing demands of other 'ethnic' groups for recognition of their place within the nation led to the appointment of the Royal Commission on Bilingualism and Biculturalism in 1963.[5] The commission was given the mandate 'to develop the Canadian Confederation on the basis of equal participation between the two founding races, taking into account the contribution made by other ethnic groups.'[6] This mandate reproduced the colonial erasure of Aboriginal peoples as the original presence in the country. The commission's report subsequently repeated this gesture in its reinforcement of the equality of the two 'charter groups' (the British and the French) as the two 'founding nations.' It also called for official recognition of the various ethnic communities in the country, leading to the adoption of multiculturalism as official state policy in 1971.[7]

Said to distinguish Canada from the assimilationist 'melting pot' tendencies prevalent in the United States, multiculturalism as official policy furthered popular perceptions of the nation having made a successful transition from a white settler colony to a multiracial, multi-ethnic, liberal-democratic society. Imagined now as welcoming 'diverse' immigrants and valuing their cultures, the nation-state came to be seen as particularly amenable to resolving ethnic and cultural divisions. This perception, it should be noted, was also shared by many immigrants.

As its critics have noted, multiculturalism's commitment to developing a distinct Canadian identity was clear enough,[8] but it was unable to balance the foundational claims of the British and French with the demands for inclusion of the multitudes of other cultural groups. The policy's inability to resolve the contradiction between the definition of the nation as bilingual and bicultural and the heterogeneous nature of the population, rendered it excessively ambiguous and internally contradictory. Anti-racist scholars have argued that despite the adoption of multiculturalism, the definition of the nation as primarily bilingual and bicultural reproduced the racialized constructs of the British and French as its real subjects.

Eva Mackey has defined the policy of multiculturalism as 'a mode of managing internal differences within the nation and, at the same time, [created] a form through which the nation could be imagined as distinct and differentiated from external others such as the United States.'[9] While it certainly cannot be disputed that Canada has reaped immense benefits from presenting itself internationally as distinct from the (more aggressive) United States, it should be emphasized that, rather than simply managing difference, official multiculturalism functioned as a mode of constituting this difference, as Himani Bannerji has pointed out. The policy constituted difference among the population primarily in cultural terms, a difference which the state then sought to govern through the policy. In other words, statist multiculturalism has proved to be more than simply a mode of reflecting cultural difference and managing it; it has actively constituted such difference as the most significant aspect of the nation's relations with its (internal) Others. Multiculturalism has sought to constitute people of colour as politically identifiable by their cultural backgrounds.[10] With this move, race became reconfigured as culture and cultural identity became crystallized as political identity, with the core of the nation continuing to be defined as bilingual and bicultural (that is, white).

In her study of Australian multiculturalism, Sara Ahmed has noted that multiculturalism enables the nation to 'reinvent' itself. Multiculturalism is 'a way of imagining the nation itself,' which allows it to live with the difference of others, while claiming this difference to enhance its own cultural superiority.[11] Multiculturalism thus allows the nation to be imagined as homogeneous in relation to the difference of cultural strangers. Further, she argues that even if the cultural stranger is welcomed, rather than expelled, by this discourse, the stranger is nevertheless fethishized as the origin of the difference.

In this chapter, I argue that the transition from an avowedly white settler national identity to a multicultural identity had far more prosaic (sometimes mundane) motivations (and limitations), as well as far more profound consequences than might be suggested by the self-exalting claims of enlightened national commitments to cultural diversity and pluralism. Many scholars of immigration have pointed out that the elimination of overt racial distinctions in immigration policy and citizenship during the 1970s was a pragmatic response to changing global economic conditions that had less to do with idealistic commitments to a cultural utopia and more with the country's growing need for labour. While I agree with this analysis, I also argue that in addition to these changes, the adoption of multiculturalism helped stabilize white supremacy by transforming its mode of articulation in a decolonizing era.

Following on the heels of the Great Depression, the Second World War wreaked havoc upon the Allied western countries. The end of the war ushered in a period of economic expansion and increased international trade, and Canada, along with other hypercapitalist countries, enjoyed a period of economic growth. Like many other countries, it was also experiencing a labour shortage, with the consequence that European sources of labour proved to be insufficient to meet the increased demand for workers in Canada, as many scholars of immigration have noted. Although European immigration continued to be encouraged,[12] it was immigration from the third world that increased significantly.

The changes in the post-war global order were more than merely economic. With large numbers of the previously colonized world acquiring national independence, followed by the growing intensity and visibility of the Civil Rights and anti–Vietnam War movements in North America, the previous immigration policies that had distinguished immigrants on the basis of their race became scandalous. These could no longer be publicly defended in the era of civil rights and decolonization.[13] The far-reaching changes to Canadian immigration policy and citizenship were based in the recognition that immigration from the third world was going to remain a constant feature of western economies for the foreseeable future. Given the (relatively) small population base of the Canadian nation and its declining birth rate, maintaining overtly racialized state policies would have had severe consequences. The outright exclusion of people of colour from political and social life was no longer tenable.

That the changes to immigration and citizenship legislation did not result from any general disavowal of racism among the majority of the population was acknowledged by Freda Hawkins in her extensive study of Canadian immigration policy.[14] She found that the changes in these policies, which had reflected a larger 'white Canada policy' until the 1960s, were not the result of 'parliamentary or popular demand,' but were instead motivated by a growing recognition among bureaucrats that 'Canada could not operate effectively within the United Nations, or in a multiracial Commonwealth, with the millstone of a racially discriminatory policy round her neck.'[15] These officials were concerned that international perceptions of such policies could have potentially damaging effects on national interests, including Canada's participation in the United Nations and the Commonwealth. They concluded that these interests would be better served by the elimination of such explicit racial categories, as would be the nation's relations with the newly independent postcolonial states in Africa, Asia, and the Middle East. Nor was this pragmatism a uniquely Canadian response. Sivanandan also identified a similar dynamic among European elites: 'Improving race relations was a way of improving business opportunities in newly-independent countries which would no longer accept British overlordship. So if you were going to work with the comprador classes in the newly-independent countries, you had to stop saying that they were inferior to you, that their cultures were inferior to yours and declare that we were all brothers under the same capitalist skin.'[16]

In the case of Canada, it should be noted that the elimination of overt racial categorization in state policy occurred only after the whiteness of the 'nation' and its 'citizens' had been consolidated by the policies of the previous era. As Hawkins well recognized, the point system was introduced in the 1960s and 1970s because Canada was not 'prepared to even think about a universal, non-discriminatory immigration policy until full national independence, a reasonably well developed political system, adequate citizenship legislation, and really encouraging economic prospects and the confidence which goes with them, had been achieved.'[17] In other words, the point system only became a possibility once the racial character of nationals, and national institutions, had been consolidated.

If increasing immigration from the third world had to be accepted as an unavoidable necessity in the interest of economic expansion[18] and, with it, the demographic shifts this would inevitably entail, it could be argued that the multiculturalism was to prove to be a far-sighted response, given the racial preoccupations of the state and nation. The liberalization of immigration policy and the adoption of official multiculturalism facilitated both a material inclusion of increased numbers of immigrants within the population *and* their simultaneous exclusion from the nation, primarily through their reification as cultural outsiders, as a number of theorists have noted.[19]

Drawing upon the important critiques of multiculturalism by Ahmed and Bannerji, this chapter examines the profound and far-reaching consequences of multiculturalism in its Canadian statist formulation. Building on both theorists' contention that multiculturalism has enabled the preservation of white domination within settler societies such as Australia and Canada, it examines how multiculturalism has been critical also in the *reconstitution* of whiteness in its distinct (and historically new) version as a culturally 'tolerant' cosmopolitan whiteness. This has facilitated a more fashionable and politically acceptable form of white supremacy, which has had greater currency within a neocolonial, neoliberal global order.

The post-colonial era was shaped by powerful political movements that sought a radical transformation of the balance of power between western powers and their previously colonized populations. The struggles of these peoples for national independence, mirrored by those of people of colour within the west for access to citizenship, were a powerful refutation of the claims of colonizers as benign bearers of modernity and civilization. The force of this refutation gave rise to a crisis of whiteness, a crisis further exacerbated by the discrediting of the scientistic theories of racism in post–Nazi Europe. The extent to which the Nazis had developed this form of racism within the heart of Europe itself led to its demise at the end of the war. Most of the hypercapitalist countries were compelled to distance themselves from these theories, with the result that the previously secure sense of whiteness became deeply destabilized, haunted by its associations with colonial genocides and Nazi policies of extermination. In these circumstances, multiculturalism was to prove critical to the rescuing of Euro/white cultural supremacy: white subjects were constituted as tolerant and respectful of difference and diversity, while non-white people were instead constructed as perpetually and irremediably monocultural, in need of being taught the virtues of tolerance and cosmopolitanism under white supervision.

The increased proximity of racialized Others that was the result of the importation of foreign labour into western countries compelled white subjects to contend more regularly with the startling successes of racial and cultural Others within their own national space. These diverse and ongoing challenges to white supremacy, whether in their overt or submerged and angst-ridden varieties, were met by nationals with renewed claims to the exaltation that multiculturalism allowed them. Even the successes of their Others could be presented as having been made possible only by the nation's newfound ethos of tolerance and inclusion.

Defining official multiculturalism as a form of 'communalizing' power of the state, the following sections examine how this power has (re)configured both the figure of the national subject and that of the immigrant Other in state policy, as well as in their respective self-constituting practices. Foucault defined the state's power as 'both an individualizing and totalizing form of power.'[20] The reach of the state can certainly be defined as 'totalizing,' and likewise, it does constitute subjects as atomized, individualized citizens. Here, however, I want to highlight another aspect of state power in settler societies that becomes evident in policies such as multiculturalism: the power of the state as a communalizing power; that is, a power which constitutes communities as discrete racial, ethnic, and cultural groups existing within its territorial borders, yet outside the symbolic bounds of the nation.

Communities of immigrants and refugees, who remain categorized as such irrespective of their place of birth, their legal citizenship status, or the length of their residence within the country, provide a particularly salient example of this communalizing power of the state. The constitution of certain sectors of the population as cultural communities within state policy seeks to homogenize them as natural social groupings, the distinguishing of which then becomes the modality of their governance. Multiculturalism constructs communities as neatly bounded, separate cultural entities, unchanged by the process of migration and dislocation. Such entities are perceived as untouched by either the external factors within which their cultural practices take place, which change the histories and destinies of the nation, or by the changing realities within the geopolitical order.[21]

For their part, immigrants from the third world who had mobilized against racism in immigration and citizenship legislation were suddenly offered the enticing possibility of greater inclusion into nationhood. Having historically experienced racial dehumanization within the institutional apparatus of the Canadian nation-state, and having been subjected to the economic underdevelopment and the racial conflicts bequeathed their countries of origin by the colonial legacy, this offer of inclusion was irresistible. If their presence was endured by the nation-state largely through exclusionist and segregationist practices in the pre-war period, their inclusion and integration in this new era was to come at the cost of their increased subservience, across generations, to the grand narrative of national supremacy. No longer openly reviled as racial inferiors, immigrants and their descendents were instead seduced by their being celebrated as a source of cultural diversity. This seduction has proved to be potent indeed. Today, the notion of discrete, neatly distinguishable cultural communities has come to be accepted as common sense by advocates of multiculturalism (national and other), and even by some of its detractors. The policy's reification of culture has disciplined and transformed those defined as cultural outsiders such that most have come to accept and reproduce their own classification in just such culturalist terms.

The Rescue of Whiteness

Many scholars have pointed to the crisis of legitimacy confronted by the Canadian state in the 1960s, a crisis that was sparked by the increasing demands of francophones in Quebec; the continuing struggles of Aboriginal peoples for self-determination; the class and gender based political movements of the period; and the increasing demands of people of colour for full citizenship. Seeking to transform itself from a settler colonial state into a liberal-democratic one, and hence claim legitimacy as guarantor of the interests of all these various sectors, official multiculturalism became 'a diffusing or a muting device'[22] for the deeply entrenched conflicts of race. However, this crisis of the Canadian state was, in fact, part of an international crisis of whiteness. The crisis permeated the nation's very sense of itself and the subjectivity of nationals. It also challenged the very notion of white supremacy on a global level.

The crisis of whiteness in the post-war period was forged by a number of factors. The rise of fascism in Europe among those who claimed to be the most civilized and advanced races in the world – including the Nazi regime, with its genocidal policies that culminated in the horrors of the concentration camps – led to a complete shattering of the legitimacy of western scientific theories of race.[23] The modern western model of the nation-state, which had defined itself as shaped by an essentially rationalist ethos, was revealed to have manifested forms that had provoked unprecedented violence and global war and thereby had undermined the entire European imperial order.

Moreover, the scientific theories used by the Nazis informed state policies not only in Germany but also in the other western countries, including Canada.[24] As a partner in the Allied forces fighting fascism, Canada claimed moral superiority over Germany along with its allies in defeating Nazism. But embarrassingly enough, the racial science used by the Nazis could be also found informing Canadian state policy. The heightened association of the Nazis with scientific and biological racism discredited this form of racism so thoroughly that every western nation-state, including Canada, was thereafter compelled to distance itself from the use of such racist science to determine state policy. The continued public use of overtly racialized policies, of the eugenicist values shaping public policy, and of the scientific theories of racial supremacy – all of which had previously enjoyed such popularity among Europeans and their descendents – became impossible to defend publicly, except among the most extreme sectors of these societies and the overtly apartheid regimes.[25]

Equally significant, western assumptions of racial and cultural superiority had become suspect as international public opinion condemned the scale of the violence used against Aboriginal peoples and their communities. Knowledge of this violence could no longer be plausibly denied or fully avoided by nationals. Aboriginal peoples were meeting with greater success in their organizing at the international level, and were turning with great visibility to the Canadian courts in asserting their claims to their land and sovereignty. The ongoing Aboriginal presence in Canada pointed to the implausibility of the national fantasy of benevolent, innocent, and liberal origins. With the worldwide struggles of Aboriginal peoples having received increased legitimacy in the international arena through their petitioning of the United Nations, the realities of the nation's genocidal practices against these peoples were being named as such by increasingly vocal and powerful forces. The growing strength of anti-colonial movements in other parts of the world increased the visibility of these struggles of Aboriginal peoples in North America: the destructiveness of colonial policies could no longer be cloaked as effectively by platitudes of civilizational and moral superiority as had once been the case.

In this circumstance, the political writings and mobilizations of critics of white supremacy posed the following challenges to western nationals.[26] What was the nature of their nation, and its state, if both had been built through commitments to preserving the values of racial supremacy and racial hierarchies, if both had organized racially motivated campaigns against those deemed their inferiors? What kind of being was the national who belonged to such a nation, who was party to the horrors that underpinned its existence, and in whose name these acts had been committed by the state? The very basis of the master narratives of nationhood and their myths of benign and innocent origins were being shaken to the core in Canada, as in the rest of the western world. Whose experiences were to be placed at the centre of the nation's narrative of its origins and progress: those of the civilized white national or of the brutalized and dispossessed Aboriginal?

Control over representations of the nation's past is as critical to maintaining legitimacy and moral authority as is control over its present, and maintaining mastery over the national narrative was critical if nationhood was to be effectively sustained. The past, as a direct link to the present, held the power to hold nationals together in a shared, collective cause and community. If the master narrative of nationhood was to shatter, who could tell what might be the full consequences of this deconstruction?

This crisis of whiteness could only have further intensified with the liberalization of immigration and citizenship legislation, measures which were based on the overt recognition that the labour of people of colour was absolutely indispensable to economic growth and to Canadian national prosperity. The increased (demographic and political) presence of those previously designated non-preferred races meant that racial proximity became a feature of daily life.[27] The diminishing of racial distance mobilized deep seated racial/national anxieties and gave rise to a different kind of dislocation of white identity.

The class composition of immigrants changed dramatically as Canada sought highly qualified and professional immigrants for permanent settlement, attracting many who had considerable expertise as entrepreneurs and professionals. The liberalization of the Trudeau era also enabled people of colour to make advances in accessing the educational and occupational opportunities previously denied them. As people of colour availed themselves of the new opportunities, they achieved significant socio-economic mobility and encountered nationals in the same sites and spaces – in the same schools, universities, executive offices, and workplaces – that nationals had previously claimed for their own. These new forms of intimate contact undoubtedly gave rise to new sets of anxieties among the nationals who considered themselves inherently superior. The proximity of people of colour within these sites challenged white entitlement and privilege, implicitly, if not explicitly. If 'they' are like 'us,' if they can become like us, can even surpass us in their notable and sometimes spectacular achievements, what makes us better? Who are we if they can become us?

The industriousness, professional and financial successes of these immigrants debunked the notion that nationals were marked by a superior commitment to excellence, a higher intelligence, and a stronger work ethic. Something else had to be taken into account. Indeed, people of colour recognized that they had to work harder, that they were held to a higher standard, and that they were repeatedly forced to prove themselves in these sites. The nationals who imposed these conditions on them also undoubtedly recognized these realities. It is inconceivable that the changed geopolitical conditions and domestic necessities would not have a profound impact on the hegemonic self-regard of whites.

In the context of this crisis, Canadian multiculturalism proved to be a timely and effective response. It opened up the possibility of recasting national identity in a manner that maintained its uniqueness; it could now be cast as being distinct from the United States and Europe, and thus not (directly) implicated in their (more visible) colonial and imperialist histories. National identity could be presented as more fluid, open-ended, and embracing, unlike the American and European homogenized, uni-dimensional identities. The policy also enabled the nation-state to claim as part of its rightful property the cultural heritage and identity of every other nation in the world from which immigrants had arrived. Multiculturalism enabled the nation to appropriate as its own the global cultural field in a manner that was to prove far-sighted, indeed.[28] It furthered the nation's international interests in the fields of trade and business, as it did in the political arena, with Canada claiming for itself the role of the international cosmopolitan, in contrast to America, the anti-communist 'Big Brother.'

In his study of Australian multiculturalism, Ghassan Hage has argued that nationals who supported multiculturalism used this support to define themselves as sophisticated, urbane, and cosmopolitan. They were able to gain ascendancy over racist nationals precisely through (re)constituting themselves as tolerant, and hence as more adaptable to changing global conditions and more amenable to availing themselves of newly emerging international opportunities. Constructing racist nationals as a minority isolated within the national body, and hence marginal to it, their embrace of multiculturalism allowed these adept nationals to contest the older damaging national imaginary and transform it for a new era.[29] Beverly Skeggs has identified a similar dynamic within British society, making the case that this move was also class based. She points out that the upper and middle classes have been able to utilize their support for multiculturalism as cultural capital in the age of globalization, unlike the working classes whom they have depicted as irremediably racist and uncouth. Elites have thereby enhanced the distinctions of their respective class identities.

As in Australia and Britain, the embrace of multiculturalism allowed Canadians to resolve the crisis of whiteness through its reorganization as tolerant, pluralist, and racially innocent, uncontaminated by its previous racist history. Because multicultural whiteness claimed to be tolerant of difference, even when besieged by a bewildering global array of diversity, it could now recast itself as uniquely committed to pluralism and thereby exalt its basic goodness. The adroit national could erase the compromised racist imaginary of the past and project this upon a traditionalist minority within the white population that might still overtly defend the older, biological conceptions of white supremacy. The old nationalist minority, cast now as incorrigibly and shamelessly racist, could be made responsible for the racist sins of the past. The racist extremists of the present, such as the neo-Nazis and extreme right-wing groups, were in like manner made solely responsible for the current sins of racism. Theirs was a blatant racism from which most nationals who embraced multiculturalism could detach themselves.

As Hage and other theorists have observed, these multiculturalist and racist nationals both shared the basic assumption that racial communities were the bearers of difference, and both imagined the national space as essentially white. Racial and ethnic others continued to be marginalized by such politics; they could be defined as provoking the majority beyond tolerance by their incessant demands for 'special' rights. Constituting themselves as 'masters of national space,' whether through opposition to multiculturalism and the rights of racial minorities or through support for multiculturalism as the primary political site for minority concerns, both viewed racial and ethnic minorities as 'objects' requiring their control.[30]

Multiculturalism masked the continuity of white privilege, even as the justification of this privilege was being profoundly eroded. The national subject remained empowered by displacing the patterns of discrimination and racial hatred onto the now disclaimed past or onto its own rejected, obstreperous, and stubborn minority in the present. Thus, multiculturalism became the solution to the crisis of whiteness that had emerged in the post-war era as the colonial world exploded in violence. Instead of a critical examination and disavowal of the colonial experience, multiculturalism enabled a projection of the destabilizing effects of the crises of white identity onto a small minority of recalcitrant whites who refused or were unable to mask their racisms. Its appeals for tolerance enabled a national amnesia regarding inconvenient histories.

Multiculturalism also enabled the suturing of the post-colonial crises by enabling a different kind of projection: that of the anxieties of an intolerant and racist whiteness onto immigrants. The heightened focus on the cultures of third world peoples – which were believed to keep them stubbornly traditional despite the nation's offer to modernize them, despite its hospitality and generosity towards them, and despite its respect for their cultures – allowed for the continued projection of the anxieties of whiteness onto 'them.' If whites were to be accused of racism, genocide, and colonial exploitation, they could now respond in kind by pointing to how much worse immigrants were, with their primitive and backward cultural practices, their corruptions, misogyny, cronyism and violence. With whiteness coming to signify tolerance, a willingness to change and a cosmopolitan sensibility, people of colour could be tied all the more readily to cultural parochialism, authoritarianism, essentialism, and intolerance.

Multiculturalism as a specific policy and a socio-political racial ideology has thus come to attest to the enduring superiority of whiteness, of its ability to transform and accommodate itself to changing times and new opportunities. It became a framework that assumed a certain rigidity in the cultures of racial others, of their enduring inferiority, immaturity, and the need for their reformulation under the tutelage of progressive – always modernizing – western superiority.

Communalizing Multiculturality

It is surely no coincidence that official multiculturalism emerged at a moment when anti-racist and anti-colonial discourses had gained considerable ground internationally. The deployment of these discourses was as central to the struggles for national independence and the mobilizations of civil rights movements as they were to the international alliances that emerged between these movements. People of colour organized transnational movements and international alliances, built multiracial organizations and convened conferences in the heyday of the revolutionary era of the 1940s through the 1960s.[31] It was a moment of unparalleled global anti-colonial solidarity. Emerging as oppositional to these efforts for self-determination, the efficacy of multiculturalism depended upon the expulsion of anti-racist and anti-colonial discourses from the horizon. Its effectiveness as a counter response in Canada was much bolstered by its adoption by the state as official policy.

In this section, I examine how the discursive regulations of multiculturalism suppressed references to race and racism and disrupted the potential for greater multiracial solidarity among communities of colour in their struggles to achieve socio-economic, *not merely cultural,* parity. By accepting and institutionalizing dubious assumptions regarding the immutability of cultural difference, cultural barriers, and cultural enhancement, multiculturalist policies, which had been directly provoked by these very considerations, eviscerated these discourses and movements contesting racial hierarchies of power.

Situating multiculturalism within the larger framework of bilingualism and biculturalism, the policy introduced by the Trudeau government privileged the English and French languages and cultures as the overarching national frame, within which were to be located the multicultures of ethnic and racial minorities.[32] Reifying the cultural identities of both the nation (as bilingual and bicultural) and its Others (as multicultures), the policy committed the state to providing specific forms of practical support to different cultural minorities.[33] In brief, the policy stated that resources were to be provided to those cultural groups who had demonstrated a desire to contribute to the national project and were committed to national unity; it identified cultural barriers as hindering full participation in Canadian society; it promulgated creative cultural interactions to further national unity; and it defined the acquisition of French- and English-language skills as adequate to the task of enabling racial and cultural minorities full participation within society. How the desire to contribute to national unity demanded by the policy was to be measured was left unspecified. It was clear, however, that multiculturalism was intended to further the nation's unity, not its transformation.

The multiculturalism policy identified the nationals' lack of familiarity with the cultures of racial minorities, and these minorities' lack of English- and French-language skills, as the most salient factors excluding them from 'full participation' in society. It thus placed the onus for racial inequalities experienced by people of colour onto their own (collective) cultural inadequacies (that is, their differences) and (individual) lack of linguistic skills. In emphasizing culture, it suppressed public discussion of the racism, both institutional and personal, which barred the full participation of people of colour within the economic and sociopolitical establishment. Most importantly, in defining the population as belonging to discrete ethnic and cultural groups, this communalizing power of the state suppressed the legal distinctions between immigrant and citizen, ideologically equating their status and identity by emphasizing only their shared membership in 'their' cultural communities. The constitution of cultural communities as homogenous entities erased the very many differences among them. The inequalities of class, gender, sexual orientation, disability, and so on were all rendered secondary and less material. Cultural difference was to be the primary modality for mediating relations among nationals, immigrants, and the state.

The multiculturalism policy was not the only instrument through which the population was organized along clearly delineated cultural lines. The state was committed to the objective that increased immigration would not undermine the nation's character or its social fabric, and the Immigration Act that institutionalized the point system reinforced the distinction between immigrants who shared the nation's cultural and social characteristics and those who did not. Among the Act's objectives were the following:

> to promote the domestic and international interests of Canada recognizing the need (a) to support the attainment of such demographic goals as may be established by the Government of Canada in respect of the size, rate of growth, structure and geographic distribution of the Canadian population;

> ... to enrich and strengthen the cultural and social fabric of Canada, taking into account the federal and bilingual character of Canada.[34]

The Act naturalized the character of the nation as bilingual and made its objective the strengthening of the 'cultural and social fabric' of whiteness in the face of increasing non-white immigration. Immigration legislation was to remain attentive to both demographic needs and the maintenance of the nation's character. Here, a historical continuity was to be maintained with state practices that sought to produce national homogeneity out of demographic heterogeneity. The category *immigrant* drew upon the historical status of *non-preferred races* as outsiders in this new liberalized era, recodifying it so that those who were previously reviled as non-preferred races were now reconfigured as culturally different communities. Viewing immigrants primarily through this lens of cultural and linguistic difference meant that all people of colour would become ideologically constructed as *immigrants* on the basis of their shared cultural and linguistic diversity. It was in this equation of immigrants with cultural and linguistic difference from the nation that processes of racialization found their new mode of expression, contributing to the suppression of the anti-racist discourse developed by people of colour in their struggles for full citizenship.[35]

The state's commitment to the preservation of the national character was further bolstered by its development of the categories of 'visible minorities' and 'newcomers' to refer to these communities of immigrants.[36] Ten non-white groups were officially designated as visible minorities: this category reinforced skin-based racial difference, opening the door to the fusing of this visible form of difference with culturally based difference.[37] The designation of people of colour as newcomers or new Canadians erased their particular individual histories, rendered secondary their legal citizenship status, and suppressed knowledge about the older histories of their communities in the country. The category newcomers suppressed the history of the racist campaigns waged by nationals during the first half of the twentieth century to ensure that these communities remained small in size and to restrain their public participation, an effort necessary to their subsequent acceptance as newcomers.[38] Ahistorical and self-contradictory, the various modalities of difference constituted by these categories intersected at various levels to crystallize as instruments of racialization.[39]

Whereas in the pre-war period, racial character and culture were treated as synonymous in state practices,[40] these new policies emphasized distinctions of culture while suppressing those of race. In their study of racism in British society, both Martin Barker and Paul Gilroy have made the case that a significant shift occurred in processes of racialization during the 1970s, the same period these changes took place in Canadian policies.[41] Characterizing this shift as the emergence of a 'new' racism, both have argued that racial hierarchies became organized through the discourse of cultural and national difference, not of biological inferiority. Defined in essentialist terms, cultural and national differences were said to make majority and minority communities incompatible. Foreigners were defined as having their natural homes and as properly belonging to their natural national groups. Instead of making an overt case for the inferiority or superiority of various peoples, this new racism equated race with nation and culture, raising questions instead about the national (in)compatibility and cultural (in)commensurability of majority and minority populations.

Sherene Razack has pointed to the operation of a similar 'culturalization of race' within Canadian society. Modern racism, she points out, is

distinguished from its nineteenth-century counterpart by the vigour with which it is consistently denied. In its modern form, overt racism, which rests on the notion of biologically based inferiority, coexists with a more covert practice of domination encoded in the assumption of cultural or acquired inferiority. This 'culturalization of racism,' whereby Black inferiority is attributed to 'cultural deficiency, social inadequacy, and technological underdevelopment,' thrives in a social climate that is officially pluralist.[42]

The discourse of Canadian multiculturalism, with its emphasis on deep and unchanging cultural difference, can be considered part of a world-wide shift to a new and culturally communalizing form of racism.

The politics of allocating multicultural funding on the spurious basis of cultural distinctions further undermined the self-defined multi-racial organizations and movements mobilized by people of colour. State-funded community organizations promoted the emergence of a class of elite cultural 'spokes(wo)men,' whose primary claim to political space was articulated within the terrain of multiculturalism. This community elite acquired a stake in the preservation of multiculturalism, and they have defended this stake vociferously. State support for community organizations facilitated the state's role as arbitrator of community representatives. These funds designated official insiders and outsiders in communities of colour. Speaking culture to power became the avenue to accessing this coveted status.

In their study of the workings of multiculturalist policy in relation to the political organizing of women of colour in the 1980s, Linda Carty and Dionne Brand have demonstrated how state-initiated (and state-funded) strategies undermined the self-organizing activities of the various anti-racist women's organizations committed to improving the economic status of working-class women. Initiating and fostering the creation of multiculturalist women's conferences and organizations, state funding enabled the containment of anti-racist organizing from below by the promotion of a middle-class elite leadership that focused more on issues of cultural identities than on socio-economic inequalities.[43] Women's anti-racist struggles were greatly undermined by such intervention, as they were by the encouragement of cultural communities to make their own separate claims for recognition and support from the multicultural bureaucracy.

The success of multiculturalism lies in its facilitation of the integration of immigrants on the nation's terms; it remains dependent on the derailment of the struggles of people of colour against the racism of the nation-state. People of colour campaigned long and hard against the racist immigration policies of the first half of the twentieth century. Like the Civil Rights movement in the United States, which had a profound affect on drawing attention to the pervasive racism that denied Black people basic civil rights,[44] anti-racist struggles in Canada contributed to a global political climate that made the overt use of racial categories in public policies difficult to sustain. Changes to immigration policy were, therefore, the result of the state's pragmatism, which prompted changes 'from above,' as well as of anti-racist struggles, which prompted changes 'from below.'

In Canada, the increased access of people of colour to citizenship was likewise the result of both their struggles for inclusion and the state's recognition of the need for harnessing their labour. People of colour organized and fought racist labour laws and racist trade unions; they pooled resources and organized community institutions to sustain their presence in the country, and they struggled for access to social entitlements.[45] The challenges they mounted against their racial domination are also part of the context within which multiculturalism was adopted as state policy.

Multiculturalism co-opted and derailed the explicitly anti-racist activism of people of colour, splitting their cross-racial alliances as it worked to contain the demands for racial equality that sought to transform the very basis of economic, social, and political power.[46] Multiculturalist policy and its after-effects on popular culture eroded the salience of anti-racist politics and discourses; it disguised the persistence of white supremacy and power in the new constitution of whiteness as signifying 'tolerance.' Multiculturalism avoided recognition of the critical intersection of institutional power and interpersonal forms of racism, demanding only tolerance at the level of interpersonal interactions. Knowledge about the nature of racism, and the role it has historically played in Canadian nation-building, has thus been made peripheral. Most public discussions of racism focus only on its individualized and interpersonal aspects and do not include the concept of power, institutional and state practices, and the centrality of these practices to national formation.

The regulatory practices of multiculturalism have led to the utter marginalization of racism as an urgent subject for redress in public policy and as a subject for theorization in the social sciences and philosophy; as well, confrontation in the media has been silenced. The level of denial of racism in daily life is of such intensity that (many) immigrants come to doubt their own experience of this phenomenon. Like national subjects, immigrants also tend to minimize and deny the racism that pervades their lives, unless it is far too overt to deny.[47] This situation is not unlike that found by feminist scholars in their examination of the experiences of women living with violence. These women generally tend to minimize – or outrightly deny – the forms and levels of violence they live with. Feminist researchers have found that women who experience male violence often tend to blame themselves, and their own behaviour, for the violence.[48] In like fashion, people of colour also tend to minimize or even deny the forms and levels of racism that shape their daily lives.

Ironically, immigrants are acutely attuned to the heterogeneity that makes up the country's population, perhaps even more so than are nationals. Immigrants are aware of their diversity, not only in relation to the dominant Euro-Canadian community but also in relation to other communities of colour. Indeed, having been made the embodiment of this diversity by the dominant culture, they live out this diversity in their daily lives and become acutely sensitive to the differences between themselves and the various other groups collapsed into the categories immigrant, refugee, and visible minorities. They are less ready to conflate these differences.

Many immigrants, echoing the politics of the dominant majority, also come to equate the prejudices held by people of colour towards each other with the racism of the dominant Euro-Canadian majority. As multiculturalism supresses recognition of the relationship between power and racism, it therefore promotes definitions of such prejudices among immigrants to be equated with, or even eclipse, the racism of the dominant majority. The actuality that few people of colour have the power to impose their prejudices upon the groups against which these are directed does not hinder such equations. Thus, if immigrants question or reject the multiculturalist frame, its discursive moves can be mobilized against them to accuse them of not respecting diversity and difference and of being racist themselves.

The 'leaders' of immigrant communities have largely stressed the positive aspects of multiculturalism, which are those directly linked to recognition of cultural heterogeneity and diversity. They also value the economic opportunities that they feel they can access – and more importantly, those that their children can access – through the official accommodation of their difference. Their strong attraction to multiculturalism speaks to the impulse of multiculturalism from below, shaped by a deep desire for inclusion. Multiculturalism has indeed promoted the advancement of certain classes of ethnic and racial professionals up the corporate ladder as Canadian and international firms have sought to maximize their cultural assets in the global market in order to promote their own interests abroad.[49] The cost of such advancement, however, has been to sustain the marginality of Aboriginal peoples.

In short, multiculturalism did not herald the end of the racialization of Canadian national identity.[50] Multiculturalism has had the effect of constituting people of colour as possessing an excess of culture that marked them as outsiders to the nation. By masking the parochiality of their whiteness as a cultural identity, nationals were instead constituted as both experiencing a dearth of their own culture and as being more accepting of cosmopolitanism by their interactions with 'multi-cultures.' Furthermore, it is within the contours of the discourse of multiculturalism, not anti-racism, that nationals and immigrants were compelled to constitute their respective forms of subjectivity.

Through National Eyes

The adoption of state multiculturalism has had enormous influence on shaping popular perceptions of cultural diversity as a 'problem' and as an issue for national concern, consideration, and management. It has reified culture as the most salient factor in intergroup dynamics, deflecting attention from the disqueting legacy of white supremacy and casting people of colour as culturally problematic.

As discussed above, anti-racist critics have argued that official multiculturalism diverted attention from the power relations that reproduce racial hierarchies, reframing these instead as conflicts arising from ignorance and cultural intolerance.[51] Immigrants, not having the same access to shaping or participating in this discourse, were to become its objects. Consequently, the socio-economic problems experienced by immigrants became defined in the national imagination as evidence of their innate cultural deficiences which became a threat to the liberal values of the nation.

Multiculturalism also enhanced those self-constituting practices of immigrants that emphasized their supposed difference from the west and from other racially denigrated communities. In other words, multiculturalism as a regulatory mechanism encouraged immigrants to imagine themselves in the same 'culturalist' tropes nationals used against them, thereby coming to see themselves through the eyes of the nation. The effectiveness of the discourse has been such that to reject its foundational assumptions by raising questions about racism is seen to be in bad form or, worse, as acting in bad faith. To do so questions the 'good' intentions of nationals in their commitment to tolerance.

The multiculturalism policy sought to define not only *who* the nation's Others were but also *what* they were. Prime Minister Trudeau's speech gestured towards this constructionist approach inherent in the policy: 'I wish to emphasize the view of the government that a policy of multiculturalism within a bilingual framework is basically the conscious support of individual freedom of choice. We are free to be ourselves. But this cannot be left to chance. It must be fostered and pursued actively.'[52] The policy committed state support for those groups willing to demonstrate their commitment to the national project and to those who would help enrich the lives of nationals. The multicultural bureaucratic apparatus determined which communities shared this goal of nurturing the national enterprise and therefore deserved the state's support. This bureaucracy's funding authenticated various aspects of these cultures while marginalizing others. In effect, then, this bureaucracy domesticated those forms of difference that would enhance the nation's sense of itself, as well as those which would nurture the nationals' sense of him/herself through the consumption of such difference. Multiculturalism required particular techniques to shape cultural communities (defining them along religious, linguistic, ethnic lines), and hence preserved these forms of difference as traditional forms. Through the politics of state funding for particular multicultural organizations, activities, programs, and events, the state asserted its determination of which practices were to be rightly considered part of the traditional culture of immigrants, worthy of being given visibility and promotion. The policy thus linked the preservation of these cultures as remnants of the past, as was spelled out in 'The Federal Response' by Trudeau.

The source countries of immigrant communities were constructed in the western imagination as pre-modern, tradition bound, and culturally backward. Immigrants themselves were likewise perceived by policymakers and the public as deficient in their accomplishment of modernity. 'Vibrant ethnic groups can give Canadians of the second, third and subsequent generations a feeling that they are connected with tradition and with human experience in various parts of the world and different periods of time,' explained 'The Federal Response' to the policy.[53] Ethnic groups were presented as connected to tradition, not modernity, and they embodied 'human experience in various parts of the world' associated with a different temporal plane (different periods of time) than the one inhabited by the nation. With their cultures defined in this manner, how could individual members of these communities escape becoming essentialized, or cultured, as it were? The policy advocated that their strangeness was not only to be tolerated but also was to be preserved and made cannibalistically available for the nation's sustenance and enrichment. The nation's nostalgia for a past lost to them could now be accessed by the forays of nationals into these communities of culture, communities defined as outside history and modernity, outside the spaces inhabited by the nation. Culture was to trap immigrants in the nostalgic fantasies of the nation.

Paul Gilroy, among others, has dismissed the notion that the cultures and identities of various populations in the Americas, that is Aboriginals, colonizers, settlers, slaves, and migrants, lived or developed their respective communities in isolation from each other. He argues that the 'the reflexive cultures and consciousnesses of the European settlers, the "Indians" they slaughtered, and the Asians they indentured were not, even in situations of the most extreme brutality, sealed off hermetically from each other.'[54] Rejecting the 'lure of ethnic absolutisms,' Gilroy instead develops the concept of the 'Black Atlantic' to highlight the 'syncretic pattern' that shaped the cultures, politics, and consciousness of these populations. The forms of identity, consciousness, and social practices developed by immigrants within Canada were likewise shaped as much by the exigencies of their insertion into the new society, by their experiences of migratory dislocation and by their interactions with nationals as they were by the 'cultural baggage' they were assumed to bring with them from their traditional homelands.

Instead of highlighting these new hybrid forms of subjectivities, the adoption of the multiculturalist policy fossilized immigrants as living remnants of the past. The policy would also help counter the alienating and depersonalizing effects of the modern life of nationals within an industrial society: 'The government will support and encourage the various cultures and ethnic groups that give structure and vitality to our society. They will be encouraged to share their cultural expression and values with other Canadians and so contribute to a richer life for us all.'[55] The state highlighted and emphasized the traditional (read conservative) aspects of immigrant communities, above their egalitarian, modern, and transformative aspects. As many have argued, definitions of both culture and community are hotly contested.

South-Asian feminists, as well as Chinese-Canadian, Black, and Aboriginal feminists, for example, have challenged practices that oppress women in the name of tradition as patriarchal, and hence as organizing power relations, rather than as expressions of timeless cultural practices.[56] These women, as well as others who have sought to challenge the hegemony of the multicultural discourse, have had to contend not only with the authoritarian forces internal to the community, which have been greatly strengthened by multiculturalist support from the state, but also with the overwhelming pervasiveness of this discourse within mainstream society.[57] If multiculturalism exalted nationals by rescuing their whiteness, giving it a new respectability, the regulatory practices of this discourse proved no less effective in shaping the discursive horizons and disciplinary practices within the other modalities it mapped out.

Sara Mills rightly cautions that not all subject positions are uniformly adopted by all members of a particular group.[58] However, all subject positions, even if oppositional to hegemonic formulations (and contesting notions) of community and culture, have to negotiate the power embedded in the discourse of multiculturalism, in the state bureaucracies and its agencies, and in the media and other institutions. Thus, people of colour have had to engage with the state and the innumerable other centres of power in which this discourse is embedded, contesting it even as their lives have become regimented by it.

Not all immigrants, of course, have sought to counter the framework of multiculturalism. Indeed, many of them have embraced it wholeheartedly as a celebration of their existence in the country. Many have sought to reflect back to the state the image of their communities as homogeneous through attempts to suppress the fissures and dissidents internal to these social groupings.[59] Fanon observed that racism often provoked Black people into an aggressively nationalist stance, such as Negritude, or into the defence of a higher status within the racial hierarchy by denigrating those situated on a lower order (the Martinican who considered her/himself superior to the Senegalese), as well as into developing the mimicry of whiteness.[60] All of these stances, and probably a great deal more, have shaped the responses of people of colour to multiculturalism and its detritus. Many immigrants have embraced their culturalization, some have rejected it, others have tried to 'pass' as Canadian, and yet others have sought to reframe this culturalist discourse within an anti-racist framework. All, however, have had to engage with it. None have escaped its reach.

In her study of the 'politics of the visible,' Eleanor Ty examined the paradox of immigrants being both 'visible' and 'invisible' within North

American cultures. She finds that many Asian North American authors and film-makers struggle with this paradox, as they do with their own 'internalization' of their Otherness. Many of these artists reproduce the Otherness of the Asian, especially with regard to Asian women, by exoticizing and mystifying them. Their representations of their own immigrant mothers feature the women as tradition bound and subject to a suffocating and pervasive cultural patriarchy.[61] For others, the dominant images produced in popular culture, by Hollywood for example, become the mirror through which they attempt to shape their own subjectivity, even as their immersion in the language of their colonizers furthers their alienation from their own sense of history and community.[62] Yet Ty also finds that some writers are able to subvert these culturalist tropes and 'move away from the spectre of the Oriental.'[63]

The reproduction of the western gaze by many (if not most) Asian North Americans, both in their accounts of their ancestors and families and of themselves, is probably inevitable, given the dominant historiography that seeks to erase traces of non-western, and most particularly, anti-western, historical perspectives and experiences. Given the paucity of more historically accurate accounts of the perspectives and practices of colonized peoples and of the experiences of immigrants from such communities, and given the lack of public space accorded these perspectives when they are expressed, people of colour in North America are greatly hampered in their efforts to contest their own self-orientalizing practices. To do so requires a constant and unrelenting hypervigilance, an ongoing psychic and political resistance against the hegemonic master narratives of the past and of the present.

Multicultural discourse marks non-western cultures as more patriarchal and backward than the west, while it simultaneously pressures immigrant men to conform to significantly strengthened masculinist codes of behaviour in the name of cultural authenticity. As a consequence, immigrant women, whose consciousness is also shaped in interaction with the master narrative, approach the men of their communities with complex expectations and anxieties. Caricatured forms of cultural practices, valorized by the state as authentic, thus discipline people of colour into reproducing the more patriarchal and politically conservative practices within their histories and communities. Both women and men come to 'see' and experience their own culture through this frame, with its peculiar versions of femininities and masculinities. They learn to see themselves through the nation's eyes, even when they seek to contest such damaging images of themselves.

In the absence of the intervention of strong counter-hegemonic, anti-racist, and anti-colonial perspectives and without consciously articulated and persistent efforts to contest the dominant multiculturalist discourse, immigrant communities are encouraged to express and experience 'their' cultures through multiculturalism's conceptual language and assumptions. The male cultural figure is presented to be in need of constraint and control; the woman requires rescue through constant education and acculturation beyond her own culture, community, and family. She needs to be tutored into an embrace of the nation's more 'liberatory' gender values and norms. This routinized representation of immigrant women acts as a form of propaganda that encourages women's alienation from their communities and families as potential sites of support and sustenance, and weakens possibilities for cross-gender solidarity. Thus, even as patriarchal relations are strengthened through immigration and citizenship policies, the gendered effects of multiculturalism undermine the possibilities for solidarity between 'cultured' women and men.

Contemporary modern Canadian (and western) culture repeatedly frames immigrants' cultural practices, religious lives, gender relations, and family structures as oppressive, ill-informed, and unhealthy, if not deadly. However, some immigrants might at times find these practices pleasurable, especially if they enhance their own status and power within their relationships in their community, deepening the complexity and heightening the anxieties of their subject and community formation.

Orientalist constructs of racialized gender have for centuries fed the assumption that the lives of non-white women are to be understood in terms starkly different from those that account for the experiences of white women, meant to represent the norm of the modern, forward-looking and flexible female gender identity.[64] Canadian society has been presented as offering immigrant women the opportunity to escape from their inherently and deeply oppressive communities and enforced traditional feminine roles. Gendered inequalities, in being reduced to a matter of cultural and traditional deficiency, have become racialized and normalized, if not overtly sanctioned, as widely pervasive within immigrant communities; the presence of (proto)feminist practices within such groups is deemed impossible. Such constructs map out the distance of women of colour from Canadian women and, in turn, from the larger national collective. Indeed, the subordination of third world women has today become a key signifier of 'their' cultural Otherness on a global scale, a marker of the core values said to separate 'them' from western nations.

Culturalism has become the overarching discursive frame, conflating the varied experiences of women with origins in continents as different as Asia, Africa, and the Americas, presenting them as all – and always – victimized by hypermasculine domination. Even as their cultural differences from the nation are emphasized and enhanced, the women's differences from each other are flattened and subsumed by the homogeneity of the categories used to classify them, that is, immigrants, refugees, or visible minorities. These women's entry into Canadian society is presented as an escape from their disadvantageous, tragic, or uninformed backgrounds and communities.

A number of theorists have argued that the construction of immigrants as the nation's Others serves not only to define them as outsiders but also to congeal the insider status of members of the nation.[65] If the presence of the nation's Others marks the boundary that holds the nation together, the presence of women of colour at these margins gives rise to a particular anxiety for nationals. Media presentations attest to this anxiety in their perpetual narrations of the cultural deficiencies that are said to control the lives of these women. News stories of women of colour largely focus on them as hapless victims: 'Cultural conflicts, arranged marriages, oppressive cultures, exotic dress and foods – these are the stock in trade of the press's coverage of racialized women.'[66] These women become the cause of considerable consternation: their adoption of Canadian ways, and a properly solicitious gratitude towards nationals for allowing them to live in their country, lend legitimacy to claims of the nation's superior multiculturalist values and its commitment to an egalitarian pluralism. These women's modernization, signalled by the level of their assimilation into Canadian society and its values, upholds such exaltations of nationhood.

Should these women 'lapse' into their cultural and traditional ways by, for example, choosing an arranged marriage or choosing to wear the hijab or chador, the superiority of the nation's cherished values become suddenly threatened. If assimilation occurs successfully, then their difference can be harmlessly preserved in the form of their exotic dress, even if only to be worn at community events; in their food, which the popular song-and-dance version of multiculturalism promotes; or in their language and religion, if practised in a private and non-politicized manner. The women can then be celebrated as the proper multicultural subjects who attest to the nation's spirit of tolerance and acceptance of diversity and who embrace the superior mores of Canadians.

The national's sense of self is routinely enhanced in spectacular fashion through her/his participation in events such Divali celebrations and

Chinese New Year parades. Hage has drawn attention, in the case of Australia, to the 'discourse of enrichment' that enables national subjects to consume the multicultures within their vicinity, through their consumption of ethnic foods and arts at multicultural fairs and restaurants, for example.[67] The vision of the framers of Canadian multiculturalism anticipated just such a provision of cultural enrichment to the nation's subjects in order to give vitality to the nation, to contribute to a richer life for nationals in various ways.[68] Prime Minister Trudeau, phantasmagorically represented even now as the quintessential urbane bohemian, envisioned the development of a national identity that would successfully accommodate itself to the fluidity and flexibility – hybridity even – demanded in the new global climate. This retooled subjectivity might welcome the cultural exchanges proffered to it, finding pleasure in, and enriching itself from, a sort of multicultural gala while remaining, at its core, staunchly Canadian.

That the national subject derives a significant form of self-enrichment from the pleasurable aspects of consuming other cultures, that is, the food, music, dance, fashions, and so on, of the other, has been pointed out by Hage and other theorists. But equally significant to this subject's exaltation are what have been defined as the negative, annoying, and disgusting aspects of these Other cultures. The 'smelly' odors and 'gaudy' colours of the Chinatowns and Little Indias in Canadian cities;[69] the crowded streets and the unwieldy immigrant drivers who meander across the roads, stop at all the wrong places, park in all the wrong spots – violate all traffic regulations; the hidden cockfights, 'gambling dens,' and drug dealers; the garbage strewn streets of ethnic markets at night; the loud voiced and excitable speech of the ethnic – these are among the more amusing, embarrassing, and troubling aspects of multicultural life. These disconcerting 'horrors,' 'tasteless' sensual excesses, and 'quaint' mannerisms of ethnics have to be avoided or mocked at all costs. The avoidance of such displays of negative cultural excesses also sustain the self-exaltation of nationals.

The national community exalts itself as the tolerant host of all this sound and fury and, in so doing, publicly deliberates and passionately opines on which encounters and exhibitions are enriching, annoying, or quaint, and which are especially revolting and threatening. It should not be assumed that the national subject, therefore, is served only by the enriching, positively vetted, elements of the immigrants' cultural lives; she/he is just as fascinated and obsessed by the disgusting elements, is also enriched by realizing his/her own distance from these. Indeed, she/he is perhaps even more obsessed with these negative aspects, for it is in the disavowal and disdain for these practices that the national subject is able to experience most fully his/her cultural superiority, his/her higher civilizational status. In disparaging the deviant, dictatorial, and ultrapatriarchal practices that are construed to be the reality of the everyday lives of immigrant communities, the national subject can experience him/herself as enjoying the freedoms, liberties, individual rights, and forms of demeanor that immigrants are considered incapable of exhibiting and appreciating.

This complex cultural terrain also shapes the subjectivities of the ethnic and racial others who seek acceptance into the nation. The strangers who can be presumed to embody and emphasize the positive aspects of their cultural life as valued by the nation and who place as much distance as possible between themselves and the negatively evaluated aspects of their cultural lives are more likely to be selectively marked for inclusion in social life. In Ahmed's words, they become the acceptable strangers, not the 'stranger' strangers who remain unassimilable: 'multiculturalism can involve a double and contradictory process of incorporation and expulsion: it may seek to differentiate between those strangers whose appearance of difference can be claimed by the nations, and those stranger strangers who may yet be expelled, whose difference may be dangerous to the well-being of even the most heterogenous of nations.'[70]

For the adroit immigrant subject who desires to become the nation's multicultural subject, deploying her/his difference effectively so that it is reassuring and not alarming, becomes a means for acquisition of some measure of acceptance by nationals. So, for example, the wearing of the salwar-kameez will be tolerated, admired even, but not the hijab. Should the immigrant subject deploy the discourse of anti-racism to challenge their pervasive inequality within socio-political institutions, she/he is derided as hostile or angry, with the proverbial chip on her/his shoulder.[71] Such contestations usually unsettle the national subject, who often voices anger, anxiety, or guilt. Therefore, the immigrant subject's cultural Otherness is more likely to be accepted if it reconfirms the national subject's sense of her/his own exaltation. It is from this space of a domesticated cultural Otherness that the immigrant subject is allowed access to the dominant society, with all of its attendant benefits.

The immigrant subject can thus safely exhibit her/his cultural strangerness or foreign-ness in public, to the extent that it reconfirms national superiority by attesting to its tolerance. A measured and cautious display guarantees the immigrant's access to recognition and acceptance, but her/his otherness must be kept under strict control to avoid eliciting disgust, revulsion, or a sense of threat.

Moreover, the immigrant who longs for acceptance into the national fold can project, with external support, the caricatured cultural self onto other immigrants as the real bearers of the devalued cultural practices. Perhaps the stake of this immigrant self who longs for national acceptance is even greater in its disavowal and derision of its own cultural practices than that of the national subject. For this subject is perpetually required to prove her/his divestment of the negative elements of her/his cultural self. The fear of 'slipping' back into the 'fresh-off-the-boat' behaviour, of lapsing into the thicker 'immigrant' accent, remains a constant possibility, an ongoing danger against which one is required to remain vigilant. These racial subjects are under constant white surveillance, that watches for just such a slip, just such a gesture, that will confirm what the 'knowing' national subject always already knows: 'they' are all really like that.

The vigilance of the culturalized subject against the slippage of its sanitized cultural self has to therefore remain constant. To draw from Fanon, the 'whitened' (cultural) mask cannot be allowed to slip to reveal the 'Black' face that lies beneath. Fanon argued that the racialization of colonized peoples affected much more than their administrative and bureaucratic control, it deeply shaped the subjectivity of colonized peoples. Like the racialization processes examined by Fanon, the (multi)culturalizing processes in Canada profoundly influence the subjectivity of immigrants, especially their racial and cultured sensibilities.

In a gesture parallel to that of the multiculturalist national who distances him/herself from racism by projecting it onto a marginalized minority and its practices, the immigrant who longs for acceptance distances him/herself by projecting onto other immigrants the caricatured cultural self and the devalued cultural practices. This immigrant absorbs the dominant society's disdain and projects it onto other immigrants, contributing more scorn and derision, ever distancing him/herself as modern, assimilated, hyphenated, and no less urbane or cosmopolitan than the national. This is the immigrant who repeatedly (and politely) points out that she/he waited in line for their turn to migrate, who played the game by the rules, not like the illegal migrants, the 'boat people,' the 'economic' migrants, and the undocumented.[72] Yet this immigrant self is involved in what Fanon described as largely a fool's errand, for as Fanon himself experienced while living in France, the racialized marking of the body cannot be overcome, no matter the sophistication of one's deportment, the undetectability of one's accent, the depth of one's longing to belong.[73] Even a young white child had the power to reduce the adult Black man to little more than his 'epidermal schema.'

Many people of colour have clearly been very attracted to the multiculturalist discourse despite their everyday experiences of racism and exclusion. Multiculturalism is the overarching frame that dominates the public sphere regarding questions of difference, and it therefore becomes the framework most readily available to them for staking their claims for inclusion. Little public space is available for discussion and debate over the changing contours of racism in the Canadian ethnoscape.[74] While most immigrants readily recognize the interpersonal forms of racism that they experience, they are ill-served by the educational system and other social institutions which deny the historical racialization of Canadian society, or the ongoing institutionalization of such racializing processes. People of colour have to struggle to access a vocabulary that can effectively address the complexities of contemporary nation-building and 'culture talk.' In fact, they are forced to contend with a vocabulary that explicitly suppresses knowledge about such complexities. Multiculturalism creates an environment such that to reject its supposedly inclusive ethos is to risk being labelled ethnocentric and culturally chauvinist, a charge that sticks more readily to people of colour than it does to the nationals exalted by the state as tolerant and committed to valuing diversity.

Although multiculturalism has been popularly defined as being antithetical to an assimilationist politics, it has actually resulted in a deeper assimilation of people of colour under white supervision. In its Canadian variety, it has allowed for the national to 'know' that the nation is *really* bilingual and bicultural (English and French). Furthermore, it is the nation's proper responsibility to oversee the practices of immigrants and to govern cultural difference: 'we' may let 'you' in, but you must become who we say you should be.

Under White SuperVision

Perhaps someone could explain to me how a native child born on the Tsawwassen Indian reserve has any less of an 'economic opportunity' than a child born metres away in Tsawwassen. Please tell me how these native children's access to education, jobs, careers and housing has been somehow restricted to the point where we must provide them with cash, land, special race-based rights and privileges to fisheries, and agricultural land where the protections for this valuable farmland are waived to support revenue-generating development. We are led to believe that without these benefits we are dooming them to a life of poverty and low economic standards.

Try to sell this argument to the immigrants of many races who come to Canada with low education levels, poor or no English and often with few resources, but still manage to find and hold jobs, create businesses, send their kids to university, and be successful, contributing Canadians.

We might have learned by now that hard work, drive, ambition and desire are the ingredients that create success, not freebies, handouts and creating artificial economic conditions. Race has nothing to do with it.

Letter to the Editor, *Vancouver Sun*[75]

Not only has multiculturalism enabled the integration of people of colour into Canadian society under white supervision, it has also generated a popular mainstream denunciation of the claims of Aboriginal peoples.[76] The popular sentiment, as the letter to the editor in the *Vancouver Sun* expresses, defines Aboriginality as amounting to no more than just one culture among many in the country, with Aboriginal peoples having no special claims, no special entitlements above those that can be claimed by other individuals. The popular sentiment also often expresses itself with an accompanying disavowal of the causal significance of race in the incidence of socio-economic privation. The Canadian state is presented as the benevolent guardian of Aboriginal peoples ('they have the same living standards and opportunities as their off reserve neighbours,' as the author also claims in the letter), and the nation as a generous host to 'newcomers.' The state is seen as having the unique propensity and responsibility to offer a race-blind prosperity for all.[77]

Hard-working and self-effacing immigrants are thus offered inclusion into the diverse nation, an inclusion that is also offered to Aboriginals, who are repeatedly imagined as one more ethnic group that has just not learned well enough how to share:

Canada is a multicultural society in terms of its fundamental values and its demographic composition. Diversity has always been a fundamental characteristic of Canadian society. From the beginning, more than 50 different Aboriginal peoples with their own unique languages and cultures interacted with each other throughout Canada. They were later joined by Europeans and people of African and Asian descent, all of whom helped to build the Canada we value today.[78]

In the government report quoted above, multiculturalism is projected back to the very origins of the nation. It is presented as shaping the relations of various Aboriginal nations with each other, while reformulating the colonial encounter as just another harmless, or even positive, encounter of cultural interaction and tolerance. The reference to Aboriginal peoples' interactions with each other prior to European contact as exemplary of multiculturalism accomplishes two things. First, the origins of the present multicultural society are projected as having existed 'from the beginning.' Second, the present claims of Aboriginal peoples are derided as a failure to both remember their own multicultural past and to accept the claims of all other racial groups as being on par with their own.

Multiculturalism has been instrumental in the reconceptualization of the nation's relations with Aboriginal peoples. The liberalization of immigration and citizenship policy took place contemporaneously with the state's refusal to provide Aboriginal populations with the educational and other resources necessary to draw them into the labour force, resources which would have enabled their economic (and political) advancement during this period. Faced with the probability that an improved socio-economic status for Aboriginal peoples could potentially increase their demands for self-determination, the nation-state considered immigration from the South a more preferable alternative. Such immigration would provide labour and further the political marginalization and economic underdevelopment of Aboriginal peoples, even during periods of economic growth.

With its emphasis on tolerance and diversity, multiculturalism has discredited Aboriginal claims to special status as the original inhabitants of the land; Aboriginality is instead devalued as only one among several cultures that needs to be harnessed for the cultural enrichment of nationals. Multiculturalism has demanded that Aboriginals extend their tolerance to the presence and claims of these other cultures.[79] Aboriginals' resistance to these politics has been recast as evidence of their ethnocentrism and essentalizing chauvinism. Indeed, Aboriginal peoples have even been accused of being racist towards Canadians and cultural Others in their insistent demands for Aboriginal rights. As Eva Mackey notes, the hegemonic multiculturalist narrative does not exclude recognition of the Aboriginal peoples in the country, nor does it erase their presence. Instead it has comfortably included their presence, featuring them prominently as the bearers of a (far older) culture and history, and as 'contributing' these to the nation of settlers Aboriginal presence has thus been used to exalt the benevolent and inclusive qualities of nationals. It has been used to more deeply sustain settler narratives of nationhood in the postmodern era, not disrupt them.[80]

The changed cultural climate in Canada, enabled by the adoption of multiculturalism, increased people of colour's access to formal citizenship and its entitlements and their inclusion into the regime of a liberal multiculturalist social formation. Increased inclusion was the reward for the race compromise forged by people of colour, and multiculturalism deepened integration into national fantasies and white domination.

Immigrants who might have self-identified along any number and combination of possible identities, including those of class, gender, and age, instead find themselves to be overdetermined culturally, over and above all other aspects of their identities. State-sponsored multiculturalism compels them to negotiate and comprehend their identities on very narrow grounds, discouraging and possibly foreclosing the possibility of alliances that might allow a systemic challenge to white dominance, patriarchy, and global corporate capitalism.

REFORM

5 Reforming Canadians: Consultations and Nationalizations

Immigration is about deciding who we are as a nation and who we want to become in the 21st century. We need a clear and practical vision of the kind of nation we want to build. And Canadians need to help shape that vision. It is important – now, more than ever – for all Canadians to engage in an open, honest discussion about immigration and our future.

Citizenship and Immigration Canada, *Canada 2005*[1]

I find myself suddenly in the world and I recognize that I have one right alone: That of demanding human behaviour from the other.

Frantz Fanon, *Black Skin, White Masks*[2]

Calling on Canadians to engage in an 'honest' and 'open' discussion about immigration and the future of the nation, the minister of Citizenship and Immigration Canada launched a national public consultation in 1994 to conduct a thorough review of the immigration program.[3] The minister of human resource development launched a concurrent review as part of a massive restructuring of social security policies.[4] The Canadian state has developed something of a tradition of organizing such public consultations regarding changes to key policy areas. These particular reviews, however, were to be much broader in scope and more extensive in their outreach.

In her deliberations on how citizens might decide upon the 'rights of others,' the political theorist Seyla Benhabib has called for a process of 'democratic iterations' by which communities of citizens can ethically engage in such determinations. By democratic iterations, she means the 'complex processes of public argument, deliberation, and learning through which universalist rights claims are contested and contextualized, invoked and revoked, throughout legal and political institutions as well as in the public sphere of liberal democracies.'[5] This chapter examines the Immigration Policy Review and the Social Security Review as examples of what can occur within such processes of democratic iterations between the national community of citizens, their state and Others in making determinations about the rights of Others.

The call for Canadians to be honest and open regarding the future of immigration signalled that the review might well prove to be painful; after all, it is mostly in relation to conflictual encounters that one is most often asked to be honest and to engage in open dialogue. Not that many Canadians had demonstrated reticence in voicing their sentiments regarding immigration or the entitlements of immigrants to social security programs.

Scapegoating Immigrants

A palpable change in the public mood – decidedly anti-immigrant and resentful of multiculturalism – had been discerned among leading politicians, media commentators, immigration experts, and ordinary Canadians across the country during the 1990s. The meteoric rise of the Reform Party to the national stage was associated with its capitalizing of this growing anti-immigrant sentiment, among other things. Multiculturalism was also being increasingly attacked for having undermined national cohesion and for having strengthened the political clout of special interest groups. The immigration program was derided for allowing wide-scale abuse of the system and for overburdening social services. Similarly, the refugee program was attacked for allowing economic migrants and bogus asylum claimants to pose as political refugees.[6]

The narrative that legitimized this popular anti-immigrant sentiment generally ran along the following lines: the nation had been a largely homogenous entity (notwithstanding the Anglo/French divide), with a neatly defined heritage and culture, until the point system allowed large-scale immigration. This heritage and culture was being eroded by the growing diversity of immigrants and by the promotion of their different cultures. National fragmentation and the erosion of Canadian values had been the result of such overly generous, but essentially foolhardy policies. Worse, the coterminous policies of affirmative action that sought to protect minorities against discrimination had gone so far that Canadians were now experiencing a 'reverse racism.' The vocal immigrant organizations and their well-intentioned, but misguided, liberal supporters were irresponsibly championing the rights of these minorities (and underqualified ones at that!) to the detriment of the meritocracy determined by the rules of fair play. Racial minorities were defined as politically astute special interest groups, trading on the guilt of white nationals for past injustices to claim special rights to further their current interests.

In her study of multiculturalism, Eva Mackey travelled across the province of Ontario during this period and observed celebrations of national events. She interviewed both organizers and participants at these events, and summarized her findings:

> [D]uring the 'identity crisis' of 1992, many white Canadians saw multiculturalism as disempowering them, and as a threat to the unity, national identity and progress of Canada. A sense of insecurity, uncertainty and crisis fed a backlash to the gains made by minorities, a backlash which was not framed as an overt defence of *whiteness*, but rather ... as a defence of . national identity and unity. Many believed that cultural pluralism weakened an already crisis-ridden and insecure national identity, and that to bolster itself Canada should be defined on the basis of Canadian-Canadian culture, and 'Canada first.'[7]

Mackey's findings were corroborated by Lisa Jakubowski, who found that the growing public anxiety regarding the consequences of cultural tolerance was closely tied to a resentment of the economic and social pressures said to be the result of increased immigration. She concluded that the large national deficit and shrinking state funds for social programs, including welfare, health care, and education, made immigrants a handy scapegoat for cutbacks to social services: 'The immigrant was socially constructed to be one who was abusive to, and a burden on, Canada and its resources' in state policy.[8] Jakubowski argues that public opinion polls reflected this increasing tendency to link immigrants with abuse of the welfare system.

The sentiment that a naive generosity had proven costly beyond the nation's means and that Canadians had been ill served by their hospitality had become increasingly popular. Now, the interests of Canadians had to be placed above those of outsiders. The times called for a tightening of belts, for greater responsibility and sobriety in meeting the new challenges of globalization. Too many immigrants had become too accustomed to living off welfare. With corporate downsizing and increasing economic uncertainty, and with Canadians being asked by governments to make sacrifices to reduce the debt, how could immigration be allowed to continue unchecked? The nation's compassion had to be measured; its excess had proved to be as detrimental as its lack.

In regard to social security, the post–Second World War consensus in favour of the welfare state had broken down in most of the hypercapitalist countries, including Canada. The end of this consensus was crystallized in the shift from the Keynesian welfare state to the neoliberal state in the 1990s. Social policy emerged as a key contentious political issue on the home front as conservatives and neoliberals alike mobilized for greater deregulation and trade liberalization.[9] The downsizing of the public sector and a minimalist federal state was the goal of these advocates of the free-trade ideology propelling globalization.[10] Foremost among the measures being advocated were the slashing of federal funds for social programs and a dramatic reduction in corporate and personal taxation levels.

Given that increasing immigration levels had been defined as critical to the nation's prosperity a mere two decades earlier and that this recognition had continued to inform the setting of the annual target levels for immigration, the public consultations organized for social security and immigration policies provided an ideal opportunity for countering the anti-immigrant sentiment identified by researchers. Presented by the state as an exercise in participatory democracy, these consultations provided a national platform for educating Canadians on the continuing need for immigration and for all members of the polity to have equal access to full citizenship. The opposite, however, was to prove to be the case.

In the following sections, I examine how the public review process served as a key institutional mechanism through which racialized discourses of nationality, citizenship, and immigration were reproduced in an effort to discipline immigrants *and* nationals into the coming restructuring process.[11] By casting immigrants as largely responsible for the economic and social problems of the nation, the reviews allowed the state to cast Canadians as its true subjects and citizens – the only real public whose concerns and opinions were worthy of consideration.

Given that immigration was going to become more, rather than less, necessary for the future, and given that this immigration was going to be predominantly from the global South, the public reviews further fuelled the anti-immigrant discourse and served at least two functions. First, they reproduced definitions of real Canadians as white nationals, and thereby maintained the historically racialized nation-state relationship in spite of an ever increasing heterogeneity among the population. Second, they legitimized unequal citizenship rights for immigrants as outsiders, and maintained the possibility of increasing the restrictions on their citizenship in the future.

The public consultations exalted Canadians as the chief beneficiaries of the coming restructuring of the two policy areas. They also became sites for the further consolidation and circulation of 'knowledge' regarding the nefarious motives and potentially abusive activities of immigrants, structuring the terrain for the 'strange encounters' between nationals and immigrants in the coming millennium. The prior framing of the specific problems for public discussion in the consultation documents presented these to participants as matters of national concern. As was to be anticipated, the framing of these particular sets of problems shaped the subsequent solutions proposed by participants – decreasing immigration levels for permanent settlement and increasing the restrictions on access to citizenship.[12]

The inclusion of overtly racist and anti-immigrant sentiments in the reviews' final reports, as well as their treatment as equally worthy of consideration for policy changes, meant that the reviews tacitly provided legitimacy to such views. With a declining national birth rate, an increasingly aging population, and a growing competitiveness among western countries to attract highly skilled immigrants, the notion that Canada could maintain its prosperity without maintaining current levels of immigration was clearly not feasible.[13] Yet this notion was promoted as part of the disciplinary practices crucial to contemporary national formation. The reviews disciplined national subjects into the restructuring of the welfare state by strengthening the relationship of the state to its nationals through the fortification of the nation's ideological boundaries against outsiders. The racialized scapegoating of immigrants was to remain an intrinsic part of the processes of governance.

Conceptualizing National Frameworks

The Immigration Policy Review (IPR) invited Canadians to discuss the impact of immigration on the nation, on cultural diversity, and on the economy and solicited their input in developing a 'Vision of Canada.'[14] The discussion paper for the consultations provided the following background information: 'In 1991, the Economic Council of Canada found that immigration had a small but positive impact on our economy.'[15] This was clearly an extraordinary starting point for a discussion on the immigration program in a settler society which was established through the migration of settlers and immigrants and which continued to rely upon immigration to replenish its population levels. Such a starting point enacted a definition of Canadians as not having been immigrants themselves. It thereby called upon white subjects (who were not defined as immigrants) as the (true) national subjects of the collective 'our' of the text. It erased the history of European colonial migrations and instead naturalized the nation's existence. A prosperous economy, beyond the need for immigration, was also being imagined. The reference to 'our' economy identified immigrants as outside its boundaries. Although immigrants were said to make some 'positive contributions,' it was not 'their' economy. This starting point for the review expelled Aboriginal peoples from the horizon; they were treated as having no particular stake in the immigration program.

Two of the three questions for discussion in the articulation of a national vision drew specific attention to cultural diversity: 'How does immigration affect the social and cultural life of Canada?' 'What are the benefits of cultural diversity?' and 'What role should immigration play in fostering the development of Canada's economy?'[16] Separating economic development from social and cultural life, the questions set the stage for an economic versus social and cultural cost-benefit analysis. The linking of social and cultural diversity with immigration implicitly defined Canadians as socially and culturally homogenous, and the explicit questioning of the benefits of cultural diversity implied that immigrants were the cause of concern because of their cultural and social diversity. In short, this first topic for discussion in the invitation to Canadians to be honest about their views placed diverse citizens outside the state–nation partnership and curtailed their ability to meaningfully engage in the process.

The second issue for discussion raised questions about the appropriate balance between the independent (also referred to as the economic) and family classes of immigrants. Participants were informed that the criteria for admission under the independent category included the education level, skills, and occupation of applicants. Immigration under this category could be easily managed through adjustments to the allocation of points in order to ensure that it met 'new immigration priorities.' The independent category was here presented as posing few problems for management, and as valuable for making economic contributions. It was not directly linked with social or cultural diversity, nor was it overtly associated with any specific costs.

The family category, however, was presented in stark contrast. No reference was made to the economic contributions of these immigrants, despite the existing official studies attesting to their value.[17] Instead, participants were informed that applicants were allowed entry as long as they met 'standards for good health and character.'[18] The information provided for this question did not specify that the family class required sponsors to meet specific financial criteria before they would qualify; or that sponsors had to commit themselves to undertake financial responsibility for their dependents under the sponsorship regulations; or that the immigration levels for this class were also controlled by annual target levels.[19] Annual plans tabled by the immigration minister set numerical targets for both the independent and family classes. Yet the family class was presented as potentially limitless, not subject to economic criteria and quite possibly uncontrollable.

When the document asked, 'Should immigration be managed according to business cycles or long-term social goals?'[20] participants were made to choose between two apparently *opposing* rather than complementary goals. When the text posed the question, 'How much importance should the principle of family reunification be given?'[21] it specifically called into question the *principle* underlying this category, signalling that the numbers of this class were not the only 'problem.' Opening up family reunification for discussion, the question gave nationals the authority to help decide whether family life should be permissible for immigrants in the future.[22] Immigrant women and their children (who were disproportionately represented in the family class) were relegated to the shadows of these questions.

Six of the ten issues delineated raised specific questions about the costs of immigration and linked 'increased' demands on social programs with immigration.[23]

- 'Have recent immigration and economic trends created needs which current programming and resources cannot meet?'
- 'Should newcomers receive materials explaining the rights and responsibilities of consuming public services?'
- 'How far are Canadians prepared to go to ensure their generosity and openness are not abused?'
- 'What are the groups, institutions, and programs which need to be protected?'

- 'What factors should we consider in shaping our immigration programs to increase economic benefits at low cost?'
- 'How do we build partnerships among all levels of government to improve the detection of abuse?'
- 'How do we build a common database on immigration to serve public policy and program goals?'[24]

These questions identified a wide range of fiscal, social, and political problems, linked them directly with immigration, and stressed the need to protect existing programs (and the Canadians these were intended to really serve) from immigrants.[25] As the immigrant family was being linked with economic costs and the abuse of Canadian generosity, Canadians were being constituted as citizen-taxpayers whose access to such programs was exercised with responsibility. All Canadians were presented as equally in danger of abuse, and thus as sharing a common interest in controlling immigrant families.

Expunged from the field of vision was the actuality that the sponsorship regulations expressly forbade the family category from accessing particular social security programs, such as social housing and social assistance, for the duration of the sponsorship period.[26] No mention was made that these regulations made sponsored immigrants second-class citizens, nor was it mentioned that sponsors, who might themselves be citizens, had to forfeit their own claims to social assistance in order to sponsor family members. Likewise, no mention was made of the various other discriminations visited upon immigrants, of the prevailing anti-immigrant public sentiment, or of the violence experienced by immigrants. Only one question was raised regarding potential discrimination, that of the non-recognition of foreign educational and professional credentials. This was said to diminish the economic contributions professional immigrants could potentially make to the nation.[27]

The launching of the IPR, with its public meetings and study circles, all conveyed the appearance of an open democratic process that would allow Canadians to raise their concerns. This image was repeatedly enhanced by the minister who reiterated his government's commitment to listen to Canadians. However, the advance determination of the questions for discussion as described above, made the public consultations the vehicle for shaping participants' perceptions and knowledge of such problems, thus further popularizing these anti-immigrant conceptions. The consultations became a mechanism by which nationals would come to *own* the subsequent policy changes as being in their own best interests.[28]

Following the public meetings, a number of reports were produced that summarized the proceedings and policy recommendations made by participants.[29] Submissions from individual participants were included alongside those from various organizations and working groups. Equal weight was said to have been given to all submissions. Indeed, so democratic was the process that even views that were 'based on contentious or perhaps, even inaccurate assumptions' were included because they 'reflected strongly held opinions.'[30] The inclusion in the final reports of recommendations based upon such inaccurate assumptions, without exposing the innacuracies meant that the organizers of the process regarded these as equally reasonable considerations for policy development. In effect, the reports granted such views legitimacy and helped disseminate them even more widely.

For its part, the Social Security Review (SSR) was organized into three major policy areas: working, learning, and security.[31] Identifying social security as a particular value shared equally by the state and Canadians, the SSR placed this value at the very heart of national identity:

Canada's social security system is a hallmark of our nation. Through it, we have defined ourselves as a country that aspires to give our children the best possible start in life, to enable all Canadians to meet their basic needs, and their families to live in dignity. It is a system dedicated to supporting the most vulnerable in our society, while creating opportunity for all Canadians to improve their lives. Social security embodies the values of justice, tolerance and compassion that mark our country.[32]

Canada's social security programs are envied throughout the world. They have helped make life better for generations of Canadians.[33]

Our social programs have always been based on compassion, and caring for those in need.[34]

The SSR asserted that social security was an integral part of the shared national inheritance, to which all Canadians had equal entitlement. Its reference to these programs as the 'envy' of other countries gestured towards both the superiority of the nation at the international level and the possibility that those who envied the system might be drawn to seek access to it. The claim that 'we' have built 'our' national social security system imagined a closed, domestic origin to the nation's prosperity, as it did a unity of interest between Canadians and 'our' state. The SSR

made no attempt to recognize, or account for, the unequal access of
Aboriginal peoples or of immigrants to social security.[35] The SSR also
refused to address the glaring lack of entitlement of domestic workers,
temporary workers, and undocumented migrants to social security programs.

In her study of the Foucauldian concept of discourse, Sara Mills has
pointed out that 'perhaps the most important structure of discourse is
less its constituent parts but rather the function of exclusion.'[36] The
master narrative of nationhood that the SSR, like the IPR, drew upon
excluded Aboriginal peoples from national concerns and erased the
reality that the social security of Canadians remained very much contingent upon the ongoing denial of Aboriginal sovereignty. Constructing
an insider status for Canadians by defining 'our' compassionate social
security programs as central to how 'we' define 'ourselves' as a nation,
the reports expelled those who did not have access to these programs
from belonging to the collective we of the SSR. The implicit message to
Canadians was that the social security of Aboriginal peoples and immigrants were not of concern to 'us': 'their' contributions were not linked
to 'our' social security and, therefore, 'their' concerns belonged elsewhere. While explicit discussions of race and racial inequality were
carefully avoided throughout these reports, references to race were
implicitly coded by the discursive strategies. The SSR starting point
erased the divisions among Canadians, such as class, ethnicity, gender,
sexuality, and disability, and presented the nation to itself as a homogenous entity.

A significant threat to national prosperity was identified as emanating
from other nations vying for Canada's place within the global system:
'Our place in the world economy is being challenged. Around the globe,
other nations are charging forward, helping well-educated, highly-
skilled workers use new technologies. Rapid change means every Canadian must keep updating existing skills and acquiring new ones.'[37] That
these nations educated their populations to produce highly educated
workers was presented as a direct threat to the interests of Canadians: 'literally billions of people in what we once called "The Third World" are
now joining the global economy, almost always on free market principles
... Markets never sleep. There are no islands anymore. And like it or not,
there is no place to hide; and information technology is "unstoppa-
ble."'[38] The prosperity of Canadians was being threatened by 'literally
billions' of third world peoples and Canadians had 'no place to hide.' It
is significant that the billions who threatened Canadian interests were

defined as only recently 'joining the global economy.' These billions – newcomers, really, to the global economy – were presented as wanting what was rightfully and historically 'ours,' what 'we' have worked hard to achieve. The statement denied the reality that third world nations had been integrated into the global economy under colonial domination for centuries and denied that their underdevelopment had resulted from this domination. The benefits accrued by Canadians from their nation's linkages to British imperial supremacy were hidden from view. Similarly absent was the reality that Canada benefited, as did other western countries, from the brain drain of the global South whereby large numbers of highly educated and skilled workers migrated to the North, taking these valuable resources with them. Further, Canada's support for the structural adjustment programs imposed upon third world countries and on the lives of billions of third world peoples – programs that were decimating national budgets for education, health care, and social services during the same period – was concealed from view.

While the SSR sought to subsume the internal divisions among Canadians by describing them as both individually and collectively facing threats from foreigners, it also spoke directly to the anxieties and economic insecurities experienced by working and low-income nationals. The statement 'there is no place to hide' sounded a warning (or maybe a threat?) to these Canadians: if they did not commit themselves to the renewed sense of partnership being promoted by their state, and if they did not accept the prescriptions of the state, they stood alone in the face of 'literally billions' of third world peoples.

The SSR reports reversed the oppressive relations that have resulted in the resources of the majority of third world peoples and Aboriginal peoples in North America underwriting the prosperity of the hypercapitalist countries. It is these peoples who were facing increased dangers from the trade liberalization and free-trade policies aggressively being pursued by the Canadian state on multiple fronts. The actuality that this state, as a member of the G7, the Organization of Economic Cooperation and Development, and the World Trade Organization, was negatively rewriting the welfare of the 'billions' living in the global South was overturned. The strengthening of western domination was thus made into a necessary condition for the continuing prosperity of Canadians; national interest was constructed as depending on the reproduction of the historical divide between the North and the South.

The SSR urged Canadians to learn to deal with these threats more effectively:

Thus, as a new century beckons, we again must push our nation's learning yardsticks further out – much further. In the balance is our ability to preserve our position as one of the world's most prosperous societies. If our standard of living is to be secure, one of our urgent tasks must be to strengthen our learning and training system. As a trading nation, for example, Canadians will need to sharpen their language skills and knowledge of other cultures, in order to reach out successfully to our trading partners. Our collective mission must be to recapture the post-war expectation of expanding prosperity and opportunity for all, with each generation better off than the last. An indispensable ingredient is better learning.[39]

Immigrants (many of them citizens) who possess the cross-cultural skills necessary to facilitate such exchanges, who speak other languages and who have lived experience of other cultures, were repeatedly placed outside the collective 'we' of the text, as the above quote demonstrates. Indeed, this exclusion from the collective 'we' relocated these immigrants among the foreigners whose languages and cultures 'we' have to learn. The acquisition of foreign languages and cultural skills were defined as valuable assets for Canadians to acquire, as long as these remained *foreign*. They had value only in as much as they furthered the express purpose of increasing international trade.

In producing the foreign threats, and the potential for increased trade and employment, the SSR reinforced the relationship between the state, its nationals-as-workers and the corporate sector: 'In the past 15 years, mounting worldwide competition and technological change have hurt the big manufacturing plants and resources-based industries that for decades paid the high-wages that allowed many Canadians to enjoy prosperity.'[40] This statement directed attention away from the increasing deregulation and liberalization of investment and trade policy and away from the corporate practices of downsizing and shedding jobs, even as corporations made enormous profits in the 'jobless recovery' of the 1990s. Instead, the economic sectors were presented as victims – much like the ordinary Canadian – of foreign threats. Presenting the interests of Canadian industries and workers as being synonymous, the corporate sector was presented as having no particular responsibility for contributing to the erosion of the prosperity of Canadian workers.[41] The solution required a pulling together of Canadians, corporations and the state, as 'we' have done in the past: 'This generation must use its ingenuity to rebuild our social programs for a new era, just as an earlier generation after the Second World War forged solutions to meet the social needs of the post-war world.'[42] The text continued: 'Notwithstanding the fluctuations of the business cycle, in the long haul unskilled and labour-intensive manufacturing is declining here as Third World producers expand.'[43]

Third world producers were defined as expanding, not the Canadian corporations whose global reach was being greatly enhanced by corporate-driven globalization. These corporations were increasing their exploitation of third world workers, of whom women were a growing number and among the most vulnerable, both internationally and. in the country.[44] The report turned this reality on its head: 'The changes sweeping through society are being driven by a fundamental reshaping of the economy in Canada and around the world. At the root of this reshaping, technological innovation is transforming the way we work and do business.'[45] The reality of class divisions between those who 'work' and those who 'do business' was erased, and instead an ideological community that collectively 'worked' and 'did business' was enacted. The unpaid, reproductive labour of women, which underpins the entire economic system, was not included in the definition of 'our' work or business. The SSR further naturalized the gendered division of labour and, in this, integrated it more deeply into the restructuring of social security.

Whereas the Immigration Policy Review presented immigrants as a challenge to the very social and cultural viability of the nation, the Social Security Review defined the specific threats to the nation as emanating from third world workers, a ballooning deficit crisis, and the failures of social programs. While neither adequately addressed the inequalities of gender, class, or race, both fuelled race-based anxieties and antipathies.[46] Both sought to transcend inequalities internal to the nation by appealing to a shared racial identity that was pivotal to the construction of a unified national interest. Both produced a partnership between the state and its nation, confirming the legitimacy of the state as equally representative of the interests of all Canadians. In this, the reports erased the reality that corporate interests were increasingly driving state policies with the rise of neoliberal globalization.[47]

Having constructed a national line of descent between previous and future generations, the SSR reports stressed the state's commitment to protecting the most vulnerable members of this nation: 'Our social security system must protect those most in need – people who can't work, low-income families struggling to get by, people who face barriers due to disability or chronic illness, especially children.'[48] While a collective responsibility for the most vulnerable Canadians was urged (at least rhetorically), no such responsibility was to be assumed for Aboriginal peoples or immigrants.

A Vision for the Nation

In response to the question 'Should we have immigration?' the views of the majority of the IPR participants were presented as cautiously supportive. Some called for an end to immigration altogether, others for a reduction in the numbers:

> Some people call for a '*moratorium on immigration*' or gradually reducing immigration until the '*doors are closed ...* '

> Many people advocate a reduction in immigration levels as they feel Canada, '... *can no longer absorb the numbers that are being admitted*,' and they are concerned about increased economic and racial tensions ...

> A policy which high-pressures immigration and is insensitive to ... social, community-level implications will, more and more, increase popular resistance and inflame intolerance ...[49]

Support for continued immigration was based on its ability to promote economic growth, thereby making Canada 'internationally competitive,' and its ability to sustain the Canadian population.[50] However, even as these economic and demographic benefits were recognized, the reports immediately and repeatedly undermined the benefits by highlighting the problems that immigrants brought with them: high unemployment; the detrimental effects of 'increasing diversity' that 'inflame(s) intolerance'; the nation's inability to absorb more immigrants; the lack of 'social' integration of immigrants and the dangers of 'increased economic and racial tensions.'[51] Predictably enough, the benefits of immigration were said to be largely economic and the problems with immigrants largely social and cultural; immigrants were seen as a source of racial divisiveness and financial costs.

The limited support for continuing immigration was made contingent upon better management of the dangers of racial diversity:

> Diversity is one of Canada's enormous strengths, but the importance of the whole must be emphasized. We must be a choir, not a cacophony ...

Diversity … is a strength so long as it is not force-fed and micro-managed …

ethnic diversity has no benefits, it only creates tension …

Many assert that Canada should be, '… celebrating what its citizens have in common instead of their differences.'

There are also concerns that Canada is becoming a country made up of special interest groups, whose own goals take precedence over the national interests of the country. Although many agree that immigrants to Canada should be able to retain their religion and cultural practices, they feel that these should not take precedence over '*Canadian traditions.*'[52]

This attribution of diversity as the characteristic only of immigrants, and therefore essentially foreign to the nation, was achieved through re-peated reiterations of Canadians' concerns: 'No other country in the world expects its tax-payers to finance the practice of ethnic diversity. Whatever behavior immigrants wish to adopt should be left to the choice of the individuals. State support to ethnic diversity sows the seeds of conflict and should be avoided.'[53] It was not mentioned that immi-grants paid taxes, nor was it acknowledged that the state support for diversity in the form of the multiculturalism policy enabled Canadian businesses to gain greater access to international markets.

After elaborating upon the divisive effects of diversity, the final report explicitly defined the contours of the national values that were pre-sented as being shared by Canadians: 'Paramount were the importance of freedom, democracy and the rule of law. Central also were the princi-ples of justice, fairness, tolerance, and respect for our fellow citizens. Equality was essential …'[54] One submission was singled out for special mention: 'Canadians value honesty and fairness. They respect hard work and people with integrity. And they are willing to give people a sec-ond or even third chance. But Canadians also expect their fellow Cana-dians to respect the system that is in place, and to not take advantage of their generosity.'[55] The vision for the nation, the definition of the Cana-dian character and its exalted values, were all elaborated upon in great detail:

Focus group participants state that '*accepting differences,*' '*ethnically diverse,*' '*tolerant,*' '*humane,*' and '*proud*' are among the specific values to which they attribute Canadian identity …

... continue the vision of our country as home to ordinary people living ordinary lives, working, paying fair taxes, supporting policies for the good of all, taking an interest in the government of our towns, provinces and the country, helping our neighbours no matter where they or their fathers come from, making their neighbourhoods and communities good and safe places to live and raise families.[56]

The persistent identification of Canadian identity, of its character and core values, made these available for all Canadians to claim as their own, regardless of their individual traits. The fleshing out of this national character as committed to tolerance, as accepting of differences, and as humane stood in marked contrast to the actual recommendations made by many of the participants to end immigration altogether, to accept immigrants only from European source countries, to end family reunification, and to contain (even eliminate) cultural and racial diversity. The frequent recommendations made to 'close the doors' to immigrants were not allowed to disrupt the exaltation of the Canadian character as fair and just. The significance of this production of a unified national character lies in its attempts to stabilize Canadian identity and its subsumption of divisions within the nation, especially during a period of far-reaching economic restructuring that, by many accounts, was deepening these very divisions.[57]

Furthermore, the national character was defined in direct relation to immigrants, who were repeatedly depicted as a threat to this character and its values:

Throughout the consultation process, Canadians have expressed concern that their Canada is disappearing; that '... *its values and lifestyle are being eroded and degraded.*'

(The current immigration policy) ignores the fragile present condition of the Canadian identity, at a time when the future of the country is uncertain. Immigration policy must not introduce even more uncertainty and ignorance about Canadian and heritage values.

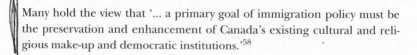

Many hold the view that '... a primary goal of immigration policy must be the preservation and enhancement of Canada's existing cultural and religious make-up and democratic institutions.'[58]

The Department of Immigration and Citizenship was itself recorded as concerned about the erosion of this national character: 'Yet, a number of thoughts were expressed with respect to Canada's character. A list of the elements of the country's basic belief system should look something like this: non-violence, justice, democracy, equality, honesty, acceptance, and fairness. There is no doubt that Departmental personnel want these core values to be retained and strengthened by immigration, not threatened.'[59] The views being expressed here did not so much imply that immigrants did not share the national character and values but that they actively threatened its erosion and degradation; immigrants were defined as devoid of these exalted values. The cultural and social stranger was thus objectified as having an ontological integrity oppositional to that of the national. Where Canadians were defined as respecting 'the rule of law,' as honest, fair, and hard-working taxpayers, immigrants were associated with abuse and seen as hostile to these high values. Not surprisingly, then, participants were said to demand the following:

> ... a government which takes effective action against abuse of our systems instead of allowing chronic abusers of our immigration and welfare systems to go unchecked.[60]

> A common opinion expressed both in written submissions and during other consultation activities is that prospective immigrants must be informed about Canadian law and values.[61]

> Careful screening overseas, to protect the public from criminal activity and health risks is strongly called for. It is argued that the rigorous implementation of the rules and control procedures will prevent abuse of the system and ensure the fair treatment of all applicants. Global cooperation is also a recurring theme in terms of our screening activities. One group suggests that, ... 'our government seek to build bridges with nations from which people are emigrating to Canada in order to prevent abuse of Canada's immigration system, and that Canada impose sanctions against countries who fail to cooperate in providing records and information concerning immigrant applicants or refugees.'[62]

> In order to conduct proper screening, one contributor suggests the creation of, 'one common database' incorporating criminal, security and immigration information that is accessible to both overseas and domestic personnel.[63]

Government officials were reported to be frustrated by the system, which they claimed undermined their ability to deal quickly and efficiently with fraud and abuse. They were evidently disturbed by the fact that some people arrived at 'our' borders with '*instructions* on how to use the system to their advantage.'[64] Because immigrants' use of the system was equated with fraud and abuse, those who did use it to 'their advantage' became a source of frustration. As did those who did not know how to use the system. These immigrants were depicted as being unable to comprehend how democracies functioned and were therefore unable to respect the rule of law! The government officials also complained that there were too many 'appeal mechanisms' in the system.[65] They reportedly called for increased cooperation between immigration and law enforcement agencies.[66] In the interest of 'the protection of society as a whole,' the officials proposed the elimination of appeal procedures and access-to-information laws, even as they simultaneously defined Canadian society as committed to the principles of fairness and justice.

Given these rather extensive elaborations on the problems arising from immigration, it was hardly surprising that the restriction of immigration in order to protect the nation was recommended by many participants.[67] And if increased restrictions and disincentives failed to dissuade prospective immigrants from applying, it was recommended that deportation be used more rigorously and effectively:

> It could be preferable to send a message that Canada is concentrating on deporting certain categories. However, some believed that beyond defined refugee and humanitarian entitlements, Canada could not afford to allow any one deportable group to remain. It was suggested that the legislation try to capture all individual deportable situations. There would be a mechanism for priorising these situations for removals. However, resources would be used to effect removals 'across the board,' resulting in 'equitable, generalised removals.'[68]

Recommendations for 'across the board' and 'equitable, generalized removals' no doubt were seen as attesting to the commitment of those who advocated such measures to the principle of fairness. In its closing pages, the final report summarized the general sentiment expressed during the consultation process:

> Similarly, many Canadians are troubled by what are viewed as threats to the integrity of the nation's health care and social assistance programs, as well

as the integrity of the immigration program itself. In particular, they are concerned that the generosity of the Canadian people has been taken advantage of. As a result of a few recent and unfortunate incidents related to immigration, many Canadians worry that the immigration systems are not working as they should, particularly as they pertain to the entry of undesirable persons and the removal of those who violate our laws. They, in effect, express a loss in confidence in the ability of immigration to provide protection from those who pose a risk to the safety of Canadians and/or Canadian institutions.[69]

The report shamelessly allowed what it called a 'few' and 'unfortunate incidents' to stand as the basis upon which to suspect the integrity of the entire immigration program and its ability to 'provide protection' 'to Canadians and/or Canadian institutions.' It made no effort to quell the 'loss of confidence' Canadians were reported to feel; which was probably being exacerbated by the report's very repetition of untruths and overtly racist sentiments.

The IPR also raised as a problem the quality of immigrants being allowed into the country, who were defined as threatening the nation's 'way of life': 'Growth as an ever increasing and self-sustaining way of life, leading to increased consumption, has been our North American way of life. All of these treasured ideas and much of what we call 'our way of life' is now ending.'[70] The 'dangers' of overpopulation were presented as a particularly serious concern:

> While a few feel that Canada has already surpassed its ideal population, many think that Canada's population should be stabilized at its current level. Still others propose that a population of 34–35 million would be about as much as Canada could sustain due to its '... *climatic conditions, geography and ecology* ...'
>
> It must be realized that Canada is not an empty country waiting to be filled up. We have a fragile ecology.[71]

The use of geographical and climatic conditions to justify the curtailment of immigration from third world countries has been a familiar practice in the history of Canadian immigration policy. Arguments that Asians and Africans were incapable of adapting to the cold northern climate were used to legitimize the restriction of their immigration in the nineteenth and twentieth centuries. The IPR gave new currency to this rationale:

The effect that population growth will have on our environment and quality of life seems to be of primary concern. Environmental deterioration, air
and water pollution, traffic congestion, increased crime rates, over bur-
dened social services, garbage disposal problems and shortages in housing,
food and energy, are some of the problems that people identify with overpopulation. They are concerned as Canada's population grows, these problems will increase in severity.[72]

This astonishing statement is notable for a number of reasons. The
sentiments being expressed were not from any specific contribution by a
particular participant. Instead, produced in this particularly alarmist
manner in the final report, these sentiments were presented as a com-
posite of 'concerns' said to be shared by participants. As I have mentioned earlier, concerns regarding the nation's declining birth rate have
been reported as an important factor in shaping immigration policy
during the 1970s. These concerns were no less relevant in the 1980s. In
light of this situation, the IPR report's reluctance to point out just how
unfounded concerns about overpopulation were, *even by the state's own
reckoning*, supports my argument that the review itself provided a
national platform for the inflamation of the anti-immigrant discourses
of the period.[73]

Furthermore, the statement began with a reference to population
growth, which was immediately *equated* with overpopulation. In establishing this equation, it could assign responsibility for environmental
deterioration, pollution, increased crime, overburdened social services,
food and housing shortages, and other social problems to immigrants.
At the same time, it directed attention away from state policies and corporate practices, both of which were weakening environmental protection regulations and reducing levels of social spending at that time.[74] By
blaming immigrants for these problems, the reality of power relations
was reversed: immigrants were attributed with enough power to devas-
tate and overwhelm the entire nation. Although population levels
were actually projected to decline in the year 2010 without continued
immigration, the statement's incorporation of such outlandish and
unfounded fears fed and promoted these fears.[75]

Interestingly enough, the concerns regarding the dangers of overpopulation did not define all population growth as problematic. Indeed,
specific recommendations were made to *increase* population growth by
providing Canadians with incentives to increase their reproduction: 'the
government [could] develop programs to encourage the population

growth within the country. For example, the government could provide financial incentives to encourage Canadians to have children.'[76] Increasing the population levels of Canadians was not the problem; it was the population levels of immigrants that was the cause for such alarmist concern. By blaming immigrants for overpopulation and enumerating the specific problems said to be associated with this, the reports reproduced for national consumption the problems third world peoples have historically been associated with in the western imagination: increased crime, disease, pollution, excessive breeding, and excessive demands on scarce resources.[77] In contrast, Canadian society was presented as 'dedicated to the preservation of a healthy environment.'[78] Indeed, one would be hard-pressed to find a more racially charged contemporary presentation of immigrants than that found in these reports.

The gendered implications of the particular problem of overpopulation are unmistakable. After all, it is women who 'populate,' and it is third world women in particular who have been associated with overpopulating the planet.[79] Debates on population issues since the 1960s have often drawn upon the Malthusian legacy to characterize the population growth in the global South as an 'explosion,' endangering the very survival of the planet. High population levels have been blamed for causing everything from economic stagnation and environmental depletion to poverty and starvation. Overpopulation has created excessive demands on scarce resources, the argument goes, and population control measures are urgently required.[80] Indeed, the 'excessive' fertility of third world women has long served in the *Canadian* imagination as presenting a threat strong enough to overwhelm the nation by polluting its whiteness. The discussion of the dangers of overpopulation in the reports reinvoked the racialized/gendered historical legitimations of previous immigration policies for the coming millennium. These dangers were used to rally Canadians to support the containment of the abundant fecundity of immigrant women, a fecundity defined as potent enough to destroy communities and cities and pollute the environments in which Canadians lived.

The Report of Working Group # 4, which was mandated to deal with the question of environmental degradation, pointed out that environmental degradation in the source countries for immigration was one of the causes of increased migration.[81] The interim and final report, however, stressed only the reverse so that immigration became the *cause* of environmental degradation in Canada. The activities of Canadian corporations abroad, which contributed to the environmental problems in

third world countries, was not raised as a concern. The Working Group's
report also reinforced racialized fears regarding overpopulation by
referring to 'massive' and 'enormous' flows of immigrants. It pointed to
'rapid population growth' in 'poor countries' and called on the Canadian government to work towards 'population stabilization by any
means acceptable to the societies concerned.'[82] The means acceptable
to ruling elites have included the forced sterilization of women and men
in India, Bangladesh, Peru, and Brazil.[83] These means have also been
acceptable to ruling elites in Britain, the United States, and Canada,
which have all practised the sterilization of certain groups of women in
their not-too-distant pasts.[84]

Given the systematic nature of such atrocities, it is shocking that the
report supported suggestions that third world women be subjected to
population control measures before these women attempted to migrate
to Canada. The problem of overpopulation was thus pinned on-
immigrant woman: their actual presence *and* their capacity to reproduce presented them as a double threat. Concerns regarding both the
quantity and quality of immigrants became very specifically and literally
inscribed onto the bodies of these women.

That the problem of overpopulation was related to concerns about the
quality of immigrants was made even clearer in subsequent sections of
the reports.[85] Repeated recommendations were made for increasing the
recruitment of independent class and of English- and French-speaking
immigrants.[86] Recommendations were also made for recruiting immigrants from the original European source countries because they would
be more compatible with the nation: 'Some people commented on the
racial mixture of immigration. They feel that Canada should be selecting
immigrants from countries having the most in common with Canada and
call for a return to the pre-1960 source countries. This, they feel, would
reduce costs associated with integration and ease racial tensions.'[87]

The report declined to point out that reverting to an earlier period of
overt racial distinctions in immigration policy would be contrary to anti-
discrimination laws. Instead, the recommendations were treated as legitimate and reasonable policy options. Fluency in English and French
were repeatedly recommended as criteria by which the quality of potential immigrants should be evaluated. Such criteria would, of course, privilege Europeans, who were defined as being of the quality deemed most
compatible with the nation.

Not all consultation participants were in agreement with the overwhelming anti-immigrant sentiments that permeated the review process

and that were highly profiled in the final reports. It is, therefore, important to note the presence of dissident views that could have seriously challenged the discursive frame of the IPR and to pay attention to their omissions from the final reports. A number of such contributions were made by participants in some of the Working Groups and at the National Conference, which challenged the common-sense, popular racialization of the category immigrants. For example, one contribution reported that 'people speak of the "immigrant problem" and the "refugee problem," and believe that immigrants "live off the fat of the taxpayer." She said these perceptions would not be prevalent if all immigrants looked like her, that is, white.'[88] However, this particular contribution, that quoted a woman who identified herself as white, was not included in the final report. Nor was it used to contest the racialization of immigrants by the numerous other participants. Similar contributions made by a few other participants who contested the definition of Canadians and immigrants as driven by opposing sets of values were likewise excluded from the final reports:

> Canada is a nation made up of indigenous peoples, descendants from generations of immigrants, and recent immigrants.[89]

> The concentration of a large number of people from one immigrant community who arrive within the space of five years is a new and big problem to some, while for others it is simply Canadian history repeating itself for the umpteenth time.[90]

These statements, which drew a parallel between recent immigration and the older migrations that established the nation, which rejected the binary construction of Canadians and immigrants, and which disrupted the discursive frame, were denied entry into the final summations. Instead, the reports ended with a reiteration of the numerous threats immigrants presented to the health and safety of Canadians and 'their' na-tional institutions. The immigrant character was defined ad nauseum as the embodiment of criminality, disease, and laziness, and of being ignorant of democratic values when not openly flaunting or defying these.

Familiar Familial Burdens

As discussed earlier, the family class was singled out as lacking in eco-

nomic contributions to the nation and as dangerous for facilitating virtually limitless immigration into the country. This class was also made
responsible for overburdening social programs and was linked to the
cultural and social diversity said to fragment the nation. In contrast, the
independent class was identified with economic contributions and presented as easily manageable. This binary framing of both classes shaped
the responses from participants so that, with few exceptions, most participants likewise reproduced such ideological constructions:

> Many people involved in the various consultation activities expressed con-
> cern with our diminishing capacity to afford immigrants who can neither
> support themselves nor be supported by their families, especially given the
> current state of our economy.[91]

> ... the proportion of family class immigrants should be reduced and that
> *the government should consider possible (additional) restrictions on the sponsoring
> of family class members.*[92]

The staff of Citizenship and Immigration Canada recommended the following: 'Weight must be given to official language ability, education levels and potential to contribute to Canada ... .Potential to contribute to
Canada must be viewed in terms of (a) ability to demonstrate willingness
to integrate socially and culturally; and (b) proven ability and demonstrated willingness to be productive economically.'[93]
   The objective of increasing the economic benefits of immigration
inevitably translated into recommendations for reducing family class
immigration, and for increasing controls over the access of sponsored
immigrants to social programs if they were to be allowed into the country.[94] Recommendations were made for a 'different mix' of immigrants
as participants argued that immigrants be required to pay for the costs
of settlement services:

> The majority agree that, if a primary objective of immigration is economic
> benefit for Canada, then we need to select a different mix of immigrants,
> concentrating on raising the levels of the independent and business cate-
> gories.[95]

> As to who should be responsible to bear the costs of integration, many feel
> that independent, sponsored and business immigrants should fund their
> own settlement needs. Some advocate a prepayment program.[96]

One group recommended that already-established 'immigrant communities' fund settlement services for incoming immigrants:

> Immigrant communities can play an important role in the integration of new arrivals. They should be encouraged in this respect, to provide language and settlement services to other immigrants, particularly where existing delivery mechanisms are underfunded or overburdened and if possible to provide Canadian job experience as a transition into the broader labour market (perhaps through a form of sponsorship). These measures will help raise the economic contribution of immigrants while reducing the costs of traditional settlement delivery mechanisms.[97]

This startling recommendation relied on the definition of existing immigrant communities as outsiders, regardless of their citizenship status, and attempted to make 'them' responsible for providing for 'their' own kind. The reality that immigrant communities, as taxpayers, were funding 'our' social programs was elided in such recommendations.

Given the opportunity to decide upon the fate of family reunification, many participants did not hesitate to use the authority granted to them by the review. The National Consultation on the Family Class, for example, called for increased enforcement of sponsorship agreements, including the enhancement of the provincial government's powers to prosecute sponsors in their enforcement of sponsorship agreements.[98] Some even recommended the introduction of a sponsorship bond and the requirement of higher income levels in order for sponsors to qualify.[99]

Participants were encouraged to discuss whether family sponsorship should be maintained and, if so, which particular relatives should to be allowed in under this class. The participants responded by stressing the necessity for sponsors to be held accountable for the financial aspects of sponsorship, and they recommended that the sponsorship regulations be more vigorously enforced. They readily claimed their 'right,' as Canadians, to help the state determine what kind of family reunification should be allowed, uncritically accepting the assumption that determinations about the fate of immigrant families should be made in the best interests of Canadians, not those of immigrants.

A proposal for introducing a 'contextualized' system for the family class was offered in the final report, which sought to evaluate applicants not only on the basis of their relationship to the sponsor but also on the basis of the 'actual emotional and material dependency or interdependency' between them:[100]

In recognition that the interests being served in family class immigration are both private and public, it was agreed that the predominant policy rationale for facilitating the immigration of family members to Canada should be to optimize the position of the sponsor within Canadian society by recognizing those relationships which are fundamental to sustained emotional and economic sharing, care, and support. If the policy rationale for admitting family members is to optimize the position of the sponsor in Canadian society, then family class immigration policy should accurately identify as family members those persons most able to contribute to the sponsor's functioning within Canadian society.[101]

The primary function of sponsored immigrants was described as supporting the integration and settlement of the sponsor, and the 'contextualized' definition of the family was described as a positive measure that would enable the sponsor to decide which family members would best contribute to his/her well-being. This measure, it was argued, would allow for non-traditional families, such as extended and same-sex couple families, to become eligible for sponsorship. Such liberal moves, however, would enhance the power of the sponsor. The sponsor would be given the power to decide upon the fate of family members on the sole basis of what would be most beneficial for the sponsor's own resettlement, not on the basis of family relationships, obligations, or the best interests of the family as a unit.

This proposal for contextualization would redefine the family relationship between the sponsor and his/her dependent so that the relationship per se would become unimportant. Instead, the relationship would be important only to the extent that it served the *individualized* interests of the sponsor. Contextualization would be a way to 'optimize the position of the sponsor,' and the group's report urged the recognition of only 'those relationships which are fundamental to sustained emotional and economic sharing, care and support.' The recommendation thus devalued the immigrant family unit as an entity, even as it undermined reciprocity within family relations, by increasing the power of the sponsor to decide which relations best served his/her own interests. The potential created here for the abuse of family members by the sponsor is obvious. The recommendation was based on the assumption that the family relationships of immigrants, or consideration of the needs of the entire family, were not legitimate and valid in themselves. The value of family members was to be determined solely by their contribution to the well-being of the sponsor, whose only value in turn was the economic contribution he/she made to the nation.

The recommendation also opened the door for greater state intervention in regulating the immigrant family. The change that was proposed would inevitably compel sponsored family members to prove to the state, in addition to the sponsor, their commitment to enhancing the sponsor's well-being. The most personal and intimate relationships between immigrant family members would hence be open to scrutiny, testing, and judgment by immigration officials, as was recognized by the recommendation's framers: 'officials would be called upon to make an holistic assessment of the authenticity of the family relationship based not upon categorical definitions, but upon flexible guidelines'[102]

As immigration officials would make the final determination on the level of the 'commitment' of the relative to be sponsored to the sponsor, the power of these officials to reshape relations among immigrant family members would become greatly enhanced. Increased regulation and surveillance of sponsored family members would be sure to follow, as these family members would be called upon to demonstrate their emotional and economic interdependency with the sponsor.

Another recommendation was made to increase the control of sponsored family members after they became residents by giving them 'conditional entry,' which could be reassessed after a certain period of residency.[103] Here, the right of the family class to permanent residence, and hence to citizenship, would likewise be made conditional.

These recommendations assumed that immigrant families were different from, and less legitimate than, Canadian families, and that their relationships and emotional bonds were less valuable. Such assumptions are deeply rooted in colonial and culturally supremacist attitudes towards third world peoples. They bring to mind the behaviour of British immigration officers who demanded (in the 1970s and 1980s) that sponsored Asian women undergo virginity tests at airports to 'prove' their 'commitment' to the fiancees who had sponsored them.[104] It has also been reported that immigration officials have asked Black couples 'whether they had enjoyed their honeymoon and whether they normally slept together,'[105] and that officials have scrutinized the private correspondences of immigrant spouses to assess whether they demonstrated adequate 'affection' for each other. It is indeed remarkable that, despite such historical excesses, participants could so uncritically advocate the reintroduction of such dehumanizing measures.

In this treatment of the family class, one cannot help but be struck by the tremendous sense of power that participants seemed to have desired, or imagined themselves to have, over the lives of immigrant families, and the ease with which they asserted this will to power. The family relations of immigrants were considered worthy by them only for their instrumentality. In other words, it was not enough that immigrants have families with whom they should be able to live out their lives. Immigrants should have to provide proof of the worthiness of their relationships and their willingness to nurture the sponsor's needs above all other considerations, in order to qualify under the family class. In other words, immigrants would have to provide proof that their family bonds were authentic and ultimately productive for the nation. In these recommendations, as in all the others, the power of the state was uncritically claimed by the participants, who, through the review process, came to experience the power of the state as *their* power to decide upon the eligibility of immigrants for family life.

Some of the submissions recommended the outright termination of family sponsorship for low-income immigrants:

> The income level for sponsorship must be high enough to provide adequately for those who are sponsored. Consideration should also be given to additional criteria to be met by the sponsor, to support the long run nature of the sponsorship – the initiative of the sponsor, employability and language skills. The Working Group was concerned that allowing individuals on welfare to sponsor members of their family added to economic costs and should be prohibited. By removing this privilege there would be an added incentive for the immigrant to find employment and integrate quickly.[106]

This recommendation shifted the responsibility for unemployment onto the immigrant's own lack of incentive, and it penalized low-income immigrants by requiring them to forfeit their right to family life. The immigrant's right to have a family should be made contingent upon their financial worth, according to many of these submissions: 'many feel that sponsored parents are often too aged to work and place a strain on the social and medical systems. In addition, many people feel that being separated from one's family is a choice that every immigrant must make when deciding to come to Canada.'[107]

A number of participants contested this dominant construction of the immigrant family as primarily a burden on social services. Their submissions noted that most adult sponsored immigrants entered the labour market soon after their arrival in the country.[108] They argued that sponsored family members made the settlement process much easier for the main applicant, thereby reducing the costs of their settlement.[109] Whereas the unpaid, reproductive labour of sponsored immigrant women was made invisible by their classification as non-economic, some submissions recognized that their labour directly reduced the overall costs of immigration. They also noted that racial inequalities and unequal access to social entitlements for sponsored immigrants were the most significant barriers to their successful integration. They made specific recommendations to increase the access of *all* immigrants to social entitlements:

> The entire settlement process should be based on the principles of access and equity. The federal government should take a leadership role in the area of anti-racism education. All federal funding for training programs should be granted on the basis of the adherence to equity principles as a criterion for funding.

> Obtaining meaningful employment is an integral part of the settlement process. Immigrants should be recognized as a target group which needs appropriate training opportunities.[110]

> When discussing public services, it is important to recognize who 'the public' is. The group felt that it was important to recognize that the public was in fact everybody in Canada. Immigrants, refugees and minorities are not a group separate from 'the public.' They have equal rights to available services ...

> Recognizing that issues of jurisdiction and reform of social policy are topical these days, the group felt that the federal government should maintain a leadership or co-ordinating role in ensuring equal access to public services by all sectors of the public including new immigrants. This is particularly important for the provision of services to assist in the integration of immigrants.[111]

These recommendations challenged the fundamental assumptions of the discourse being promoted by the IPR. However, through their strategic expulsion from the final reports, the voices of these participants did not disrupt the IPR agenda. Indeed, the knowledge being produced was based on the active suppression of the very few perspectives that advocated greater equality for immigrants. In this way, the review process gave the power to speak only to those participants whose contributions reaffirmed the anti-immigrant sentiments that dominated public culture.

Economic costs and benefits were also of significant concern in the Social Security Review. However, the SSR review's treatment of these issues was very different from that of the IPR. The SSR defined the deficit crisis as a major problem that threatened national prosperity and that demanded nothing short of an entire restructuring of the social security system: 'As a nation we have overspent in recent decades, building up debt.'[112] The deficit crisis was presented as a collective problem, the 'we' of the reports was said to have overspent in the previous decades and all were equally responsible.[113] The presentation by the finance minister went further in attributing responsibility to every Canadian for the deficit crises: 'The debt is money we owe ... That is a burden we all bear.'[114] Another report (A New Framework for Economic Policy) reads, 'We have created the deficit and debt problem ourselves. The wound is self-inflicted. It must be healed.'[115] Indeed, the amount for which each Canadian was said to be responsible was calculated precisely:

> For three entire decades, after the Second World War, all we knew was high growth, high productivity, high income growth, and low unemployment. We had it easy for too long and we missed the signals that times were changing ... And as we were missing those signals, what did we do? We borrowed to paper over the problem – borrowing first from ourselves, then from foreigners – and always from the future. It is compelling to note that the last overall public sector surplus recorded in Canada was two decades ago. From 1981 until this year – a mere thirteen years – federal and provincial government debt increased six-fold to almost $700 billion – now more that $24,000 for each and every Canadian. For two decades now, we have spent more than we saved.[116]

No mention was made of the generous support provided through public finances to corporations as contributing to the debt crisis.[117] Instead, the collective extravagance of Canadians was defined as threatening to bankrupt the future of our children, and to limit the state's ability to provide for the well-being of future generations.[118] With the debt established as a collective responsibility, the only option for resolving the crisis was a drastic reduction in social spending.[119] This 'necessity' for reducing social spending was reiterated throughout the reports and presented as a non-negotiable option: the nation had been irresponsible, excessive in its spending, and it was now the state's responsibility to get it back on track.[120] Deficit reduction was presented as a priority only because of the state's commitment to preserving the prosperity of all Canadians.

The creation of a deficit crisis, made possible largely through the reduction of corporate taxes that significantly reduced state revenues and high interest rates, has been examined by a number of theorists as a strategy pursued by the state to create a low-wage economy.[121] The SSR texts reversed this actuality by making every Canadian personally accountable for the deficit and, in the process, harnessed public anxieties about economic insecurity and high unemployment. These anxieties were redirected against foreigners and their nations, both of whom were named as the only direct beneficiaries of the deficit crisis.[122] Foreigners were said to benefit from the indebtedness of Canadians, and these foreigners threatened the social security of the nation. 'They' controlled international markets and threatened 'our' economic sovereignty. Shielding the practices of corporations, of international financial institutions, and even of the neoliberal state, the SSR presented the debt burden as threatening the security of the entire national community.[123]

Although the SSR defined Canadians as responsible for the deficit crisis, the problem was said to be a result of their generosity: both nation and state were presented as motivated only by their compassionate national values. Consequently, the blame, if any, lay in the nation's excessive care. Moreover, the very social programs that they had so generously funded had failed Canadians: 'Today's social security system doesn't deliver enough of what Canadians need, and spends too much money in the wrong places.'[124] Income assistance programs were highlighted as particularly problematic.[125] Previously defined as the precious entitlement of citizenship and a means to protect individuals from the unpredictability of economic cycles, these programs were now redefined as *causing* unemployment and dependency. The review targeted the 'female' track of social security programs for major cutbacks, as women made disproportionate claims to income-assistance programs because of their unequal participation in the paid labour force.[126]

Even as the SSR defined dependency on social security programs as a problem, it was careful not to assign blame to Canadians individually. The reports upheld the work ethic as a national value of Canadians, which social programs had eroded by encouraging dependency. Canadians were routinely depicted as wanting to work, while the failures of social programs had held them back. Canadians and the state were depicted as victims of these programs. Unemployed Canadians were defined as 'the victims of structural unemployment' and as suffering from a 'skills deficit.'[127] The economic framework argued that social programs had become 'dead ends of dependence rather than roads to recovery.'[128] While dependency on social assistance was certainly treated as a problem, it was not constructed as something inherent in Canadians.[129] The SSR reports defined Canadians as deserving, even if somewhat naïve, citizens. Immigrants, however, were extended no such generosity. The IPR used any claims that immigrants might make for social assistance as proof of their inherent unworthiness and why they not be allowed into the country and granted citizenship.

By overlooking the relationship between immigration policy and social security policy in the organization of citizenship rights, the SSR did not present the racialized inequalities organized through this relationship as a problem that required the attention of Canadians. The contributions of immigrant women to the social security system, through their labour and taxes, were not acknowledged. The separation between the SSR, as dealing with the social security of Canadians, and the IPR, as dealing with immigrants, further reinforced the ideological distance between these groups: the SSR was presented as dealing with 'our' issues and the IPR as dealing with 'their' issues. The objective of the SSR was defined as the restructuring of social security policy for the twenty-first century on the principles of fairness and justice. That these principles were not to be applied to Aboriginal peoples or to immigrants was amply demonstrated by both the IPR and SSR strategies that simply eliminated their concerns from the discursive frame.

Participatory Citizenry, Responsive State

The SSR called on Canadians to ensure that their state lived up to its responsibility because 'governments have lost a clear sense of economic leadership – a vision of what their role must be in the modern economy – and where they should leave action to others.'[130] For its part, the state would ensure that Canadians lived within their means. Indeed, the state was presented as actually taking a lesson from Canadians in cutting social spending: 'Canadians live within their means. Government should live within its means too.'[131] Urging Canadians to ensure that their state acted responsibly, the review reiterated the state's commitment to the democratic participation of its citizenry: 'Government by necessity has the final word. We think it is important to give Canadians the first say.'[132]

Both the SSR and IPR reviews constructed the state as a benevolent patriarch, concerned only with the prosperity of the nation even if Canadians themselves refused to recognize the necessity for the coming restructuring. The economic framework presented a stern face of this state as patriarch, which was compelled to save Canadians from themselves: 'Most of us did not choose to enter public life because of a burning desire to dismantle government programs. We came into government to help build a better Canada – a Canada of jobs and growth. That is our only goal. And it is because of that – not in spite of that – that we must act decisively on the debt challenge today.'[133] Cuts to social spending were made as a matter of 'morality' and 'justice.' For those who opposed the spending cuts, the finance minister had a clear message: 'And if people come before you and say that now is not the time to cut, ask them to describe the morality and the justice of letting the debt continue to run wild, unchecked, ruining the future of our children.'[134]

The national interest was defined as collective, in relation to which the opposition of individuals who might not support the restructuring was made to appear as individualistic, immoral, and irresponsible. Many Canadians did, in fact, oppose the cutbacks to social security programs, but the discursive framing of social security, as popularized through the public consultations, allowed them no hearing. Unable to influence the public consultations, these opponents organized demonstrations and disrupted a number of the public meetings. However, such acts remained outside the review process; they were not allowed into the review's carefully crafted space.

Significantly, the IPR met with little public opposition, unlike the SSR. Thus, even the opponents of cuts to social security reproduced the divisions instituted by the state between 'us' and 'them': they organized demonstrations against the cuts that would erode the entitlements of Canadians, but left unaddressed the erosion of immigrants' access to social security and citizenship.

The discourse popularized through the IPR allowed both right-wing, anti-immigrant views and more liberal views, which valued 'tolerance,' to be woven into an ersatz consensus. Since immigrants were assumed to engage in massive abuse of social services and since their presence was assumed to intensify racial tension, the obvious solution was to restrict the immigration from the global South. The historical construction of such immigrants as outsiders to the nation made this solution politically acceptable to the nation.

The very basis for the creation of social programs, especially social assistance, was the recognition that individuals are not responsible for the economic conditions that create unemployment and poverty, and that they need protection from the volatility of the economic cycles that give rise to these problems. Defining immigrants as strangers, however, legitimized their unequal rights to such programs. Whether immigrants actually made undue and excessive claims to social programs, or whether they routinely broke sponsorship agreements, as the IPR claimed they did, was beside the point.[135] The point was that the state *legitimized* and *normalized* unequal rights and entitlements for all immigrants, so that it appeared completely normal and natural that 'they' should not have the same rights as 'us.'

Exalting Canadians in overtly racialized ways, the state sought to engage them, through the public consultations, into its domain for the twenty-first century. Both the IPR and SSR enabled the state to present itself as the legitimate defender of the national interest against foreign threats, against immigrants in general, and against immigrant women and their families in particular. The public consultations were an exercise in closing the ranks of the nation. Because Aboriginal peoples and immigrants were represented as outside the nation, the links that exist in actuality between the Indian Act, immigration policy and social security policy in the organization of the nation, its citizens, and their social security were broken.

On 1 November 1994, the IPR concluded with the minister of Immigration and Citizenship tabling the annual report to Parliament for the years 1995 to 2000. It was entitled *A Broader Vision: Immigration and Citizenship.* He also presented *Into the Twenty-first Century: A Strategy for Immigration and Citizenship,* a long-term strategy that was to be the basis for immigration policy for the coming century. As such, the significance of the IPR cannot be underestimated. The SSR was abruptly halted, and the finance minister introduced major changes (and cuts) to funding for social program through the federal budget.[136] In implementing these changes, the state claimed to be acting only on the wishes expressed by Canadians during the consultations: 'Today we are making the decisions that Canadians expect of us and participants in the consultations asked us to make.'[137] The desire of Canadians for democratic participation and appeals to ethical responsibility notwithstanding, these reviews demonstrate that the ground from which citizens-as-nationals, Aboriginal peoples, and immigrants are allowed to speak is today so uneven that the very possibility for 'democratic iterations' between them is rendered all but impossible.

TERROR

6 Nationality in the Age of Global Terror

The tradition of the oppressed teaches us that the 'state of emergency' in which we live is not the exception but the rule. We must attain to a conception of history that is in keeping with this insight. Then we shall clearly realize that it is our task to bring about a real state of emergency, and this will improve our position in the struggle against Fascism. One reason why Fascism has a chance is that in the name of progress its opponents treat it as a historical norm. The current amazement that the things we are experiencing are 'still' possible in the twentieth century is *not* philosophical. This amazement is not the beginning of knowledge – unless it is the knowledge that the view of history which gives rise to it is untenable.

Walter Benjamin, *Selected Writings*[1]

A photograph of a crowd of chador-clad women, holding signs that read Islam Yes; Seqular [*sic*] No, appeared in the *Globe and Mail*, the older and more reputable of Canada's two national newspapers. The headline over the photograph read: 'The West and the Worst.'[2] These women, who were demonstrating in Tehran against the post–9/11 banning of the headscarf in France, are presented to the reader as 'the worst.' The women were rejecting the representations of the 'west' as the 'best' that have become ubiquitous in the global 'war on terror.' Rising concerns about the threat Islamists are said to present to the west are being met on a number of levels in the hypercapitalist world, which include the implementation of anti-terrorism measures as well as attempts to persuade (sometimes even compel) such women to adopt western values and fashion. These women challenge the deeply cherished idea of western superiority that is symbolized most clearly in the figure of the unveiled woman, eagerly partaking of the freedoms said to be abundant in western societies. They also contest the popular construction of the war as quasi-feminist in its stated concern to 'liberate' Muslim women.

In the era of the global 'war on terror,' the 'good' Muslim woman is the one who will readily propagate western gender and sexual norms, while condemning her co-religionists, both women and men, for refusing to laud the magnanimity of the west towards Muslim women. As Sherene Razack has noted, the Muslim woman is constructed as the victim who needs to be rescued from her religion and culture, protected from the men in her family and community.[3] This Muslim woman can be redeemed, she can be brought into the embrace of civilization. With the launch of the U.S.-led war on Afghanistan, the quintessential image of this good woman in the North American media was that of the burqa-clad Afghan woman, voiceless and passive, only too grateful to be rescued. She proved her 'goodness' by obligingly lifting her burqa for the foreign media crews accompanying the foreign occupation forces. As such images proliferated in the media, it became clear that one battle in the ideological war was to be waged on the terrain of gender relations, and that rallying western populations around fantasies of saving Muslim women would be more effective than rallying them around the overtly imperialist policies of securing U.S. control over oil and natural gas supplies. It also became clear that the media were to play a critical role in this battleground.

War on Terror and Empire-Building

The after-effects of the 9/11 attacks and the subsequent wars have been of longer duration and have had a deeper consequence in Canada than might have been initially anticipated. 'We are all Americans now' was the boldly declared sentiment expressed overwhelmingly in and by the media immediately following the attacks.[4] This fervent and visceral emotional identification with America was clearly an effort to share grief and solidarity with that nation. But it also enabled a claiming of the dangers said to emanate from an enemy defined as anti-western, fanatic, and uncivilized in nature. Indeed, it did not take long for the finger of suspicion to be pointed at such non-westerners within Canada's borders: 'Terrorists Crept in from Canada,' *The Province* in Vancouver declared unhesitatingly *one day* after the attacks. The headline covered almost a quarter of the entire front page, and one image – that of the collapsed

World Trade Center – dominated the rest of that page in the reporting of this piece of news-as-fact.[5]

Following the lead of the Bush administration, Jean Chrétien's Liberal government swiftly implemented a number of anti-terrorism measures in Canada, and sent Canadian troops into Afghanistan in the aftermath of the attacks.[6] The government was more cautious in its direct support of the second war, the invasion and occupation of Iraq, but it continued to support the United States in its larger global ambitions. Prime Minister Chrétien's successor, Paul Martin, maintained this support and Canada's active participation.[7] With their election in 2006, the Conservatives stated their greater support for the American administration, and increased the number of Canadian troops deployed in Afghanistan. This government enhanced the Canadian role in front-line operations in the most intransigent zones in Afghanistan as American troops were withdrawn from these areas. Canadian troops were serving as part of the U.S.-led operation 'Enduring Freedom' and not as part of a NATO mission. They thus became an integral part of the occupation forces.

Prime Minister Stephen Harper chose to visit Canadian troops in Afghanistan in his first public appearance after his election. His visit was highly publicized by the media to help shore up public support for the war. Prime Minister Harper identified three main reasons for Canada's increased participation in Afghanistan: to 'defend Canada's national interest'; to 'show Canadian leadership'; and to 'help Afghanistan.' In response, an editorial in the *Globe and Mail* intoned: 'Canada has a noble tradition of helping the needy.' The editor went on to argue that 'Afghanistan was once a leading incubator for terrorism and could be again if international troops don't help stabilize the country ... Canada has a strong history of international engagement, acting both as a defender of freedom and as a mediator and peace-keeper.'[8] Such self-exaltations are deeply reshaping the national imaginary so that assuming a more militaristic presence in the world is deemed as a reflection of the nation's innate masculine nobility, its virile 'goodness.' All major Canadian political parties agree on Canada's participation in what has become a U.S.-led, Anglo-North-American occupation of Afghanistan. What disagreement is to be found among these parties concerns only the extent (should troop levels be reduced? how long will they remain in that country?) and form (should Canada wait for the NATO mission to begin? should the troops be deployed only in 'humanitarian' missions or in combat operations as well?) of this participation, not the participation itself.

The foreign policy and anti-terrorism measures adopted by successive Canadian governments, particularly the country's participation in the occupation of Afghanistan, have made al Qaeda and the Taliban 'enemies' not just of the U.S. but also of the Canadian nation, and of that fictive universal 'international community.' Within North America, these anti-terrorism measures have morphed into institutionalized suspicion of Muslim immigrants and refugees as the greatest threat to the security of both the Canadian and American nations. Indeed, entire Muslim communities in North America are routinely taken to task publicly for fostering this lethal 'enemy' within their bosom. Canada has become a 'haven' for terrorists, according to the many politicians, bureaucrats, media commentators, and other experts who repeatedly lambast immigration and refugee policies as lax and irresponsible and who present the flow of immigrants as a threat to national security.[9] The Madrid bombings in March 2004 and the London bombings of July 2005 have only added fuel to the fire of the national (and western) animus directed against Muslims and Islam.

In this chapter, I argue that the United States is attempting to assert its *national* sovereignty as a *globalized* sovereignty in its imperial ambitions. Many theorists have argued that the sovereignty of nation-states has been seriously eroded by globalization processes. Michael Hardt and Antonio Negri have made the case that the end of the cold war and the escalation of globalization in the last decades of the twentieth century ushered in the Age of Empire, with the emergence of a very distinctive, decentralized global form of sovereignty.[10] This form of sovereignty emerged from the opening up of previously demarcated national frontiers to supranational entities of governance and has given rise to new and changing forms of identities and subjectivities. As insightful as Hardt and Negri's analysis of global imperial sovereignty is, it fails to address the racialized and gendered dimensions of the new forms and functions of this sovereignty.

The *national* sovereignty of the sole superpower, the United States, is being redefined as a globalized sovereignty, and it is the American *nation-state* which, as the sole superpower, is unilaterally deciding where and when its interests are under threat. The doctrine of pre-emption developed by the Bush administration seeks to proactively defend American interests at a planetary level against *possible* future actions by its opponents. The deployment of U.S. military power, funded through a budget greater than that of the rest of the world's combined military spending, is central to this assertion of globalized American sovereignty.

Consequently, through the war on terror, the United States is destroying the rights of Muslims wherever it identifies them as enemies, and wherever its army and law enforcement officials can secure control over their bodies.

Whether through the bombing sorties and house raids in Afghanistan and Iraq (with their mounting civilian deaths) or through targeted assassination, collective punishment, abduction, secret rendition, torture, security certificates and incarceration, this assertion of U.S. sovereignty is being facilitated through the collusion of obeisant partners like Canada. In redefining the scope of its global reach, the United States has claimed for itself the 'right' to override the citizenship of Muslims in other states, including Canada. By using its middle power status and its international stature as a more 'compassionate' nation, the Canadian nation-state is supporting this expansion of the American Empire and helping hunt down, incarcerate, and destroy the Muslim enemy as and where defined by the United States.

Supporting the expansion of the American Empire abroad, the anti-terrorism measures implemented in Canada are thus profoundly re-shaping the meaning of Canadian nationality and citizenship. Casting the nation as primarily western in nature, these measures enable the citizenship rights of (those who look like) Muslims to be suspended by the Canadian state and even stripped away by the American state. The deployment of the discourse of terrorism in the media, constituting Muslims as the global enemy, is pivotal to the success of this restructuring of nationality and citizenship. Presenting the anti-terrorism measures as critical to protecting national security and the war in Afghanistan as an effort to liberate Muslim women, the media has helped justify the war as being waged primarily against hypermisogynist and medieval male fanatics. Hence, the media's effective gendering of the discourse of the war on terror exalts Canadian (and all other western) nationals as possessing superior civilizational values, with these values making them the targets of terror.

This final chapter examines how the figure of the deadly and fanatic Muslim is being recast in and by the media as the most dangerous threat to the Canadian nation, with his/her immutable civilizational inferiority as the threat that demands neutralization. Simultaneously, these discursive measures recast Canadian nationality such that the civilizational superiority of the national subject, which now includes feminist gender values, is presented as threatening its very survival. The nation of western citizens imagines itself as terrorized by the irrational hatred of the

murderous and misogynist stranger, even as it increases its own involve-
ment in the invasions and occupations commanded by American
Empire-building.

Mediating Nationality

The war on terror began with an attack on the United States that was
transformed into a spectacular media event. Transmitted around the
world as they were unfolding, the attacks on the Twin Towers in New
York City transfixed audiences in country after country and highlighted
the critical importance of media to global governance.

Canadian media reporting in the aftermath of 9/11 has been
described as 'sensational,' 'emotional,' and 'repetitive' by T.Y. Ismael
and J. Measor. The authors conclude that the media have 'uniformly
failed to perform their traditional watchdog function over the Canadian
government in analyzing and presenting alternatives to the selection of
government policy.'[11] Identifying 'the lack of context' and the prevalence of 'racist notions' as particularly problematic, Ismael and Measor's
study echoes the earlier findings of Edward Said and Karim H. Karim,
each of whom traced the resilience of 'centuries-old primary stereotypes,' particularly that of the 'violent' Muslim in North American
media reporting. Karim has further noted that media discourses 'accord
an implicit primacy to nation-states, particularly to elite nations such as
the American superpower.' In so doing, the media make 'invisible' the
'wholesale violence' of these elite nations while 'highlighting' the violence of 'sub-national groups.'[12]

Misrepresentations of Muslims and Islam are certainly rife within
North American media, as are orientalist constructs of non-western populations. Selective definitions of violence and terrorism clearly serve to
divert attention away from the murderous foreign policies of the United
States and Canada, and of their European precursors in the Middle East
and Central Asia.[13] Drawing upon these critiques of the media, the following sections analyse how Canadian print media are deploying the
discourse of terrorism to mediate the ground for the 'strange encounters' – to borrow from Ahmed – between a terrorized and innocent west
and the hateful Muslim who threatens its destruction.[14]

Benedict Anderson has highlighted the important role of print media
in the historical constitution of nations as 'imagined communities.' The
development of this media facilitated the emergence of a sense of
shared temporal and spatial simultaneity among nationals. Further,

Anderson argued, print media enabled ruling elites to propagate the notion of a shared history and common future among the population and to define its own interests as being synonymous with *the* public inter-est.[15] For his part, Arjun Appadurai has argued that the electronic media have become pivotal to the 'work of the imagination,' profoundly affecting ideas of self, community, and identity at the level of daily life.[16] In his examination of the cultural aspects of globalization, Appadurai argues that, as far reaching as the changes brought about by print media were in the past, these were nonetheless 'only modest precursors' to the tremendous changes being wrought by the media in the current phase of globalization.[17]

The electronic media have become a pivotal vehicle of globalization, enabling various forms of agency to be enacted through its shaping of 'imagined selves and imagined worlds' at the transnational and transcul-tural levels.[18] With the majority of populations depending largely on the media for their knowledge about – and understanding of – current events and, most particularly, of international affairs, the media enable not only the imagining of the nation but also the imagining of its inter-national interests, the nature of its enemies and allies, as well as their multiple convergences and conflicts.

In their study of the Canadian media, communications scholars Rob-ert Hackett and Yuezhi Zhao have pointed out that 'journalism is argu-ably the most important form of public knowledge in contemporary society.'[19] Despite the tremendous growth of diverse forms of media, including television, film, radio, and the Internet, print media continue to exert an inordinate influence in the shaping of public discourses and the setting of political agendas. Newspapers are at the foundation of the 'information pyramid,' and their reports provide much of the informa-tion used by other media sources.[20] Hackett and Gruneau have noted that, compared with newspapers, 'no other mass medium offers the same combined possibilities for accessibility, in-depth analysis, potential diversity of viewpoints, and sustained reflection on important political and economic issues.'[21] Despite their declining sales, especially among the young, the broadsheets nonetheless provide a useful forum where elites can engage with one another in public discussions regarding cur-rent events and policy formulations.

The last decade of the twentieth century witnessed an increased merging of political, corporate, and media elites in Canada, with the lib-eral ideal of a relatively autonomous media having been all but fully eclipsed. The role of the corporate media in popularizing neoconserva-

tive critiques of the Keynesian welfare state, and in shattering the ideological consensus in favour of the welfare system, has been analysed by a
number of scholars and social activists.[22] This increasing concentration
of media ownership became a major concern during that period, as did
the increasingly interventionist stance adopted by the owners of the
media.[23]

In the case of the United States, the concentration of media ownership reached historically unprecedented levels, leading Ben Bagdikian
to make the following observation:

> In the last five years, a small number of the country's largest industrial cor-
> porations has acquired more public communications power – including
> ownership of the news – than any private businesses have ever before pos-
> sessed in world history ... Using both old and new technology, by owning
> each other's shares, engaging in joint ventures as partners, and other forms
> of cooperation, this handful of giants has created what is, in effect, a new
> communications cartel within the United States ... At issue is the possession
> of power to surround almost every man, woman and child in the country
> with controlled images and words, to socialize each new generation of
> Americans, to alter the political agenda of the country ... to exert influence
> that in many ways is greater than that of schools, religion, parents, and
> even government itself.[24]

If this was the case with the American media, media ownership in Canada was concentrated in *even fewer hands* during the same period. Media
analysts note that while 43.7 per cent of daily newspapers sold in the
United States in 1996 were controlled by ten companies, a comparable
share in Canada was owned by only one company, Hollinger Inc.[25] To
appreciate more fully the broad reach and deep influence of a handful
of media barons, it should be noted that ninety-three out of every one
hundred English-language newspapers sold in Canada were published
by only four companies.[26] While the overt censorship of news reporting
and direct control of editorial content that is often asserted by media
owners is an ongoing concern, much more insidious are the effects of
the naturalized assumptions shared and propagated by and within the
media.[27] These assumptions, naturalized in the reporting of the war on
terror, have been paramount in shaping the common-sense understandings nationals have come to acquire about the war and in shaping the
ways in which nationality is constituted.

Nationalizing the 'West'

One morning, three years after the 9/11 attacks on the United States, a period during which not a single terrorist attack was launched in Canada, the readers of the the *Globe and Mail* were presented with the following front-page headline: *Emergency. Code Red. Code Red. Without Missing a Beat, the Children Run to a Corner and Huddle Behind Their Teacher's Desk.*[28] The headline was accompanied by a photograph of fifteen second-grade students, indeed huddled with a teacher behind her desk. The news report described a drill at an elementary school in rural Ontario to 'prepare children for whatever danger lurks in a panicky age of school shootings and terrorist attacks.' The school was said to be located 'in the middle of nowhere, surrounded by farmer's fields,' and, even the reporter covering the event observed, 'It [was] about the last place on earth imaginable as the target for a gunman or a crazed, knife-wielding student.' Nevertheless, the drill was conducted to prepare staff and students for Columbine-style shootings and 'Beslan-style terrorist attacks.'

The alarmist comparison to Beslan was clearly unwarranted (after all, Aboriginal peoples living under occupation in Canada have no such record of armed hostage-taking in recent memory, unlike the Chechens living under Russian occupation), and the danger of Columbine-style shootings was also highly exaggerated (although one copycat shooting did take place in a school in Alberta). The peculiarity of the situation did not escape commentators: 'Why not train them on what to do if they're struck by lightning? It's more likely to happen,' pointed out an astute criminologist interviewed for the story. Another expert on school violence was reported to 'acknowledge there are no more reportings of school violence than there were before,' but, undeterred by this acknowledgement, he went on assert, 'it's clear to us the intensity of the violence is higher.'[29]

The news report's fusing of two such significantly different kinds of incidents reveals the heightened anxieties in Canadian society about a generic 'terrorist threat' said to be omnipresent in the age of the global war. The prominence given this piece of news, the front-page photograph featuring little (white) children whose safety was of national concern, and the countless other such news reports continue to fuel such anxieties, presenting the terrorist threat as urgent and as confronting not only the United States, but all 'civilized' nations, including, of course, Canada. The young children featured in the report, children who were being taught to fear terrorists, embody the innocence of the nation, which must protect its most precious resource: its children. Their youth and whiteness symbolize the purity and vulnerability of the exalted nation that experiences itself as terrorized, its future survival at stake.

In a radio interview in Vancouver, the chief of the Vancouver Police Department said he was very 'worried' about terrorism: 'If I was to tell your listeners what ... our intelligence is telling us and what I know, I tell you there would be some sleepless nights.'[30] He advised listeners 'to be vigilant. Read the newspapers, watch the news, determine what you think is unsafe behaviour and support the police.' If this broadcast leaves little doubt that the terrorist threat is not only global but also local, it likewise leaves little doubt about where the enemy is to be found lurking. The chief stated: 'We are a huge, metropolitan city that's home to a variety of different issues that go on here, and I think it's just vigilant and good common sense for the police to encourage citizens to be aware of all kinds of things.' It is in the 'huge' metropolitan centres of the nation – populated by large communities of people of colour – where the 'threat' is said to have buried itself. The vigilant national, then, must be alert to a wide spectrum of danger.

A number of scholars have persuasively argued that race is spatialized, and that with the inner-city's association with crime, drugs, violence, and urban decay, this space has been made synonymous with the perilous colonial zones of previous centuries: 'The inner city is racialized space, the zone in which all that is not respectable is contained.'[31] In the post–9/11 public discourses articulated in media reports, a new civic responsibility is being assigned to the responsible national-cum-citizen (who is not a terrorist). The new burden of citizenship now includes a constant hypervigilance – and a readiness to spring into action – against the inner-city based 'terrorist' (who is not civilized, even if passing as a citizen). Increased collaboration between the real national-as-citizen and the law enforcement agencies of the state is presented as vital to the elimination of this threat to the security of both.

Following the 9/11 attacks, President Bush made the case that the immediate cause for these was the murderous envy of the terrorists, who were contemptuous of the democracy and freedoms that abound in the west. The explanation that 'evildoers' hate 'our' freedoms was uncritically accepted and widely repeated by political and media elites.

There are people who hate America, they hate what we stand for, they hate the fact that Democrats and Republicans both love our country equally. They hate the idea that we worship freely. They hate the concept that we debate issues in the open. They hate freedom. They just hate it. And they are going to hurt us; they are.[32]

History has called America and our allies to action, and it is both our responsibility and our privilege to fight freedom's fight.[33]

In these statements, and countless other such banal musings regularly reported in the media, Bush drew – unwittingly perhaps – upon the Enlightenment legacy as well as the Hegelian concept of history as the inexorable march of the west towards freedom and progress.[34] With the rise of reason and rational government, history's call was met by western civilization in the form of the bourgeois liberal-democratic order, with the rest of the world following under benevolent European – and subsequently Euro-American – tutelage.

Bush's representation of the American nation as the leader of the west, as a beacon of democracy and freedom in the world, was used mercilessly by the media to silence critics of U.S. foreign policy. By their relentless exaltations of the west, the media legitimized the invasions and occupations of the war on terror as being freedom's fight: 'we' are civilized and free, 'they' are filled with hatred and envy.[35] The strategy of the Bush administration to cast the war in such epic civilizational terms was enthusiastically advanced in and by the media.

In an incisive essay, Stuart Hall has argued that the concepts of east and west do not refer principally to geography. Rather, they belong to a system of representation that is rooted in the myths and fantastical projections of Europeans in their historical conquest of territories, and in their colonization of the peoples whom they subsequently defined as belonging to an intrinsically different order of humanity.[36] Describing the ways in which the concept of the west functions, Hall has highlighted its four critical aspects: the classification of societies into separate categories; the conjuring up of certain images of these societies, i.e., developed, industrialized, urban; the establishment of a standard for comparison; and the provision of evaluative criteria, i.e., developed equals 'good,' underdeveloped equals 'bad.'[37] The enthusiastic invocation and popularization of the concept of the west by the media thus constantly mobilizes these four aspects of its implicit meaning for mass consumption.

Whereas the discourse of the 'west and the rest' treats the development of the west as 'the result of forces largely internal to Europe's history and formation,' Hall further points out that this 'development' was instead very much a 'global story.'[38] It was in relation with – and in contrast to – the 'rest' that the 'west' developed its own sense of identity. Similarly, it was through their appropriations of the wealth of their colonies that Europe's 'national' economies were developed. In his study of the relationship between the west as Occident and the East as Orient, and particularly the Islamic Orient, Edward Said named the discursive formulation of this relation of Europe to its Others as orientalism, the essence of which was posited as the 'ineradicable distinction between Western superiority and Oriental inferiority.'[39] Constructing the west as internally homogenous and united in its interests, this discourse constituted those who were not of the west, and the Islamic Orient in particular, as inherently incommensurable. As in the past, the current exaltations of the west in the ideological war rely less on the conquest of the enormous wealth of the enemy, which includes the vast oil and natural gas resources of the Middle East and Central Asia, than on the demonization of Muslims.

Third world feminist critiques of the concept of the west have argued that this is deeply gendered: the bourgeois-liberal gender order became a critical signifier of the modernity of the west, a standard against which to measure the purported traditionality of the 'rest' as irremediably and violently patriarchal.[40] Claiming to be unique in its subscription to women's equality, and in proffering greater rights and freedoms to women, the west has been popularly presented as the sole site of these rights and freedoms. Whereas the equality of women within public life is said to be among its most cherished values,[41] the non-west is routinely presented as the pre-eminent site for terrible gender oppression and violence against women, where forced marriages, dowry deaths, honour killings, genital mutilation, and other such practices are said to characterize women's lives. These forms of violence against third world women are generalized as inextricable aspects of their cultures while the forms of violence western women are subjected to are either ignored or minimized, never popularly defined as emblematic of western cultures.[42] Notwithstanding the existence of the various forms of patriarchal practices and misogynist violence prevalent within the modern societies of the west, European powers have historically used particular patriarchal practices within non-western societies to justify their conquest and colonization.[43]

As its colonial and imperialist antecedents had done in previous centuries, the war on terror dramatically interjected gender into the centre of global political debates at the dawn of the twenty-first century. The Bush administration identified the liberation of Afghan women as a key policy objective in its war, second only to the uprooting of the al Qaeda network. The rationale of saving Muslim women and girls thus became central to mobilizing popular support for the war on Afghanistan and for the participation of Canadian troops in this 'good' war.

The media responded to this racialized-gendered strategy of the Bush administration by flooding news reports with images of veiled Muslim women. The burqa-clad Afghan woman became the icon of victimized and passive Muslim womanhood, overwhelming and displacing all other descriptions of these women. In this context, the veil and burqa came to signify not only the patriarchal oppression of the women but also the justice implicit in the war and the 'feminist' sensibility of the nationals who waged and supported it, in uniform or otherwise. The media's promotion of this racial-gendered discourse of the west drastically curtailed public space for opposition to the war. Similarly impeded was any examination of how the militaristic violence affected the lives of the women who were to be saved.

The representation of their nations as primarily western was a crucial element in the transformation of the 9/11 attacks into a global crisis by the hypercapitalist powers, and of the formulation of the war as a global war. 'Shocked world leaders called the suicide assaults on New York's World Trade Center and the Pentagon in Washington a declaration of war on civilization,' reported the *National Post*.[44] Canadian elites were also quick to embrace such a formulation. 'Despite our differences [with the U.S.] we have common interests, a common language, common heritage and a common culture – as emblazoned on the Peace Arch: "We are children of a common mother.".... The enemy we face together is anti-modern medieval religious fanaticism,' opined a group of experts.[45] Even commentators with liberal leanings who called for calm after the 9/11 attacks and cautioned against 'the search for scapegoats,' reproduced this framing of events. The attacks, argued one such commentator, were 'far more' than an attack on the U.S.:

It's also an attack on the notion of civil society itself and, at yet another level, it is an assault on advanced civilization as a precept ... If the attackers do indeed prove to be Islamic fundamentalists waging a renewed jihad against the U.S., it will mark a new flaring of tensions between Christian

Europe and the Islamic Middle East that have endured for 1,500 years and still convulse the Balkans today.[46]

Little disagreement was to be found in the assumptions shared by politicians, columnists, editorialists, and other 'experts.'[47] 'Those who are responsible are most likely men from remote desert lands. Men from ancient tribal cultures built on blood and revenge. Men whose unshakeable beliefs and implacable hatreds go back many centuries further than the United States and its young ideas of democracy, pluralism and freedom,' explained a prominent woman journalist.[48] Indeed, the active participation of women, and of feminists, in the reproduction of this discursive frame granted greater legitimacy to its gendered racializations.

An intense identification with the U.S. was presented by the media as widespread not only among elites but also among the larger population.[49] Vigils, memorials, and other local events were reported upon in great detail, while anti-war marches and demonstrations were either ignored or ridiculed. Exalting nationals as western and civilized, such reporting emphasized the shared racial identity and global interests of Canadians and Americans, constituting both as belonging to a superior order of humanity. Such racial bonding naturalized the cause of the conflict and helped suppress public discussion of the attacks as a direct response to particular U.S. policies in the Middle East, as was claimed by the al Qaeda network held responsible for orchestrating the attacks.

Further, this racial bonding constructed any opposition to U.S. foreign policy as a refusal to support these policies and as an implicit attack on the Canadian nation and its values.[50] Such opposition became equated with support for, if not actual complicity with, terrorism, as numerous reporters and editorialists gave Bush's pre-emptive strategy wider legitimacy and international credibility. Endorsing this as the only frame for Canadian responses, the war in Afghanistan was presented as equally vital for the preservation of the Canadian nation.

The media's exaltation of western civilization and denigration of Muslims drew upon Samuel Huntington's infamous thesis of a violent 'clash of civilizations' between the west and Islam. Huntington argues that the two are absolutely irreconcilable, ignoring the historical evidence used by many commentators who argue the opposite.[51] Tariq Modood, among other scholars, rejects Huntington's thesis, arguing instead that 'Islam, with its faith in the revelations of Abraham, Moses, Jesus and Mohammad, belongs to the same tradition as Christianity and Judaism.' In support of this position, Modood cites obvious similarities, such as the shared 'monotheism, legalism and communitarianism' of these religions, as well as many of their shared dietary regulations.[52] While the extent of the similarities shared by these religions is clearly a matter for debate, as is the question of the internal heterogeneity of each, the discourse of the west, in its reborn guise as the 'clash of civilizations,' was presented by the media as self-evidently true.

Media reporting thus helped mask the long-term economic and geopolitical ambitions underlying the policy directives of the United States (and Canada) towards Afghanistan, Iraq, and other Middle Eastern and Central Asian countries.[53] As Mahmood Mamdani argues, the 'culture talk' inherent in Huntington's thesis avoids a historical and political analysis of the current conflict and 'downplays the crucial encounter with colonial power,' which shapes the current relationship of the U.S. to the Middle East and Central Asia.[54] Mamdani asserts that contemporary militant Islamist movements are the outcome of *contemporary* geopolitical realities, including the cold war hostilities between the U.S. and the Soviets, and the CIA's support for the revival of the concept of armed Jihad through its alliances with the various Mujahideen factions in Afghanistan during the Soviet occupation. The consequences of European and American colonial and imperial domination of the third world thus provide a more accurate frame for understanding the current international conflict.[55]

Another significant factor identified by Mamdani was the pattern of American support for the use of terror against civilian populations in its counter-insurgency strategies in a number of countries – including Angola, Nicaragua, and Afghanistan – after its defeat in Vietnam. The ·U.S. routinely equates militant nationalism in the third world, driven by the quest for independence from colonial and imperial domination, with communism, and thus justifies violent intervention to suppress such resistance wherever it emerged. Political analysis of this sort, readily available, was completely marginalized by the print media. Instead, a selective pro-war analysis was used to disseminate and popularize the Bush administration's perspective as the only rational one. War with incorrigible Muslims was presented as inevitable and potentially endless to protect the exalted bodies of innocent nationals and their co-civilizationalists.

Even if somewhat muted, this recasting of Canadian national identity has not stalled in the years after the 9/11 attacks.[56] 'We are a haven to several underground terrorist groups. And, of course, we are part of the West, which Osama bin Laden and his cohorts see as their oppressor,' argued a leading media commentator, one year after the attacks.[57] 'We have always said that Canada is under threat, that the attacks on Sept. 11 were an attack on democracy and we have always known ... that this was a fact and that this was continuing,' stated the then Liberal deputy prime minister.[58] 'All urban, industrialized, democratic societies are vulnerable to terrorism,' opined an expert on security and intelligence issues.[59] Calling for the United States to adopt a more multilateralist approach, a Conservative ex-prime minister advocated 'a new sense of partnership with nations holding similar values. After all, terrorists can strike from Tokyo to Toronto. Canadians, Europeans and others share American commitments to democracy, human rights and the basis [sic] tenets of economic liberalism.'[60]

Prime Minister Stephen Harper, during his highly publicized visit to Afghanistan, stated: 'The truth is, Canada is not an island. We live in a dangerous world and we have to show leadership in that world and that's what we're doing and that's what I am trying to do.'[61] This prime minister has repeatedly linked the presence of Canadian troops in Afghanistan with the attacks of 9/11, and presented them as being directed against Canadians.[62] The *Globe and Mail* helped the prime minister sell the nation's increased participation in the war: 'Part of Canada's role in southern Afghanistan is to stop them over there before they can wreak havoc back here,' it asserted.[63]

Terrorist attacks against western powers in recent history have largely been in direct response to the imperialist aggressions and colonial occupations of particular powers: attacks by the Irish against the British, by the Algerians against the French, by Palestinians against the Israelis, by Chechens against the Russians, by al Qaeda against the U.S., and most recently, by Islamists in Madrid (Spain) and London (Britain), for their respective governments' participation in the invasion and occupation of Iraq. In light of this history, it can be anticipated that the more fervently the Canadian state seeks to intensify its 'new sense of partnership' with the United States, the more Canadians participate in invading and occupying other countries, the more likely it is that the nation-state will become a target for retaliatory attacks. Instead of promoting discussion of these changing realities, the media promotes a paranoid and generic fear which feeds the delusional fantasies of western civilizational superiority.

In order to avoid critical examinations of the potential consequences of equating U.S. and Canadian foreign policy objectives and their respective national interests, the media endlessly repeat the perspectives of those committed to an intensification of these equations by stoking alarmist national fantasies. Peter C. Newman, a prominent writer and public figure, argued in a recent column: 'If future terrorists such as members of al-Qaeda or one of the rogue states currently developing atomic bombs, North Korea and Iran, decide to stage a terminal strike against North America, their weapons of mass-destruction would most likely come by sea in unmarked containers abroad stateless hulls, the deadly payloads secreted in undetectable lead-lined detonation devices.'[64] Newman was not above raising the level of public fear-mongering by articulating deeply paranoid musings that present the nation to itself as terrorized: 'Although the al-Qaeda merchant fleet usually carries grains and cement, it is easily transferable to more lethal assignments. But since these ships are under observation, a more likely scenario is that al-Qaeda operatives would hijack legitimate merchant ships, kill their crews, and rush them into North American harbours, carrying the toxic, city-destroying loads hidden in their holds.' This apocalyptic fantasy ends with a chilling warning to his fellow nationals: 'The threat is simply too huge, too uncontrollable to be contained, no matter who mans the harbours.'[65] Although al Qaeda has stated its intention to strike the United States again, as well as its allies in the wars in Afghanistan and Iraq, the delusional narratives of Canadian vulnerability make it difficult to sensibly assess the level of threat that might actually exist, given the serious decimation of al Qaeda's organizational structure and the seizure of its resources.[66]

Moreover, the print media's routine promotion of statements that normalize the equation of U.S. and Canadian values and interests allow for Canadian nationality to be imagined as a more robust, potent, and masculinized force even as the nation is presented as committed to feminist values abroad. 'I don't think there's a better example in decades of Canada really standing up, going to the front line and articulating our values – not just our opposition to terror, our advancement of democracy, but basic humanitarian values,' the current prime minister stated, articulating such musculinist imaginings. 'This is just a tremendous mission where we're showing leadership, and leadership that is taking on danger and advancing the kind of things that go to the heart of what Canada is all about as a country.'[67]

Under the military might of the United States, the Canadian nation-state is reclaiming and reliving its own colonial-style military efficacy, denounced now as having softened through prior peacekeeping missions in Somalia, Bosnia, and the genocidal debacle in Rwanda.[68] Promising that '[w]e won't run away,' the prime minister pointed out, 'You can't lead from the bleachers. I want Canada to be a leader.'[69] In this newly imagined aggressive persona, the cultural capital the nation has accrued in the past – through its successful self-presentation as the 'peacekeeper' of the international community – is being deployed to serve the American Empire. This enhancement of Canada's power and influence at the international level depends on its assertion of its racial bonds with the U.S. and its participation in the current remaking of the world order. The United States is perceived as the muscle-flexing 'Big Brother,' feared and resented in most of the 'non-western' world, particularly so in the Middle East and Central Asia. In contrast, the Canadian nation-state is widely perceived as the compassionate middle power, with a commitment to peacekeeping rooted in its distinct national values. Canada's participation in the war on terror helps sanitize the image of U.S. power.

Canadian support for the United States is sometimes accompanied by some criticism, but the acceptance of the discourse of the west to legitimize the war remains unchallenged. This discourse, and the claim that Afghanistan is 'our' war, are exempletive of what Inderpal Grewal has so aptly termed 'transnational nationalism.' The media's promotion of the war as 'ours' invites Canadians to imagine their interests as consistent with those of the United States. Such exaltation provokes a powerfully emotive response to both the United States and to the enemy. Canadian nationality and the western-ness of its 'civilizational values' thus merge into each other as the more abstract concept of the west becomes locatable in the corporeality of this national subject.

The phenomenon of western racial bonding has a long history, and it is useful here to turn to Ella Shohat and Robert Stam's discussion of the imperial ideologies of an earlier era: 'Europeans were encouraged to identify not only with single European nations but also with the racial solidarity implied by the imperial project as a whole' in the heyday of colonialism.[70] The Bush administration's reassertion of the category the west draws upon, and simultaneously strengthens, a racial imperial solidarity for the contemporary era. Grasping the depth of this solidarity is necessary if the impact of the war on terror on Canadian nationality is to be adequately comprehended.

Racializing the 'Enemy'

If the civilizational narratives that frame the war on terror promote a racial solidarity within the west then this bonding relies primarily on its

racial coding of the enemy as non-western. With this narrative's representation of Islam as the quintessential Other of the west, the category
Muslim has been constituted in this war as not only religious and political but also as a racialized category. This omnipresent enemy is defined
in numerous ways that depict it as monstrous. The enemy has been
described a: 'a terrorist underworld – including groups like Hamas,
Hezbollah, Islamic Jihad, Jaish-I-Mohammed – it operates in remote jungles and deserts, and hides in the centers of large cities.'[71] Members of
these groups are known as 'evil-doers,'[72] hiding 'in the shadows' with 'no
regard for human life.'[73] They are 'hydra-headed,'[74] and need to be
'hunt[ed] down' and 'smoke[d] out of their holes.'[75] Such rhetoric reinvokes the figure of the 'crazed savage' imagined in the earlier colonial
encounter between Europe and its Other, the indigene. The war on terror has dragged this figure out of the depths of the collective psyche of
the nation to where it had been relegated in the med-twentieth century.

Although much of the overtly racialized language used to describe
this enemy originated from the Bush administration, Canadian elites
and media commentators used such rhetoric to assert their own
western-ness.[76] The Chief of Defence Staff, for example, described the
'opponents' of Canadian troops in Afghanistan as 'detestable murderers
and scumbags, I'll tell you that right up front. They detest our freedoms,
they detest our society, they detest our liberties.'[77] An overtly racialized
discourse, not tolerated in polite public spaces following the liberalization of the 1960s, can now be heard articulated unchecked, as long as it
targets Muslims and Islam. By the uncritical repetition of this language,
the Canadian media facilitated the spread of this racialized discourse
outside the borders of the U.S., popularizing it and endowing it with
international legitimacy.

'Racism,' Ella Shohat and Robert Stam have argued,

> involves a double movement of aggression and narcissism; the insult to the
> accused is doubled by a compliment to the accuser. Racist thinking is tauto-
> logical and circular; we are powerful because we are right, and we are right
> because we are powerful. It is also essentializing, ahistorical, and metaphys-
> ical, projecting difference across historical time: 'They are all that way, and
> they will always be that way.'[78]

The contemporary language that describes the enemy of the west as
animal-like, and hence as implicitly less-than-human, exalts the west-
erners threatened by 'them' as fully human. Presented as culturally

irremediable and ontologically predisposed to hatred and violence, the war rhetoric draws an equation between the actual perpetrators of the 9/11 attacks with all the other Muslim strangers as their racial and civilizational cohorts.

An interesting example of such racialized equations of the terrorist threat can be found in a recent report prepared for the influential conservative think tank, the Fraser Institute, by a former Canadian ambassador to the Middle East and Asia. The report recommended a stronger adoption of 'Canadian values' by 'new' immigrants as a specific counterterrorism measure: 'If they find such acceptance difficult, they should not come here in the first place.'[79]

As reported in the *Montreal Gazette* and the *National Post*, this diplomat, also identified as a 'counter-terrorism policy co-ordinator at Foreign Affairs,' urged that such immigrants be required to take an oath,

> swearing that they are not only fully committed to Canadian values and will give their complete allegiance and loyalty to Canada, but that their actions in the future will reflect these commitments ... Special attention must be given to working with the Muslim community, since radical Islamic terrorists are currently the greatest danger to Canada's security.[80]

With the attachment of immigrants to 'Canadian' values long having been deemed suspect, this alleged lack of attachment was here associated with a radical potential for terrorism among new immigrants, and also among the Muslim community.

If gender has been a key signifier of the civilizational superiority of the west, the threat to the nation said to be posed by this religio-racial enemy was also imagined as gendered. It was not only fanatic and hypermasculine Muslim men who were constituted as terrorizing the nation with their inborn propensity to blow up buildings and planes, and indeed, even their own bodies, Muslim women were also constituted as posing a very particular kind of threat. As Mamdani, and others, have noted, Muslims in the post–9/11 period have been defined as being either good or bad Muslims:

> After an unguarded reference to pursuing a 'crusade,' President Bush moved to distinguish between 'good Muslims' and 'bad Muslims.' From this point of view, 'bad Muslims' were clearly responsible for terrorism. At the same time, the president seemed to assure Americans that 'good Muslims' were anxious to clear their names and consciences of this horrible

crime and would undoubtedly support 'us' in a war against 'them.' But this could not hide the central message of such discourse: unless proved to be 'good,' every Muslim was presumed to be bad. All Muslims were now under obligation to prove their credentials by joining in a war against 'bad Muslims.'[81]

Gender relations have been central to the drawing of this distinction. The good Muslims are the assimilated ones; they berate other Muslims for their cultural backwardness and, most particularly, they berate the women for revealing such backwardness by wearing the headscarf, the chador, or the veil. These good Muslims are styled (and style themselves) as the anti-hijabis. They acquiesce to American imperial interests, vociferously defend these, and know their proper place as supplicants to the west. They are appropriately grateful for having been allowed to partake in its civilizational project, and they want to aid the west in its quest to liberate their co-religionists, especially the women, around the world.

However, significant media coverage was also given to the bad Muslim woman, the one who dares to defy western gender norms, who refuses to condemn her religion and its adherents. This is the woman who is not imperilled, but who imperils the west by her embrace of Islam, or by her resistance to occupation and imperialist aggression. She is the 'Black widow' of Chechnya, the suicide bomber of Palestine, the 'Doctor Germ' and 'Mrs Anthrax' of Iraq. This Muslim woman is not to be rescued: she is unrepentant. The worst of these women, as depicted in the photograph discussed at the beginning of this chapter, are the ones who refuse to unveil themselves. They are labelled as fanatical and oblivious to male domination. Their embrace of Islam is seen as an affront to the freedoms enjoyed by western women. Such an embrace of Islam is only tolerable to the nation of civilized subjects if it is accompanied with the simultaneous, but more ardent, embrace of superior western values and norms.

The presence of women of colour has long been a site of anxiety for the Canadian nation, as I have discussed in previous chapters. Women's bodies, as the markers of racial, cultural, and national difference, have been constructed as primarily responsible for transmitting such difference onto subsequent generations throughout the nation's history.[82] News reports of these women in the media prior to 9/11 largely focused on them as 'victims' of what Uma Narayan has fittingly termed 'death by culture.'[83] In the post–9/11 period, such historical anxieties have coalesced around the figure of the Muslim woman, who has become the cause for particular national consternation, her body the site for the waging of the clash of civilizations. Not only are these women represented as subject to 'death by culture' themselves, they are now ascribed with the potential to bring death *to* the nation *by* their culture. The adoption by Muslim women of western values, of western dress and lifestyles, lends credibility to the nation's claims to civilizational superiority, and Muslim women's modernization, signalled by the level of their assimilation and gratitude, upholds such claims. However, should these women reject such markers of their gratitude by, for example, adopting the wearing of the headscarf, burqa, or the chador, the superiority and alleged universality of western values become destabilized. Unfortunately for the good Muslims (women and men), no matter how deep their gratitude to the nation, no matter how ardent their embrace of western civilizational norms, the new anti-terrorism measures continue to make them as equally suspect as the bad Muslims.[84]

Along with the 'terrorists,' the 'bad' Muslims include those who refuse the westernization of their bodies and minds, who resist the domination of their societies, and who insist on adherence to their faith as the inspiration for their values and politics. These Muslims are 'guilty' by religious and cultural association, regardless of their actual stance on international politics or the use of violence by particular movements in particular contexts. Such a strategy of dividing the good natives from the bad has a long history in Canada, being rooted in the foundational moment of nationhood when 'noble savages' were distinguished from the 'barbaric savages' among Native peoples. The construct of the barbaric savage was used then, as it is now, to justify the genocidal violence unleashed against them. The construct of the noble savage was used to make a case for their assimilation and cultural extinction.[85] In a gesture reminiscent of this history, the constructions of good and bad Muslims enable nationals to remember (and re-enact) the pleasures of carrying their white (wo)man's burden in a new historical moment.

Moreover, the racialization of the category 'Muslim' made it inevitable that racialized Others inside the country would come to be linked directly with the enemy outside the borders of the nation-state. After all, the enemy was said to live not only in jungles and caves but also in the inner cities, to be found at airports and in shopping malls, in apartment buildings and schools, and on buses and trains. In making 'their' cultural hatreds the most salient feature defining them, the Muslim strangers within, even if claiming the legal status of citizens, comes to be construed as not only not sharing the threat faced by the nation, *they* are the threat to the nation.

So it was that while the men who carried out the attacks of 9/11 were principally Saudi citizens, it was Pakistanis, Indians, Parsis, Hindus, Sikhs, Arabs – many of them citizens of the United States and Canada – who were attacked, harassed, confined, marked for surveillance and deported by law enforcement officials and by ordinary nationals. The racialization of the enemy was so virulent that after the London bombings in 2005, a young Brazilian man, Jean Charles de Menezes, initially identified as a Pakistani and Asian by eyewitnesses, was shot to death by the British security forces.

Disturbing as the many reported acts of physical violence against those who look like Muslims were in Canada, these have been far outnumbered by the normalization of overtly anti-Muslim practices at the level of daily social life. Such practices include the unrelenting public exaltations of the west in popular culture as well as the interminable maligning of Muslim men as hate-filled misogynists and Muslim women as abject victims and hapless dupes. These exaltations and denigrations provide justification for the harassment of immigrants and refugees even as they legitimize the foreign policies of the nation and its allies.

Post–9/11, high-ranking politicians, military and media spokespeople publicly advocate for the use of racial profiling, security certificates, and the suspension of the rights of terrorist suspects as being absolutely vital to protect national security. As discussed in chapter 1, Giorgio Agamben has pointed out that the paradox of sovereignty is that the sovereign stands 'at the same time, outside and inside the juridical order' with 'the power to suspend the validity of the law.'[86] The war on terror has allowed such a state of exception to be imposed on Muslims suspected of 'links to terrorism' in Canada, as elsewhere, such that the suspension of the law has allowed the introduction of measures previously deemed outside the juridical order. Agamben cautions us to remember that the suspension of the law does not mean that the state of emergency creates a 'lawless' arena.[87] Rather, this arena remains related to the law in that the law is deemed to no longer apply to it.

In the case of racial profiling, the state of exception imposed upon Muslims has removed the legal protections previously accorded them, thus placing them in a perilous situation as the targets of the anti-terrorism measures zealously undertaken by law enforcement agencies and hypervigilant nationals. Racial profiling is, of course, not a new practice in Canada, having been used against Aboriginal peoples, Japanese-

Canadians during their internment, Jewish refugees during the Second World War, and most recently, against Black men in their treatment by the police. Nevertheless, such profiling was publicly treated as an aberration after the liberalization policies of the 1960s and 1970s, unfortunate violations of the liberal-democratic ideal of equal treatment. The current public lauding of this 'valuable tool of law enforcement'[88] brings to the fore the historically problematic relationship of people of colour to 'western' liberal-democracy.[89]

Making racial profiling a politically acceptable technique of governance is to inscribe suspicion and illegality onto the bodies of those who 'look' like 'Muslims.' Raising concerns about the legality of such profiling in the Canadian context, Sujit Chowdhry has argued that its advocates have not specified who will be subjected to it, whether it will be Arabs, Muslims, or everybody from the Middle East.[90] Yet it is precisely this lack of specificity that gives racial profiling its potency; it allows an inordinate amount of discretionary power in the hands of law enforcement officials to be used to target entire sections of the population as circumstances change and political priorities fluctuate in a war said to be of unforeseeable duration.

Such profiling is engaged in by law enforcement agencies and by zealous nationals within daily social life. Immediately following 9/11, the dangers posed by the 'terrorist threat' were said to be most immediate at the nation's territorial borders and, in light of the methods used for the attacks, at flight-training schools and airports.[91] Border control measures aimed at Muslims were tightened, as were security measures at airports. Soon after, however, the potential sites identified by officials for future attacks began to encroach into the localized sites of daily life. With each new warning came the attendant call on nationals-as-citizens to increase their individual surveillance of such sites.[92]

Riad Saloojee, executive director of the Council on American-Islamic Relations (Canada), reported being told by a landlord that he (Mr Saloojee) should 'understand' that the landlord was 'reluctant' to rent his premises to a Muslim.[93] In another case, twenty-one Indians and Pakistanis training at a flight school in Ontario were arrested as 'suspected terrorists.'[94] Most of these men were later released, and some were found to have committed only minor immigration violations. The charges made against them alleged that they had links to terrorist organizations and were reported in a highly sensationalized manner in the media. The charges proved to be unfounded, but the reputations, careers, and relationships of many of these men were profoundly damaged.

In another instance, the widely celebrated author of South Asian origin, Rohinton Mistry, who has become somewhat of an international symbol of the successes of Canadian multiculturalism, canceled his U.S. book tour in frustration after having been targeted for 'overzealous scrutiny' at U.S. airports.[95] Stating that the measures adopted for such scrutiny were 'degrading' and gave him 'visions of Guantanamo,' Mistry related how he had been repeatedly targeted during his travels to the United States. A federal minister, also of South Asian origin and likewise considered a symbol of the positive aspects of multiculturalism, voiced his strong opposition to racial profiling, revealing that he, too, had been subjected to this practice in the past.[96]

The institutionalization of racial profiling has not abated in the years following the 9/11 attacks.[97] A Liberal senator, herself a Muslim who said she had experienced such profiling, called it an 'understandable' measure, albeit one which should not be allowed to become permanent. Her 'advice' to other Muslims was this: 'It's not meant towards you. I would rather that people be careful and people felt safe. I want people to fly. It is very important for our economy to get back to normal.'[98] This senator drew upon her impeccable multiculturalist credentials to justify the practice; the few public opponents of the practice have not been able to disrupt the commonsense position deployed by and in the media in support of it. Indeed, the media's reporting of the opposition to this practice by prominent persons like Mistry is used to further the exaltation of the nation as well-intentioned in its general impulse, but ultimately naïve in its commitment to protecting the very minorities who have proved themselves to be a threat. The public advocacy of this practice deepens its normalization as it places nationals on guard against an enemy said to be operating everywhere around them.[99] The use of such profiling enables elites to mobilize the nation through, and into, a racialized animus: racially oriented surveillance from 'above' calculatedly stokes the flames of racism from 'below.' The relationship between nation and state is hereby reinforced on the basis of a shared vigilance against those who 'look' like Muslims.[100]

The use of particular technologies of surveillance at airports and borders (where new security measures such as the removal of shoes at airport security checkpoints and the patting down of bellies has already become routine, as has the increased surveillance of young Muslim men who carry rucksacks or wear padded jackets) said to be necessitated by the *form* of the 9/11 attacks (i.e., suicide bombings), constitutes the Muslim traveller/immigrant as a potential suicide bomber in the national imaginary. The figure of the Muslim stranger is recast by such surveillance techniques as the archetype of the current global menace in the western imagination, the 'suicide bomber.' The actual citizenship of the Muslim thus defined can be made irrelevant. Such measures decontextualize and depoliticize the actual practices of particular suicide bombers, treating the bodies of all immigrants and refugees who look like Muslims as literal ticking bombs.

Such profiling does not distinguish between those people of colour who are born in these countries, those who are citizens, and those who are not. It treats anyone who looks like a Muslim as potentially suspect, unless proved otherwise, and seems set to shape our lives (and rights) for the future. Most disturbingly, racial profiling has the inevitable outcome of changing individual attitudes and behaviours of nationals-as-citizens against those popularly presented (and perceived) to be 'enemies.' Racial profiling puts people of colour 'back' in 'their' place as outsiders-to-the-nation, stripping away pretensions of inclusion within the liberal-democratic order.

Citizenship in the Age of Terror

The state of exception instituted by the anti-terrorism measures specifically targeted the legal rights and protections of Muslim subjects. 'The security of both countries [the United States and Canada] remains vulnerable to a Canadian asylum system that seems designed to openly welcome potential terrorists,' claimed a former Canadian ambassador after 9/11.[101] Immigration and refugee laws were said to have made Canada a 'terrorists' haven,' second only 'to the United States for terrorist infiltration.' 'Although none of the terrorists came from Canada, the existence of terrorist cells has been well documented. The threat continues today', reported another newspaper.[102]

Following the 9/11 attacks, hundreds – if not thousands – of immigrants and refugees were rounded up for detention in both the U.S. and Canada for being security threats.[103] As the terms 'sleeper cell' and 'home-grown terrorists' entered the popular lexicon, the panic created by their deployment meant that Muslims who might have lived their entire lives in Canada also became suspect. Sleeper cells might remain dormant for up to twenty years, experts hurried to explain, thus extending suspicion to all Muslim communities, most of whose members have entered the country since the liberalization of immigration and citizenship policies in the 1970s. Experts continue to proffer absurd scenarios in which Muslims are said to have come to Canada, not to seek more prosperous lives for themselves and their families but to prepare for mass murder twenty and thirty years hence!

A number of disturbing incidents point to the erosion of the citizenship rights of Muslims in Canada. In October, 2002, the U.S. announced that individuals travelling into the country from a list that included Iran, Iraq, Syria, Libya, and Sudan, among others, were to be photographed and fingerprinted at the borders. The new rules were to apply also to Canadian citizens who were born in these particular countries, regardless of their actual citizenship status. These particular technologies of surveillance are symbolically associated with criminality (mug shots and fingerprinting), and their application to these particular persons-in-transit constituted all such persons as potentially criminal.

Dubbing the application of these technologies a form of 'bio-political tattooing,' Giorgio Agamben publicly cancelled his own travel plans to the United States. He also called for others to likewise oppose the normalization of such technologies:

> Some years ago I had written that the West's political paradigm was no longer the city state, but the concentration camp, and that we had passed from Athens to Auschwitz. It was obviously a philosophical thesis, and not historic recital, because one could not confuse phenomenon that it is proper, on the contrary, to distinguish.
>
> I would have liked to suggest that the tattooing at Auschwitz undoubtedly seemed the most normal and economic way to regulate the enrolment and registration of deported persons into concentration camps. The bio-political tattooing the United States imposes now to enter its territory could well be the precursor to what we will be asked to accept later as the normal identity registration of a good citizen in the state's gears and mechanisms.[104]

Agamben noted that such technologies of surveillance are first introduced in relation to the dangers said to be posed by 'foreigners,' and are subsequently applied routinely to citizens. In North America, however, the distinction between foreigner and citizen is not as clearcut as Agamben suggests.

In response to the new regulations originating in the United States, the Canadian government issued a travel advisory, cautioning those among its citizens born in the countries listed not to travel to the United States, unless such travel was absolutely necessary. This move was denounced by conservative politicians and commentators in Canada. It also angered many in the United States, including the Bush administration and the right-wing talk show host, Pat Buchanan, who was prompted to call Canada a 'Soviet Canuckistan.'[105] In this particular case, the racial profiling of Muslims originated in U.S. policy. However, the Canadian state responded by issuing the travel advisory to Canadian citizens with origins in the countries on the U.S. list, *not to all its citizens*, and thereby replicated the racialized distinction. Although the Canadian response could be read as a criticism of the new U.S. policy, or an attempt to protect Canadian citizens born in the specified countries from being subjected to such intrusive practices, in effect, it promoted the same racialized distinctions among its citizens. Muslim citizens were here (re)defined by both the U.S. and Canada as occupying a separate category of (religious?) citizenship. Such a redefinition went unreported in the media.

The case of Maher Arar, a Canadian citizen of Syrian origin, presents yet another disquieting example of the erosion of the citizenship rights of Muslims. While travelling back to Canada from a holiday in Tunisia, Mr Arar, an engineer living in Ottawa, was detained in New York City on allegations of having links to 'terrorism.' Although traveling on a Canadian passport, and despite his request to be returned to Canada, he was instead deported from the United States to Syria. There, he was detained for over a year and was tortured while in custody. Following intense lobbying by his wife and his family's supporters, he was finally released and returned to Canada. Upon his return, Mr Arar charged that Canadian authorities had colluded with U.S. agencies in his deportation to Syria. He has not been officially charged with any terrorist or criminal offences, but damaging allegations continued to be made against him anonymously by Canadian law enforcement agents and these were widely reported in the media.

Mr Arar had acquired Canadian citizenship and had lived most of his adult life in Canada, but his request to U.S. authorities to be sent back to Canada was ignored. Instead, he was sent 'back' to where he 'came from.' In another more recent case, secret hearings were reported to be planned in Canada for an Egyptian-Canadian who was 'suspected of making surveillance videos of Toronto's subway system and the CN Tower.'[106] Neither the date nor the location of the hearings was disclosed. In another case, a Muslim school-bus driver, who was investigated for terrorism but never actually charged with terrorist activity, was reported to have launched a civil lawsuit alleging that 'Canadian security services shared his personal information with Egyptian authorities, and [was] thereby responsible for his two-week detainment and alleged harsh treatment in Cairo.'[107] These cases demonstrate that allegations of links to terrorist activity or to organizations listed as engaged in such activity, no matter how unsubstantiated the 'suspicion' or how flimsy the 'evidence,' are being used by Canadian authorities to strip away the civil liberties and legal rights of Muslim citizens.

Such cases demonstrate the Canadian state's abdication of responsibility for these citizens defined as being 'culturally' prone to terrorism by the United States. In addition to the changes in border control policies, Mr Arar's case also demonstrates how cavalierly the United States has claimed the unilateral power to decide whether the Canadian citizenship (or indeed, the citizenship of any other country) of Muslims is to be upheld, or whether it is to be abrogated. Whether it is the suspension of detainee rights at Guantanamo Bay, or the 'bio-tattooing' of Muslims, or the deportation of Canadian citizens to other countries, the U.S. is today asserting a globalized sovereignty that overrides the citizenship rights proffered by other states to their respective citizens. In Canada, such an audacious move has met very little resistance. Indeed, thus far, the Canadian state has facilitated the assertion of such a globalized sovereignty by the United States.

In the Arar case, a public inquiry led by Mr Justice O'Connor criticized the RCMP for its role in the detention and deportation of Mr Arar to Syria. This report, released in September 2006, found that the RCMP had 'improperly passed along erroneous anti-terrorism intelligence to the United States that very likely led to Mr. Arar's deportation to the Middle East in 2002.'[108] A dramatic apology was made to Mr Arar and his family for the 'nightmare' they had experienced by the RCMP Commissioner when he testified before the House of Commons Public Safety Committee after the release of the inquiry's findings.[109] While it is clearly beyond the scope of this chapter to analyse more fully the treatment of Mr Arar by the state and its agencies, it should be noted that the public exoneration of Mr Arar took place within a climate of worldwide public revulsion at the use of torture in the war on terror, captured so graphically by the photographs of detainees at Abu Ghraib. The media coverage of the inquiry's findings, while rightly criticizing the RCMP and the Liberal government for their treatment of this case, remained silent on the larger implications of the extension of U.S. sovereignty over Canadian citizenship. Likewise, the similarities between the Arar case and those of a number of other (Muslim) Canadian citizens plunged into the 'nightmare' suffered by Mr Arar was not pursued in any significant manner.[110]

Most importantly, the media have largely refrained from publicly examining their own role in the initial demonization of Mr Arar, nor have they reviewed their own conduct in the highly sensationalized reporting of 'terror' suspects arrested and detained subsequent to the Arar detention. In other words, the Arar case was treated as problematic only because the RCMP got the 'wrong' man, not for the profound restructuring of Canadian citizenship that it pointed to. The impact of Justice O'Connor's findings on restoring Mr Arar's standing and reputation cannot be downplayed. But it cannot be ignored that the exposure of the falsity of charges made against 'terror' suspects has not evoked a more measured response from the state or media in subsequent cases. Sensationalized reporting continues unabated, while unsubstantiated charges and anonymous allegations are repeated with an irresponsibility bordering on malice.

Citizenship within particular nation-states has been one of the pillars organizing the rights of individuals within the international system of law. Whatever protection this system offered in the past is today endangered for Muslim citizens, simply on the basis of their religious-turned-political identity. Canada, by its assistance in implementing the new expansive notion of U.S. militarized sovereignty, is contributing directly to the broadening of the reach of U.S. operations.

If the figure of the Muslim is today being used to represent the most potent threat to national security, the racialization of the categories 'Muslim' and 'immigrant' means that all people of colour who 'look' like 'Muslims' (that is, who are Black and Brown), are being constituted as part of this danger, regardless of their legal status. Racialization renders the distinction between citizen and immigrant all but meaningless in the eyes of nationals, who in the post–9/11 era imagine themselves to be 'terrorized,' perceiving the threat to their survival as emanating equally from both.

Although many Muslim immigrants and refugees have been detained in Canada for ostensibly posing threats to national security, almost none have been charged with anything more than (minor) immigration violations. As mentioned earlier, the twenty-one terrorist suspects who were rounded up with much media fanfare in Ontario in September 2003 were later released. It was subsequently reported that 'the Ministry has not produced any evidence against any of the 21 showing they are a security threat.'[111] While such practices have netted few terrorists, they have had serious consequences for those detained, as well as for all Muslims who fear increased surveillance and targeting by law enforcement officials.

Such measures have greatly increased the suspicions directed by nationals against all immigrants, fortifying the limits of the nation and sending a chill among many. Muslim communities, which now fear for the legal status and the physical safety of their members. The media has contributed in no small measure to the growing anti-Muslim racism in North America and to the erosion of their citizenship rights. The distance between 'immigrants' and 'real' Canadians has thus vastly increased since 9/11, with unforeseeable consequences for the future.

Conclusion

The historical emergence of the national subject as citizen, with clearly delineated rights and entitlements, is celebrated in hegemonic liberal discourses as emblematic of the advances towards human progress and equality promised by Enlightenment values and modernist projects. In contrast, I have argued that the constitution of the human being as national subject and citizen has had devastating consequences for this subject's excluded Others, as well as for the interactions among them. I have defined exaltation as the political process that constitutes the national subject as belonging to a higher order of humanity. In the case of settler societies like Canada, the triangulated relationship between whites, Aboriginal peoples and immigrants, organized through the juridical order and the institution of citizenship, has sustained the reproduction of the colonial hierarchies underpinning white supremacy. The socio-political horizons described in the preceeding pages continue to chart out the trajectory of nationality into the present.

In this book, I have asked the question, *What does the Canadian nation imagine itself to be?* Analysing some of the key characteristics widely attributed to the nation, I have historicized such exaltations and highlighted the racialization processes that sustain national-formation. The constitution of the national subject as the embodiment of the nation's distinctive characteristics and values has furthered the notion that Canadians are ontologically different from outsiders and, hence, are intrinsically deserving of greater rights and entitlements. The common humanity that could shape the social relations among nationals, Aboriginal peoples, and immigrants is implicitly denied by such exaltations.

Far too often, 'race-neutral' discourses and policies are put forward in Canada as remedies to the racial histories invested in the nation(al)'s foundation. Denunciations of scientistic discourses, which rely primarily upon biological conceptions of racial inferiority, are prolific and celebrations of cultural difference are instead valorized as a national value. Contemporary racism is treated as arising mainly from the prejudices and ill-informed actions of ignorant – but largely well meaning – Canadians, or as the poisonous and hate-filled practices of a handful of diehard bigots and ultraright fringe groups. The mainstream of Canadian society is generally defined as tolerant and balanced in its approach.

In contrast, I have traced the constitution of Canadian national identity through different historical junctures to argue that this identity has been deeply racialized since its inception in colonial violence, and that it remains inextricably infused with the colonial tropes of white racial supremacy and western civilizational superiority. Exaltation facilitates the constitution of the national subject as a racial subject by inscribing it as such into institutional mechanisms and by foreclosing the possibilities for coevality and mutual reciprocity among the national and his/her respective Others.

In tandem with the state practices and policies discussed in this book, the self-constituting practices of national subjects that have been shaped by their habitations of exalted subject positions have been central to the efficacy of governance. Dwelling in these subject positions has enabled the human being to constitute itself as a *national* subject, and as such, has allowed this subject access to rights and privileges even while deepening its collusion with the state in reproducing coloniality. Claiming exalted subject positions remains key to the integration of individuals into nationality, and hence into the reproduction of its racial hierarchies.

The founding of the Canadian nation was, of course, predicated upon a narrative of racial supremacy as national superiority, and was accomplished through the concomitant ejection of Aboriginal peoples from the newly constituted Euro-Canadian nation. This narrative remains firmly ensconced within the 'strange encounters' of the national with the Native. Moreover, the exclusion of most people of colour from full citizenship further consolidated the symbolic identity of the nation as white. As people of colour achieved inclusion into Canadian citizenship, they did so at the cost of becoming complicit in the further marginalization of Aboriginal populations. The inclusion of people of colour has been accommodated more as an afterthought than as a fundamental reworking of the institution of citizenship. Their complicity in furthering colonial projects remains inevitable without a fundamental transformation of the institution itself.

The transformation of the racialized nature of the national-formation requires a fundamental redefinition of the relationships of *all* non-indigenous populations to Aboriginal peoples. The fatal flaws in the institution of citizenship cannot be remedied by simply expanding access to previously excluded groups. Canadian citizenship remains predicated upon the erasure of Aboriginal sovereignty, and unless this institution can be transformed in relation to the realization of Aboriginal sovereignty, it will remain an instrument of colonial dispossession. Whether such an institution can indeed be transformed, and to what degree, or whether some new phenomenon will emerge to resolve its fatal flaws, the necessity of freeing the powers of imagination to envision such a future is critical.

Overtly brazen assertions of the racial superiority of Canadians, widely celebrated until the mid-twentieth century, were somewhat tempered following the liberalization of the settler society prompted by increased migrations from the global South, as well as by the public attention commanded by the anti-colonial struggles of indigenous peoples, the national independence movements of the colonial world, and the Civil Rights and anti-racist movements in the hypercapitalist world. However, the liberalization of Canadian society did not demolish, but rather reformulated, the institution of white supremacy.

The facticity of the heterogeneous nature of the population continues to be evaded by state policies that remain committed to reproducing the racial homogeniety that sustains the nation-state's imagining of itself as primarily 'white' and 'western'. In this endeavour, the U.S. led war on terrorism is a boon to governing elites who have made it the occasion to further consolidate the construct of the true national as a western subject, while constructing the not insignificant presence of people of colour as a potentially deadly threat to the nation. The present danger that global terror is said to present to the nation reinvokes and fuses the historical fears of the various 'threats' that outsiders have always been imagined to visit upon the nation. The conflation of these various threats, and of the different groups they are said to emanate from, shape the terrain on which the present war is being waged.

Tapping into the anxieties of nationals whose claims of commitment to cultural pluralism were shaken by the 9/11 attacks on the United States, and whose racial superiority was likewise destabilized by the brutality of the war on terror, the current security-obsessed climate is providing a new public sanction for the growing anti-Muslim racism, as well as for the assertive claims of western civilizational superiority. Muslim communities in the country have acquired access to Canadian citizenship, but what is the security of this citizenship if the Muslim is constituted as a threat to the nation? How long will this citizenship protect the Muslim? The present demonization of Muslims (whether citizens, immigrants, or refugees) and the refusal to engage with serious and informed critiques of Canadian and American foreign policies in and by the mainstream media enable ruling elites to legitimize and sustain the 'new' world order with its perpetual wars under U.S. dominance.

Contemporary media reinforcements of the 'terrorist threat' as emanating from a non-western enemy, whose hate is directed against the entire west, has enabled the intensification of the transnational racial alliances that uphold white supremacy at a global level. A national Canadian identity is thus being reinscribed as synonymous with a transnational western identity. In other words, in order to be a real citizen, the subject either has to be western or has to unquestioningly subscribe to the claim of the west being the 'best.' Facilitating the right of global mobility long enjoyed by white subjects, and of a global entitlement that allows them access to the best part of the planet's resources, has historically been central to the mission of this west. That mission is today finding expression in the new invasions and occupations under the aegis of the American Empire, with Canada being an indispensable, and thus far a willing, accomplice. How well and for how long such an alliance might last remains to be seen, as does the question of how effectively the concept of the west can be restored to a place of global hegemony without the ongoing resort to military power that undermines such claims to civilizational superiority.

The impact of the war on terror on hegemonic imaginings of Canadian nationality, its allies and its interests, will have far-reaching and profound consequences. The divisive and overtly colonial legacy encapsulated in the concept of the west has acquired a robust resurgence, with non-westerners subjected to a barrage of the self-exaltations that it allows. The definition of the nation's interests as compatible – if not completely synonymous – with that of the United States, strengthens white racial bonding, boding ill for the future of all outsiders to this western fraternity. The resurgence of this nostalgic discourse enables all who are included as true national subjects to assert their individual claims to civilizational superiority in their encounters with non-western Others. The most obvious danger of the resurgence of this discourse is the intensification of racial and ethnic polarization inside Canada and at the global level. It further marginalizes immigrants and refugees in religious and cultural and civilizational terms, irrespective of their actual legal citizenship status. The reality that communities of Muslims live within the nation's territorial borders, that they have migrated in significant numbers since the liberalization of immigration policies in the 1970s, and that they have thus far posed no danger whatsoever to the nation is rendered irrelevant as the concept of the west becomes more deeply entrenched in daily life. With every assertion of its superiority, banal or otherwise, the distance between those of the 'west' and the 'rest' grows wider.

With a falling national birth rate, a growing birth rate among Aboriginal peoples, and the continuing need for immigrant labour, the possibility that non-white populations will once again become an allied and powerful enough presence to transform white supremacy remains real. This possible future gives rise to a crisis of whiteness in all settler societies that will grow more stark with every new generation. The potential of this changing demographic to transform the racial composition of the nation, as well as its symbolic identity, remains a distinct possibility in the forseeable future. It is from this crisis of whiteness that the actual threat of racial violence arises at the planetary level.

The intensification of the racially exclusionary aspects of Canadian immigration and citizenship legislation remains an option for containing such threats to the whiteness of the nation. Integrating immigrants more deeply into the racial and cultural hierarchy that sustains white supremacy might forestall such a future temporarily. Constituting the only good immigrant as the supplicant to the nation is the strategy currently operating to accomplish their complicity.

This book is not a full genealogy of the Canadian national subject. Mapping out this genealogy more completely is a task that remains to be undertaken, and the more that task remains unattended, the more necessary it becomes. What I have sought to do here is to lift the suffocating blanket of compassion imposed by nationals upon Aboriginal peoples and immigrants in daily strange encounters so that all can breath a little more easily.

In this work, I have sought to give new language to the experiences of the nation's various Others. The key point I have made is that particular subject positions, which exalt the humanity of their claimants, are made available to nationals even as they are closed off to other human beings through the networks of power. As the reproduction of the nation attests, nationals have, in the main, inhabited these subject positions. How enthusiastically and uncritically nationals do this, and whether they choose to contest or reject their nationality, is not the question addressed in this study. That, too, is a project for another day. For now, I have delineated one technique that reproduces nationality, exaltation, and I have done so with the hope that this project contributes to the erosion of its efficacy.

Appendix

Organization of the Social Security and Immigration Policy Reviews

My commitment is to listen to and work with all Canadians, different governments, groups and organizations so that we can develop in partnership a social framework that makes sense, is effective and is founded on the basic Canadian values of compassion and justice ...

While governments can and must provide leadership, they must answer to the people. All Canadians must share in finding the solutions we need to the problems of working, learning and security in the 1990s and beyond. This is an essential task to complete, if we are to preserve a social security system worthy of Canadians and equal to the times.[1]

Having defined social security and immigration as policy areas of key concern for the nation, the ministers of both departments called upon Canadians, as members of the nation, to work with the state in managing these 'problem' areas.[2] Defined as 'one of the most thorough and comprehensive Parliamentary reviews ever undertaken on Canadian social programs,'[3] the Social Security Review (SSR) was organized through a number of texts, chief among which was the document *Agenda: Jobs and Growth, Improving Social Security in Canada*, also known as The Green Paper.[4] The Parliamentary Standing Committee on Human Resources Development Canada was mandated to organize public consultations to define specific policy recommendations, and a Ministerial Task Force was appointed to work with the minister.[5]

After the tabling of The Green Paper, the finance minister presented the economic framework to the Parliamentary Standing Committee on Finance in October 1994, outlining the framework for the coming restructuring.[6] Following his presentation, the Parliamentary Standing Committee on Finance organized pre-budget consultations across the country. The main avenues for further consultations were to be these Parliamentary Standing Committees, which were to summarize and synthesize contributions regarding specific policy recommendations, following which there would be 'further public debate and negotiations with the provinces,' resulting in the tabling of legislation for policy reforms.[7] Additionally, Canadians were urged to express their views to their Members of Parliament and to participate in the concurrent public consultations and seminars. They were also urged to submit individual workbooks distributed by the ministry, and a number of organizations were provided funding to hold their own consultations.[8] The principles underlying the review were defined as creating opportunity in a rapidly changing global economy; investing in people; building mutual responsibility; preventing future problems; putting people first; greater fairness; and affordability.[9] The review itself was organized into three major policy areas: working, learning and security.[10]

The Immigration Policy Review (IPR) was organized somewhat differently. Whereas annual consultations on the immigration program have been organized since the 1970s,[11] the IPR was significantly unlike these, in that its mandate was to develop a strategy for immigration policy for the twenty-first century. As the Department of Immigration and Citizenship stated, the public consultations were intended to reach out to as many Canadians as possible.[12] This extensive review was deemed necessary as a result of the 'challenges' presented by changing global conditions to the 'effective management' of the immigration program.[13] The objectives outlined were twofold: first, 'to engage Canadians in an informed, constructive and positive discussion,' and second, to engage a 'broader spectrum' of Canadians in the process, not just the 'traditional stakeholders' in 'making choices and decisions that impact their communities and their country.'[14]

Ten issues were decided upon for discussion in the public consultations, as were the 'elements of an approach to consultation which would lead to the most productive discussion of these issues.'[15] Ten Working Groups of between ten to twenty 'experts' were appointed to examine each issue with their colleagues and other associations, and to submit reports with specific policy recommendations.[16] The co-convenors of the groups also met with the minister to make their respective recommendations in person. Issue #1, 'A Vision of Canada,' was assigned to the Parliamentary Standing Committee on Citizenship and Immigration, and a National Consultation on Family Class Immigration was also convened to deal specifically with this category.

In addition to the working groups, federal immigration officials organized consultations with provincial governments during May 1994, and deputy ministers at the federal/provincial/territorial levels met to develop their recommendations in July and October 1994. As with the SSR, Canadians were invited to participate in the public meetings and through direct written submissions to the Consultations Task Force.[17] Seven 'town-hall-type' public meetings were co-hosted by organizations solicited by the department, with over 1,600 participants in total.[18] Many Members of Parliament organized public meetings in their ridings, as did a number of other organizations and institutions.[20] School boards were asked to engage students in the discussion, and the minister also participated in open-line talk shows on radio and television stations and met with editorial boards of newspapers in the numerous communities he visited. The staff of Citizenship and Immigration, both inside the country and overseas, were asked to participate, and a series of focus groups were also organized by Insight Research Canada. Finally, a two-day National Conference was organized at the Government Conference Centre in Ottawa, with over 200 participants. In total, the department estimated that over 10,000 people participated directly in consultations between February and September 1994. Countless others were reached through the extensive media coverage of the review.

Notes

Introduction

1 Still intent on having Canadians navigate a 'new' world, this is how Mr Lloyd Axworthy, former minister of human resource development and of foreign affairs (1993–6) in the Chrétien Liberal government, envisioned the nation's 'special' role on the global stage. Lloyd Axworthy, *Navigating a New World: Canada's Global Future* (Toronto: Alfred A. Knopf, 2003), 1–7.

2 See R. Adamoski, D.E. Chunn, and R. Menzies, eds., *Contesting Canadian Citizenship: Historical Readings* (Peterborough, ON: Broadview Press, 2002).

3 The Foucauldian definition of the subject has been thus described by Prado: 'The new conception of the subject has two aspects. The first is that an individual is subject in the sense of *being subject* to regulation by other individuals, institutions and the state. The second aspect is that an individual is a subject on the sense of *experiencing subjectivity*, of being aware. But being a subject in this second sense is not merely being aware or conscious. It includes having aims, desires, and – most important in the present context – a self-image or sense of who and what one is. Throughout Foucault's discussions of subjects and subjectivity, particularly in his genealogical works, the notion of 'the subject' includes both of these aspects. 'Subject' and 'subjectivity' are used in ways that are deliberately ambiguous between the subject as a member of a governed society and as a self-aware identity.' C.G. Prado *Starting with Foucault: An Introduction to Genealogy* (Boulder, CO: Westview Press, 2000), 56.

4 An excellent example of the paranoia about outsiders wanting access only to the nation's resources is the widespread tendency to suspect refugees fleeing political persecution of 'really' being 'economic' migrants and to discount their claims on this basis. The popular stereotype of the 'bogus' asylum

258 Notes to page 4

claimant articulates this paranoia and suspicion most succinctly. For an
excellent discussion of this point in relation to women asylum claimants in
Canada, see Sherene H. Razack, *Looking White People in the Eye: Gender Race
and Culture in the Courtrooms and Classrooms* (Toronto: University of Toronto
Press, 1998), chap. 4.

5 Sara Ahmed, *Strange Encounters: Embodied Others in Post-Coloniality* (London:
Routledge, 2000).

6 In 1908, James S. Woodsworth, the first leader of the left-leaning political
party, the Co-operative Commonwealth Federation (CCF), penned a 'pioneer sociological study' on immigrants, *Strangers within Our Gates*. He began
by describing what the 'ordinary' Canadian 'knew' about the immigrant:
'What does the ordinary Canadian know about our immigrants? He classifies
all men as white and foreigners. The foreigners he thinks of as the men who
dig the sewers and get into trouble at the police court. They are all supposed
to dress in outlandish garb, to speak a barbarian tongue, and to smell abom-
inably' (9). Woodsworth sought to provide more accurate information about
these strangers, but 'strangers' they remained nonetheless, as the title he
chose for this work emphasizes. Woodsworth referred to other prominent
Canadians, including one Josiah Strong, as equally concerned about these
strangers: 'We may well ask whether this insweeping immigration is to for-
eignize us, or we are to Americanize it. Our safety demands the assimilation
of these strange populations, and the process of assimilation becomes slower
and more difficult as the proportion of foreigners increases' (233). J.S.
Woodsworth, *Strangers within Our Gates: Or Coming Canadians* (1909; reprint,
Toronto: University of Toronto Press, 1972).

7 Homi Bhabha has underscored the importance of narration in the cultural
construction of the nation. H. Bhabha, *The Location of Culture* (London:
Routledge, 1994).

8 This narrative of nationhood permeates numerous myths and public
accounts of 'Canadian-ness.' Eva Mackey has noted its presence in the myth
of the benevolent Mountie, 'based on the idea that the process of civilising
the frontier occurred in a gentler, less violent, manner in Canada than the
USA, because of British systems of justice, the benevolent and tolerant
behaviour of the Mounties,' in Eva Mackey, *The House of Difference: Cultural
Politics and National Identity in Canada* (Toronto: University of Toronto, Press,
2002) 76–7. She quotes Douglas Cardinal, the architect of the Canadian
Museum of Civilization, who reproduces this mythic national-ness: 'Canadians, with their roots in several different cultures, now are evolving a new culture. Their cultures are merging and a greater understanding and
appreciation are becoming part of Canada's national character. Our chal-

lenge should be to express the goals and aspirations of our society in our structure so that they will be physical manifestations of the best of our multi-cultural society' (75). For greater elaboration on the myths of the white set-tler society, see S. Razack, ed., *Race, Space, and the Law: Unmapping a White Settler Society* (Toronto: Between the Lines, 2002).

9 Benedict Anderson, *Imagined Communities* (London: Verso, 1996).

10 For excellent critiques of western ontologies, see Frantz Fanon, *Black Skin, White Masks* (London: Pluto Press, 1986); Edward Said, *Orientalism: Western Conceptions of the Orient* (London: Penguin, 1978); Stuart Hall, 'Who Needs Identity?' in S. Hall and P. du Gay, eds., *Questions of Cultural Identity* (London: Sage, 1996) 1–17; and Ahmed, *Strange Encounters*.

11 See M. Foucault, *The History of Sexuality: An Introduction*, vol. 1 (New York: Vintage, 1990); Prado, *Starting with Foucault*; Hall, 'Who Needs Identity?'; Fanon, *Black Skin, White Masks*.

12 In *The History of Sexuality*, Foucault defines discourse as follows: 'Indeed, it is in discourse that power and knowledge are joined together. And for this very reason, we must conceive discourse as a series of discontinuous segments whose tactical function is neither uniform nor stable. To be more precise, we must not imagine a world of discourse divided between accepted discourse and excluded discourse, or between the dominant discourse and the domi-nated one; but as a multiplicity of discursive elements that can come into play in various strategies. It is this distribution that we must reconstruct, with the things said and those concealed, the enunciations required and those forbidden, that it comprises; with the variants and different effects – accord-ing to who is speaking, his position of power, the institutional context in which he happens to be situated – that it implies; and in the shifts and reuti-lizations of identical formulas for contrary objectives that it also includes. Discourses are not once and for all subservient to power or raised up against it, any more than silences are. We must make allowance for the complex and unstable process whereby discourse can be both an instrument and an effect of power, but also a hindrance, a stumbling-block, a point of resistance and a starting point for an opposing strategy. Discourse transmits and produces power; it reinforces it, but also undermines and exposes it, renders it fragile and makes it possible to thwart it' (100–101).

Explicating Foucault's complex use of the concept of discourse, Sara Mills identifies three ways in which he defines it: (1) as 'the domain of all state-ments,' i.e., including all 'utterances and texts'; (2) as 'an individualizable group of statements,' i.e., 'groups of utterances which seem to be regulated in some way and which seem to have a coherence and a force to them in common', and (3) as 'a regulated practice which accounts for a number of statements,' i.e., 'he is less interested in the actual utterances/texts that are produced than in the rules and structures which produce particular utterances and texts.' See Sara Mills, *Discourse* (London: Routledge, 1997), 7.

13 J.D. Faubion expands on Foucault's notion of bio-power: 'This form of power that applies itself to immediate everyday life categorizes the individual, marks him by his own individuality, attaches him to his own identity, imposes a law of truth on him that he must recognize and others have to recognize in him. It is a form of power that makes individuals subjects.' J.D. Faubion, ed., *Michel Foucault: Power* (New York: The New Press, 1994), 331. Prado explains that Foucault's concept of the constructed 'subject' treats it as just one method of organization of the self: 'Because of the constitutive role of discourse and the possibilities thus afforded, he [Foucault] maintains that 'the subject ... is obviously only one of the possibilities of organizing a consciousness of self.' He asks whether 'the subject is the only form of existence possible,' and whether there might not be 'experiences in which the subject ... is not given any more,' which might not be subject-centred. For instance, we might have been multiple 'personalities' and conscious from different perspectives in a way that we presently think is pathological. Nonetheless, however difficult to imagine, Foucault conceives of the subject as historical, as a particular, and as a kind.' Prado, *Starting with Foucault*, 79.

14 Foucault, quoted in ibid., 71.

15 Foucault identified the myriad of discursive practices pervasive within society, those embedded within social institutions as well as those within the intimate spaces of the self, as practices constitutive of the subject, ibid.

16 Prado explains that in the *History of Sexuality*, Foucault 'stresses that the deployment of sexuality reflected a crucial change in how people are managed and their behaviour regulated. The change was from "dealing simply with legal subjects over whom the ultimate dominion was "death" to a "taking charge of life."' Ibid., 105.

17 For an interesting discussion of feminist responses, see Margaret A. McLaren, *Feminism, Foucault, and Embodied Subjectivity* (Albany: State University of New York Press, 2002).

18 My use of the notion of a 'structure of humanity' is informed by Raymond Williams's work on the 'structure of feeling.' For an excellent discussion of this concept, see Jennifer Harding and E. Deidre Pribham, 'Losing Our Cool? Following Williams and Grossberg on Emotions,' *Cultural Studies* 18, no. 6. (2004), 863–83.

19 In *Capital*, Marx defined as commodity fetishism the process by which material objects are imputed with a value that comes to be seen as their natural

property, and not the result of the social relations which lead to the production of these objects as commodities. For a good summary of Marx's theory of commodity fetishism, see T. Bottomore et al., *A Dictionary of Marxist Thought* (Cambridge, MA: Harvard University Press, 1983).

20 Achille Mbembe *On the Postcolony* (Berkeley: University of California Press, 2001), 25.

21 Ibid., 26.

22 Achille Mbembe, 'Necropolitics,' *Public Culture: Violence and Redemption* 15, no. 1 (Winter 2003), 11.

23 See Fanon, *Black Skin, White Masks*. See also N. Gibson, 'Losing Sight of the Real,' in R. Bernasconi and S. Cook, eds., *Race & Racism in Continental Philosophy* (Bloomington: Indiana University Press, 2003), 129–50.

24 Fanon, *Black Skin, White Masks*, 110.

25 W.E.B. Du Bois, *The Souls of Black Folks* (New York: Bantham, 1989), 3.

26 Fanon, *Black Skin, White Masks*, xv.

27 Fanon describes the crushing effect of his encounter with the white child: '"Look, a Negro!" It was an external stimulus that flicked over me as I passed by. I made a tight smile. "Look, a Negro!" It was true it amused me. "Look, a Negro!" The circle was drawing a bit tighter. I made no secret of my amusement. "Mama, see the Negro! I'm frightened!" Frightened! Frightened! Now they were beginning to be afraid of me. I made up my mind to laugh myself to tears, but laughter had become impossible.'" Ibid., 111–12.

28 Bonita Lawrence, *'Real' Indians and Others: Mixed-Blood Urban Native Peoples and Indigenous Nationhood* (Vancouver: UBC Press, 2004).

29 Ibid., 1.

30 Ibid., 5. Lawrence notes that Native peoples were treated as 'contemporary interlopers ... because they held paying jobs, lived in houses, consumed pizza and other European foods, and in general lived contemporary lives' (4).

31 In *Strange Encounters*, Ahmed makes the following point about the role of the stranger: 'To be alien in a particular nation, is to hesitate at a different border: the alien here is the one who does not belong in a nation space, and who is already defined as such by the Law. The alien is hence only a category within a given community of citizens or subjects: as the outsider inside, the alien takes on a spatial function, establishing relations of proximity and distance within the home (land). Aliens allow the demarcation of spaces of belonging: by coming too close to home, they establish the very necessity of policing the borders of knowable and inhabitable terrains' (3).

32 Ibid., 21. Ahmed goes on to discuss some of the dangers said to emanate

from the figure of the stranger: 'The stranger is clearly figured in a variety of discourses, including the crime prevention and personal safety discourse of "stranger danger" ... In such a discourse, which is clearly a field of knowledge that marks out what is safe as well as what is dangerous, the stranger is always a figure, stalking the streets: there are some-bodies who simply are strangers, and who pose danger in their very co-presence in a given street. The assumption that we can tell the difference between strangers and neighbours which is central to, for example, neighbourhood watch programmes, functions to conceal forms of social difference. By defining "us" against any-body who is a stranger, what is concealed is that some-bodies are already recognized as stranger and more dangerous than other bodies' (3–4).

33 Ahmed explains: 'By analysing recognition in this way, I am suggesting that the (lawful) subject is not simply constituted by being recognized by the other, which is the primary post-Hegelian model of recognition ... Rather, I am suggesting that it is the recognition of others that is central to the constitution of the subject. The very act through which the subject differentiates between others is the moment that the subject comes to inhabit or dwell in the world. The subject is not, then, simply differentiated from the (its) other, but comes into being by learning how to differentiate between others. This recognition operates as *a visual economy*: it involves ways of *seeing the difference* between familiar and strange others as they are (re)presented to the subject. As a mode of subject constitution, recognition involves differentiating between others on the basis of how they "appear."' Ibid., 24.

34 See Women, Immigration and Nationality Group (WING), *World's Apart: Women Under Immigration and Nationality Law* (London: Pluto Press, 1985); Teresa Hayter, *Open Borders: The Case against Immigration Controls* (London: Pluto Press, 2000); and B. Singh Bolaria, and Peter S. Li, *Racial Oppression in Canada* (Toronto: Garamond Press, 1985). An important exception to this approach has been the work of Aihwa Ong, who has developed the concept of 'flexible citizenship' in examining the transnational practices of elite Chinese immigrants, including their holding of multiple passports, as they seek to maximize their access to power, capital, and status by negotiating the different forms of sovereign power to which they are subject. See A. Ong, *Flexible Citizenship: The Cultural Logics of Transnationality* (Durham, NC: Duke University Press, 1999).

35 Chinese Canadian National Council (CCNC), *Jin Guo: Voices of Chinese Canadian Women* (Toronto: The Women's Book Committee, CCNC, 1992). See also Bolaria and Li, *Racial Oppression in Canada*; and Norman Buchignani, and Doreen Indra, with Ram Srivastava *Continuous Journey* (Toronto: McClelland and Stewart, 1985).

36 I do not wish to suggest that there is no heterogeneity within the category 'immigrant.' Immigrants come from very different historical experiences and diverse backgrounds and are also marked by the social relations of gender, class, sexuality, disability, and so on. However, the category immigrant subsumes these differences by imposing a homogeneity onto them.

37 This is how Elie Kedourie defined the modernist doctrine of nationalism: '... a doctrine invented in Europe at the beginning of the nineteenth century. It pretends to supply a criterion for the determination of the unit of population proper to enjoy a government exclusively its own, for the legitimate exercise of power in the state, and for the right of organization of a society of states. Briefly, the doctrine holds that humanity is naturally divided into nations, that nations are known by certain characteristics which can be ascertained, and that the only legitimate type of government is national self-government.' Quoted in G. Eley, and R.G. Suny, eds., *Becoming National: A Reader* (New York: Oxford University Press, 1996), 6.

38 For a recent and very popular version of this narrative, see *A People's History of Canada*. The television docudrama series was conceived and produced by Mark Starowicz and CBC-TV News, 2001. It initially was broadcast on the Canadian Broadcasting Corporation in 2000, and repeatedly broadcast since on multiple channels in multiple languages. Canadian nationhood is complicated by the often conflictual relationship between the two contending colonizing powers, the French and the British. While the two powers had conflicting interests with regard to their respective control of the territory and the cultural identity of the emerging nation, both powers shared a common goal in their commitment to the colonization of Aboriginal peoples. Hegemonic Canadian nationhood has remained fraught with the historical tensions between these two national groups, but the whiteness of the two groups has also created a racial commonality between them in regard to their dealings with Aboriginal populations and with immigrants.

39 See E. Balibar and I. Wallerstein, eds., *Race, Nation, Class: Ambiguous Identities* (London: Verso, 1991), 37–68.

40 Benedict Anderson, *Imagined Communities* (London: Verso, 1991), 6–7.

41 P. Chatterjee, 'Nationalist Thought and the Colonial World' in *The Partha Chatterjee Omnibus* (New Delhi: Oxford University Press, 1999), 17.

42 Peter Fitzpatrick, 'Introduction,' in P. Fitzpatrick, ed., *Nationalism, Racism and the Rule of Law* (Aldershot, UK: Dartmouth Publishing, 1995), xv–xvi.

43 Peter Fitzpatrick, "'We Know What It Is When You Do Not Ask Us': Nationalism as Racism," in Fitzpatrick, ed., *Nationalism, Racism and the Rule of Law*, 3–26.

44 Ibid., 15.

45 Ibid., 17. Fitzpatrick, like others, has pointed out that the building of the nation, its coherence and integrity, both manufacture and rely upon 'a pervasive and refined racism' (4).

46 Ahmed, *Strange Encounters*, 8–9.

47 Peter O'Neil, 'Vancouver Could See Race Riots: Study Says,' *Vancouver Sun*, 23 September 2002, A1.

48 Frank Luba, 'Report: Keep Immigrants Out of the Big Three Cities,' *The Province*, 24 September 2002, A6.

49 In a similar vein to the study mentioned above, numerous 'experts' on immigration regularly and vociferously argue that Canadians are ill served by overly generous immigration and refugee protection policies that allow unscrupulous immigrants and bogus refugee claimants to gain access to the nation's precious resources. See Daniel Stoffman, *Who Gets In: What's Wrong with Canada's Immigration Program, and How to Fix It* (Toronto: Macfarlane Walter and Ross, 2002). Immigrants are also routinely said to masquerade as refugees. Canada's oldest national newspaper informed its readers in an editorial that 'immigrants are routinely granted refugee status despite coming from peaceful democracies such as Hungary and Mexico.' Editorial, 'Rejecting Song Dae Ri,' *Globe and Mail*, 4 February 2004, A18.

  Most recently, the minister of citizenship and immigration claimed that economic migrants were widely posing as refugees. Vowing to reform refugee policy, she argued, 'There's a problem and everyone knows there's a problem ... From what I've seen, people [in the refugee system] are economic migrants more than anything else.' See Marina Jimenez, 'Minister Targets Bogus Refugees,' *Globe and Mail*, 11 November 2004, A1. Canadian immigration policy, long defined as humanitarian and compassionate, is argued to no longer serve the nation's interest. Advocating the restriction of this policy to allow only the entry of the 'right' kind of immigrants, that is, skilled workers who contribute to the nation's prosperity, immigration policy is popularly presented as allowing too many unskilled immigrants into the country, along with their numerous dependents.

50 Foucault, quoted in Prado, *Starting with Foucault*, 77.

51 Ibid., 76.

52 Prado elaborates on the Foucauldian concept of the 'development of political technology': 'What is new in Foucault's consideration of pervasive management is description of how it is achieved not just through restrictions, but through enabling conceptions, definitions, and descriptions that generate and support behaviour-governing norms. What is also new, and intellectually jarring, is description of this degree of management as requiring the complicity of those managed. Complicity is required because what needs to be

achieved are not only obedience to the law, but also what is more clearly the-matized in *The History of Sexuality*. That is the deep internalization of a care-fully orchestrated value-laden understanding of the self.' Ibid., 55.

Foucault explains his thesis that power is 'everywhere': 'The analysis, made in terms of power, must not assume that the sovereignty of the state, the form of the law, or the over-all unity of a domination are given at the outset: rather, these are only the terminal form power takes. It seems to me that power must be understood in the first instance as the multiplicity of force relations immanent in the sphere in which they operate and which consti-tute their own organization; as the process which, through ceaseless strug-gles and confrontations, transforms, strengthens, or reverses them; as the support which these force relations find in one another, thus forming a chain or a system, or on the contrary, the disjunctions and contradictions which isolate them from one another; and lastly, as the strategies in which they take effect, whose general design or institutional crystallization is embodied in the state apparatus, in the formulation of the law, in the various social hegemonies. Power's condition of possibility ... even in its more 'peripheral' effects, and which also makes it possible to use its mechanisms as a grid of intelligibility of the social order, must not be sought in the pri-mary existence of a central point, in a unique source of sovereignty from which secondary and descendant forms would emanate; it is the moving sub-strate of force relations which, by virtue of their inequality, constantly engen-der states of power, but the latter are always local and unstable. The omnipresence of power: not because it has the privilege of consolidating everything under its invincible unity, but because it is produced from one moment to the next, at every point, or rather in every relation from one point to another. Power is everywhere, not because it embraces everything, but because it comes from everywhere.' *The History of Sexuality*, 92–3.

53 Chatterjee, *The Partha Chatterjee Omnibus*, 18.
54 For further discussion of the racialization of rights, see P. Chatterjee, *The Nation and Its Fragments: Colonial and Postcolonial Histories* (New Delhi: Oxford University Press, 1995); Mbembe, 'Necropolitics,' 11; M. Omi and H. Winant, *Racial Formation in the United States: From the 1960s to the 1990s* (New York: Routledge, 1994); D.T. Goldberg, *The Racial State* (Malden, MA: Black-well, 2002).
55 Goldberg explains: 'Seemingly by contrast, but in fact relatedly, colonizing states like Britain and the Netherlands proceeded on an assumption of inter-nalized population homogeneity, of ethnoracial sameness and of externaliz-ing difference. They were able to sustain at least a semblance of the charade by purporting nominally to keep the different out and at bay lest they undo

by infecting the rationality of brotherhood, thus toppling reason's rule. The creation and promotion of difference is the necessary condition of repro- ducing homogenized sameness; and (re-) producing homogeneity necessar- ily promotes the externalization of difference to produce its effect.' Goldberg, *The Racial State*, 31.

56 Ibid., 2, 4.

57 Omi and Winant describe this role of the racialized state: 'Through policies which are explicitly or implicitly racial, state institutions organize and rein- force the racial politics of everyday life ... They organize racial identities by means of education, family law, and the procedures for punishment, treat- ment, and surveillance of the criminal, deviant and ill.' *Racial Formation in the United States*, 83.

58 H. Winant, *Racial Conditions* (Minneapolis: University of Minnesota, 1994), xi.

59 See Himani Bannerji, *The Dark Side of the Nation: Essays on Multiculturalism, Nationalism and Gender* (Toronto: Women's Press, 2000).

60 In *The Partha Chatterjee Omnibus*, Chatterjee examines the controversies related to the Ilbert Bill Affair (18) and the Nil Durpan Affair in this analysis (22).

61 Ibid., 24.

62 Ghassan Hage, *White Nation: Fantasies of White Supremacy in a Multicultural Society* (London: Routledge, 2000).

1. Founding a Lawful Nation

1 Frantz Fanon, *The Wretched of the Eart* (New York: Grove Press, 1963), 38–9.

2 This is how Prime Minister MacKenzie King paid tribute to the Canadians who had made nationhood possible upon the creation of the first Citizen- ship Act in 1947: 'The vision and courage of men and women have trans- formed our country, almost within living memory, from small and virtually unknown regions of forest and farm into one of the great industrial nations of the world.' The prime minister's comments erase the reality that 'our' country was stolen from Aboriginal peoples and make invisible the existence of indigenous societies by designating Canada as having been among the 'virtually unknown regions' of the world. See MacKenzie King, 'Text of the Prime Minister's Speech,' *Ottawa Citizen*, 4 January 1947. A contemporary version of this myth of a new people building a new world informs the much acclaimed television docudrama, *A People's History of Canada*, Canadian Broadcasting Corporation, in 2000.

3 It should be noted that the insistence on the rule of law as a legitimizing

principle for colonization was pervasive within the British empire. David Cannadine outlines this dominant imperial historiography: '[T]he British Empire was a formally constituted political entity, and from that perspective its history was for the most part concerned with law, governance and constitutional evolution. In the hands of such historians as Arthur Barriedale Keith and Sir Kenneth Wheare, the dominant theme of the empire story was the export of British constitutional practices and their successful establishment in newly evolving nations around the globe. Thanks largely to Lord Durham (so this argument ran), British-style responsible government was established in Canada in the 1840s, and it subsequently spread to Australia, New Zealand and South Africa, whose constitutional equality with the mother country was eventually acknowledged in the Statute of Westminster, passed in 1931.' David Cannadine, *Ornamentalism: How the British Saw Their Empire* (Oxford: Oxford University Press, 2001), xiv.

4 Fanon, *The Wretched of the Earth* (36).

5 Ali Behdad, 'Eroticism, Colonialism and Violence,' in Hent de Vries and S. Weber, eds., *Violence, Identity, and Self-Determination* (Stanford: Stanford University Press, 1997), 202.

6 Walter Benjamin, *Selected Writings*, ed. M. Bullock and M. Jennings, vol. 1 (Cambridge, MA: Harvard University Press, 1996), 248.

7 Ibid. Emphasis in original.

8 Giorgio Agamben, *Homo Sacer: Sovereign Power and Bare Life* (Stanford: Stanford University Press, 1997), 15.

9 Ibid., 17–18. Emphasis in original.

10 Foucault, *The History of Sexuality* (88–9).

11 See Fanon, *The Wretched of the Earth*, and Mbembe, *On the Postcolony.*

12 I am indebted to Dara Culhane for suggesting the use of this term. See her *The Pleasure of the Crown: Anthropology, Law and First Nations* (Burnaby, BC: Talonbooks, 1998).

13 Mbembe, *On the Postcolony*, 26. Emphasis in original.

14 Agamben, *Homo Sacer.* Homo sacer was a figure in ancient Roman law: 'The sacred man is the one whom the people have judged on account of a crime. It is not permitted to sacrifice this man, yet he who kills him will not be condemned for homicide; in the first tribunition law, in fact, it is noted that 'if someone kills the one who is sacred according to the plebiscite, it will not be considered homicide.' This is why it is customary for a bad or impure man to be called sacred' (71).

15 Ibid., 82.

16 Ibid., 1.

17 This is a position adopted by progressive social movements in Canada,

including the women's and labour movements. The concept recognizes the British, French, and Aboriginal peoples as having founded the nation together. I should point out that many of the women's organizations that I have worked with in the past, including the National Action Committee on the Status of Women, where I served as president of the organization, subscribed to this concept.

18 A number of theorists have argued this point. See Culhane, *The Pleasure of the Crown.*

19 Quoted in Ronald Wright, *Stolen Continents: The 'New World' Through Indian Eyes* (Toronto: Penguin, 1993), 4.

20 Ibid., 8.

21 For an excellent discussion of the relationship of law to colonization in Canada, see Culhane, *The Pleasure of the Crown.*

22 Mbembe, *On the Postcolony,* 16.

23 Ibid., 25. Fitzpatrick's recognition that the law has been an absolutely vital instrument of nation-formation supports Mbembe's thesis. In becoming identified with the nation-state, Fitzpatrick argues, the law came to override other forms of authority. See Fitzpatrick, ed., 'Introduction,' *Nationalism, Racism and the Rule of Law.*

24 Mbembe, *On the Postcolony,* 25.

25 See Elizabeth Vibert, 'Real Men Hunt Buffalo: Masculinity, Race and Class in British Fur Trader's Narratives,' in Joy Parr and Mark Rosenfeld, eds., *Gender and History in Canada* (Toronto: Copp Clark, 1996), 50–68; Wright, *Stolen Continents*; Boyce Richardson, *Peoples of Terra Nullius: Betrayal and Rebirth in Aboriginal Canada* (Vancouver: Douglas and McIntyre, 1993); Culhane, *The Pleasure of the Crown.* Historians have documented that the initial contact between the Europeans – the French and the British – and the Aboriginal peoples in what came to be known as Canada resulted in the development of the fur trade. These Europeans were more interested in acquiring furs for the European market than in permanent settlement, but the traders and the missionaries, who soon developed their own domains within the colonies, were to be the 'advance guard of colonialism' as the fur trade gave way to colonization proper as their settlements increased (Vibert, 'Real Men Hunt Buffalo'). The attendant dispossession of Aboriginal peoples' territories and economic resources was integral to the settlement policies of white settler colonies within the British Empire, including the United States, Canada, New Zealand, and Australia.

26 'Mundo la reves' is how Felipe Waman Puma, an Inca contemporary of Shakespeare, referred to the post-conquest world in which he lived (Wright, *Stolen Continents,* 8). For accounts of the colonization of the Americas, see

also Richardson, *Peoples of Terra Nulius*; Howard Zinn, *A People's History of the United States* (New York: Harper Collins, 1980); Eduardo Galeano, *Open Veins of Latin America: Five Centuries of the Pillage of a Continent* (New York: Monthly Review Press, 1973); Joyce A. Green, 'Towards a Détente with History: Confronting Canada's Colonial Legacy,' *International Journal of Canadian Studies* 12 (Fall 1995), 85–105.

27 Vandana Shiva has described this violence as follows: 'Denying other cultures their rights on the basis of their difference from European culture was convenient for taking away their resources and wealth. The Church authorized European monarchs to attack, conquer, and subdue non-believers, to capture their goods and their territories, and to transfer their lands and properties. Five hundred years ago, Columbus carried this worldview to the New World. And millions of people and thousands of other living species lost their right to exist under the first wave of globalization,' in Vandana Shiva, *Biopiracy: The Plunder of Nature and Knowledge* (Toronto: Between the Lines, 1997), 106.

28 Richardson, *Peoples of Terra Nullius*, 27.

29 Governor Cornwallis of Nova Scotia announced in 1749: 'His Majesty's Council do promise a reward of ten Guineas for every Indian Micmac taken or killed, to be paid upon producing such Savage taken or his scalp (as in the custom of the America) if killed to the Officer Commanding at Halifax, Annapolis Royal or Minas.' In Dean Neu and Richard Therrien, *Accounting for Genocide: Canada's Bureaucratic Assault on Aboriginal People* (Halifax: Fernwood, 2003), 30.

30 This is how Bonita Lawrence describes the 'destructive processes' brought into play to destroy Native societies: 'These processes have included deliberately introduced diseases and alcoholism, wholesale land appropriation, resource plundering practices, the deliberate use of starvation tactics, settler violence and organized military violence to subjugate communities and suppress resistance, centuries of widespread and concerted attacks on Indigenous spiritual and ceremonial life, and finally the theft of Native children, first into residential schools and then into the foster care system.' B. Lawrence, *'Real' Indians and Others: Mixed-Blood Urban Native Peoples and Indigenous Nationhood* (Vancouver: UBC Press, 2004), 17.

31 The scale of this genocide has been called 'the most appalling holocaust in human history' by Boyce Richardson, *Peoples of Terra Nullius*, 3. Ronald Wright estimates the population of Native Americans to have been around 100 million in 1492 (*Stolen Continents*, 4). Eduardo Galeano estimates the population of the Americas at 70 million, which was reduced to 3.5 million within a century and a half (*Open Veins of Latin America*, 50). Howard Zinn

estimates that the population in North America was 10 million prior to the coming of Columbus, and was brought down to less than one million (*A People's History of the United States*, 16). The diseases brought by the Europeans, such as smallpox, devastated these populations. Although the full effect of these diseases on the depopulation of indigenous societies is not known, there is little doubt about the intense violence and brutality of the European conquest in the extensive historical literature. Ward Churchill has also specifically examined the violence against Indigenous peoples in North America. See Ward Churchill, *A Little Matter of Genocide: Holocaust and Denial in the Americas 1492 to the Present* (San Francisco: City Light Books, 1997).

32 Bonita Lawrence expands on the use of this threat: 'Looking north of the border, the fact that Canada was able to pacify the Indigenous peoples of half a continent on a virtually nonexistent military budget cannot be understood without taking into account how British officials have *always* used the threat of warfare and its attendant starvation south of the border to control Native populations in Canada. In a sense Canada piggybacked off of American Manifest Destiny, using the starvation and territorial limitation brought about by the destruction of the buffalo and the Indian wars to the south to force treaties on captured populations in the north, all the while maintaining a posture of innocence and denial about the fundamentally violent nature of the colonial process in Canada' (*'Real' Indians and Others*, 30).

33 To the idea of 'discovery,' Dehatkadons, chief of the Onondaga Iroquois, responded: 'You cannot discover an inhabited land. Otherwise I could cross the Atlantic and "discover" England' (Wright, *Stolen Continents*, 5).

34 For a fuller discussion of these concepts, see Green, 'Towards a Détente with History'; Culhane, *The Pleasure of the Crown*; Wright, *Stolen Continents*; and Richardson, *People of Terra Nullius*.

35 Papal Bulls, the Columbus Charter, and the patents granted by European monarchs laid the juridical and moral foundations for the colonization and extermination of non-European peoples. For one example, the Papal Bull of Donation was granted by Pope Alexander VI to Queen Isabelle of Castille and King Ferdinand of Aragon in 1493. The Bull gave all lands 'discovered and to be discovered, one hundred leagues to the West and South of the Azores towards India' not owned by a Christian king to these two monarchs (Shiva, *Biopiracy*, 1).

36 For example, the Spanish King, Charles V, called upon Juan Gines de Sepulveda, a philosopher, and Bartolomeo de Las Casas, a Dominican monk, at the Conference of Valladolid in 1550 to ascertain whether conquest and settlement could be undertaken justly (Culhane, *The Pleasure of the Crown*, 37–8). In this conference, Sepulveda argued that the racial inferiority of

indigenous peoples allowed their subjugation by the superior European
races while Las Casas held the position that indigenous peoples 'possessed
an evolved culture' and could be colonized only if the intent was to Chris-
tianize them.

37 Spanish conquistadors took the step of reading aloud to the peoples they
intended to conquer a truly extraordinary document, the *Requiromento*. Its
recitation apparently removed 'the stain of innocent blood from the Spanish
king's immortal soul.' The conquistador Francisco Pizarro recited the following words from this *Requiromento* to the Incas: 'I, Francisco Pizarro, servant of
the high and mighty kings of Castile and Leon, conquerors of barbarian peoples, and being their messenger and Captain, hereby notify and inform you
... that God Our Lord, One and Eternal, created Heaven and Earth and a
man and a woman from whom you and I and all the people of the world are
descended ... Because of the great multitude begotten from these over the
past five thousand and some years since the world was made ... God placed
one called Saint Peter in charge over all these peoples ... And so I request
and require you ... to recognize the Church as your Mistress and as Govern-
ess of the World and Universe, and the High Priest, called the Pope, in Her
name, and his Majesty [King of Spain] in her place, as Ruler and Lord King
... And if you do not do this ... with the help of God I shall come mightily
against you, and I shall make war on you everywhere and in every way that I
can, and I shall subject you to the yoke and obedience of the Church and his
Majesty, and I shall seize your women and children, and I shall make them
slaves, to sell and dispose of as His Majesty commands, and I shall do all the
evil and damage to you that I am able. And I insist that the deaths and
destruction that result from this will be your fault.' To this declaration, the
chiefs of Sinu are reported to have replied: 'The holy father has indeed been
generous with others' property.' Quoted in Wright, *Stolen Continents*, 65–6.

38 Peter Fitzpatrick, '"We Know What It Is When You Do Not Ask Us": Nationalism as Racism,' in Fitzpatrick, ed., *Nationalism, Racism and the Rule of Law*, iii.

39 Quoted in James S. Frideres, *Native People in Canada: Contemporary Conflicts*
(Scarborough, ON: Prentice-Hall, 1983), 2.

40 Antony Anghie points out that although Hugo Grotius is generally said to be
the 'principal forerunner of modern international law,' he was deeply
indebted to Francisco de Vitoria's conceptualization of international law.
Antony Anghie, 'Francisco de Vitoria and the Colonial Origins of International Law,' in E. Darian-Smith and P. Fitzpatrick, eds., *Laws of the Post Colonial* (Ann Arbor: The University of Michigan Press, 1999), 90. Emphasis in
original.

41 Vitoria stated: 'If after the Spaniards have used all diligence, both in deed

and in word, to show that nothing will come from them to interfere with the peace and well-being of the aborigines, the latter nevertheless persist in their hostility and do their best to destroy the Spaniards, they can make war on the Indians, no longer as innocent folk, but as against forsworn enemies and may enforce against them all the rights of war, despoiling them of their goods, reducing them to captivity, deposing of their former lords and setting up new ones, yet wherewithal observance of proportion as regards the nature of the circumstances and of the wrongs done to them.' Ibid., 98.

42 Ibid., 100.

43 Culhane, *The Pleasure of the Crown*, 39.

44 Ibid.

45 Culhane discusses the centrality of the 1608 *Calvin's Case* regarding the colonization of Ireland, which held that 'if a Christian King should conquer a kingdom of an infidel, and bring them under his subjection, there ipso facto the laws of the infidels are abrogated, for that they be not only against Christianity, but against the law of God and of nature.' Ibid., 47.

46 Ibid., 48. Emphasis in original.

47 See ibid., 54, and Wright, *Stolen Continents*, 54.

48 Daiva Stasiulis and Radha Jhappan have pointed out that this 'protection was warranted by the political necessity to keep the peace under settler colonialism.' Daiva Stasiulis and Radha Jhappan, 'The Fractious Politics of a Settler Society: Canada' in Daiva Stasiulis and Nira Yuval-Davis, eds., *Unsettling Settler Societies: Articulations of Gender, Race, Ethnicity and Class* (London: Sage, 1995), 107.

While the Royal Proclamation is often cited as recognizing Aboriginal presence and entitlement, and is said to have defined indigenous peoples as 'autonomous and self-governing,' Eva Mackey points to the 'self-deception and hypocrisy' that infuse these claims, arguing that many who made such claims also 'expressed gratitude that Providence had sent epidemics and intertribal wars to sweep away the native populations of Southern Ontario and Quebec, thus leaving the regions for French and English settlers.' Mackey, *The House of Difference*, 25.

49 Culhane, *The Pleasure of the Crown*, 55.

50 In addition to the Royal Proclamation, Lord Sumner's Dictum of 1919, which held that indigenous people's claims to land had to be evaluated with reference to their level of evolution within the context of the Social Darwinist framework of human development, has been pertinent to Aboriginal land claims. Ibid., 67–8.

51 These indigenous societies in the Americas included 'nomadic hunting groups, settled farming communities, and dazzling civilizations with cities as

large as any then on earth' (Wright, *Stolen Continents*, 5). For readers interested in a substantive discussion of the varied economic, cultural and military systems among the various indigenous peoples, Ronald Wright's book provides an excellent read. Anthropologist Dara Culhane in *The Pleasure of the Crown* has pointed out that before the settlement of Europeans in the Americas, approximately 500 Aboriginal nations had lived in various social formations on the lands that are known today as North America (42).

52 Women are known to have held high political, social and moral authority in Aboriginal societies and were actively engaged in trading and other economic activities. They were spiritual leaders in some societies and hosted such important ceremonies as potlatches. See Marjorie Mitchell and Anna Franklin, 'When You Don't Know the Language, Listen to the Silence: An Historical Overview of Native Indian Women in BC,' in Barbara K. Latham and Roberta J. Pazdro, eds., *Not Just Pin Money: Selected Essays in the History of Women's Work in British Columbia* (Victoria: Camosun College, 1984); Sylvia Van Kirk, 'The Impact of White Women on Fur Trade Society,' in S. Trofimenkoff and A. Prentice, eds, *The Neglected Majority: Essays in Canadian Women's History* (McClelland and Stewart, 1977); Stasiulis and Jhappan, 'The Fractious Politics of a Settler Society'; Donna K. Goodleaf, '"Under Military Occupation": Indigenous Women, State Violence and Community Resistance,' in Linda Carty, ed., *And Still We Rise: Feminist Political Mobilizing in Contemporary Canada* (Toronto: Women's Press, 1993), 225–42. The presence and extent of patriarchal relations within pre-contact Aboriginal communities has been the source of considerable debate. There is evidence in British Columbia of patterns of matrilineal descent and kinship among the Haida, the Tsimshian, and the Northern Kwagiulth. Among the Coast Salish, the Nootka, Bella Bella, Bella Coola, and Southern Kwagiulth, a bilateral form of social organization has been recorded (Mitchell and Franklin, 'When You Don't Know the Language, Listen to the Silence').

Backhouse tells us that among the Mohawk, women controlled their own property after marriage, had full custody of children, and had the right to divorce. Constance Backhouse, *Colour-Coded: A Legal History of Racism in Canada, 1900–1950* (Toronto: University of Toronto Press, 1999), 108.

53 For a study of five of these societies and their respective cultures, the Aztecs/ Mexica (Mexico), the Maya (Guatemala and Yucatan), the Incas (Peru), the Cherokees (U.S.), and the Iroquois (Great Lakes), see Wright's *Stolen Continents*. The Mohawk adjudicative process in 1807 is described as follows: 'Among us we have no prisons, we have no pompous parade of courts; we have no written laws, and yet judges are revered among us as they are among you, and their decisions are highly regarded. Property, to say the least, is well

guarded, and crimes are as impartially punished. We have among us no splendid villains above the control of our laws. Daring wickedness is never suffered to triumph over helpless innocence. The estates of widows and orphans are never devoured by enterprising sharpers. In a word, we have no robbery under color of law.' Cited in Backhouse, *Colour-Coded*, 108.

54 Patricia Monture-Angus, *Thunder in My Soul: A Mohawk Woman Speaks* (Halifax: Fernwood Press, 1995), 34–5.

55 Agamben, *Homo Sacer.*

56 Val Napolean, 'Extinction by Number: Colonialism Made Easy,' *Canadian Journal of Law and Society* 16, no. 1 (2001), 113–45. See also Lawrence, *'Real' Indian's and Others.*

57 Goodleaf, '"Under Military Occupation,"' 226.

58 Joyce Green summarizes the colonial practices institutionalized in this Act: 'The way in which Aboriginal nations have been made Other is typical of colonial endeavours, and has served to both justify colonial actions and to deny the historical and contemporary completeness of aboriginal existence in Canada. Colonialism's project, in Michael Stevenson's words, "was, and still is, to lay waste a people and destroy their culture in order to undermine the integrity of their existence and appropriate their riches." It is pursued via "total war" legitimized not only through racist construction but through creation of language celebrating colonial identities while constructing the colonized as antithesis of human decency and development, thereby establishing a justification for their physical, historical and cultural annihilation. This language "becomes the basis for the forming of national identity and for providing the state with an organising ideology" whose racist, imperialist concepts become institutionalized as the "democratic nation-state" in which hatred of the Other is bureaucratized. That is, racism becomes part of the structural base of the state, permeating the cultural life of the dominant society both by its exclusive narrative of dominant experience and mythology, and by its stereotypical rendering of the "Other" as peripheral and unidimensional.' Green, 'Towards a Détente with History,' 12. The Indian Act represented this 'bureaucratized hatred,' organizing colonial governance through the ideological transformation of Aboriginal peoples into Indians, as well as entrenching unequal rights for Indian men and women.

59 See Jo-Anne Fiske, 'Political Status of Native Indian Women: Contradictory Implications of Canadian State Policy,' *American Indian Culture and Research Journal* 19, no. 2 (1995), 1–30; Mitchell and Franklin, 'When You Don't Know the Language, Listen to the Silence'; Stasiulis and Jhappan, 'The Fractious Politics of a Settler Society,'; Green, 'Towards a Détente with History.' Upon marriage to non-indigenous men, indigenous women would lose their

Indian status and the right to live on reserves. Marriage outside their community resulted in legal estrangement from their communities, and their children were also disinherited. Aboriginal men, however, did not lose status by marrying outside their communities. Instead, the non-Aboriginal women they married acquired Indian status and their children were not disinherited. In this manner, the Act created 'competing interests between women and men' within Aboriginal communities (Fiske, 'Political Status of Native Indian Women,' 4). The Act also stipulated that Aboriginal women of 'bad moral character' would lose rights to their husband's estates. The power to judge the women's 'moral character' was placed in the hands of white male administrators. See Sarah Carter, 'Categories and Terrains of Exclusion: Constructing the 'Indian Woman' in the Early Settlement Era in Western Canada,' in Parr and Rosenfeld, eds., *Gender and History in Canada*, 30–49.

60 Napolean, 'Extinction by Number,' 115.

61 The relative 'freedom' of Aboriginal women when compared with the status of European women was a 'matter of considerable anxiety to European men and a prime target for the Christianizing drive of missionaries' (Stasiulis and Jhappan, 'The Fractious Politics of a Settler Society,' 101). The introduction by the Canadian state of the male-dominated band-council structure for the internal administration of Aboriginal peoples was part of the attempt to re/formulate indigenous patriarchies. Until 1951, Aboriginal women were 'excluded from the band electorate' and were 'barred from public meetings' (Fiske, 'Political Status of Native Indian Women,' 6).

62 Lawrence, *'Real' Indians and Others*, 33.

63 Report of the Royal Commission on Aboriginal Peoples, quoted in Napolean, 'Extinction by Number,' 127.

64 Napolean, 'Extinction by Number.'

65 See Lawrence, *'Real' Indians and Others*, 46–7.

66 See ibid., chap. 2, for an excellent discussion of how the Indian Act affected gender.

67 See Lee Maracle, 'Racism, Sexism and Patriarchy,' in Himani Bannerji, ed., *Returning the Gaze: Essays on Racism, Feminism and Politics* (Toronto: Sister Vision Press, 1993); and Fiske, 'Political Status of Native Indian Women.' Jeanette Lavell and Yvonne Bedard, who had lost their status, challenged the Act in 1971. The Supreme Court ruled that the Act did not discriminate against Aboriginal women. Sandra Lovelace, who had also lost her status, went to the Human Rights Commission of the United Nations with her case. The Commission found Canada to have violated her rights and, in 1980, bands were allowed to suspend this discriminatory section of the Indian Act.

However, this change only 'shifted' the discrimination from the woman onto her children in subsequent generations. Napolean, 'Extinction by Number.'

68 Lawrence, *'Real' Indians and Others*, 25.

69 As Dara Culhane reminds us, 'When Aboriginal people say today that they have to go to court to prove they exist, they are speaking not just poetically, but also *literally.*' *The Pleasure of the Crown*, 48. Emphasis in original.

70 For a detailed study of the creation of the reserve system in British Columbia, see Cole Harris, *Making Native Space: Colonialism, Resistance, and Reserves in British Columbia* (Vancouver: UBC Press, 2002).

71 Monture-Angus, *Thunder in My Soul*, 31.

72 Aboriginal societies referred to America as Great Island or Turtle Island. Wright, *Stolen Continents*.

73 Gayatri Spivak uses the term 'epistemic violence' to refer to the process of developing western knowledge to legitimate domination of non-western cultures. For a useful explanation of Spivak's use of this term, see Stephen Morton, *Gayatri Chakravorty Spivak* (New York: Routledge, 2003), 19.

74 In British Columbia alone, ten different ethnic groups spoke thirty different Aboriginal languages. Mitchell and Franklin, 'When You Don't Know the Language, Listen to the Silence.'

75 See Churchill Ward, *Fantasies of the Master Race* (San Francisco: City Light Books, 1998).

76 Those who dared to keep these rituals and practices alive had to pay a heavy price, as evidenced in the treatment of Dakota Wanduta in Manitoba in 1903, where the Dakota had dared to perform the outlawed Grass Dance. In 1884, the Canadian state began to prohibit and criminalize the performance of ceremonial Indian dances, dances which were 'inextricably linked with the social, political and economic life–blood of the community, and dances underscored the core of Aboriginal resistance to cultural assimilation' (Backhouse, *Colour-Coded*, 64–5). Calling such ceremonies 'debauchery of the worst kind,' Prime Minister John A. Macdonald introduced legislation prohibiting them. With the ceremonial dances banned as spectacles of 'savagery,' the first chief to be convicted and imprisoned under this law in 1889 was the Kwakiutl chief, Hamasak. The law remained in effect until 1951.

77 Fiske, 'Political Status of Native Indian Women'; Green, 'Towards a Détente in History'; Carter, 'Categories and Terrains of Exclusion'; Mitchell and Franklin, 'When You Don't Know the Language, Listen to the Silence.'

78 See Backhouse, *Colour-Coded*, chap. 2. The first statute to define status in 1850 included the following: '1. persons of Indian blood, reputed to belong to the particular body or tribe, and their descendents; 2. persons intermarried with such Indians and residing among them and their descendents; 3.

persons residing among such Indians whose parents on either side were or are Indians, or entitled to be considered as such; and 4. persons adopted in infancy by such Indians, and residing in the village or upon the lands of such tribe or body of Indians, and their descendents' (21). In 1876, an Indian was defined in the Indian Act as 'any male person of Indian blood reputed to belong to a particular band, any child of such person, and any woman who is or was lawfully married to such person' (ibid.). The Act also specified that the legal category 'person' did not include Indians.

79 In her study of Canadian legal history, Constance Backhouse tells us, 'There was no consultation with First Nations on definitional matters' regarding their 'Indian status' (*Colour-Coded*, 22). Backhouse documents how a jurisdictional dispute between the federal government and the Quebec government regarding the provision of relief supplies to the Inuit led the Supreme Court of Canada to decide in 1939 that 'Eskimos' were indeed 'Indians' in *Re Eskimo*. She points out that although the Supreme Court 'is specifically authorized to direct that ... "interested parties" be heard, and it can appoint counsel to represent interests otherwise unrepresented ... no one seems to have thought that representatives of the Inuit or First Nations communities constituted "interested parties"' (35). The ruling found that the Inuit, renamed Eskimos, were really Indians (see 18–55).

80 Backhouse, *Colour-Coded*, 15. Backhouse notes that it 'was only on the rarest of occasions that certain legislators, lawyers, and judges attempted to stem the systemic discrimination that permeated Canadian law, refuting the excesses of Canadian racism.'

81 See ibid., chap. 4, 103–31.

82 Ibid., 123.

83 Culhane, *The Pleasure of the Crown*, 2.

84 Culhane defines the White and Bob case as the first such case (*The Pleasure of the Crown*, 74). She also discusses many of the early cases in the country in chapter 6.

85 It should be remembered that Indians who obtained university education or degrees in law lost this status, that is, they could no longer claim Indian status because they had proved themselves capable of being educated. As Lawrence points out, compulsory enfranchisement was imposed upon Native peoples to better control them: 'Native people could be enfranchised for acquiring an education, for serving in the armed forces, or for leaving reserves for long periods of time to maintain employment.' *'Real' Indians and Others*, 31.

86 The Indian Act was amended in 1910 to forbid the use of band funds for land claims without the approval of the superintendent of Indian Affairs,

that is, without the Canadian state's permission. In 1927, solicitations and donations for such claims were criminalized. Ibid., 36.

87 Dara Culhane, personal communication with the author, November 2004.

88 See Backhouse, *Colour-Coded*, 130–1.

89 Ibid., 123.

90 Ibid., 119. This view was held in law, notwithstanding that the Iroquois Confederacy is considered by many to have been the political model adopted by the settlers for developing the (federal) political union of the American colonies. Noting that colonists took 'Indian ideas as well as Indian land,' Ronald Wright explains that the Onondaga sachem, Canasatego, suggested this idea to 'the bickering commissioners of Pennsylvania, Virginia and Maryland.' Benjamin Franklin took notes from Canasatego's speech, and later wrote, 'It would be a very strange thing if Six Nations of ignorant savages should be capable of forming a scheme for such a union, and be able to execute it in such a manner as that it has subsisted for ages and appears indissoluble; and yet that like union should be impracticable for ten or a dozen English colonies.' Quoted in Wright, *Stolen Continents*, 116.

91 Gerald Robert Vizenor, *Fugitive Poses: Native American Indian Scenes of Absence and Presence* (Lincoln: University of Nebraska Press, 1998), 25. Emphasis in the original.

92 Harris, *Making Native Space*, 146–7.

93 For instance, after 1870 when the Hudson Bay Company lands were turned over to the Dominion, the Canadian state helped clear indigenous peoples off the lands, initiating a program of 'free homesteads' to settle the West' (Carter, 'Categories and Terrains of Exclusion'). Settlers were recruited by the Canadian state in England, with promises of 'free land and easy wealth as inducements to immigration' (Green, 'Towards a Détente with History,' 88). At this time, the Aboriginal and Metis populations in the West were greater than that of Euro-Canadians. For example, in the district of Alberta in 1885, Aboriginal and Metis peoples numbered around 9,500, and the 'new' arrivals numbered 4,900 (Carter, 'Catgories and Terrains of Exclusion,' 32). See also Noel Dyck, *What is the Indian 'Problem': Tutelage and Resistance in Canadian Indian Administration* (St John's, NL: Institute of Social and Economic Research, 1991).

94 Harris, *Making Native Space*, xvii.

95 Ibid., xv.

96 Ibid., xvi. Sproat later became the Indian Reserve Commissioner in British Columbia, although his sympathies for the Aboriginals resulted in his tenure being of short duration. Although Sproat believed the myth that Aboriginal peoples were doomed to extinction, he advocated a more humane approach

towards them than was popularly tolerable by the settler population in the
province.

97 Ibid.

98 A stark example of Europeans forsaking potentially more humane relationships with Aboriginal peoples in the interests of securing a white nationality
is provided by fur traders/settlers who had Aboriginal wives. During the fur
trade which preceded settlement, French and British men were in a minority and they engaged in relationships, including marriage, with Aboriginal
women. These relationships were crucial to the survival of the men in
'Indian country,' and they were also of great economic importance with
women, acting as liaisons and peacemakers, enabling the men to secure
valuable trade and political alliances with indigenous peoples. See Van
Kirk, 'The Impact of White Women on Fur Trade Society'; Mitchell and
Franklin, 'When You Don't Know the Language, Listen to the Silence';
Carter, 'Categories and Terrains of Exclusion.' Such relations were to later
serve the interests of colonial powers. See Sylvia Van Kirk, '*Many Tender
Ties': Women in Fur-Trade Society* (Winnipeg: Watson Dwyer, 1980).

99 These constructs can be found in the works of Jean Jacques Rousseau and
Thomas Hobbes. Rousseau's work theorized the 'noble savage' as the pre-
cursor of the rational citizen of the social contract, while the construct of
the 'savage savage' informed the work of Hobbes, who argued for a strong
state to control the brutalities which characterized the 'state of nature.' See
Vizenor, *Fugitive Poses;* Daniel Francis, *The Imaginary Indian: The Image of the
Indian in Canadian Culture* (Vancouver: Arsenal Pulp Press, 1992), 5; and
Culhane, *The Pleasure of the Crown,* for discussion of these constructs.

100 Francis, *The Imaginary Indian.*

101 Wright, *Stolen Continents,* xi.

102 See Carter, 'Categories and Terrain of Exclusion,' 30.

103 Lawrence, *'Real' Indians and Others,* 23. Eva Mackey concurs with this observation: 'since the formation of the Dominion of Canada in 1867, images of
nature, the wilderness, and the north have defined Canadian national identity, often in racialised terms as white settler identity. In 1990s' Canada such
images which combine nature and nation remain ubiquitous, although they
are now coupled with images of cultural pluralism which do not simply
include but highlight Canada's Aboriginal peoples and multiculturalism'
(72).

104 See Mackey, *The History of Difference,* chap. 4, 71–90. Mackey examines how
Douglas Cardinal, the architect of the Canadian Museum of Civilization,
described his vision in his design statement: 'His proposal takes the form
of a narrative, beginning with the emergence of the land from the sea and

the creation of "a culture ... entwined with the forces of nature." Here he is obviously referring to Canada's Aboriginal peoples. Later, people arrive "from across the oceans ... from diverse cultures all over the world, drawn to the beauty and *bounty of this land.*" Although at first, he says they only "visited and *took from the land* to reinforce their empires," they later stayed and "*gave to the land* their sweat and hardships"' (75). Emphasis in the original.

105 'In both 1990s' narratives of nationhood, as presented in the Canadian Museum of Civilization and the *Spirit of a Nation* performance, Aboriginal peoples become equated with the land and with nature' (ibid., 77). See also Francis, *The Imaginary Indian.*

106 Mair was appointed by the government to negotiations of Treaty Number Eight in Northern Alberta. Quoted in Francis, *The Imaginary Indian,* 3–4.

107 The painting, *The Death of General Wolfe* by Benjamin West – as well as those by Paul Kane, the 'first artist in Canada to take the Native population as his subject' – created a 'fiction,' Francis argues (ibid., 17). Although artists routinely added foreign artifacts and clothing to the bodies of the Aboriginal peoples they depicted, their works were popularly presented as 'truthful' and accurate depictions. See ibid., chap. 2, 16–43.

108 Mackey attests to the enduring power of the work of the Group of Seven: 'The wilderness paintings of the Group of Seven represent and embody the origin of Canadian modern art and have a revered place in the symbolic construction of nationhood today ... Their work as a whole is characterized by its wild and unpeopled northern landscapes, as their central imagery is the rugged and rocky terrain of the pre-Cambrian shield and the northern woods ... The power that this imagery still holds today is borne out by my own experience. When I was in Northern Ontario during fieldwork, I found myself calling the pine trees "Group of Seven trees," and feeling that their presence confirmed that I was now really in the "*true* Canada" the "*true* North." The natural world, for me also, was seen through the lens of these quintessential nationalist texts' (*The House of Difference,* 40). The power of the Group of Seven to continue representing the 'Art for a Nation' remains unparalleled in contemporary exhibitions of their work, such as the Art Gallery of Ontario's February to May 1996 exhibition, 'The Oh! Canada Project.' Rinaldo Walcott argues that the racial geography of the actual exhibit reproduced 'the same old story of exclusion and marginalization with a new twist (exclusion on the inside).' So it was that the Group of Seven's paintings were housed in a privileged location, while the works of 'community-based' artists were displayed in a peripheral, marginal space with other distractions occupying centre space, such as interactive educa-

tional materials. Rinaldo Walcott, 'Lament for a Nation: The Racial Geography of the 'Oh! Canada Project,''' *Fuse* 19, no. 4 (1996), 15–23.

Mackey assesses the construction of the national self in Margaret Atwood's work as follows: 'For Atwood this preoccupation with defining the "self" of Canada is itself framed within a discourse of victimisation, of being colonised by others. Canadians, according to Atwood, need to build a sense of self because they have been denied full personhood as a result of British colonialism or American cultural imperialism.' Nature is seen as a brutal force, a 'monster,' betraying the settlers who expected a more benign environment. 'Submission to, and victimisation by, nature as ignoble, untamed and monstrous savage define Canadianness' (*The House of Difference*, 46–7).

109 Mackey argues that the theme of settlers 'giving back to the land' features strongly in such narratives: 'In these narratives the process of "giving to the land" through colonial progress is presented as if it were similar to the pre-colonial relationship between Aboriginal people and the land, and on a continuum with what Native people wanted. It is presented as if settlers and Aboriginal people were really, after all, involved in the same sort of transformative, yet ecologically sound endeavour.' This transformation resulted in settlers being defined as living in "harmony" with nature, while Aboriginal peoples became defined as being 'more like settlers' (ibid., 80).

110 Daniel Francis discusses the work of Egerton Ryerson Young, who recounted the following story about going fishing with a doctor in the lake country. '"Wait a minute, doctor," I said. "I can add to the wild beauty of the place something that will please your artistic eye." Young had two Natives paddle out to a nearby island where he asked them to strike poses on the rocks, their fishing lines in the water, while Young and his friend admired them. "I confess I was entranced by the loveliness of the sight," he wrote. For Young, Indians were figures in a landscape, placed there by an all-knowing God to enhance the romanticism of the scenery' (*The Imaginery Indian*, 51).

111 Quoted in Morton, *Gayatri Chakravorty Spivak*, 18.

112 Mahamood Mamdani, *When Victims Become Killers: Colonialism, Nativism, and the Genocide in Rwanda* (Princeton, NJ: Princeton University Press, 2001), 22.

113 Culhane points out that settlers would have been affected by social evolutionary ideas which would have defined their integration into Aboriginal societies as a step 'backwards, both in historical time and in human psychological development' (*The Pleasure of the Crown*, 43). She also refers to James Tully, who points out that recognition of Aboriginal forms of property and of Aboriginal equality with Europeans would have made settlement impossible (53).

114 Irving Powless, Jr., Onondaga Chief, cited in Backhouse, *Colour-Coded*, 131.

115 Quoted in Francis, *The Imaginery Indian*, 6. Francis goes on to note: 'I would have thought, however, that in the three hundred and forty years separating Thomas Hobbes and Judge McEachern, our understanding of aboriginal culture might be seen to have improved. But obviously not' (7). Nor is Judge McEachern alone in subscribing to these views. Legal arguments still continue to be made by the province of British Columbia, which include claims that Aboriginal title exists only if created by the sovereign; that Aboriginals were 'too primitive' for the sovereign to have created such title; and that First Nations were 'minimally evolved nomads lacking law or government when Europeans first arrived.' Although historians and legal scholars dismiss these as 'implausible,' 'indefensible,' and 'ridiculous' notions, Culhane notes that these positions have 'been argued repeatedly by prestigious lawyers, and declared "fact" by eminent judges, for 30 years' (*The Pleasure of the Crown*, 75).

116 Lawrence, *'Real' Indians and Others*, 5.

117 On 18 November 2004, the Supreme Court ruled in two cases that governments were required to consult with Aboriginal peoples who were involved in the process of making land claims. K. Makin, 'Landmark Rulings Made on Native Claims,' *Globe and Mail*, 19 November 2004, A7. As the *Vancouver Sun* reported, the rulings of the Court stated governments had 'a duty to consult aboriginal peoples and accommodate their interests.' The consultations should be 'meaningful,' but the ruling also stated that 'there is no duty to reach agreement.' Aboriginal peoples 'must not frustrate the Crown's reasonable good faith attempts, nor should they take unreasonable positions to thwart government from making decisions or acting in cases where, despite meaningful consultation, agreement is not reached.' While the 'Crown is not rendered impotent ... It may continue to manage the resource in question, pending claims resolution.' The Court also stated, 'The Crown cannot cavalierly run roughshod over aboriginal interests.' See V. Palmer, 'Land-Claim Rulings Throw Cold Water on Both Sides' Hard-Liners,' *Vancouver Sun*, 19 November 2004, A3.

118 Culhane, *The Pleasure of the Crown*, 86.

2. Nationals, Citizens, and Others

1 A Liberal Member of Parliament (1906), quoted in Peter Ward, *White Canada Forever: Popular Attitudes and Public Policy toward Orientals in British Columbia* (Montreal: McGill-Queen's University Press, 2002), 84.

2 John Ibbitson, 'Canada's Immigrant challenge,' *Globe and Mail,* 11 March 2005, A4.

3 Seyla Benhabib, *The Rights of Others: Aliens, Residents and Citizens* (Cambridge: Cambridge University Press, 2004).

4 Benhabib draws on the analysis of Katrin Flikschuh, who discussed Kant's recognition of three interrelated but distinct rights: rights of persons and the state; rights between states; and rights between persons and foreign states. Ibid., 25.

5 This right particularly cannot be denied to strangers who face 'destruction.' Kant's notion of this right has 'become incorporated into the Geneva Convention on the Status of Refugees as the principle of "non-refoulement."' Ibid., 35.

6 Ibid., 50. Arendt traced the source of totalitarianism to European colonization of Africa.

7 Ibid., 61.

8 Ibid., 2.

9 Ibid., 19–21.

10 Ibid., 21.

11 Menzies, Adamoski, and Chunn identify three major paradigms of citizenship: civic republicanism, which defines the citizen as a responsible and active participant in the public sphere and governance; liberal individualism, which defines citizenship as a status, such that 'requirements from the state do not extend beyond 'freedom and security'; and neo-liberalism, informed by Marshall's conception of social and welfare citizenship. See R. Menzies, R. Adamoski, and D. Chunn. 'Rethinking the Citizen in Canadian Social History,' in R. Adamoski, D. Chunn, and R. Menzies, eds., *Contesting Canadian Citizenship: Historical Readings* (Peterborough, ON: Broadview Press, 2002), 11–42.

12 Benhabib refers to the work of Amartya Sen, but only to strengthen her case against the desirability of a radical redistribution at the global level. See Benhabib, *The Rights of Others*, chap. 3.

13 Ibid., 105.

14 Ibid., 107.

15 A. Brah, *Cartographies of Diaspora: Contesting Identities* (London: Routledge, 1996), 21.

16 Paul A. Silverstein, *Algeria in France: Transpolitics, Race and Nation* (Bloomington: Indiana University Press, 2004).

17 During the nineteenth century, 'race' had a different meaning than it was to assume during the twentieth century. So, for example, the Irish, the Jews, the Polish, the Hungarians, and so on were all defined as racially inferior to the

British and French, and their immigration to North America was not looked upon favourably. However, during the twentieth century, these other European groups were integrated into the racialized category 'white' in Canada (Bannerji, *The Dark Side of the Nation*). See also E. Shohat, and R. Stam, *Unthinking Eurocentrism: Multiculturalism and the Media* (London: Routledge, 1994).

18 Whether the assumptions underpinning Benhabib's theory of citizenship and universal human rights can be unproblematically applied to any liberal democracy is a question clearly beyond the scope of this study.

19 The Canadian government produced brochures and maps that were distributed to recruiting agents and through the media to attract European settlers, among other measures. See Freda Hawkins, *Critical Years in Immigration: Canada and Australia Compared* (Montreal: McGill-Queen's University Press, 1989); Clifford Sifton, 'Only Farmers Need Apply,' in Howard Palmer, ed., *Immigration and the Rise of Multiculturalism* (Toronto: Copp Clark Publishing, 1975), 34–8; H. Troper, 'American Immigration to Canada, 1896–1914,' in Palmer, ed., *Immigration and the Rise of Multiculturalism*, 38–43.

20 Ethnicity and race were often conflated during this period, with the British and the French defining themselves as different races than other Europeans. Whereas Britain, the United States, and France, and 'to a lesser extent' northern and western Europe had been among the 'preferred' source countries, immigrants were subsequently accepted from among some of the other previously 'non-preferred' races of Europe, specifically the Ukrainians, Italians, Poles, and Hutterites. See Lisa Marie Jakubowski, *Immigration and the Legalization of Racism* (Halifax: Fernwood Publishing, 1997), 11–12. See also Stasiulis and Jhappan, 'The Fractious Politics of a Settler Society'; Bolaria and Li, *Racial Oppression in Canada*; Ward, *White Canada Forever.*

21 As Mahmood Mamdani has noted: 'If the law recognizes you as a member of an ethnicity, and state institutions treat you as a member of that ethnicity, then you become an ethnic being, legally and institutionally. In contrast, if the law recognizes you as a member of a racial group, then your relationship to the state, and to other legally defined groups, is mediated through the law and the state. It is a consequence of your legally inscribed identity. If your inclusion or exclusion from a regime of rights or entitlements is based on your race or ethnicity, as defined by law, then this becomes a central defining fact for you the individual and your group. From this point of view, both race and ethnicity need to be understood as political – and not cultural, or even biological – identities.' Mamdani, *When Victims Become Killers*, 22.

22 See Bannerji, *The Dark Side of the Nation.*

23 See T.H. Marshall, 'Citizenship and Social Class,' in T.H. Marshall and Tom

Bottomore, *Citizenship and Social Class* (London: Pluto Press, 1992), 18. Marshall's conceptualization of citizenship in this essay, delivered at Cambridge in 1949, continues to remain one of the most influential works in contemporary debates on citizenship. He defined citizenship as encapsulating three distinct categories of individual rights: civil (including freedom of speech, the right to own property, etc.); political (including the right to vote, to belong to political parties, etc.); and social (the right to social entitlements such as unemployment insurance, social assistance, etc.). Marshall's theory examined the relationship between the inequalities generated within the sphere of the economy, and the 'equality' conferred on individuals by the institution of citizenship within the political sphere. He argued that citizenship rights would help counter the economic inequalities of class (3–51).

24 See Tom Bottomore, 'Citizenship and Social Class, Forty Years On,' in Marshall and Bottomore, *Citizenship and Social Class*, 55–93; Friedrich Kratochwil, 'Citizenship: On the Border of Order,' *Alternatives* 19 (1994), 485–506; Michael Mann, 'Ruling Class Strategies and Citizenship,' *Sociology* 21, no. 3 (1987), 339–54; Ramesh Mishra, *Society and Social Policy: Theoretical Perspectives on Welfare* (London: Macmillan Press, 1977); D. Taylor, 'Citizenship and Social Power,' *Critical Social Policy* 9, no. 2, Issue 26 (1989), 19–31.

25 Taylor, 'Citizenship and Social Power.'

26 Carol Pateman, *The Sexual Contract* (Cambridge: Polity Press, 1988).

27 A right is defined as 'a moral or legal entitlement to have or do something' in the *Oxford English Dictionary*, 2d ed. A rite is defined as 'a body of customary observances characteristic of a Church or a part of it ... a social custom, practice, or conventional act' (1516).

28 Drawing upon the theories of Durkheim, Goffman, and Collins, this is how Bellah defines the secular ritual at the heart of social interactions: 'In this process of ritual interaction the members of the group, through their shared experience, feel a sense of membership, however fleeting, with a sense of boundary between those sharing the experience and all those outside it; they feel some sense of moral obligation to each other, which is symbolized by whatever they focused on during the interaction; and finally, they are charged with what Collins calls emotional energy but which he identifies with what Durkheim called moral force. Since, according to Collins, all of social life consists of strings of such ritual interactions, then ritual becomes the most fundamental category for the understanding of social action.' R.N. Bellah, 'The Ritual Roots of Society and Culture,' in M. Dillon, *Handbook of the Sociology of Religion* (Cambridge: Cambridge University Press, 2003), 31–44.

29 Woodsworth, *Strangers within Our Gates*. The first quote is from Phillips Brooks, quoted in Woodsworth, 231–2.

30 See Anderson, *Imagined Communities*, and also Saskia Sassen, *The Mobility of Labor and Capital: A Study in International Investment and Labor Flow* (New York: Cambridge University Press, 1988); Lydia Potts, *The World Labour Market: A History of Migration* (London: Zed Books, 1990).

31 For example, the Empire Settlement Act of 1922 committed Britain to work with Dominion governments and private agencies to develop emigration and settlement programs into those colonies. See W.A. Carrothers, *Emigration from the British Isles* (London: P.S. King and Son, 1929); Hawkins, *Critical Years in Immigration*; William Peterson, 'Canada's Immigration: The Ideological Background,' in Palmer, ed., *Immigration and the Rise of Multiculturalism*, 22–33.

32 Robert A. Huttenback, *Racism and Empire: White Settlers and Colored Immigrants in the British Self-Governing Colonies 1830–1910* (Ithaca, NY: Cornell University Press, 1976), 26.

33 The race of the ruling elite was the basis upon which Canada acquired its independence from the British state: 'the "gifts" of liberal democratic government and relative political autonomy so that (Canada) might develop within a shared framework of civilization and moral and material standards. Hence, although Canada (and the other so-called "white dominions") shared with the so-called "dependent colonies" a peripheral position in the international political economy prior to the twentieth century, as a cultural, social and political entity, it was a chip off the metropolitan block' (Stasiulis and Jhappan, 'The Fractious Politics of a Settler Society,' 97). See also Green, 'Towards a Détente with History,' 85–105; and Hawkins, *Critical Years in Immigration*.

34 Stasiulis and Jhappan, 'The Fractious Politics of a Settler Society,' 109.

35 Green, 'Towards a Détente with History,' 92.

36 R.K. Carty, and P. Ward, 'The Making of a Canadian Political Citizenship,' in R.K. Carty, and P. Ward, eds., *National Politics and Community in Canada* (Vancouver: University of British Columbia Press, 1986), 65–79. See also Charles Ungerleider, 'Immigration, Multiculturalism, and Citizenship: The Development of the Canadian Social Justice Infrastructure,' *Canadian Ethnic Studies* 24, no. 3 (1992), 7– 22. Examining the development of Canadian citizenship, Carty and Ward have pointed out that 'most policies encouraging migration reflected the assumption that northwestern Europeans and Americans of like descent made the best prospective citizens' (68). For a discussion of The Naturalization Act, Canada 1881 and the 1885 'Citizenship debates,' which dealt with the question of the extension of the Federal fran-

chise to women, Natives and Asians, see Veronica Strong-Boag, 'The Citizenship Debates: The 1885 Franchise Act,' in Adamoski, Chunn, and Menzies,
eds., *Contesting Canadian Citizenship*, 69–94.

37 Dyck, *What Is the 'Indian' Problem*, 3.

38 Carter, 'Categories and Terrains of Exclusion,' 32.

39 In tracing the development of intellectual property rights within the global
system of relations, Vandana Shiva has argued that communal property
rights existed in colonized societies prior to colonization. Colonization introduced private property rights, which led to the destruction of many of these
indigenous customary rights. Such 'customary' rights had been developed by
diverse societies and were based in value systems different from, and in
opposition to, private property rights. While the exact content of these customary rights varied across societies and require detailed historical study, colonization greatly undermined these rights where they were not destroyed
completely (see her *Biopiracy*). See also Goodleaf, '"Under Military Occupation."'

40 See Lawrence, *'Real' Indians and Others*.

41 The Gradual Civilization Act of 1857 offered 'voluntary' enfranchise-ment to
Aboriginal peoples. It required that an Indian be 'schooled, debt-free, and
'of good moral character' before he could be enfranchised – at which point
he would receive twenty hectares of land, freehold tenure, from his former
reserve' (Lawrence, *'Real' Indians and Others*, 31). The Indian Advancement
Act of 1884 'envisioned the voluntary transformation of reserves into model
municipalities, much like those of settlers' (Strong-Boag, 'The Citizenship
Debates,' 81).

42 Aboriginal women acquired enfranchisement in the 1960s. Lee Maracle has
argued that the enfranchisement of Aboriginal women was not the result of
any liberatory impulse of the Canadian state: 'It was not because anyone seriously considered us people entitled to full citizenship that changed things
but the threat of a mass movement of Natives' (Maracle, 'Racism, Sexism and
Patriarchy,' 150).

43 At the time of Confederation, the legal status of 'Canadian citizens' was that
of British subjects with domicile in Canada (Carty and Ward, 'The Making of
a Canadian Political Citizenship'; Ungerleider, 'Immigration, Multiculturalism, and Citizenship'). The 'Canadian' population was 60 per cent British
and 30 per cent French. Warren E. Kalbach, 'A Demographic Overview of
Racial and Ethnic Groups in Canada,' in Peter Li, ed., *Race and Ethnic Relations in Canada* (Toronto: Oxford University Press, 1990, 18. The ruling elite,
of course, came from these two 'races.'

44 Such supports included access to 'cheap' land, financial grants, assisted pas-

sages and assistance with settlement and employment. See Green, 'Towards a Détente with History'; Hawkins, *Critical Years in Immigration*; Joy Parr, 'The Skilled Emigrant and Her Kin: Gender, Culture, and Labour Recruitment,' *Canadian Historical Review* 68, no. 4 (1987), 529–51; Vibert, 'Real Men Hunt Buffalo'; Dyck, *What Is the 'Indian' Problem*. Clifford Sifton, who developed the immigration branch in the ministry of the interior in the government of Wilfrid Laurier in the 1890s, was not bashful in declaring his government's objectives:

> In those days, settlers were sought from three sources: one was the United States. The American settlers did not need sifting; they were of the finest quality and the most desirable settlers. In Great Britain we confined our efforts very largely to the North of England and Scotland, and for the purpose of sifting the settlers we doubled the bonuses to the agents in the North of England and cut down as much as possible in the South. The result was that we got a fairly steady stream of people from the North of England and from Scotland and they were the very best settlers in the world ... Our work was largely done in the North. Then, came the continent where the great emigrating centre was Hamburg. Steamships got there to load up with people who are desirous of leaving Europe ... We made an arrangement with the booking agencies in Hamburg, under which they winnowed out this flood of people, picked out the agriculturalists and peasants and sent them to Canada, sending nobody else. We paid, I think, $5 per head for the farmer and $2 per head for the other members of the family (Sifton, 'Only Farmers Need Apply,' 34–5).

Sifton seems to have taken considerable pride in having made 'a determined and successful effort' to 'free' Aboriginal lands for 'immediate settlement,' and despite his claims to the contrary, the 'sifting' of American settlers did in fact occur in his government's refusal to grant land to Black immigrants from the United States. Sifton explained how the state's policies to ensure the supply of labour and the creation of a 'national' market came together with its priorities for white nation-building in policies which recruited settlers from particular European races and classes. The state sought out farmers and those 'accustomed to pioneering life,' while leaving out 'artisans, mechanics, labourers, small shopkeepers' (Hawkins, *Critical Years in Immigration*). To be excluded from permanent settlement in Sifton's campaigns were *all* non-Europeans, irrespective of their class.

Sifton's campaigns were also gendered. The ideal woman, which these campaigns sought to recruit, was defined as the wife of the good 'quality' settler who would become the nation's 'backbone': 'I think a stalwart peasant in a sheep-skin coat, born on the soil, whose forefathers have been farmers for generations, with a stout wife and a half-a-dozen children is good quality,' he stated (Sifton, 'Only Farmers Need Apply,' 35). Although the European women who were actually recruited would have severely tested Sifton's ideal, his comments express the official recognition of the importance of the role of women in nation-building. Sifton later served as the minister of indian affairs, in which capacity he was to 'champion a policy of transferring unused Indian reserve lands into the hands of Euro-Canadian land speculators who were "clambering" to "acquire valuable reserve lands"' (Dyck, *What Is the 'Indian' Problem*). The interests of non-Indians, and in particular, their access to lands, were paramount in the administration of Aboriginal peoples by the colonial state. In 1909, the minister reported to Parliament that 700,000 acres of reserve lands were acquired by the Crown and sold off for three dollars an acre. After the First World War, another 68,000 acres of land were redistributed in a soldier settlement scheme (ibid.).

45 In 1911, Stephen Leacock described these unwanted arrivals as follows: 'They are, in great measure, mere herds of the proletariat of Europe, the lowest classes of industrial society, without home and work, fit objects indeed for philanthropic pity, but indifferent material from which to build the commonwealth of the future.' See S. Leacock, 'The Immigration Problem,' in Palmer, ed., *Immigration and the Rise of Multiculturalism*, 48. See also Vibert, 'Real Men Hunt Buffalo'; Peterson 'Canada's Immigration.'

46 Stasiulis and Jhappan, 'The Fractious Politics of a Settler Society.'

47 Anderson, *Imagined Communities*.

48 Stasiulis and Jhappan, 'The Fractious Politics of a Settler Society.'

49 Vibert, 'Real Men Hunt Buffalo'; Carter, 'Categories and Terrains of Exclusion.'

50 Carter, 'Categories and Terrains of Exclusion,' 30.

51 This is what has come to be known as the 'first wave' of Euro-Canadian feminism. In their commitment to a racialized national project, the women were 'little different' from their male counterparts (see the 'Introduction' in Susan Mann Trofimenkoff and Alison Prentice, eds., *The Neglected Majority: Essays in Canadian Women's History* (Toronto: McClelland and Stewart, 1977). Many women's organizations actively supported the immigration restrictions to keep non-preferred races, both men and women, out of the colony. For example, the National Council of Women voted to bar Asian women from entry, as did the Christian Ministerial Association, for 'fear' Canada would become a 'hindu colony.' See Mahinder Kaur Doman, 'A Note on Asian Indian Women in British Columbia 1900–1935,' in Barbara K. Latham and Roberta J. Pazdro, eds., *Not Just Pin Money: Selected Essays on the History of Women's Work in British Columbia* (Victoria: Camosun College, 1984), 99–104.

Emily Murphy, a renowned Canadian feminist, believed in the superiority of the 'Nordic' races and published a book in 1922 on the dangers of white women being enticed into sex through the use of opium. This book was part of an anti-Chinese campaign. The activists of the Woman's Christian Temperance Union wore white ribbons as a symbol of milk (an anti-alcohol statement) and for the racial purity of the country. See Marianna Valverde, 'When the Mother of the Race is Free,' in Franca Iacovetta and Marianna Valverde, eds., *Gender Conflicts: New Essays in Women's History* (Toronto: University of Toronto Press, 1992), 3–26. Strong-Boag describes the more radical feminists among this first wave who, in order to mobilize broader support for political rights for women, also tended to work with the less progressive reform-minded organizations. See Veronica Strong-Boag, '"Setting the Stage": National Organization and the Women's Movement in the Late Nineteenth Century,' in Trofimenkoff and Prentice, eds., *The Neglected Majority*, 87–103.

52 The example of the National Council of Women demonstrates how close ties with the ruling elite increased the success of these women's political organizing. The Governor General's wife was solicited as the Council's first president, and Lady Thompson, wife of the prime minister, along with Madame Laurier, wife of the leader of the opposition, became honorary members.

53 The National Council of Women envisioned their role in this particular manner. Strong-Boag, '"Setting the Stage,"' 102.

54 Buchignani and Indra, *Continuous Journey*.

55 B. Singh Bolaria, and Peter S. Li, *Racial Oppression in Canada* (Toronto: Garamond Press, 1985); Ward, *White Canada Forever*.

56 Ward, *White Canada Forever*, 92.

57 The concept of the 'social imaginary' has been defined by Charles Taylor as follows: 'The social imaginary is not a set of ideas; rather, it is what enables, through making sense of, the practices of a society.' See Charles Taylor, 'Modern Social Imaginaries,' *Public Culture* 14, no. 1 (Winter 2002), 91–124.

58 Ward, *White Canada Forever*, 9–10.

59 For discussion of the anti-Asian campaigns, see ibid.; Bolaria and Li, *Racial Oppression in Canada*; Chinese Canadian National Council, *Jin Guo*.

60 Hawkins, *Critical Years in Immigration*, 22–3.

61 See Bolaria and Li, *Racial Oppression in Canada*; Palmer, *Immigration and the Rise of Multiculturalism*; Stasiulis and Jhappan, 'The Fractious Politics of a Settler Society.' Although relatively small in numbers, these immigrants worked in the economy's most important sectors, including building the actual physical infrastructure which made the westward expansion and the development of a market economy possible. These non-preferred races built the railway,

worked in the agricultural and resource extraction sectors as fruit pickers, as labourers in logging camps, lumber yards and saw mills, in mining, fishing, canning, and in the steel and other manufacturing plants. See Agnes Calliste, 'Race, Gender and Canadian Immigration Policy: Blacks from the Caribbean, 1900–1932,' in Joy Parr and Mark Rosenfeld, eds., *Gender and History in Canada* (Toronto: Copp Clark, 1996), 70–87; Ajit Adhopia, *The Hindus of Canada* (New Delhi: Inderlekh Publications, 1993); Sucheta Mazumdar, 'Colonial Impact and Punjabi Emigration to the United States,' in Lucie Cheng and Edna Bonacich, eds., *Labor Immigration under Capitalism: Asian Workers in the United States Before World War II* (Berkeley: University of California Press, 1984), 316–36; Bolaria and Li, *Racial Oppression in Canada*; Buchignani and Indra, *Continuous Journey*; Ward, *White Canada Forever.*

62 See Hawkins, *Critical Years in Immigration*; Adhopia, *The Hindus of Canada*; and Tamara Adilman, 'A Preliminary Sketch of Chinese Women and Work in British Columbia 1858–1950,' in Latham and Pazdro, eds., *Not Just Pin Money*, 53–78. These scholars discuss the widespread fears that the Chinese were waiting to 'overpower' and 'outnumber' white Canadians. Adilman describes the environment of 'hysteria' that prevailed as fears of Asians planning to 'invade' British Columbia were whipped up by politicians. The findings of the 1907 Royal Commission, however, reveal how unfounded these 'fears' were. It concluded that immigration from India was an organized phenomenon, promoted by the activities of nationals. The Royal Commission identified three main reasons for this immigration between the years 1904–1906: shipping companies were promoting migration to Canada for their own business interests; information about economic opportunities in Canada and the U.S.A. was being widely distributed in the rural areas of Punjab and Bengal in a bid to recruit migrants; and individual agents were running lucrative businesses bringing immigrants over, securing them employment and organizing their settlement. Although none of these activities were illegal, they were defined as 'unpatriotic to the Empire' by MacKenzie King (see Adhopia, *The Hindus of Canada*).

63 Annie Demirjian, Douglas Gray, and David Wright, *The 1947 Canadian Citizenship Act: Issues and Significance*, prepared for Citizenship and Immigration Canada (Ottawa: Consulting and Audit Canada, 1996).

64 These three classes are defined as follows:
   (i) natural-born citizens, including children born outside the country with Canadian fathers and children born out of 'wedlock' to Canadian mothers (*Canadian Citizenship Act, 1947* (CCA) An Act Respecting Citizenship, Nationality, Naturalization and Status of Aliens. Ottawa: Edmond Cloutier. Sections 4 and 5).

(ii) naturalized citizens: British subjects with Canadian domicile, 'domicile' being defined as five years residence; women married to Canadian citizens; British subjects admitted into Canada for permanent residence (CCA, 1947, Section 9).

(iii) citizens granted a citizenship Certificate by the Minister by virtue of the following: coming of age at 18 years and filing an intention to become citizens; spouses of, and resident with, Canadian citizens or British subjects. In order to acquire this certificate, applicants had to meet the following conditions: prove they were lawfully admitted for permanent residence; demonstrate their residency in Canada for four of the previous six years, including the year immediately prior to the application; demonstrate their good character; demonstrate adequate knowledge of English or French, and if unable to do so, prove that they had been resident in Canada for a period of twenty years; demonstrate that they intended to reside permanently in Canada or intended to enter the public service (CCA, 1947, Section 10).

65 'The Governor in Council may order that any person other than a natural-born Canadian citizen shall cease to be a Canadian citizen if, upon a report from the Minister, he is satisfied that the said person either: (a) has, during any war in which Canada is or has been engaged, unlawfully traded or communicated with the enemy or with a subject of an enemy state or has been engaged in or associated with any business which to his knowledge is carried on in such manner as to assist the enemy in such war ... (d) if out of Canada, has shown himself by act or speech to be disaffected or disloyal to His Majesty, or, if in Canada, has been convicted of treason or sedition by a court of competent jurisdiction' (section 21(1)).

66 Demirjian, Gray, and Wright, *The 1947 Canadian Citizenship Act.*

67 Barbara Roberts, *Whence They Came: Deportation from Canada 1900–1935* (Ottawa: University of Ottawa Press, 1988).

68 John Porter, *The Vertical Mosaic* (Toronto: University of Toronto Press, 1966).

69 King, 'Text of the Prime Minister's Speech.'

70 Quoted in Jakubowski, *Immigration and the Legalization of Racism,* 17.

71 Some Black people were brought to Canada as slaves, and others came as Loyalists and pioneers as early as the seventeenth century (Bolaria and Li, *Racial Oppression in Canada*). The first Chinese migrants to come to Canada are recorded to have arrived in 1858. See Peter Li, *The Chinese in Canada* (Toronto: Oxford University Press, 1998), 3.

72 See L. Lowe, *Immigrant Acts: On Asian American Cultural Politics* (Durham, NC: Duke University Press, 1998).

73 See Hawkins, *Critical Years in Immigration*; Ungerleider, 'Immigration, Multiculturalism, and Citizenship'; Stasiulis and Jhappan, 'The Fractious Politics of a

Settler Society'; Jakubowski, *Immigration and the Legalization of Racism*; Bolaria and Li, *Racial Oppression in Canada*.

74 Paul Gordon, *Policing Immigration: Britain's Internal Controls* (London: Pluto Press, 1985); Women, Immigration and Nationality Group (WING), *World's Apart*; Potts, *The World Labour Market*; Mazumdar, 'Colonial Impact and Punjabi Emigration ...'

75 Bolaria and Li, *Racial Oppression in Canada*; Buchignani and Indra, *Continuous Journey*. For example, the 1923 Immigration Act required all Chinese in Canada to register and obtain a certificate from the state, whatever their legal status. Naturalization was made very difficult for Chinese immigrants so that between 1915 and 1930, only 349 Chinese immigrants were naturalized. An Order in Council was passed in 1931 that required all Chinese applying for citizenship to get consent from the minister of the interior in China (Bolaria and Li, *Racial Oppression in Canada*, 87–8). Chinese immigrants, *as a race*, were also not allowed to acquire Crown lands, hand logger's licences or liquor licences, and had to pay special poll taxes. South Asians were subjected to similar treatment: they were denied the franchise and defined as 'alien residents,' subject to deportation. All Asians were denied the right to vote until 1947 on the basis of their racial identity.

76 For example, the Chinese population in British Columbia fluctuated from being about 15 per cent to 40 per cent of the population in the 1860s (Ward, *White Canada Forever*, 14). The Chinese were about 17.1 per cent of the population in 1870, but by 1921 they had been reduced to 5.1 per cent of the population. In 1901, Asians in the province were 10.9 per cent of the total population. However, by 1941, they had been reduced to 5.2 per cent of the population (ibid., 170–1).

77 Amy Chua identifies a historical pattern of ethnic minorities gaining control over vital sectors of the economy in most of the 'developing world,' giving rise to deep-seated hostility to their economic domination among majority communities. See A. Chua, *World on Fire: How Exploring Free Market Democracy Breeds Ethnic Hatred and Global Instability* (New York: Anchor Books, 2004).

78 By 1759, there were over 1,000 Black slaves in New France and by 1767 there were 104 in Nova Scotia. In 1783, Loyalists brought 2,000 more Black slaves into the country (Bolaria and Li, *Racial Oppression in Canada*, 166). The Royal Commission on Bilingualism and Biculturalism noted the following about the history of Black migration: 'Negroes came to new France and to the Provinces of British North America in the 18th century chiefly as slaves. In the 19th century, they formed sizable settlements as freedmen and fugitives in the Maritimes, in southwestern Ontario, and in Victoria. Many returned to the United States in the 1860s, during and after the Civil War.

The 1871 census figure of 21,500 for Canada probably represents a drop in the negro population from an earlier period. The 1881, 1901, and 1911 censuses record further declines' (*Immigration and the Rise of Multiculturalism*). In the case of British Columbia, Sir James Douglas, whose father was a Glasgow-born merchant who had settled in British Guiana on his family's sugar plantations, and whose mother was a creole, became the governor in 1851. In 1855 American prospectors began to enter the then British territory, and Douglas encouraged the migration of Black settlers to counter this growing American presence. See Crawford Kilian, *Go Do Something Beautiful: The Black Pioneers of British Columbia* (Vancouver: Douglas and McIntyre, 1978).

79 Bolaria and Li, *Racial Oppression in Canada*, 168.
80 Palmer, *Immigration and the Rise of Multiculturalism*.
81 Hawkins, *Critical Years in Immigration*.
82 The construction of the railway led to 17,000 Chinese workers being recruited between 1876 and 1884 (Adilman, 'A Preliminary Sketch of Chinese Women ... ,' 55). See also Mazumdar, 'Colonial Impact and Punjabi Emigration ... '; Jabukowshi, *Immigration and the Legalization of Racism*.
83 See Porter, *The Vertical Mosaic*. The labour of Chinese men was so critical to building this railway and the risks of this work so great that the 1970 Report on Bilingualism and Biculturalism stated, 'It has been said that a Chinese is buried beneath every mile of track of the railway through the mountains of British Columbia' (Palmer, *Immigration and the Rise of Multiculturalism*, 6).
84 Bolaria and Li, *Racial Oppression in Canada*, 86.
85 The head tax was initially set at $10 and steadily increased over the years to $50 between 1896 and 1900; $100 for the next three years; and $500 from 1904 to 1923. See Hawkins, *Critical Years in Immigration*; Adilman, 'A Preliminary Sketch of Chinese Women ...'; Ungerleider, 'Immigration, Multiculturalism, and Citizenship'; and Jesuit Refugee Service, 'Racism and Xenophobia against Refugees and Immigrants in Canada,' Occasional Paper No. 1 (Toronto: JRS, 1995). As Bolaria and Li point out, 'The head tax was a compromise over a basic dilemma which involved a desire to maintain the convenience of using Chinese labour on the one hand, and an unwillingness to recognize the rights of Chinese on the other. It was a means to ensure that the supply of Chinese labour would not be completely severed, while at the same time, to officially endorse the second-class entrance status of the Chinese. Such an endorsement helped to sustain the marginal participation of the Chinese in the Canadian economy' (*Racial Oppression in Canada*, 90).
86 See Hawkins, *Critical Years in Immigration*; Undgerleider, 'Immigration, Multiculturalism, and Citizenships.' In addition to reducing the immigration of the Chinese, the head tax was also a lucrative source of revenue for the state.

Between 1886 and 1924, special registrations required of Chinese immigrants and the head tax brought in revenues amounting to $22.5 million (Bolaria and Li, *Racial Oppression in Canada*, 90).

87 This legislation required immigrants to travel from the country of origin to Canada in an uninterrupted journey. At that time, only one steamship company offered continuous passage to Canada, and this company was persuaded by the state to discontinue selling tickets (Buchignani and Indra, *Continuous Journey*; Mazumdar 'Colonial Impact and Punjabi Emigration ...'; and Adhopia, *The Hindus of Canada*. Tickets were not sold even to those South Asians who were already settled in Canada and were visiting the country of their origin.

88 Ungerleider, 'Immigration, Multiculturalism, and Citizenship,' 9. In 1910, a $200 head tax on South Asians was introduced.

89 Hawkins, *Critical Years in Immigration*; Jakubowski, *Immigration and the Legalization of Racism*.

90 Ungerleider, 'Immigration, Multiculturalism, and Citizenship,' 9.

91 Adhopia, *The Hindus of Canada*; Buchignani and Indra, *Continuous Journey*; Adilman, 'A Preliminary Sketch of Chinese Women ...'; Doman, 'A Note on Asian Indian Women ...'; and Alma Estable, *Immigrant Women in Canada: Current Issues* (Ottawa: The Canadian Advisory Council on the Status of Women, 1986).

92 Chinese and South Asian immigrants organized campaigns against the various head taxes and the Chinese Exclusion Act. They confronted racist immigration laws head on, as most famously demonstrated in the case of the *Komagatu Maru*. See Adhopia, *The Hindus of Canada*; Buchignani and Indra, *Continuous Journey*.

93 The Japanese, for example, were engaged in salmon fishing and berry farming to such an extent that they were considered to present a serious threat to the interests of whites in these sectors. In 1919, Japanese-Canadians held almost half of the fishing licences in British Columbia. Ward, *White Canada Forever.*

94 Ibid., 16.

95 This situation changed in 1908 when immigration from Japan was made subject to a 'Gentlemen's Agreement,' which allowed only returning Japanese immigrants and their families, along with their employees, to enter the country. This agreement lasted until 1940. The example of Japanese-Canadians is also significant because Japanese women's immigration was at a rate higher than that of men. The women were allowed to come as 'picture brides' for Japanese men who had been allowed to migrate earlier, between 1890 and 1907. See K. Victor Ujimoto, 'Multiculturalism and the Global Information

Society,' in Vic Satzewich, ed., *Deconstructing a Nation: Immigration, Multiculturalism and Racism in '90s Canada* (Halifax: Fernwood 1985), 351–8.

96 In 1942, 22,000 Japanese-Canadian women, men, and children in British Columbia were given twenty-four hours to vacate their homes. Branded as 'enemy aliens,' their businesses, houses, and other belongings were confiscated by the state. The proceeds of the sale of their property were used to finance the costs of their internment. Seventy-five per cent of them had been born in Canada and were 'citizens' by birth and by domicile. But this status was not sufficient to prevent 4,000 of them from being deported to Japan. Order in Council PC1486 gave authority to the RCMP to remove 'persons of Japanese racial origin,' to conduct searches without warrants, along with the power to enforce a curfew and to impound their cars, radios, cameras and firearms. See Roy Miki, and C. Kobayashi, *Justice in Our Time: The Japanese Canadian Redress Settlement* (Vancouver: National Association of Japanese Canadians, 1991); Morris Davis, and Joseph F. Krauter, *The Other Canadians: Profiles of Six Minorities* (Toronto: Metheun, 1971). The internment was legitimized on the basis of the 'race' of the Japanese community, and the incident used to justify this suspension of their citizenship was the bombing of Pearl Harbour by Japan on 7 December 1941. The stark choice given to Japanese-Canadians was that of internment and dispersal from British Columbia, or repatriation to Japan.

97 As noted by Ward: 'The pattern of the mobilizing for this outburst is also revealing, for, by and large, British Columbians reached their conclusions about the Japanese menace with little prompting. More or less simultaneously, thousands recognized an obvious threat and identified the equally obvious solution. In the generation of this consensus, neither popular leaders nor popular journalism played a predominant role. Halford Wilson and MacGregor Macintosh, once the two chief critics of the west coast Japanese, were submerged beneath the rising tide of hostility. In fact, the protest movement had no preeminent leaders whatsoever. Nor did provincial papers become leaders of opinion, even though some took up the popular cry. During the crisis west coast journalism helped sustain the prevailing mood, but most papers merely reflected the popular mind. In other words, the outburst was both widespread and largely spontaneous' (*White Canada Forever,* 158–9). The organizations which came together to demand the expulsion of Japanese-Canadians reveals a race alliance forged across class and gender lines: it included women's and workers' organizations, as it did the Vancouver Real Estate Exchange, the BC Poultry Industries Committee, the North Burnaby Liberal Association, among many others (ibid., 159).

98 Demirjian, Gray, and Wright, *The 1947 Canadian Citizenship Act.*

99 The Immigration Act 1976–77, contained a specific non-discrimination
    clause on the following grounds: 'to ensure that any person who seeks
    admission to Canada on either a permanent or temporary basis is subject to
    standards of admission that do not discriminate on the grounds of race,
    national or ethnic origin, colour, religion or sex' (section 3(f)).
100 As the name indicates, immigrants were to be assessed on the allocation of
    points for their skills and the educational and occupational qualifications
    they possessed. Additionally, family members of immigrants and citizens
    were also allowed to immigrate. This 'family class' immigration is discussed
    in chapter 3.
101 The Act defined these categories as follows: (1) the family class, based upon
    the reunification of immediate family members of citizens and landed
    immigrants; and assisted relatives who did not have enough points to qual-
    ify under the independent category, but who were nominated by a relative
    in Canada for sponsorship; (2) independent applicants, whose eligibility
    was to be determined through the point system, with points being allocated
    on the basis of their skills (this class included assisted relatives), and (3) ref-
    ugees, who feared persecution and met the United Nations definition of
    'convention refugees.' Additional categories under which immigration was
    also organized were the Non-Immigrant Employment Authorization Pro-
    gram (NIEAP), introduced in 1973, and the domestic worker category. The
    NIEAP allowed workers to enter the country on temporary work permits.
    See Nandita Sharma, 'Cheap Myths and Bonded Lives: Freedom and Citi-
    zenship in Canadian Society,' *Beyond Law* 6, Issue 17 (1997), 35–62; Singh
    B. Bolaria, 'From Immigrant Settlers to Migrant Transients: Foreign Profes-
    sionals in Canada,' in Satzewich, ed., *Deconstructing a Nation*, 211–28; and
    Daiva Stasiulis, 'The Political Economy of Race, Ethnicity and Migration,'
    in Wallace Clement, ed., *Understanding Canada: Building the New Political
    Economy* (Montreal: McGill-Queen's University Press, 1997), 141–71.
    Domestic workers were allowed into the country as temporary workers
    between 1973 and 1981. Prior to 1973, domestic workers were allowed to
    enter as landed immigrants. However, this enabled many of them to find
    work in other occupations because of the low wages and unfavourable work-
    ing conditions in domestic work. Since 1981, domestic workers have been
    allowed to apply for landed status after having worked in Canada as domes-
    tic workers for two years. See Sedef Arat-Koc, 'Immigration Policies,
    Migrant Domestic Workers and the Definition of Citizenship in Canada,' in
    Satzewich, ed., *Deconstructing a Nation*, 229–42; Abigail Bakan, 'The Interna-
    tional Market for Female Labour and Individual Deskilling: West Indian
    Women Workers in Toronto,' *Canadian Journal of Latin American and Carib-*

bean Studies 12, no. 24 (1987), 69–85; and Makeda Silvera, 'Speaking óf Women's Lives and Imperialist Economics: Two Introductions from *Silenced*,' in Himani Bannerji, eds., *Returning the Gaze: Essays on Racism, Feminism and Politics* (Toronto: Sister Vision Press, 1993), 242–69. These two categories have been made 'invisible' as they are rarely publicly referred to in discussions of the immigration program. In 1986, another category of immigrants was created, that of the 'business immigrant,' or the 'entrepreneur' category. Applicants under this category were required to have a 'personal net worth of at least $500,000,' and invest an amount in the range of $150,000 to $500,000 in order to qualify. See Lloyd L. Wong and Nancy S. Netting, 'Business Immigrant to Canada: Social Impact and Racism,' in Satzewich, ed., *Deconstructing a Nation*, 93–122.

102 J. Brodie, 'Three Stories of Canadian Citizenship,' in Adamoski, Chunn, and Menzies, eds., *Contesting Canadian Citizenship*, 43–65. The most salient change (for the purpose of this study) was that the residency requirement for eligibility to citizenship was reduced to three years, and the twenty-year residency requirement for applicants who did not speak English or French was eliminated (Demirjian, Gray, and Wright, *The 1947 Canadian Citizenship Act*).

103 Demerjian, Gray, and Wright, *The 1947 Canadian Citizenship Act*.

104 Alan G. Green and David A. Green, 'The Economic Goals of Canada's Immigration Policy, Past and Present' (paper presented at the British Columbia Centre For Excellence on Immigration, Vancouver, 1997); and Hawkins, *Critical Years in Immigration*.

105 Yasmeen Abu-Laban, 'Keeping 'em Out: Gender, Race and Class Biases in Canadian Immigration Policy,' in Joan Anderson, Avigail Eisenberg, Sherrill Grace, and Veronica Strong-Boag, eds., *Painting the Maple: Essays on Race, Gender, and the Construction of Canada* (Vancouver: University of British Columbia Press, 1998), 69–82; Tania Das Gupta, 'Families of Native Peoples, Immigrants, and People of Colour,' in Nancy Mandell and Anne Duffy, eds., *Canadian Families: Diversity, Conflict and Change* (Toronto: Harcourt Brace, 1995), 141–74; Roxana Ng, 'Gendering Policy Research on Immigration,' in *Gendering Immigration: Integration Policy Research Workshop Proceedings and a Selective Review of Policy Research Literature 1987–1996* (Ottawa: Status of Women Canada, 1998), 13–22; and Roxana Ng and Janet Strout, *Services for Immigrant Women: Report and Evaluation of a Series of Four Workshops Conducted in the Summer, 1977* (Vancouver: Women's Research Centre, 1977). Between 1951 and 1957, 91.39 per cent of immigration recruitment expenses went to 'developed' countries, and between 1962 and 1969, 78.2 per cent went to the same. Likewise, there were five immigration offices in the United King-

dom and ten in the United States in 1981, compared with one in India and one for the entire continent of Africa (Jakubowski, *Immigration and the Legalization of Racism*, 18–20). The Act allowed immigration officers to grant points for the personal suitability of applicants and also gave them powers to override the point system entirely in certain cases. These powers allowed the personal prejudices of officers to be exercised in their allocation of points to prospective immigrants, argue these scholars. In the 1970s, then immigration lawyer and subsequent Attorney General and premier of British Columbia, Ujjal Dosanjh, identified precisely these discretionary powers as one of the major factors in the discriminatory treatment of 'visible minorities.' At a workshop for service providers held in 1977, Dosanjh pointed out that 'visible minorities' are disproportionately detained and investigated by immigration officials (Ng and Strout, *Services for Immigrant Women*). See also Abu-Laban, 'Keeping 'em Out.'

106 See Green, 'Towards a Détente with History'; Lawrence, *'Real' Indians and Others.* Also see R. Bateman, 'Comparative Thoughts on the Politics of Aboriginal Assimilation,' *BC Studies: The British Columbian Quarterly*, no. 114 (Summer 1997), 59–83.

107 See Bateman, 'Comparative Thoughts ...' for a discussion of such public attitudes in Canada and the United States.

108 A. Sivanandan, *A Different Hunger: Writings on Black Resistance* (London: Pluto Press, 1982).

109 Paul Gilroy, *There Ain't No Black in the Union Jack* (Chicago: University of Chicago Press, 1991); Waqar I. Ahmad and Charles Husband, 'Religious Identity, Citizenship, and Welfare: The Case of Muslims in Britain,' *The American Journal of Islamic Social Sciences* 10, no. 2 (1993), 217–33; Gordon, *Policing Immigration*; and WING, *World's Apart*.

110 Ahmad and Husband, 'Religious Indentity, Citizenship, and Welfare,' 219.

111 Norman Ginsburg, *Divisions of Welfare: A Critical Introduction to Comparative Social Policy* (London: Sage, 1992); Amina Mama, *The Hidden Struggle: Statutory and Voluntary Sector Responses to Violence against Black Women in the Home* (London: London Race and Housing Research Unit, 1989).

112 Marshall, 'Citizenship and Social Class.' Most contemporary discussions take Marshall's theorization of citizenship, rooted in liberal political theory, as their point of departure.

3. The Welfare of Nationals

1 Human Resources Development Canada (HRDC), *Agenda: Jobs and Growth: Improving Social Security in Canada, A Discussion Paper* (The Green Paper)

(Ottawa: Minister of Supply and Services Canada, 1994), 9. See also the discussion of the Social Security Review documents in chapter 5. These documents repeatedly affirm compassion and care as a core national value of the nation-state in the post-war period.

2 Alvin Finkel, 'The Origins of the Welfare State in Canada,' in Leo Panitch, ed., *The Canadian State: Political Economy and Political Power* (Toronto: University of Toronto Press, 1977), 433–70; John Clarke, Allan Cochrane, and Carol Smart, *Ideologies of Welfare: From Dreams to Disillusion* (London: Routledge, 1992); Jane Ursel, *Private Lives, Public Policy: 100 Years of State Intervention in the Family* (Toronto: Women's Press, 1992); and Ramesh Mishra, *Society and Social Policy: Theoretical Perspectives on Welfare* (London: Macmillan, 1977).

3 Mishra, *Society and Social Policy*. Clarke, Cochrane, and Smart in *Ideologies of Welfare* identified four major ideological themes in Britain during the late nineteenth century: (1) laissez-faire individualism, which opposed state intervention in the free market; (2) Fabianism, which supported state intervention to solve social problems by delivering social services based upon 'professional expertise'; (3) socialism, whose support for social programs was somewhat ambiguous because of the impact of these in lessening support for socialist revolution; and (4) finally feminism, which sought to empower women and reduce their economic inequalities through their access to social programs.

4 Finkel, 'The Origins of the Welfare State in Canada'; Clarke, Cochrane, and Smart, *Ideologies of Welfare*; Ursel, *Private Lives, Public Policy*; and Mishra, *Society and Social Policy*.

5 Ursel, *Public Lives, Private Policy*; Nancy Fraser and Linda Gordon, 'Contract Versus Charity,' *Socialist Review* 22, no. 3 (1992), 45–65.

6 Social programs have reinforced the gendered division of labour in society, feminist scholars have found. Although these programs have indeed provided vital support for women's labour within the family, they have also perpetuated women's inequalities by keeping them primarily responsible for this labour, subjecting women to 'public patriarchy' in addition to the 'private patriarchy.' For a very useful explication of the concept of public patriarchy, see Nancy Fraser, *Unruly Practices* (Minneapolis: University of Minnesota Press, 1989), 146. For feminist critiques of the welfare state, see also Ursel, *Public Lives, Private Policy*; Megan Davies, '"Services Rendered, Rearing Children for the State": Mothers' Pensions in British Columbia 1919–1931,' in Barbara K. Latham and Roberta J. Pazdro, eds., *Not Just Pin Money: Selected Essays on the History of Women's Work in British Columbia* (Victoria: Camosun College, 1984), 249–64; Ruth Lister, 'Citizenship Engendered,' *Critical Social Policy* 11, no. 2 (32) (1991), 65–71; and Sylvia Walby, 'Is Citizenship Gendered?' *Sociology* 28, no. 2 (1994), 379–95.

7 The sense of entitlement has been greatly eroded during the 1990s, with social assistance programs becoming highly stigmatized, as have been the claimants of these programs. The restructuring of the Canadian social security system during the 1990s is discussed in chapter 5.

8 Ward Churchill, *Kill the Indian, Save the Man: The Genocidal Impact of American Indian Residential Schools* (San Francisco: City Lights Books, 2004).

9 Linda Gordon, *Pitied But Not Entitled: Single Mothers and the History of Welfare* (Cambridge, MA: Harvard University Prss, 1994), 132. Gordon points out that Black women who built 'welfare' institutions in their communities were committed to supporting Black women's role in mothering. The effects of slavery had been devastating for Black families and had undermined the role of Black women as mothers. An urgent concern for Black women was the mothering of their children. While white reformers were also concerned with the role of mothering, Gordon argues that the race concerns of white feminists and Black feminists from the 1890s to 1935 sprang from very different motivations and had different consequences. White women shared the same assumptions as white men and helped to maintain white supremacy within the global capitalist system. Black women's concerns for the upliftment of their race were based on an oppositional politics that challenged the racial supremacy of whites. Patricia Hill Collins concurs that Black women were committed to the upliftment of their race in the community institutions they built. See Patricia Hill Collins, *Black Feminist Thought: Knowledge, Consciousness and the Politics of Empowerment* (New York: Routledge, 1991), 100–107.

10 Goodleaf, '"Under Military Occupation"'; Maracle, 'Racism, Sexism and Patriarchy' and Sharon McIvor, 'A Social Policy Agenda for First Nations Women,' in Frank Tester, Chris McNiven, and Robert Case, eds., *Critical Choices, Turbulent Times* (Vancouver: The School of Social Work, University of British Columbia, 1996), 100–107.

11 The cyclical nature of capitalist growth had become devastatingly clear during the Depression, and the 'new' liberals made a case that the state had an obligation to protect its citizens from the sometimes catastrophic consequences of economic cycles over which these individuals had no control. John Maynard Keynes and Lord Beveridge were among the 'new' liberals who developed the theoretical and intellectual foundations of the welfare state. Keynesian economic policies and the Beveridge Report – dubbed the 'blueprint' for the welfare state – were to have significant impact on the development of welfare states in Canada. For Canada, see Ursel, *Private Lives, Public Policy*; Finkel, 'The Origins of the Welfare State in Canada'; Davies, '"Services Rendered ..."'; for the United States, see Gordon, *Pitied But Not Entitled*. For Australia, see Jan Jindy Pettman, 'Border Crossings/Shifting

Identities: Minorities, Gender, and the State in International Perspective,' in
Michael J. Shapiro and Hayward R. Alker, eds., *Challenging Boundaries: Global
Flows, Territorial Identities* (Minneapolis: University of Minnesota Press, 1996),
261–84. See also Francesca Klug, '"Oh to be in England": The British Case
Study,' in Nira Yuval-Davis and Floya Anthias, eds., *Women-Nation-State* (New
York: St. Martin's Press, 1989), 16–35; Robert C. Lieberman, 'Race and Lim-
its of Solidarity,' in Sanford F. Schram, Joe Soss, and Richard C. Fording,
eds., *Race and the Politics of Welfare Reform* (Ann Arbor: University of Michigan
Press, 2003), 23–46; Jane Lewis, 'The Working-Class Wife and Mother and
State Intervention, 1870–1918,' in Jane Lewis, ed., *Labour and Love: Women's
Experience of Home and Family, 1850–1940* (Oxford: Basil Blackwell, 1986), 99–
122; Clarke, Cochrane, and Smart, *Ideologies of Welfare*; Ginsburg, *Divisions of
Welfare*; S. Nasir, '"Race," Gender and Social Policy,' in C. Hallett, ed., *Women
and Social Policy* (London: Prentice Hall,1996), 15–30.
12 Finkel, 'The Origins of the Welfare State in Canada'; Mishra, *Society and
Social Policy*; Ursel, *Private Lives, Public Policy*; Clarke, Cochrane and Smart,
Ideologies of Welfare.
13 Mishra, *Society and Social Policy*. Lieberman describes this concern in the following manner: 'The welfare state traces its origins to a political moment in
which imperial conquest and colonial rule were at the centre of political life.
Both enterprises were part of the process by which European states negotiated the transition toward mass politics and democracy, which required new
means for securing the allegiance of the working class and creating an 'imagined community' among citizens' ('Race and Limits of Solidarity,' 30).
14 Katherine Arnup has pointed out that 68 per cent of men who came forward
were rejected as 'unfit' for enlistment in the armed forces in the First World
War. See Arnup 'Education for Motherhood: Creating Modern Mothers and
Model Citizens,' in Adamoski, Chunn, and Menzies, eds., *Contesting Canadian Citizenship*, 249.
15 Mishra, *Society and Social Policy*, 73.
16 More than 60,000 Canadians were killed in the First World War, and 'countless others' were left with disabilities. 'Families were fragmented, and thousands of mothers were left to raise children on their own, with little financial
aid' (Arnup, 'Education for Motherhood,' 248).
17 See Clarke, Cochrane, and Smart, *Ideologies of Welfare*; Leo Panitch, 'The Role
and Nature of the Canadian State,' in Leo Panitch, *The Canadian State: Political Economy and Political Power* (Toronto: University of Toronto Press, 1977),
3–27.
18 T.H. Marshall argued that citizenship had been evolving in a 'continuous
progress' for three centuries, in the 'modern drive' towards equality. He

defined the development of the social entitlements of the welfare state as essential to the ability of citizens to access their political and civil rights more fully. See 'Citizenship and Social Class.'

19 Ginsburg, *Divisions of Welfare*, 165–6. The Beveridge Report of 1943 was quite forthright in its commitment to strengthen the nation and called for the provision of support for the role of British women as mothers of the race and nation. It linked the well-being of race *as* nation to the well-being of women and the family, valorizing the role of women within the family as a form of 'national service' See Clarke, Cochrane, and Smart, *Ideologies of Welfare*. During this period, immigration was defined as necessary primarily to provide labour for the economy, but not to expand the population base of the nation. The Women, Immigration and Nationality Group's (WING) report noted that immigration from Britain's Black and Asian colonies was significant in the provision of the labour necessary for economic expansion during the first half of the twentieth century. However, the Royal Commission on Population (1950s) rejected the idea that the British nation could be replenished through such immigration. The commission's report argued that 'British traditions, manners and ideas' were very important and would suffer from immigration, as this would 'reduce the proportion of home-bred stock in the population' (WING, *World's Apart*, 4). WING was formed at a conference organized in Britain in 1982 to bring together women activists campaigning against racism and sexism in immigration and nationality laws. Seven members of this group researched the history of British nationality and immigration laws in the writing of the report.

20 Arnup argues that the declining birth rate in Canada and increased immigration prompted concerns about 'race suicide' within the country ('Education fro Motherhood,' 249).

21 See Laura Anne Stoler, *Race and the Education of Desire* (Durham, NC: Duke University Press, 1995); Ann McClintock, *Imperial Leather* (New York: Routledge, 1995); Iacovetta and Valverde, eds., *Gender Conflicts*; and Enakshi Dua, '"The Hindu Woman's Question": Canadian Nation Building and the Social Construction of Gender for South-Asian Canadian Women,' in Agnes Calliste and George Dei, eds., *Anti-Racist Feminism* (Halifax: Fernwood Publishing, 2000).

22 Patricia Hill Collins, 'It's All in the Family: Intersections of Gender, Race, and Nation,' Uma Narayan and Sandra Harding, eds., *Decentering the Center: Philosophy for a Multicultural, Postcolonial and Feminist World* (Bloomington: Indiana University Press, 2000), 156–76.

23 Ibid., 157.

24 See Enakshi Dua, 'Beyond Diversity: Exploring the Ways in which the Dis-

course of Race Has Shaped the Institution of the Nuclear Family,' in Enakshi Dua and Angela Robertson, eds., *Scratching the Surface: Canadian Anti-Racist Feminist Thought* (Toronto: Women's Press, 1999), 237–59. Das Gupta, 'Families of Native Peoples ...'; Maracle, 'Racism, Sexism and Patriarchy'; and Angela Davis, *Women, Race and Class* (New York: Vintage Books, 1983).

25 Finkel, 'The Origins of the Welfare State in Canada,' 346. He concludes that the driving force behind the creation of the welfare state was the need for the state to 'stabilize destabilized economies' and not the redistribution of wealth (348).

26 Ursel, *Private Lives, Public Policy.*

27 See Finkel, 'The Origins of the Welfare State in Canada,' 351. It was also in this spirit that the president of the Bank of Montreal, for example, expressed his support for unemployment and social insurance programs in a letter to the government in 1934: 'May I suggest to you that *for our general self-preservation* some such arrangement will have to be worked out in Canada and that if it can be done soon so much the better' (349). Finkel also cites the 1939 Royal Commission on Dominion-Provincial Relations, which expressed the following reasoning for the growing support among conservatives for social programs:

> Since the Great War, the Great Depression has been the chief stimulus to labour legislation and social insurance. The note sounded has not been so much the ideal of social justice as political and economic financial expediency. For instance, the shorter working week was favoured in unexpected quarters not because it would give the workers more leisure and possibilities for a fuller life but because it would spread work; and the current singling out of unemployment insurance for governmental attention in many countries is dictated by the appalling costs of direct relief and the hope that unemployment insurance benefits will give some protection to public treasuries in future depressions and will, by sustaining purchasing power, tend to mitigate these depressions (348).

28 Rather than placing limits on capital, the welfare state supported capitalism in two significant ways: structurally, it created favourable conditions for capital accumulation by reducing the costs to capital for the reproduction of the workforce and by stabilizing consumption patterns through income support programs; and politically, it legitimized the functions of the state as representing the interests of all its citizens, and not just the capitalist class. See, for example, Iris Marion Young, *Justice and the Politics of Difference* (Princeton, NJ: Princeton University Press, 1990). Theorists have also pointed out that the social programs of the welfare state were collectively funded by working

classes through taxation so that the welfare state resulted not in a 'vertical' redistribution of wealth between classes but a 'horizontal' redistribution. See, for example, Ginsburg, *Division of Welfare*, and Mishra, *Society and Social Policy*.

29 Arnup has noted that the participation of Canadian women in the war effort was integral to their enfranchisement and subsequent increased access to citizenship rights: 'The war provided the ideal opportunity for women to demonstrate their capacity to fulfill this new role [in the public sphere]. Through their participation on the home front, caring for their families while their husbands fought overseas, running voluntary organizations, and, to a limited extent, operating factories, women were deemed worthy of the ultimate reward of citizenship: the vote. While numerous factors, including the need to create an electorate favourable to conscription, led to women's enfranchisement at this time, it was women's wartime service that was used to justify granting women the franchise in 1918' ('Education for Motherhood,' 251).

30 Lister, 'Citizenship Engendered'; Ursel, *Private Lives, Public Policy*; Gordon, *Pitied But Not Entitled*; Clarke, Cochrane, and Smart, *Ideologies of Welfare*; Ginsburg, *Divisions of Welfare*.

31 Gordon, *Pitied But Not Entitled*; Strong Boag, '"Setting the Stage."'

32 Arnup, 'Education for Motherhood.'

33 Ursel, *Private Lives, Public Policy*.

34 This compromise has resulted in women working the double day, which means their labour is assigned to both the spheres of production and reproduction. Moreover, the continuing wage gap has helped to maintain women's economic dependence on men. While Ursel's analysis does not acknowledge the role of the women's movement in the creation of the welfare state, a number of feminist theorists concur with her conclusion that the welfare state preserved the gendered inequalities of the wage system. See Gordon, *Pitied But Not Entitled*; Walby, 'Is Citizenship Engendered?'; Lister, 'Citizenship Engendered'; and Nancy Fraser, *Unruly Practices* (Minneapolis: University of Minnesota Press, 1989).

35 Eugenicist concerns were widespread in Canada up to the mid-twentieth century. In his study of the eugenics movement between 1885 and 1945, Angus McLaren demonstrates that these concerns regarding 'race,' 'quality,' and 'purity' were shared by organizations like the Toronto League for Race Betterment, medical associations, and individuals like socialist leader Tommy Douglas and the feminist leader Agnes MacPhail. See Angus McLaren, *Our Own Master Race: Eugenics in Canada, 1855–1945* (Toronto: McClelland and Stewart, 1990).

36 For discussion of these measures, see Dyck, *What Is the 'Indian' Problem*; Hawk-

ins, *Critical Years in Immigration*; Ministry of Immigration and Colonization (MIC), *The Houseworker in Canada: Opportunities for Success, Work and Wages, Where To Go and What To Take* (Ottawa: MIC, 1928); Women's Migration and Overseas Appointments Society (WMOAS), *New Horizons: A Hundred Years of Women's Migration* (London: Her Majesty's Stationery Office, 1963); Helen I. Cowan, *British Immigration before Confederation* (Ottawa: The Canadian Historical Association, 1968); and Carrothers, *Emigration from the British Isles.*

37 WMOAS, *New Horizons.*

38 For one example, the ministry of immigration and colonization produced a pamphlet in 1928 to recruit British women as 'houseworkers.' The pamphlet described Canada as 'a land of opportunity' and provided general information about the country, along with specific information about work opportunities, wage levels, and working conditions. The climate was described as 'particularly suited to the white race,' and British women were told they would be 'welcomed' by the 'people.' It provided information about the emigration agents in Britain who could provide assistance to interested women, and prospective emigrants were informed that arrangements could be made for them to stay at Canadian Women's Hostels upon arrival, where they could also acquire training before going into service. These hostels were located in major centres across the country, and they were supported by the government for women emigrants from the Mother Country. Assisted passages were offered under the Empire Settlement Scheme, as were free medical examinations for the 'right type' of applicant. The British government, the Canadian government and steamship companies contributed funds under this scheme. Women officers appointed by the director of emigration and conductresses employed by steamship companies 'assisted' the women in their migration. See MIC, *The Houseworker in Canada.*

39 See Joy Parr's 'The Skilled Emigrant and Her Kin' that studies the recruitment of women hosiery workers by the Penman's Company between 1907 and 1928. Her assessment of the impact of migration on these women's lives is interesting: 'Within the new regime, women's prospects in particular were better in Canada than in Britain' (535). Immigration gave the women opportunities for 'better paying and more steady' work in Canada. The women were given tickets and 'modest cash advances' by their employer, and among them were widows for whom 'emigration was a way to keep the family solvent and together' (543–4).

40 That maternal feminists valorized women's role as mothers is well recognized in the historical record, as is the recognition that they did this in an overtly racialized manner. Most of them participated in the colonial and anti-immigration campaigns of the day. In the 1870s, the maternal feminists who

dominated the feminist movement built organizations, both local and national, to work for the good of the family and the nation. The growth of organizations such as the National Council of Women demonstrated the 'growing national self-confidence' of the women who participated in its activities, and the association of 'homes and nations,' of the 'family and state,' was the 'leitmotif' of these 'feminist-nationalists' (Strong-Boag, '"Setting the Stage,"' 101). The 'ideal of female moral superiority' they promoted was one that they shared with church organizations and other social groups. The Woman's Christian Temperance Union, the Young Women's Christian Association, the Girls Friendly Society, the Dominion Order of King's Daughters, Women's Missionary Societies, and other church organizations were among the many organizations established by these women (ibid.). See also Iacovetta and Valverde, *Gender Conflicts*.

41 Arnup, 'Education for Motherhood.'
42 Dua, 'The Hindu Woman's Question.'
43 See M. Evans and G.R. Wekerle, eds., *Women and the Welfare State: Challenges and Change* (Toronto: University of Toronto Press, 1997).
44 Finkel, 'The Origins of the Welfare State in Canada,' 345; Ursel, *Private Lives, Public Policy*; Mishra, *Society and Social Policy*.
45 Gordon, *Pitied But Not Entitled*, 287.
46 Evans and Wekerle, *Women and the Welfare State*, 3.
47 Quoted in Suzanne Fournier and Ernie Crey, *Stolen from Our Embrace: The Abduction of First Nations Children and the Restoration of Aboriginal Communities* (Vancouver: Douglas and McIntyre, 1997), 51–2.
48 Tania Das Gupta, 'Families of Native People, Immigrants, and People of Colour,' in B. Crow, and L. Gotell, eds., *Open Boundaries: A Canadian Women's Studies Reader* (Toronto: Prentice Hall, 2005), 199–216.
49 Lawrence, *'Real' Indians and Others*.
50 Churchill, *Kill the Indian, Save the Man*, 12.
51 Duncan Campbell Scott, quoted in ibid., 16.
52 See chapter 2 in Fournier and Crey, *Stolen From Our Embrace*. Also see Ronald Chrisjohn and Sherri Young, with Michael Maraun, *The Circle Game: Shadows and Substance in the Indian Residential School Experience in Canada* (Penticton, BC: Theytus Books, 1997).
53 See Arnup, 'Education for Motherhood.'
54 Jean Barman, 'Taming Aboriginal Sexuality: Gender, Power, and Race in British Columbia, 1850–1900,' *BC Studies: The British Columbian Quarterly*, Special Issue, Numbers 115/116 (Autumn/Winter 1997/98), 237–66.
55 Ibid.
56 See chapter 10 in Monture-Angus, *Thunder in My Soul*.

57 Quoted in Fournier and Crey, *Stolen from Our Embrace*, 49.

58 An army officer, Captain Richard Henry Pratt, who had worked as warden of an army prison, was appointed to 'create' and 'supervise' the residential school system in the United States. Ward Churchill argues that although the Canadian system was not run by an army officer or prison warden, it was modelled on the same principles as the American system (*Kill the Indian, Save the Man*, 13–14).

59 As Fournier and Crey describe this situation: 'Official policy called for children to be isolated, not only from their family and homelands, but also, once at school, from their friends and siblings. Isolation made children more vulnerable to the massive brainwashing that was undertaken to replace their 'pagan superstitions' with Christianity, and their 'free and easy mode of life' with relentless labour and routine. 'There should be an object for the employment of every moment,' an 1891 federal report urged. Studies were confined to only half a day until well after the Second World War, and religion dominated every waking moment. Even recreation was controlled by European rules to teach 'obedience to discipline ... Expressions of Aboriginal culture and individuality were harshly punished. As soon as children entered school, their traditional long hair was shorn or shaved off; they were assigned a number and an English name, and warned not to let a word of their language pass their lips' (*Stolen from Our Embrace*, 56–7).

60 Churchill argues that the schools functioned largely as labour camps, and that there was little difference between the industrial and non-industrial schools (*Kill the Indian, Save the Man*, 44–51). Girls were taught domestic duties such as sewing, laundry, cooking and cleaning, while boys were employed in agriculture, carpentry, shoemaking, and blacksmithing. See also Fournier and Crey, *Stolen from Our Embrace*.

61 Churchill, *Kill the Indian, Save the Man*, 34–7.

62 Quoted in Neu and Therrien, *Accounting for Genocide*, 4.

63 Thirty thousand litigants were reported as suing the federal government and churches for the abuse they were subjected to in the residential school system. See Kirk Makin, 'Implications Huge for Other Organizations,' *Globe and Mail*, 26 March 2004, A4.

64 For a list of documented acts perpetrated in residential schools, see chapter 3 in Chrisjohn and Young, *The Circle Game*.

65 The following examples from presentations made to the Royal Commission on Aboriginal Peoples attest to the depth of this denial: 'British/European missionaries were convinced that their unique culture and faith expression must represent the truest reflection of Christianity and, therefore, of God's will. The Church felt it had a Christian responsibility to help the First

Nations assimilate into the political, economic and social structures of the British Empire ... Educating and converting children soon became a key component in meeting this responsibility' (from testimony submitted by the Anglican Church). 'Missionaries arrived with armies and merchants of the fur trade. Most missionaries sincerely desired to share their most precious gift – their faith. They were generous, courageous, and often holy men and women. While some of their actions may be criticized today in light of new understandings, they tried to act with love and compassion ... Although not the sole instigators, missionary and educational activities contributed to the weakening of the spirit of the Aboriginal Peoples' (from submission of the Permanent Council of the Canadian Conference of Catholic Bishops). Quoted in Chrisjohn and Young, *The Circle Game*, 10–11.

66 The *Montreal Star* and *Saturday Night* magazine reported on the very high death rates of Aboriginal children (24 per cent was the national death rate, rising to 42 per cent when children sent home to die after becoming ill were taken into account) found by a medical inspection in 1907 (Fournier and Crey, *Stolen from Our Embrace*, 40). Ward Churchill, Ronald Chrisjohn, and Sherri Young concur that the effects of the residential school system were well known to the political establishment.

67 Pointing out that applying the United Nations Genocide Convention to the residential school system would reveal it to have been a part of the genocidal policies of the state, Chrisjohn and Young's condemnation of the system is unequivocal: 'A nation that would do such a thing to other groups of people is not a nation of tolerant, industrious, god-fearing peace-keepers, but one of greedy, grasping, homicidal thieves' (*The Circle Game*, 57). They point out that although the facts regarding the extent of the abuse are not in dispute, the acts committed against Aboriginal children in those institutions never-theless continue to be defined as aberrations and mistakes. They point out that these acts amounted to crimes, and that the contemporary focus on pro-viding therapy to survivors of the residential school system diverts attention away from the criminal nature of these acts. They ask, '... lawyers, judges, officers of the law ... does no one here recognize that crimes have been com-mitted? We have searched in vain the testimony of those experts in criminal matters for any suggestion that the aggressive uncovering and prosecution of criminals should form any part of an appropriate response to issues of Indian Residential Schooling. Precisely how typical of the law enforcement and criminal justice systems is this attitude? Is 'therapy for the victim' the bottom line in criminal law for, say, bank robbery, tax fraud, or insider trad-ing?' (15–16).

68 Arnup, 'Education for Motherhood.'

69 Dr Helen MacMurchy, the first chief of the federal division of child welfare, quoted in ibid., 249.
70 Churchill, *Kill the Indian, Save the Man*, 18.
71 Chrisjohn and Young, *The Circle Game*, 76.
72 Towards the end of the 1960s, 30 per cent to 40 per cent of all children taken into care were Aboriginal, although they made up less than 4 per cent of the national population (Fournier and Crey, *Stolen from Our Embrace*, 83). For one example, a community in BC 'lost almost an entire generation' (ibid., 86). Aboriginal children made up 20 per cent of children in foster care in the country in 1979, although the Aboriginal population was 6 per cent of the total population. In Manitoba, the Native population was 12 per cent, whereas 60 per cent of children in foster care were Native. In Kenora, Ontario, 80 per cent of Native children were in care in the 1970s (Das Gupta, 'Families of Native Peoples, Immigrants and People of Colour,' 202). In 1977, 39 per cent of children in care in British Columbia were Aboriginal, 44 per cent in Alberta, 51.5 per cent in Saskatchewan, and 60 per cent in Manitoba (Monture-Angus, *Thunder in My Soul*, 192). The apprehension of Aboriginal children has worsened since the 1970s, with a report prepared for the Indian affairs minister in 2005 stating that 30 per cent to 40 per cent of all children in care are status Indian children. The documents note an increase of 71.5 per cent in the number of on-reserve children being placed in care between 1995 and 2001. One reason for the increase noted in the report is that First Nations agencies are 'woefully underfunded.' See B. Curry, 'Natives Make Up 30–40 per cent of Kids in the State's care,' *Vancouver Sun*, 5 January 2005, A4. The relatively recent development of First Nations agencies that deal directly with child apprehension and adoption is beyond the scope of this study.
73 Hudson and McKenzie, discussed in Das Gupta, 'Families of Native Peoples, Immigrants, and People of Colur.'
74 The 'ideology of motherhood' refers to the 'constellation of ideas and images in western capitalist societies that constitute dominant ideas of motherhood against which women's lives are judged.' See Marlee Kline, 'Complicating the Ideology of Motherhood: Child Welfare Law and First Nations Women,' in Crow and Gotell, eds., *Open Boundaries*, 190.
75 B. Wearing, quoted in ibid.
76 Arnup, 'Education for Motherhood,' 251–2.
77 Barman, 'Taming Aboriginal Sexuality.'
78 Anthropologist Jo-Anne Fiske has also pointed out that 'welfare-colonialism' has resulted in massive 'unemployment' and 'underdevelopment' on reserves, and that this has had serious effects on Aboriginal women's rights ('Political Status of Native Indian Women,' 8).

79 See M.D. Stout and G.D. Kipling, *Aboriginal Women in Canada: Strategic Research Directions for Policy Development* (Ottawa: Status of Women Canada, 1998).

80 Kline found that with regard to Aboriginal women, the system functions in the following ways: 'At both the initial stage of child welfare proceedings, when it is determined whether a child is in need of protection, and at the dispositional stage, when support services and/or alternative care placements are ordered, courts draw on ideological conceptions of motherhood which form part of the commonsense knowledge of judges. This happens in two interconnected ways. First, judges focus on and blame *individual* First Nations mothers for the difficulties they face without recognizing the roots of these difficulties in the history and current structures of colonialism and racial oppression. Second, the dominant ideology of motherhood operates to impose dominant cultural values and practices in relation to child-raising on First Nations, and correspondingly devalue First Nations values and practices in this context' ('Complicating the Ideology of Motherhood,' 192). Emphasis in original.

81 Fournier and Crey, *Stolen from Our Embrace*, 81.

82 After 1982, restrictions were imposed on out-of-province and international adoptions (ibid., 89).

83 Amendments were made to section 88 of the Indian Act in 1951, which 'stipulated that all laws of general application in force in a province should apply on reserves, unless they conflicted with treaties or federal laws.' This amendment delegated authority for Aboriginal health, welfare and education to provincial governments, although the federal government continued to remain financially responsible for these services (ibid., 83).

84 Ibid., 84.

85 Ibid., 89.

86 Monture-Angus, *Thunder in My Soul*, 196.

87 Bill Curry, 'Natives Make up 30–40% of Kids in the State's Care,' *Vancouver Sun*, 5 January 2005, A4.

88 See C. Baines, P. Evans, and S. Neysmith, eds., *Women's Caring: Feminist Perspectives on Social Welfare* (Toronto: McClelland and Stewart, 1991).

89 Punam Khosla, *Review of the Situation of Women Canada, 1993* (Toronto: The National Action Committee on the Status of Women, 1993).

90 G. Lewis, *'Race,' Gender, Social Welfare: Encounters in a Postcolonial Society* (Oxford: Polity Press, 2000).

91 Tania Das Gupta, *Racism and Paid Work* (Toronto: Garamond Press, 1996).

92 Arnup, 'Education for Motherhood,' 258.

93 Baines, Evans, and Neysmith, *Women's Caring*, 16.

94 Arnup, 'Education for Motherhood,' 263.

95 Kerstin Roger, '"Making" White Women through the Privatization of Education on Health and Well-Being in the Context of Psychotherapy,' in Calliste and Dei, eds., *Anti-Racist Feminism*, 123.

96 Ibid., 135.

97 This interviewee explained her reservations as follows: 'Even after the information, I'm seeking it out, there's people out there that are saying well *you don't fit in.* I've had profs where I've asked that question in Native Studies or otherwise and got told well we don't want your help ... And as far as I am concerned, I *have to try to fit in,* and I mean maybe one day I'll be the minority. You know, *I want to fit in. I don't want to have no rights, like you (Natives) had no rights.* Like, if one day I'm to come to Saskatchewan, and you (Native) people make up the majority of the population, which could very well be, I'd like to know that *I'm going to fit in* somewhere. *I don't want to be treated the way you've been treated,* you know.' Carol Schick, 'Keeping the Ivory Tower White: Discourses of Racial Domination.' In Sherene H. Razack, ed., *Race, Space, and the Law: Unmapping a White Settler Society* (Toronto: Between the Lines, 2002), 99–119.

98 Robert Adamoski, 'The Child – the Citizen – the Nation: The Rhetoric and Experience of Wardship in Early Twentieth-Century British Columbia,' in Adamoski, Chunn, and Menzies, *Contesting Canadian Citizenship*, 318. In his study of the records of the first cohort placed in the wardship of Vancouver Children's Aid Society (founded in 1901 under the Children's Protection Act), Robert Adamoski found that '[t]he early history of what has become Canada's child welfare system highlights the complex effects that children's race, gender and social status had on estimations of how best to prepare them to assume their appropriate station in Canadian society ... "rescue" did not bring equality or independence ... The stated goals of the Vancouver Children's Aid Society – the preservation and socialization of the child, the citizen, and the nation – explicitly functioned to differentiate between the bases of working-class male and female citizenship, and to exclude those deemed unworthy of full participation in Canadian society' (332).

99 Fournier and Crey, *Stolen from Our Embrace*, 85.

100 See Lieberman, 'Race and Limits of Solidarity.'

101 Quoted in Fournier and Crey, *Stolen from Our Embrace*, 93.

102 See Franca Iacovetta, 'Making "New Canadians": Social Workers, Women, and the Reshaping of Immigrant Families,' in Iacovetta and Valverde, eds., *Gender Conflicts*, 261–303. Iacovetta's study examines the historical experiences of non-British European immigrant women and their families with professional counsellors at the International Institute of Metropolitan Toronto, a social service agency, during the 1950s and 1960s. In the case of this

particular agency, it did not begin serving immigrants of colour until the late 1960s.

103 Ibid.

104 Arnup notes that even public health nurses 'played a key role in teaching 'Canadian ways' to new immigrants' ('Education for Motherhood,' 258).

105 As one supervisor of group services from the International Institute of Metropolitan Toronto commented about such activities: 'Every activity ... is designed to foster and promote the integration of Old and New Canadians. It is interesting to observe that historical conflicts are resolved in this setting, within the special groups and in the general activities, as they could not be resolved elsewhere. The atmosphere ... is such that all members, through fellowship, avoid the expression of prejudice in pursuit of their common goal as Canadian citizens. Deliberately we cultivate freedom of expression and try to show that this personal freedom can thrive only in mutual self-respect. This general philosophy we foster as the groundwork for the Institute member when he drops his membership to integrate into the community at large.' Quoted in Iacovetta, 'Making "New Canadians,"' 269–70.

106 Adilman, 'A Preliminary Sketch of Chinese Women ...'; Adhopia, *The Hindus of Canada*.

107 Chinese merchants, clergymen, their wives and families were exempt from paying the head tax. This exemption allowed the men to bring women as 'relatives' whom they then 'offered' to working men. Many of the women and young girls brought by these merchants were from very poor families, and at least 100 to 200 of them came to Canada every year between 1887 and the early 1900s (Adilman, 'A Preliminary sketch of Chinese Women ...,' 57). Some merchant's wives are reported to have bought girls in China and brought them over as their daughters. See Karen Van Dieren, 'The Response of the WMS to the Immigration of Asian Women 1888–1942,' in Latham and Pazdro, eds., *Not Just Pin Money*, 79–98. Like the Chinese migrants, South Asian entrepreneurs were sometimes allowed to bring their families. A South Asian agent, Devichand, is reported to have lived in Canada with his wife and child at a time when the workers he recruited were not allowed to bring their families (Adhopia, *The Hindus of Canada*). Some enterprising Chinese working men are reported to have set up stalls at markets, creating their own small businesses so that they could bring their families (CCNC, *Jin Guo*).

108 Whereas 97 per cent of all foreign-born women immigrating into Canada before 1961 were from Britain, the U.S., and other European countries, this

pattern began to change during the 1960s. See Stasiulis, 'The Political Economy of Race, Ethnicity and Migration,' 142.

109 For example, the head tax became the 'most important constraint' on the immigration of Chinese women. Men were willing to lend money to other men in the expectation of being repaid, whereas very few women could be expected to repay this money (Adilman, 'A Preliminary Sketch of Chinese Women ...').

110 Dua, 'Beyond Diversity,' 255.

111 Dua, 'The Hindu Woman's Question,' 62.

112 Ibid. See also Davis, *Women, Race and Class*; Hill Collins, 'It's All in the Family'; and bell hooks, *Ain't I a Woman* (Boston: South End Press, 2000).

113 For example, there were 2,790 Chinese men for every 100 Chinese women in the country in 1911; 1,533 men for 100 women in 1921; 1,241 men for every 100 women in 1931; and 785 men for every 100 women in 1941. For South Asian immigrants, only eighteen women are recorded as being in the country up until 1920. Five thousand South Asian men immigrated before the Second World War, but only 400 women and 423 children immigrated during this period. See Bolaria and Li, *Racial Oppression in Canada*, 147.

114 Bernice Moreau explains how important access to education was for Black women in Nova Scotia in the early twentieth century: 'For the Black Nova Scotian women whom I interviewed, citizenship implied the positive recognition of their humanity, their femininity, and their racial difference. It also hinged on their freedom to pursue education, economic opportunities and legal and civil rights, as well as the privileges and opportunities enjoyed by the White citizens of the province,' Bernie Moreau, 'Black Nova Scotian Women's Schooling and Citizenship: An Education of Violence,' in Adamoski, Chunn, and Menzies, eds., *Contesting Canadian Citizenship*, 297.

115 Some of the earliest South Asian organizations campaigned against racist immigration laws and lobbied the state for family reunification. In 1939, community leaders went to Ottawa to lobby the government to allow a 'small number' of illegal immigrants to stay in the country (Adhopia, *The Hindus of Canada*). See also Buchignani and Indra, *Continous Journey*. They also campaigned against the $200 head tax until it was finally lifted in 1924, and for citizenship and the right to vote. Activists in British Columbia had strong links with activists in the United States and India, and they organized across borders to end British rule in India. By the 1920s, a network of Sikh *gurdwaras* existed in Vancouver, New Westminster, Victoria, Nanaimo, Golden, Abbotsford, Fraser Mills, and Paldi, which were accessible to all South Asians. In addition to being sites of worship, these *gurdwaras* also

served as meeting places for community members and as centres for political organizing.

An important issue for South Asian immigrants in the early twentieth century was access to housing. The intense racism and xenophobia they experienced meant that they were excluded from mainstream society and were socially isolated. Access to housing was such a severe problem that many men lived in makeshift tents and cooked on the pavements. When they were fortunate enough to find housing, they lived in overcrowded conditions. It was only by providing economic and 'psychological' support for each other that they were able to survive (Adhopia, *The Hindus of Canada*). They provided support to community members so that '[f]rom 1909 on, South Asians rarely applied for any sort of public relief. A thousand South Asians were out of work during the winter of 1909, but even hostile government observers were forced to admit that they were well provided for' (Buchignani and Indra, *Continuous Journey*, 34).

In 1939, the Chinese-Canadian community likewise campaigned against the various head taxes and the Exclusion Act. The Chinese Labour Association of Vancouver fought against the Exclusion Act, arguing for family reunification (Adilman, 'A Preliminary Sketch of Chinese Women ...'). Japanese-Canadians also fought against their internment and later campaigned for redress for the injustices to which they had been subjected. Such community organizations formed a vital network of support, providing financial support to newcomers, assisting them in securing employment and housing, and those who were employed provided support for the sick and the unemployed. Funds were raised from within these communities, and services were provided by volunteers. See also Ng and Strout, *Services for Immigrant Women*; CCNC, *Jin Guo*; and Miki and Kobayashi, *Justice in Our Time* for more details on this community activism.

116 For instance, South Asian women were involved in the challenge to the discriminatory continuous passage requirement, and the passengers of the Komagata Maru included some women. The South-Asian women living in Vancouver were also active in providing vital support to the passengers on the boat while it was detained in Vancouver harbour (Adhopia, *The Hindus of Canada*). Likewise, Japanese-Canadian women fought against the internment of their community, as well as for redress from the Canadian government after the internment ended (Miki and Kobayashi, *Justice in Our Time*). In the campaigns organized by Chinese-Canadians, a woman named Mrs J. has been identified as a key delegate to a meeting of community leaders with the federal government to lobby for repeal of the Chinese Exclusion Act. In a film made by Dora Nipp, *Under the Willow Tree*, she explains that the

woman who was part of the Chinese delegation was included as a 'token,' but ended up speaking for the community because she was seated at the side of the prime minister who had to turn to her because he could not hear otherwise. See R. Wong, in 'Willows Bend but Don't Break: Review of Dora Nipp's *Under the Willow Tree*,' *Kinesis* (July/August 1997), 21.

117 Iacovetta, 'Making "New Canadians,"' 267.

118 See Evans and Wekerle, *Women and the Welfare State*, 5–6.

119 Janine Brodie, 'Three Stories of Canadian Citizenship,' in Adamoski, Chunn, and Menzies, eds., *Contesting Canadian Citizenship*, 61.

120 This chapter does not examine the refugee program, nor the temporary employment and domestic workers programs as these remain outside the scope of my present study.

121 Marjorie Cohen, 'The Razor's Edge: Feminism's Effect on Economics,' *International Journal of Women's Studies* 8, no. 3 (1985), 286–98; Martha Mac-Donald, 'What Is Feminist Economics?' *Beyond Law* 5, no. 14 (1996), 11–36; Maria Mies, *Patriarchy and Accumulation on a World Scale* (London: Zed Books, 1986); Rhonda Williams, 'Race, Deconstruction and the Emergent Agenda of Feminist Economic Theory,' in Marianne A. Ferber and Julie A. Nelson, eds., *Beyond Economic Man: Feminist Theory and Economics* (Chicago: University of Chicago Press, 1993), 144–53.

122 The family category allowed citizens and landed immigrants to sponsor specific relatives as their 'dependents.' The list of relatives eligible for sponsorship under this category changes periodically.

123 Men who entered the country under the family category could escape their 'dependent' status *as men*. Defined as workers and economic agents, and socially as heads of households, this 'maleness' allowed them to overcome their 'dependent' status once they were in the country. For sponsored women, on the other hand, their actual status as *women* reinforced their 'dependent' status as sponsored immigrants. Further, the ideological practices of the Act that nationalized white immigrants as *future citizens* on the basis of their social, cultural, and linguistic compatibility with the nation meant that white 'immigrant' women were not constructed as an economic burden or a threat to the nation's character. The racialized status of these women meant that they were distinguished by the Act from immigrant women even when both groups entered the country under the same official classification. Therefore, it was women of colour who, as immigrant women, had come to be most strongly associated with the family category: indeed, immigrant women came to personify this category.

124 Monica Boyd, 'Immigration and Income Security Policies in Canada: Implications for Elderly Immigrant Women,' *Population Research and Policy Review*

8, no. 1 (1989), 5–24. Monica Boyd, 'Foreign-Born, Female, Old and Poor,' *Canadian Woman Studies* 12, no. 4 (1992), 50–2; Das Gupta, 'Families of Native Peoples, Immigrants, and People of Colour'; Ng, and Strout, *Services for Immigrant Women*; and Royal Commission on Status of Women, *The Status of Women in Canada* (Ottawa: RCSW, 1973).

During the 1980s, immigration under the family category was significantly greater than that under the independent category, and while women represented over half of all immigrants, they were more likely to enter as part of the family class. Between 1981 and 1986, 50.1 per cent of all women entered under the family class, compared with 39.4 per cent of all men; 12.6 per cent of women entered as refugees, 9 per cent as assisted relatives, 2.2 per cent as retirees, 5.8 per cent under the business category, and 20.4 per cent under a category called Other; 37.4 per cent of the women entered under the 'independent' class, but these included assisted relatives who were nominated by relatives, as well as women who were retired. See Monica Boyd, *Migrant Women in Canada: Profiles and Policies* (Ottawa: Employment and Immigration Canada, 1987), 56. In the year 1983, for example, 'almost three times as many immigrant women were dependent immigrants as were admitted as independents.' See Roxana Ng and Alma Estable, 'Immigrant Women in the Labour Force: An Overview of Present Knowledge and Research Gaps,' *Resources for Feminist Research* 30 (1987), 29–33. In 1988, the majority of family class immigrants were women, accounting for 59 per cent, and most male immigrants under this category were likely to be children and retired parents (Ng, 'Gendering Policy Research on Immigration,' 17).

125 The employment and immigration regulations stated that 'family class applicants are not assessed under the point system; but they must meet the basic standards of good health and character. As well, before an immigrant visa can be issued to such applicants, the sponsoring relative in Canada is required to sign an undertaking of support. In this statement, the sponsor promises to provide for the lodging, care, and maintenance of the applicant and accompanying dependents for a period of up to ten years.' See Employment and Immigration Canada (EIC), *Canada's Immigration Law: An Overview* (Ottawa: Minister of Supply and Services Canada, 1983), 10. Family members allowed under this category included spouses, unmarried and dependent children, fiance(e)s, dependent parents under sixty years of age, parents and grandparents over the age of sixty and their dependents, and unmarried dependent orphaned siblings, grandchildren, and nieces and nephews. Sponsors with no other relatives in Canada could identify any one family member for sponsorship (ibid.). In addition to sponsored family

members, the Act allowed independent applicants who did not have
enough points to qualify under the point system to enter the country as
'assisted' relatives, as long as they had sound employment prospects and a
sponsor willing to undertake responsibility for supporting them.

126 Monica Boyd, *Gender, Visible Minority and Immigrant Earnings Inequality: Reassessing an Employment Equity Premise* (Ottawa: Carleton University Press,
1991), 6. Boyd concludes that 'there exists no overall settlement/integration policy for immigrants, in general, and for immigrant women in particular' ('Immigration and Income Security Policies in Canada,' 14). Roxana
Ng argues that the work patterns of immigrant women become entrenched
in the decade during which the sponsorship agreement remains in effect.
These patterns become much harder to break out of once the sponsorship
period ends. See Roxana Ng, *The Politics of Community Services* (Toronto:
Garamond Press, 1988).

127 The Act states that this stipulation applies where an immigrant 'willfully
fails to support himself or any dependent member of his family in Canada'
section 27(f). Little information is available about the extent to which this
stipulation was monitored in the 1970s and 1980s. In the 1990s, the federal
government committed itself to closely monitoring this stipulation through
greater cooperation with provincial governments.

128 A series of workshops conducted in Vancouver in 1977 revealed a high
degree of ambiguity among service providers regarding the question of
whether sponsored immigrants were eligible for social entitlements, and if
so, which ones. In one case, a sixty-six-year-old sponsored male, who had a
wife with a disability and four children, applied for unemployment insurance and was refused. He went to an agency which was unsuccessful in helping him claim UIC and CPP and referred him to welfare services, unsure
whether he qualified for welfare assistance. In another case, a sponsored
immigrant woman in her eighties went to an agency after she was made to
leave her son's home. The agency was told she could not claim social assistance because she was sponsored. The agency finally found lodging for the
woman through emergency services, but received a call from the immigration department two days later refusing the department's responsibility for
these expenses. Such cases demonstrate that the question of the access of
sponsored immigrants to social security programs remained unclear to service providers engaged in front line service provision. See Ng and Strout,
Services for Immigrant Women.

129 In her study of the claims of immigrants to welfare programs in British
Columbia in 1989, Susanna Lui-Gurr found that sponsored immigrants who
attempted to claim social assistance were required to prove that their spon-

sorship had irretrievably broken down. Lui-Gurr does not specify exactly what kind of proof was required. In examining the access of immigrant families to welfare programs, she defines immigrants as all non-Canadian born individuals. Presumably, many of these 'immigrants' might well be citizens. See Susanna Lui-Gurr, 'The British Columbia Experience with immigrants and Welfare Dependency, 1989,' in Don J. DeVoretz, ed., *Diminishing Returns: The Economics of Canada's Recent Immigration Policy* (Ottawa: C.D. Howe Institute, 1995), 128–65.

130 Monica Boyd's research comes to a similar conclusion: 'sponsorship is viewed by the federal and provincial governments as a commitment that the designated immigrants will not require economic assistance. This can be the basis for denying access to welfare assistance programs. Depending on the interpretation of provincial and municipal regulations, immigrant women who experience marital violence and breakdown and who need to find alternative housing and income, can be denied immediate access to legal aid, publicly subsidized housing, or income assistance until the issuing authorities are satisfied that the sponsorship relation is broken. Thus, a sponsored entry status can enhance the tendency of women to remain in an abusive setting because it reduces access to social assistance programs' (Boyd, *Gender, Visible Minority and Immigrant Earnings Inequality,* 7).

131 In order to qualify as sponsors, citizens and landed immigrants had to demonstrate they would be financially self-supporting and able to undertake financial responsibility for their sponsored relatives. See EIC, *Canada's Immigration Law.*

132 Sponsored dependents were not entitled to access social assistance programs, and if they made such claims, their sponsors could be deported. As Ng, 'Gendering Policy Research on Immigration,' and Boyd, *Gender, Visible Minority and Immigrant Earnings Inequality,* point out, deportation has remained relatively rare in such cases. However, both also point out that the threat that male family members could face deportation has kept many sponsored immigrant women trapped in abusive relationships. This is similar to the situation in Britain, where studies demonstrate that Black people have had unequal access to social programs and that the welfare state has institutionalized racism within British society, rather than challenged it. A number of these studies indicate that even when Black people have had legal entitlement to social services, the fear that any claims may lead to a reassessment of their immigration status, or that of their families, works as a powerful disincentive to make such claims.

Ginsburg, *Division of Welfare,* has identified the following ways in which racism has effected the provision of social services in Britain: widespread stereotyping of all Black people and the non-recognition of their specific needs; non-recognition of Black people as legitimate claimants; and pressures on service providers from the larger society which results in lesser access to entitlements for Black people. These forms of racism have created a 'lesser welfare citizenship,' he argues. See also Ahmad and Husband, 'Religious Identity, Citizenship, and Welfare'; Mama, *The Hidden Struggle*; Ian Law, *Racism, Ethnicity and Social Policy* (London: Prentice Hall, 1996); Klug, '"Oh to be in England"'; Gordon, *Policing Immigration*; and WING, *World's Apart.*

133 Numerous studies have found that immigrant women who have entered the country under the family category joined the paid work force relatively quickly after their arrival. See Ng and Estable, 'Immigrant Women in the Labour Force'; John T. Samuel, *Family Class Immigrants to Canada, 1981–1984: Labour Force Activity Aspects* (Ottawa: Employment and Immigration Canada, 1986); and Khosla, *Review of the Situation of Women Canada, 1993.* Immigrant women and immigrant men have had higher labour-force participation rates than Canadian-born women and men, but they have tended to earn lower wages and have been denied many of the opportunities for economic advancement enjoyed by their white counterparts. See Estable, *Immigrant Women in Canada – Current Issues.* A study examining the earnings of Black men estimated that they were paid 15 per cent less on average than their white counterparts. See 'Black Earn 15 per cent less than Whites, New Study Says,' *Vancouver Sun,* 10 February 1997, A4. Immigrant families, therefore, have been less likely than Canadian families to rely on one income.

134 In the instances where sponsored immigrant women were given access to training programs, their official dependent status barred them from receiving income assistance or training allowances. Lack of access to language training programs and to skills upgrading courses limit the employment opportunities available to immigrant women. See Nahla Abdo, '"Gender" is not a "Dummy": Research Methods in Immigration and Refugee Studies,' in Roxana Ng, ed., *Gendering Immigration: Integration Policy Research Workshop Proceedings and a Selective Review of Policy Research Literature 1987–1996* (Ottawa: Status of Women Canada, 1998), 41–50. See also Boyd, ('Immigratin and Income Security Policies in Canada,') and Estable *Immigrant Women in Canada – Current Issues.* For example, basic training allowances under the Canadian Job Strategy Program, funded by Employment and Immigration Canada in the 1980s, were not accessible to sponsored immigrants, and neither were living and travel allowances (Boyd, *Gender, Visible Minority and Immigrant Earning Equality,* 7). In this way, the women most likely to need

language training programs were denied access as a result of their immigration status.

135 See Abu-Laban, 'Keeping 'em Out'; Das Gupta, 'Families of Native Peoples, Immigrants, and People of Colour'; Ng, *The Politics of Community Service*; and Ng and Strout, *Services for Immigrant Women*. A study of South Asian women in British Columbia conducted by the India Mahila Association (IMA) identified the lack of independent access to financial support as a key factor that trapped the women in violent and abusive relationships: 'One of the major barriers identified by the women was their dependency on their husbands which was determined from the outset of their relationship. All except one of the women came to Canada as sponsored immigrants and while five were sponsored by a close relative, nine out of the fourteen were sponsored directly by their husbands. In these cases, the husbands abandoned their responsibilities of sponsorship support to help settle their wives in Canada. Instead, they transformed the sponsorship into a form of new power over their wives. This created nearly insurmountable inequity in their relationships and made the women socially, psychologically and financially dependent on their husbands.' India Mahila Association, *Spousal Abuse: Experiences of 15 Canadian South Asian Women* (Vancouver: IMA and Feminist Research Education Development and Action, 1994). Also see Mama, *The Hidden Struggle*; and R. Emerson Dobash and Russell Dobash, eds., *Rethinking Violence against Women* (Thousand Oaks, CA: Sage, 1998).

136 The labour-force participation patterns of immigrant women will have severe consequences for their access to old-age security programs as they grow older. Boyd has demonstrated that immigrant women are 'the most vulnerable to poverty in old age' (Boyd, 'Foreign-Born, Female, Old and Poor,' 51). Access to these programs is based on labour-force participation as well as on the length of residence in Canada. As a consequence of their participation in low-paid, gender-segregated work, immigrant women often do not qualify for maximum benefits in the 'male' contributory social insurance programs like the Canada Pension Plan. Many immigrant women's access to income security programs like Old Age Security and the Guaranteed Income Supplement is reduced because eligibility requires a ten-year residency in the country. As a result of these factors, Boyd found that 'foreign-born women aged 67 and older who arrived after 1975 received no OAS or GIS benefits' (ibid., 51). Most of these women immigrated from countries other than the United States, Britain, and Europe, and as Boyd concludes, 'foreign-born elderly women are less likely than their Canadian-born female or foreign-born male counterparts to be receiving pension or income security benefits' (ibid.). The racialized/gendered consequences of

immigration policies, (lack of) access to job-training programs and social
security programs have shaped, and further compounded, the inequalities
these women have experienced – and continue to experience – within the
'national' economy.

137 See G.S. Basran, 'Indo-Canadian Families Historical Constraints and Contemporary Contradictions,' *Journal of Comparative Family Studies* 24, no. 3
(1993), 339–51; Das Gupta, 'Families of Native Peoples, Immigrants, and
People of Colour'; and Estable, *Immigrant Woman in Canada – Current
Issues.*

138 The Cross Cultural Communication Centre found that the 'normal processing time' for family class immigrants from the U.S. and Britain was 71 to
116 days; India 203 to 413 days; Guyana 518 days; Trinidad and Tobago 462
days; and Zaire 637 days. Cited in Das Gupta, 'Families of Native Peoples,
Immigrants, and People of Colour,' 210.

139 Davis, *Women, Race and Class,* and Hill Collins, *Black Feminist Thought.*

140 Valerie Amos, and Parmar Pratibha, 'Challenging Imperial Feminism,' *Fem-
inist Review,* no. 17 (1984), 3–20; Mama, *The Hidden Struggle;* and Amina
Mama, 'Black Women, the Economic Crises and the British State,' *Feminist
Review,* no. 17 (1984), 21–36.

141 See Nancy Mandell, 'Women, Families and Intimate Relations,' in Nancy
Mandell, ed., *Feminist Issues: Race, Class, and Sexuality* (Toronto: Prentice
Hall, 2001), 193–218.

142 F. Henry, C. Tator, W. Mattis, and T. Rees, *Colour of Democracy: Racism in
Canadian Society* (Toronto: Harcourt Brace, 1995), chap. 6, note that these
professions remain dominated by white professionals, with people of
colour concentrated in the lower ranks. Their study of this important sector concludes: 'White human-service practitioners use a variety of ration-
ales to deny, ignore, and minimize the issue of racism in their
organizations, their professional values and practices, and their personal
belief systems and relationships ... mainstream agencies continue to operate within an assimilationist monocultural model of service delivery that
views the pluralism of Canadian society as being irrelevant to their man-
dates, policies, structures and operations. Despite the growing number of
anti-racism policies developed by agencies such as the United Way and
municipal and provincial agencies, there is little evidence of a willingness
to alter the ideology that shapes human-service delivery' (168). The problems they identified within this sector include 'lack of access to appropriate programs and services; ethnocentric values and counseling practices;
devaluing of the skills and credentials of minority practitioners; inadequate funding for ethno-racial community based agencies; lack of minor-

ity representation in social agencies; monocultural or ad hoc multicultural model of service delivery' (154).

143 See Usha George, 'Toward Anti-Racism in Social Work in the Canadian Context,' in Calliste and Dei, eds., *Anti-Racist Feminism*, 111–22.

144 Usha George argues that 'immigrant groups do not use many important health and social services because of barriers' (ibid., 112).

145 Gordon, *Pitied But Not Entitled*, 293.

4. Multiculturalism and the Liberalizing Nation

1 See 'The Federal Response,' Appendix to Hansard, 8 October 1971, retrieved 3 February 2004 from www.canadahistory.com/sections/ documents/trudeau_-n_multiculturalism.htm.

2 Fanon, *Black Skin, White Masks*, 112.

3 Message from Gerry Weiner, minister of state for multiculturalism, quoted in L.W. Roberts and R.A. Clifton, 'Multiculturalism in Canada: A Sociological Perspective,' in Peter Li, ed., *Race and Ethnic Relations in Canada* (Toronto: Oxford University Press, 1990), 143.

4 Hedy Fry, then secretary of state for multiculturalism, defined multiculturalism in this manner. See A. Cardozo and M. Louis, eds., *The Battle over Multiculturalism: Does It Help or Hinder Canadian Unity?* vol. 1 (Ottawa: Pearson Shonoma Institute, 1997), 35.

5 See Hawkins, *Critical Years in Immigration*; Palmer, *Immigration and the Rise of Multiculturalism*; Bannerji, *The Dark Side of the Nation*; Mackey, *The House of Difference*.

6 Hawkins, *Critical Years in Immigration*.

7 See Prime Minister Trudeau's Speech to the House of Commons, 8 October 1971, retrieved 3 February 2004 from www.pch.gc.ca/progs/pubs/ Speeches/08osb_e.cfm.

8 'The Federal Response' stated: 'The government is concerned with preserving human rights, developing Canadian identity, strengthening citizenship participation, reinforcing Canadian unity and encouraging cultural diversification within a bilingual framework ... The Government will promote creative encounters and interchange among all Canadian cultural groups in the interest of national unity.' See 'The Federal Response.'

9 Mackey, *The House of Difference*, 50.

10 In *the Dark Side of the Nation*, Bannerji argues that multiculturalism reifies 'culture,' elevating a 'cultural' identity over that of class and gender, among others. My examination of multiculturalism is much indebted to Bannerji's work.

11 Ahmed, *Strange Encounters*, 95.

12 See Hawkins, *Critical Years in Immigration*; Jakubowski, *Immigration and the Legalization of Racism*; Boyd, *Gender, Visible Minority and Immigrant Earnings Inequality*; Green and Green, 'The Economic Goals of Canada's Immigration Policy, Past and Present'; Stasiulis, 'the Political Economy of Race, Ethnicity and Migration.' Eva Mackey points out that as late as 1964, a minister of immigration visited northern Europe, 'looking for immigrants to "balance" the flow' (*The House of Difference*, 53).

13 The Immigration Regulations of 1962 introduced changes emphasizing labour-market needs, focusing on the education, occupation, and skill levels of prospective immigrants. In 1967, the point system was introduced. It later became entrenched in the Immigration Act 1976–77. As its name indicates, the new system was to assess applicants through the allocation of points for their skills, education, and occupational qualifications. Additionally, family members were also to be allowed to immigrate. The point system is discussed in chapters 2 and 3.

14 Hawkins, *Critical Years in Immigration*.

15 Ibid.

16 A. Sivanandan, *Communities of Resistance: Writings on Black Struggles for Socialism* (London: Verso, 1990), 11. African and Asian leaders had come to power through their respective national independence movements which denounced the racial/colonial subjugation of their populations. Subsequently, the formation of the Commonwealth had resulted in these nationalist leaders claiming their place at the table as equals.

17 Hawkins, *Critical Years in Immigration*, 258.

18 Stasiulis and Jhappan have argued that Canadian nation-building had to contend with two conflicting goals: satisfying the need for labour while maintaining the nation's Euro-Canadian character ('The Fractious Politics of a Settler Society'). These conflicting goals continue to plague nation-building.

19 See Bannerji, *The Dark Side of the Nation*; Tania Das Gupta, 'The Politics of Multiculturalism: "Immigrant Women" and the Canadian State,' in Enakshi Dua and Angela Robertson, eds., *Scratching the Surface: Canadian Anti-Racist Thought* (Toronto: Women's Press, 1999), 187–206.

20 Faubion, *Michel Foucault*, 332.

21 In deconstructing the concept of 'community,' Bannerji has argued that communities are social formations constituted by both external and internal forces: 'if, instead of naturalizing "community," we see it as a formation, an ideological, that is, cultural and political practice, it becomes possible for us to develop a critique of the social organization, social relations and moral regulations which go into the making of it' (*The Dark Side of the Nation*, 154).

External forces mark out these 'communities' as different from the majority, whereas internal forces seek to suppress the internal divisions among members to constitute the community as internally homogenous.

22 See Bannerji, ibid.; and Roxana Ng, 'Multiculturalism as Ideology: A Textual Analysis,' in Marie Campbell and Ann Manicom, eds., *Knowledge, Experience, and Ruling Relations: Studies in the Social Organization of Knowledge* (Toronto: University of Toronto Press, 1995). This is how Bannerji defines the challenges faced by the state: 'The Canadian state, for example, has a lot of work to do. It not only has to mediate and express the usual inequalities of a class and patriarchal society, but also the ones created through colonialism and racism which inflect class and patriarchy. It has to maintain some notions of individual rights and citizenship, along with a historically racialized hierarchy of labour importation and regulation and what David Theo Goldberg has called "racist culture."' Bannerji, *The Dark Side of the Nation*, 5, citing Goldberg, *The Racial State.*

23 See John Solomos and Les Back, *Racism and Society* (New York: St. Martin's Press, 1996).

24 See McLaren, *Our Own Master Race.* See also *The Sterilization of Leilani Muir*, dir. Glynis Whiting and prod. Graydon Macrea and Jerry Krepakevich (The Northwest Centre and the National Film Board of Canada, 1996), filmstrip. The oppression and extermination of peoples with disabilities also has a long and painful history, along with the genocide of Aboriginal peoples, the organization of reserves as the sites for their elimation, the organization of the slave trade in the Americas, and the other massacres in the colonies.

25 Solomos and Back, *Racism and Society.*

26 The writings and activism of W.E.B. Du Bois, Aimee Cesaire, Frantz Fanon, Richard Wright, James Baldwin, and Marcus Garvey are among the most prominent of these works.

27 Audre Lorde has described in excruciating detail what the costs of such close proximity can be. See 'The Uses of Anger: Women Responding to Racism' and 'Eye to Eye: Black Women, Hatred, and Anger,' in *Sister Outsider: Essays and Speeches by Audre Lorde* (Trumansberg, NY: The Crossing Press, 1984).

28 This point is made also by Eva Mackey in *The House of Difference.* She argues that by the 1990s multiculturalism had placed Canada in an advantageous position: 'This is the nation reshaped for the 1990s, not in the old model of culturally homogeneous, but as collective hybridity engaged in a shared and progress-oriented project. All the individual ethnic identities which, if left to their own devices, are unstable, ambiguous and "in-between" (in fact so unstable that they create chaos and destruction), are presented as if they

need the project of nation-building (defined as caring for the land) to give them an anchor and a goal, a goal that in turn creates the heterogeneous (hybrid) yet unified nation. [T]his is not a liberatory hybridity mobilized to create "anti-nationalist histories of the people" of the kind Bhabha [*The Location of Culture*, 38–9] envisages. Rather it constructs the *nation itself* as a "Third Space" of hybridity, a hybrid space which nevertheless reshapes central and well-worn nationalist ideologies in which Aboriginal people are representatives of nature and helpmates to the settlers. Further, in this space, the modern project of progress is still the key to nation-building' (82–3).

29 Beverley Skeggs makes the case that it is the white working-class poor in Britain who have been constructed as 'a barrier to the progress of "multicultural modernization,"' while the middle class is presented as the facilitator of this modernization, having the cultural resources necessary to promote the nation's interests in a globalizing era. See Beverley Skeggs, *Class, Self and Culture* (London: Routledge, 2004), 90–95. In *White Nation*, Hage defines as 'cosmopolite' the figure of the white multiculturalist who successfully embraces multiculturalism.

30 Hage, *White Nation*; Bannerji, *The Dark Side of the Nation*.

31 The development of the Pan-African movement, the Non-Aligned movement and the Bandung Conference are among the most pertinent examples of the international attempts at self-determination by previously colonized and enslaved populations.

32 Even as the royal commission sought to balance its treatment of bilingualism and biculturalism with multiculturalism, the contradictions that the multiculturalism policy sought to juggle were obvious: 'The distinction between language and culture has never been clearly defined. The very name of the royal commission whose recommendations we now seek to implement tends to indicate that bilingualism and biculturalism are indivisible. But, biculturalism does not properly describe our society; multiculturalism is more accurate. The Official Languages Act designated two languages, English and French, as the official languages of Canada for the purposes of all institutions of the Parliament and government of Canada, no reference was made to cultures, and this act does not impinge on the role of all languages as instruments of the various Canadian cultures. Nor, on the other hand, should the recognition of the cultural value of many languages weaken the position of Canada's two official languages. Their use by all of the citizens of Canada will continue to be promoted and encouraged' ('The Federal Response'). Moreover, referring to the French and English as also having 'ethnic backgrounds,' the contradiction in their definition of 'ethnic' groups *as well as* the 'founding nations' was not examined further.

33 In his speech to the House of Commons on 8 October 1971, Prime Minister
   Trudeau stated: 'In implementing a policy of multiculturalism within a bilingual framework, the government will provide support in four ways. First,
   resources permitting, the government will seek to assist all Canadian cultural
   groups that have demonstrated a desire and effort to continue to develop a
   capacity to grow and contribute to Canada, and a clear need for assistance,
   the small and weak groups no less than the strong and highly organized. Second, the government will assist members of all cultural groups to overcome
   cultural barriers to full participation in Canadian society. Third, the government will promote creative encounters and interchange among all Canadian
   cultural groups in the interest of national unity. Fourth, the government will
   continue to assist immigrants to acquire at least one of Canada's official languages in order to become full participants in Canadian society.' I have used
   excerpts from the speech in this chapter, as well as from 'The Federal
   Response.'

34 Immigration Act, 1976–77, 3 (a) and (b).

35 For excellent discussions of this 'new' racism in its culturalist version, see
   Martin Barker, *The New Racism* (London: Junction Books, 1981); and Gilroy,
   There Ain't No Black in the Union Jack.

36 Bannerji has discussed the impact of these two categories in the making of
   the 'outsider' status of racial minorities (*The Dark Side of the Nation*).

37 Visible minorities were defined in the Employment Equity Act in the following terms: 'persons, other than Aboriginal peoples, who are non-Caucasian
   in race or non-white in colour.' Blacks, Chinese, Filipinos, Japanese, Kore-
   ans. Latin Americans, Other Pacific Islanders, Indo-Pakistanis (i.e., South
   Asians, South East Asians and West Asians), and Arabs are the groups named
   as visible minorities. See V. Esses and R.C. Gardiner, 'Multiculturalism in
   Canada: Context and Current Status.' Special Issue: Ethnic Relations in a
   Multicultural Society, *Canadian Journal of Behavioural Science* 28 (1996), 2,
   retrieved 3 March 2004 from www.cpa.ca/cjbsnew/1996/vol28-3.html. Linda
   Carty and Dionne Brand have analysed the creation of the category 'visible
   minority women' by the state through the politics of funding immigrant
   women's conferences and organizations in the 1980s. See Linda Carty and
   Dionne Brand, '"Visible Minority Women": A Creation of the Canadian
   State,' in Himani Bannerji, ed., *Returning the Gaze: Essays on Racism, Feminism
   and Politics* (Toronto: Sister Vision Press, 1993), 207–22.

38 Government agencies routinely refer to immigrants as 'newcomers.' For a
   recent example, the *Toronto Star* reported on a Citizenship and Immigration
   Canada report that proposed that 'new' Canadians should be required to be
   photographed and fingerprinted so that their identity papers could include

biometric information' about them. See Jim Bronskill, 'I.D. Proposals Spark Concern,' *Toronto Star*, 6 September 2004, A1.

39 See Bannerji, *The Dark Side of the Nation*; Carty and Brand, '"Visible Minority Women."'

40 See Mackey, *The House of Difference*, 51. Mackey makes this assessment based on her analysis of the 1941 Macmillan War Pamphlets, Canadian Series, *The New Canadian Loyalists*.

41 Barker, *The New Racism*; Gilroy, *There Ain't No Black in the Union Jack*.

42 See Razack, *Looking White People in the Eye*, 60.

43 Carty and Brand, '"Visible Minority Women."'

44 Omi and Winant, *Racial formation in the United States*.

45 See Adhopia, *The Hindus of Canada*; CCNC, *Jin Guo*; Buchignani and Indra, *Continuous Journey*; Bolaria and Li, *Racial Oppression in Canada*; May Yee, 'Finding the Way Home through Issues of Gender, Race and Class,' in Bannerji, ed., *Returning the Gaze*, 3–44; and Winnie Wun Wun, 'In the Margins: Challenging Racism in the Labour Movement' (MA thesis, University of Toronto, 1995).

46 In *The Dark Side of the Nation*, Bannerji makes the point that multiculturalism thwarts the possibilities for anti-racist alliances among communities of colour by fragmenting them along ethnic and cultural lines. Also see Carty and Brand '"Visible Minority Women."'

47 Taylor, Ruggiero, and Louis found that 'members of minority groups tend to perceive more discrimination directed at their group in general than at them personally as members of that group' for two reasons: (1) 'a shared stereotype about the prevalence of group discrimination, possibly fostered by media coverage,' and (2) 'a tendency to minimize perceptions of personal discrimination.' See D.M. Taylor, K.M. Ruggiero, and W.R. Louis, 'Personal/ Group Discrimination Discrepancy: Towards a Two-Factor Explanation,' Special Issue: Ethnic Relations in a Multicultural Society, *Canadian Journal of Behavioural Science* 28 (1996), retrieved 3 March 2004 from www.cpa.ca/ cjbnew/1996/ful_taylor.html. See also Esses and Gardner, 'Multiculturalism in Canada,' 3.

48 Marianne Hester, Liz Kelly, and Jill Radford, *Women, Violence, and Male Power: Feminist Activism, Research, and Practice* (Philadelphia: Open University Press, 1996).

49 This maximization of the cultural capital of professionals was to become a crucial advantage for the corporate sector in the 1990s, with globalization's promotion of 'free trade.' Chapter 5 discusses this point in greater detail.

50 See Bannerji, *The Dark Side of the Nation*; Das Gupta, 'The Politics of Multiculturalism'; Mackey, *The House of Difference*; Hage, *White Nation*.

51 Bannerji, *The Dark Side of the Nation.*

52 Prime Minister Trudeau's Speech to the House of Commons, 2.

53 'The Federal Response.'

54 Paul Gilroy, *The Black Atlantic: Modernity and Double Consciousness* (Cambridge, MA: Harvard University Press, 1993), 2.

55 Prime Minister Trudeau's speech to the House of Commons.

56 For a very useful discussion of some of the challenges facing South Asian women who have opposed violence, see Bannerji, *The Dark Side of the Nation,* chap. 5.

57 Examining the nature of the silence that suppresses overt recognition of violence against women in the South Asian community, Bannerji suggests what some of the reasons for this might be: 'One of the reasons for this paradoxical silence may be that public utterance puts us in a situation of responsibility – it makes us accountable to and for others and ourselves. After all, what we say in print, in any public medium, is fixed in form, content, and time. It becomes part of an acknowledged, even official realist, liable to be seen as a distinct political position. We are no longer just overheard or peeped into. The doors of the community open as we speak "out." So, obviously, we are wary, not only about what we say in public, but where and how we say it. We want to assess the location and reception of our public statements, our disclosures and discussions in the arena of social communication. We are, if anything, overly sensitive towards the ideological strands or networks into which they will be woven, how our statements will be received by those who are not "us," particularly those "others" who consider us not people but as "ethnic communities"' (*The Dark Side of the Nation,* 153).

58 Mills, *Discourse.*

59 This is a critique developed by Bannerji: 'Inscribed and instituted politically from the outside, the communities themselves also suppress internal sources of division and seek to present themselves, at least in their representational endeavours, as seamless realities.' She defines 'community' not only as a social and ideological category but also as a category of the state (*The Dark Side of the Nation,* 151–74).

60 See Fanon, *Black Skin, White Masks,* also Bhabha, *The Location of Culture.*

61 Eleanor Ty points out that Denise Chong, for example, has 'internalized her otherness' which can be seen most clearly in Chong's representation of her grandmother, May-ying: 'The sense of the alterity and otherness of her ancestors comes across at times in her telling, revealing the way she has internalized her own otherness' (44). Ty finds a similar tendency at work in Shirley Gok-lin Lim's *Among the White Moon Faces* and Amy Tan's *The Kitchen God's Wife.* Even as Chong and these other authors seek to contest the dominant

historiography and exclusions of Asians within North America, they remain
constrained by the very orientalist tropes which organize these exclusions.
See Eleanor Ty, *The Politics of the Visible in Asian North American Narratives*
(Toronto: University of Toronto Press, 2004).

62 Ty discusses how the protagonist in Bienvenido Santos's *The Man Who
(Thought He) Looked Like Robert Taylor* attempts to fashion himself, and his
masculinity, in the image of a popular (white) Hollywood actor: 'Through
Sol's story, Santos reveals how the culture of the United States has colonized
and influenced Filipinos to such a degree that there is no subject outside of
the desires created by these illusions. For Sol, pictorial, literary, and filmic
rendition of people and places, largely created by American institutions and
corporations, become as immediate and as real as his experiences in life'
(ibid., 55–6).

63 Ibid., 187. Among examples of such works, Ty includes Hiromi Goto's *Chorus
of Mushrooms* and Wayson Choy's *The Jade Peony.*

64 See Uma Narayan, *Dislocating Cultures: Identities, Traditions, and Third World
Feminism* (New York: Routledge, 1997).

65 Etienne Balibar and Immanuel Wallerstein, *Race, Nation, Class: Ambiguous
Identities* (London: Verso, 1991); Lowe, *Immigrant Acts*; and Sunera Thobani,
'Racism, Women's Equality and Social Policy Reform,' in Luciana Ricciutelli
et al., eds., *Confronting the Cuts: A Sourcebook for Women in Ontario* (Toronto:
Inanna Publications, 1998), 23–8.

66 Yasmin Jiwani, 'On the Outskirts of Empire: Race and Gender in Canadian
TV News,' in V. Strong-Boag, S.E. Grace, V. Eisenberg, and J. Anderson, eds.,
Painting the Maple: Essays on Race, Gender and the Construction of Canada (Van-
couver: University of British Columbia Press, 1998), 61.

67 This is how Hage defines the discourse of enrichment: 'the point being
made is not simply that the discourse of enrichment places the dominant
culture in a more important position then other migrant cultures. More
importantly, this discourse also assigns to migrant cultures a different *mode of
existence* to Anglo-Celtic culture. While the dominant White culture merely
and unquestionably *exists*, migrant cultures exist *for* the latter. Their value, or
the viability of their preservation as far as the White Australians are concerned, lies in their function as enriching cultures' (*White Nation*, 121).
Emphasis in the original.

68 Prime Minister Trudeau stated in his speech to the House of Commons:
'The government will support and encourage the various cultures and ethnic
groups that give structure and vitality to our society. They will be encouraged
to share their cultural expressions and values with other Canadians and so
contribute to a richer life for us all' (Speech to the House of Commons, 1).

69 The issue of 'smelly' restaurants recently created quite a stir in Vancouver, British Columbia, as some condominium owners sought to shut down a Persian restaurant in their vicinity. The municipal government announced that it was considering changing its by-laws 'so that businesses that offend some people's sense of small can be fined up to $10,000.' To this, the restaurant owner responded, 'How are we going to measure this smell, this odour? Which nose is going to tell me which smell is good or bad? Based on whose nose complaint?' See Canadian Broadcasting Corporation, *CBC News*, 'Smelly Eateries Face Fines in West Vancouver,' 24 November 2004, retrieved 5 January 2005 from http://www.cbc.ca/story/canada/national/2004/11/23/smell-restaurant-041123.

70 Ahmed, *Strange Encounters*, 97.

71 The popular stereotype of the 'angry' woman of colour illustrates this particular construct.

72 So, for one recent example, the arrival in British Columbia of a boatload of undocumented migrants from China in 1998 sparked off a public outcry against them. Many immigrant 'leaders,' as well as immigrant organizations, lent their support for the speedy deportation of these migrants.

73 Fanon discusses these experiences in *Black Skin, White Masks*, chap. 5.

74 For a discussion of this term, see A. Appadurai, *Modernity at Large: Cultural Dimensions of Globalization*. Minneapolis: University of Minnesota Press, 1996.

75 *Vancouver Sun*, 19 March 2004, A15.

76 See Bannerji, *The Dark Side of the Nation*.

77 Hage analyzes a popular children's book, *The Stew that Grew*, to demonstrate how the white national is constructed as the one who knows the 'true' value of these different cultures, and thus knows just what the right balance is and how to put it together. See *White Nation*, chap. 4.

78 Department of Canadian Heritage, *Annual Report on the Operation of the Canadian Multicultural Act, 2003–04* (Ottawa: Department of Canadian Heritage, 2004).

79 See Bannerji, *The Dark Side of the Nation*, and Mackey, *The House of Difference*.

80 Mackey specifically discusses how the Canadian Museum of Civilization and the performance, *Spirit of a Nation*, highlight Canada's pluralism and cultural diversity, while sustaining settler narratives. See Mackey, *The House of Difference*, chap. 4.

5. Reforming Canadians

1 Citizenship and Immigration Canada, *Canada 2005: A Strategy for Citizenship and Immigration, Conference Proceedings* (Ottawa: CIC, 2004), 1.

2 Fanon, *Black Skin, White Masks*, 229.

3 At the time I was president of the National Action Committee on the Status of Women, Canada's then largest feminist organization, and represented the organization in the reviews of both policy areas.

4 A number of other policy areas were also identified for review, including foreign policy. However, this chapter examines the reviews of only the two policy areas of social security and immigration.

5 Benhabib, *The Rights of Others*, 19–21.

6 See Mackey, *The House of Difference*, chaps. 5, 6, and 7. Also see Jabukowski for a discussion of the growing anti-immigrant sentiment during this period that constructed the immigrant as abusive to, and a burden on, Canada and its national resources (*Immigration and the Legalization of Racism*, 64). Jakubowski notes that in the political climate of the 1990s, with Canadians feeling 'vulnerable economically,' the government introduced Bill C-86, arguing that it would allow more effective 'management' of immigrants. She also examined public opinion polls of the period, which, she argues, reflected an increasing tendency to equate immigrants with abuse of the welfare system. The rise of the Reform Party during the 1990s is related to its capitalization of this growing anti-immigrant sentiment.

7 Mackey, *The House of Difference*, 142. Emphasis in original.

8 Jakubowski, *Immigration and the Legalization of Racism*, 64. These fears had been identified in an earlier study of immigration policy by Freda Hawkins in *Critical Years in Immigration*. She defined the following as being among the major concerns of the immigration department during the 1980s: managing the program effectively to stop its exploitation by criminal and irresponsible elements; controlling illegal immigrants 'without harassing them in a manner unacceptable to the public'; and ensuring harmonious race relations.

9 The reasons for this breakdown were: (1) prolonged recessions and the high unemployment levels since the 1970s, which undermined the Keynesian economic policies underpinning the welfare state; (2) growing financial pressures on social security as a result of the recessions of the period, pressures to which the state responded by reducing social spending; and (3) a concerted political assault from the political right which advocated a return to laissez-faire policies and a minimalist state. See Clarke, Cochrane, and Smart, *Ideologies of Welfare*; Janine Brodie, *Politics on the Margins* (Halifax: Fernwood, 1995); Andrew Johnson, Stephen McBride, and Patrick Smith, eds., *Continuities and Discontinuities: The Political Economy of Social Welfare and Labour Market Policies in Canada* (Toronto: University of Toronto Press, 1994); Ginsburg, *Divisions of Welfare*; Jane Pulkingham and Gordon Ternowetsky, eds., *Remaking Canadian Social Policy* (Halifax: Fernwood, 1996); Ken Battle and Sheri

Torjman, 'Desperately Seeking Substance: A Commentary on the Social Security Review,' in Pulkingham and Ternowetsky, eds., *Remaking Canadian Social Policy*, 52–66; and Sylvia Bashevkin, *Welfare Hot Buttons: Women, Work, and Social Policy Reform* (Toronto: University of Toronto Press, 2002).

10 See Janine Brodie, 'Canadian Women, Changing State Forms, and Public Policy,' in Janine Brodie, ed., *Women and Canadian Public Policy* (Toronto: Harcourt Brace, 1996); Marjorie Cohen, *Women and Economic Structures* (Ottawa: The Canadian Centre for Policy Alternatives, 1991); and Stephen McBride, and John Shields, *Dismantling a Nation* (Halifax: Fernwood, 1993).

The chief executive officers of 150 top Canadian corporations had come together to form the Business Council on National Issues in order to bring 'structural adjustment to Canada' by first getting the state to adopt fiscal policies which escalated the debt crises, and subsequently using the resulting crises to call for a dismantling of social programs. See Diana Ralph, 'How to Beat the Corporate Agenda: Strategies for Social Justice,' in Pulkingham and Ternowetsky eds., *Remaking Canadian Social Policy*, 290.

11 The process for the organization of both reviews is outlined in the appendix.

12 Both sets of reviews were intended to be preludes to the restructuring of their respective policy areas for the twenty-first century. As such, both will have far-reaching consequences.

13 The U.N. Population Fund calculated Canada's average fertility rate to be 1.48 child per woman, that is, below replacement level, a decade *after* the IPR in the year 2004. In reporting this finding, John Ibbitson noted: 'We rely on immigration to supplant the paucity of babies.' See John Ibbitson, 'Canada's Vanishing Peoples,' *Globe and Mail*, 21 September 2004, A4.

14 My examination of the conceptual framework of the IPR refers primarily to Citizenship and Immigration Canada, *Canada and Immigration: Facts and Issues* (Ottawa: CIC, 1994). This document set out the ten issues for public discussion and provided background information for each. Produced in popular tabloid form, it was circulated widely during the public consultations, as outlined in the appendix.

15 Ibid., 3.

16 Ibid.

17 For one example of an 'official' study, the chief of demographic policy for Employment and Immigration Canada had found that: 'Although the primary goal of Family Class immigration is social, the majority of such immigrants sooner or later participate in the economic activity of the country' (Samuel, *Family Class Immigrants to Canada*, 2).

18 CIC, *Canada and Immigration*, 3.

19 For example, in June 1989, immigration policy allowed sponsorship of sin-

334 Notes to pages 185–6

gle, adult offspring of sponsors. They were previously not defined as eligible for family sponsorship, and as this change attracted more applicants than the department had anticipated, changes were introduced in April 1992 to reduce their eligibility. Citizenship and Immigration Canada. *A Broader Vision: Immigration and Citizenship Plan 1995–2000, Annual Report to Parliament* (Ottawa: Minister of Supply and Services Canada, 1994), 8.

20 CIC, *Canada and Immigration*, 3.

21 Ibid.

22 The text also raised the 'problem' of controlling the refugee program, but it did so within the context of restating Canada's international obligations to accept refugees. Therefore, the text did not question the principle of *whether* Canada should continue accepting refugees. By questioning the *principle* of family reunification, the text questioned the very need for the existence of the family class itself.

23 Issue Nos. 5, 6, 7, 8, 9, and 10. In the background to the first issue, it was pointed out that immigrants were less likely to claim welfare and other benefits than Canadians, and that they contributed more in taxes than they consumed in social services. But this information was not used in the framing of the questions for discussion, and the rest of the document (apart from this one reference) reiterated the view that immigrants presented a burden on social services. CIC, *Canada and Immigration*.

24 Ibid., 3–6.

25 The range of institutions across which the 'problems' of immigration had to be managed were specified for Working Groups #6A and 6B. They included housing, health, education, social assistance, and policing. Three out of the ten issues directly presented immigrants as threatening national institutions by being engaged in the 'abuse' of social services, specifically, Issue Nos. 7, 9, and 10 (ibid.).

26 See the sponsorship regulations as outlined in Employment and Immigration Canada, *Canada's Immigration Law.*

27 CIC, *Canada and Immigration*, 5. The widespread nature of the problem of accreditation has been documented in a number of studies. See Bakan, 'The International Market for Female Labour and Individual Deskilling'; and Ng and Strout, *Services for Immigrant Women.* Not one of the ten issues referred to the unequal treatment of the workers who entered the country under the Live-in Care Giver Program or the Non-Immigrant Employment Authorization Program, which allowed such workers to enter the country for temporary periods. See Arat-Koc, 'Immigration Policies, Migrant Domestic Workers and the Definition of Citizenship in Canada'; and Bolaria, 'From Immigrant Settlers to Migrant Transients.' This significant development in Canada's

immigration policy of separating off deserving workers, who are allowed into the country under the independent category for permanent residence, and undeserving workers, who are allowed in as migrant workers, was left off the national agenda.

28 Hawkins has described how the Department of Manpower and Immigration initiated a national discussion through the Green Paper in the 1970s. She defines the major problems with that process as follows: (1) very little research was available on immigration; (2) the Green Paper and the national discussion were 'seen much less as a way of seeking information and guidance from the Canadian public on immigration policy, than as a means of *educating* the provinces and public on the critical decisions in immigration and population which would have to be made in Canada in the very near future'; and, (3) one of the major changes being considered by the minister and the department, the merging of the Department of Manpower and Immigration with the Unemployment Commission was 'never put to the public at all.' She notes that the minister did not want the public debate to reach the 'average Canadian' because 'the Minister and Cabinet did not trust the average Canadian to respond in a positive way on this issue' (*Critical Years in Immigration*, 630; emphasis in the original). The IPR public consultations became a forum to 'educate' nationals about the dangers presented by immigrants. Unlike the earlier consultations, however, a substantial body of research existed on the topic of immigration in the last decade of the twentieth century, and the growing anti-immigrant sentiment was likewise publicly visible.

29 CIC published an interim report summarizing the submissions made during the consultations until mid-August 1994. See Citizenship and Immigration Canada, *Canada 2005: A Strategy for Citizenship and Immigration: Background Document* (Ottawa, CIC: 1994). A further consultation was organized at the National Conference in September 1994. After this conference, a final report was published: Citizenship and Immigration, *Immigration Consultation Report* (Ottawa: Minister of Supply and Services Canada, 1994). It is almost identical to the interim one, with a few changes incorporating contributions from the National Conference. Both reports summarized participants' responses to the ten issues and included specific policy recommendations.

30 CIC, *Immigration Consultations Report*, 15. Equal weight, however, was not given to all contributions by the reports. Submissions of the working groups, which discussed the unequal treatment of immigrants and made specific recommendations to rectify such treatment, were given no space in the final reports, while recommendations based on 'inaccurate' information were given ample space.

31 Specific attention will be paid in this discussion to the third policy area, social security, as this area is most directly related to the present study. Social security programs define the most basic entitlement to the welfare state – social assistance – and thus these programs reflect most clearly the consequences of belonging to the social collective. A number of academics have written quite extensively about the SSR, addressing its effects on class and gender relations. See Battle and Torjman, 'Desperately Seeking Substance'; Gloria Geller and Jan Joel, 'Struggling for Citizenship in the Global Economy: Bond Raters Versus Women and Children,' in Pulkingham and Ternowetsky, eds., *Remaking Canadian Social Policy*, 303–16; Therese Jennissen, 'The Federal Social Security Review, Process and Related Events (December 1993–June 1995): A Chronology,' in Pulkingham and Ternowetsky, eds., *Remaking Canadian Social Policy*, 30–2; Katherine Scott, *Women and the CHST: A Profile of Women Receiving Social Assistance in 1994* (Ottawa: Status of Women Canada, 1998); Richard Shillington, 'The Tax System and Social Policy Reform,' in Pulkingham and Ternowetsky, eds., *Remaking Canadian Social Policy*, 100–111; and Shelagh Day and Gwen Brodsky, *Women and the Equality Deficit: The Impact of Restructuring Canada's Social Programs* (Ottawa: Status of Women Canada, 1998). My contribution to this literature is to make race and nation central categories of analysis.

32 Human Resource Development Canada (HRDC), *Agenda: Jobs and Growth: Improving Social Security in Canada, A Discussion Paper* (The Green Paper) (Ottawa: Minister of Supply and Services Canada, 1994), 7.

33 Human Resources Development Canada (HRDC), *Agenda: Jobs and Growth: Improving Social Security in Canada, Discussion Paper Summary* (Ottawa: HRDC, 1994), 5.

34 Ibid.

35 The only direct reference made by the SSR texts to immigrants was a reference to the non-recognition of the education and skills of immigrants. Treated as a loss to the national economy, a specific recommendation was made to remedy this situation: 'Immigrants to Canada face special barriers to the portability of learning credentials. At present, immigrants face serious complications in seeking to establish their learning status in Canada. Some provinces have taken steps to help individuals gain recognition of foreign credentials. The federal government is interested in working with the provinces, employers and unions, and voluntary groups to develop a Canada-wide system of credits recognition to assist immigrants to find and keep meaningful employment, commensurate with their skills and knowledge' (HRDC, The Green Paper, 67).

While accreditation would undoubtedly assist in countering the racialized deskilling of immigrants, the many other ways in which the labour of immigrants is devalued and 'cheapened' by the conditions of their entry certainly cannot not be addressed by this measure alone. Accreditation would disproportionately favour highly skilled and professional immigrants while continuing to devalue the family class and domestic workers, the majority of whom are women.

36 See Mills, *Discourse*, 56.

37 HRDC, *Agenda: Discussion Paper Summary*, 17.

38 Department of Finance, *A New Framework for Economic Policy: A Presentation by The Honourable Paul Martin, P.C., M.P. (October 17, 1994)* (Ottawa: Finance, Government of Canada, 1994), 2–3.

39 HRDC, The Green Paper, 58.

40 Ibid., 9.

41 The text noted, 'Increasingly, our competitors are not the enterprises and workers down the street or in the next province, or even across the border, but those across the ocean, in the Pacific Rim or Europe' (ibid., 10). The strategy being deployed here defined 'us' as including the state, nation, manufacturing and resource industries, and workers. 'Our' competitors were presented as existing all over the globe. The actuality that the corporate-driven free-trade policies implemented by the state were easing the flow of capital and commodities across borders was made invisible.

42 Ibid., 9.

43 Ibid., 15.

44 Swasti Mitter, *Common Bond, Common Fate: Women in the Global Economy* (London: Pluto Press, 1986).

45 HRDC, The Green Paper, 15.

46 A number of theorists have noted that the SSR did not undertake a gender sensitive analysis, nor did it pay attention to class inequalities. 'Data that point to the relative status of Canadian women in the workplace, the home, the family and the community are readily available and clearly indicate that, in general, the majority of women occupy a status subordinate to men. Moreover, there are data available that speak to the differential impact that various social policies have on women (including the impact on specific categories of women) in relation to men. The designers of the framework for the social security review, however, did not take this into account and instead focused on non-gendered categories such as "the family," "the household," and "the labour force" – terms which effectively obfuscate the unequal status of women relative to men in Canadian society' (Jennissen, 'The Federal Social Security Review ...,' 239). See also Day and Brodsky, *Women and the Equality Deficit*; Geller and Joel, 'Struggling for Citizenship in the Global

Economy'; Pulkingham and Ternowetsky, *Remaking Canadian Social Policy*;
Scott, *Women and the CHST.*

Leah Vosko draws attention to the gender specific consequences of social
programs like unemployment insurance. She argues that the changes proposed in the SSR would strengthen the creation of a two-tiered system that
would privilege the access of 'regular' full-time workers to this program while
compounding the inequalities of 'irregular' women workers who are disproportionately employed in 'non-standard' work. See Leah Vosko, '*Irregular*
Workers: *New* Involuntary Social Exiles: Women and U.I. Reform,' in Pulkingham and Ternowetsky, eds., *Remaking Canadian Social Policy*, 256–72. Geller
and Joel argue that the restructuring of the welfare state represented a 'war
on equality' and was forcing women 'to see ourselves, not as citizens, but as
economic man' ('Struggling for Citizenship in the Global Economy,' 303).

47 See Linda McQuaig, *The Wealthy Banker's Wife: The Assault on Equality in Canada* (Toronto: Penguin Books, 1993); Maude Barlow and Bruce Campbell,
Straight through the Heart (Toronto: HarperCollins, 1993).

48 HRDC, *Agenda: Discussion Paper Summary*, 20.

49 CIC, *Immigration Consultations Report*, 16–17. Emphases in the original.

50 Ibid., 16.

51 Ibid., 17.

52 Ibid., 19. Emphasis in the original.

53 Ibid., 20.

54 Ibid., 21. These Canadian values were said to have been echoed in submission after submission, including those from Working Group #2, the staff of
the Department of Citizenship and Immigration Canada, and the department's overseas posts.

55 Ibid., 20.

56 Ibid., 20–1. Emphases in the original.

57 Although the growing economic polarization of the 1990s was documented
in a number of studies, discussion of this polarization was not taken up in the
review. For examples of such studies, see Brodie, *Politics on the Margins*;
Ralph, 'How to Beat the Corporate Agenda'; and Khosla, *Review of the Situation of Women Canada, 1993.*

58 See CIC, *Immigration Consultations Report*, 22–3. Emphasis in the original.

59 Citizenship and Immigration Canada, *Employee Consultation Report* (Ottawa:
CIC, 1994).

60 CIC, *Canada 2005: Background Document*, 42.

61 Ibid., 40.

62 CIC, *Immigration Consultations Report*, 55. Emphasis in the original.

63 Ibid. Emphasis in the original.

64 CIC, *Employee Consultation Report*, 6.
65 Ibid.
66 Such recommendations included the following: 'Increased information shar-
    ing among enforcement agencies and greater access to a comprehensive
    criminal database that is international in scope is suggested by many. Some
    recommend having one file for each person containing all government held
    information for that person. While some proposals related to information
    technology may be contrary to federal and provincial privacy and access to
    information legislation, several are of the view that this is one area where the
    protection of society as a whole takes precedence over individual rights'
    (ibid., 8).
67 Other suggestions stated: 'There was consensus that Canada could be more
    clever in the disincentives it employs to minimise use of its immigration pro-
    grammes. One suggestion was to target 'vulnerable groups' much in the way
    they are targeted by unscrupulous immigration consultants and lawyers.
    Reaching out to these groups, in their home countries, to properly inform
    them of laws and conditions in Canada is required,' Citizenship and Immi-
    grantion Canada, *The Report of Working Group #7: 'How Do We Establish a Frame-
    work for Enforcement in the Immigration/Refugee Systems that Meets Public
    Expectations and Respects the Integrity of the Program?'* (Ottawa: CIC, 1994), 6–7.
68 Ibid., 6.
69 CIC, *Immigration Consultations Report*, 80.
70 Ibid., 17.
71 Ibid., 18. Emphasis in the original.
72 Ibid.
73 Freda Hawkins has pointed out that the immigration bureaucracy clearly
    recognized the necessity for maintaining the immigration levels of the
    period during the 1980s. Immigration officials and politicians anticipated
    that immigration would remain an important policy area as a result of the
    low national population base and the declining birthrate. Canada faced
    'the prospect of future population decline,' Hawkins notes. She quotes the
    American demographer Leon Bouvier, who argued that fertility levels in
    developed countries since 1970 were very low: 'as of 1984, the rate in most
    developed countries shows no evidence of climbing back to the point
    where population growth, or at least population replacement, can be
    assured over the long run' (*Critical Years in Immigration*, 269). A back-
    ground paper tabled with the annual report to Parliament in 1984 pre-
    dicted that even if the annual net immigration remained at 50,000, the
    fertility rate of 1.7 would ensure that Canada's population would begin to
    decline in the year 2021. It was predicted that in order to maintain the pop-

ulation level, annual immigration levels of at least 125,000 would have to be maintained in the long run (ibid., 270).

74 See Maude Barlow and Bruce Campbell, *Straight through the Heart* (Toronto: HarperCollins, 1993).

75 CIC, *Canada and Immigration*, 3.

76 CIC, *Immigration Consultations Report*, 18.

77 Leila Ahmed, *Women and Gender in Islam: Historical Roots of a Modern Debate* (New Haven: Yale University Press, 1992); Mies, *Patriarchy and Accumulation on a World Scale*; and Said, *Orientalism*.

78 CIC, *Immigration Consultations Report*, 21.

79 Third world women have been the target of population control programs in India, Bangladesh, and Brazil, as well as in advanced capitalist countries such as the United States and Britain. See Sonia Correa, *Population and Reproductive Rights: Feminist Perspectives from the South* (London: Zed Books, 1994); B. Mintzes, A. Hardon, and J. Hanhart, eds., *Norplant: Under Her Skin* (Delft, The Netherlands: Eburon, 1993); Carmen Barroso and Cristina Bruschini, 'Building Politics from Personal Lives: Discussions on Sexuality among Poor Women In Brazil,' in Chandra Mohanty, Ann Russo, and Lourdes Torres, eds., *Third World Women and the Politics of Feminism* (Bloomington: Indiana University Press, 1991), 153–72; Amos and Parmar, 'Challenging Imperial Feminism'; E. Barbee and M. Little, 'Health, Social Class and African-American Women,' in S. James et al., ed., *Theorizing Black Feminisms: The Visionary Pragmatism of Black Women* (London: Routledge, 1994), 182–99.

80 Barroso and Bruschini, 'Building Politics from Personal Lives'; and Correa, *Population and Reproductive Rights*.

81 Citizenship and Immigration Canada, *The Report of Working Group #4: 'How Do We Achieve a Coherent Strategy within Canada and among Nations to Deal with International Migration Pressures?'* (Ottawa: CIC, 1994), ii.

82 Ibid., 4–5.

83 Barroso and Bruschini, 'Building Politics from Personal Lives'; Correa, *Population and Reproductive Rights*; Mintzes et al., eds., *Norplant*.

84 Amos and Parmar, 'Challenging Imperial Feminist'; McLaren, *Our Own Master Race*; and Amrit Wilson, *Finding a Voice: Asian Women in Britain* (London: Virago, 1978).

85 Participants were said to have raised the following concern: 'Canadians told us that they are deeply concerned that the system and processes of the immigration program are not working as they should. More specifically, they are concerned that the focus has become one of quantity rather than quality' (CIC, *Canada 2005: Background Document*, 61).

86 CIC, *Immigration Consultations Report*, 26, 65.

87 Ibid., 26.
88 Citizenship and Immigration Canada, *Canada 2005: A Strategy for Citizenship and Immigration, Conference Proceedings* (Ottawa: CIC, 1994), 6.
89 Citizenship and Immigration Canada, *The Report of Working Group #5: 'What Are the Key Elements of a Strategy for Intergrating Newcomers into Canadian Society?'* (Ottawa: CIC, 1994), 23.
90 Citizenship and Immigration Canada, *The Report of Working Group #6B: 'How Do We Integrate Immigration Policy and Program Delivery with Areas Such as Housing, Health, Education and Training ...?'* (Ottawa: CIC, 1994), 1.
91 CIC, *Canada 2005: Background Document*, 16.
92 CIC, *Immigration Consultations Report*, 29. Emphasis in the original.
93 Ibid., 26.
94 The IPR further devalued this category by repeatedly focusing on its economic 'costs,' thereby encouraging recommendations such as the following: 'The predominant view with respect to social services, especially health care, is that immigrants (not including refugees) should not have unlimited access to services immediately upon their arrival' (CIC, *Employee Consultation Report*, 6). 'Another common view is that *a few communities bear a disproportionate cost of integration*.' Many submissions argued that due to the overwhelming needs of both immigrant children and adults for language training, the education system was *'under siege'*. A number also argued that as a result of this burden on the school system, many Canadian-born children were forgoing their regular school curriculum (CIC, *Immigration Consultations Report* 52; emphasis in the original); 'immigrant children, particularly refugee children, have needs beyond learning English ... These children and their families need support beyond what local boards can provide given present financial realities' (ibid., 46); and 'many employees agree that all levels of government, as well as the agencies and organizations involved in the provision of social services, must share information more readily and to a greater extent. This would not only result in more effective and focused service delivery, but also reduce the opportunity for abuse' (CIC, *Employee Consultation Report*, 6).
95 CIC, *Employee Consultation Report*, 7.
96 Ibid., 4. The report from Working Group #8 pointed out, 'There is increasing concern that immigrants are not respecting these responsibilities (of sponsorship), thus placing demands on already over-burdened social support programs, funded by Canadian taxpayers.' See Citizenship and Immigration Canada, *The Report of Working Group #8: 'How Do We Realize the Benefits of Immigration to Canada in Areas Such as Regional Impact Workforce Skills, Job Creation and International Competitiveness?'* (Ottawa: CIC, 1994), 10–11.

97 CIC, *The Report of Working Group #8*, 11.

98 One recommendation stated: 'The jurisdictional concerns said to stymie regular litigation by provinces to recover social welfare payments to sponsorees from their sponsors in accordance with their undertakings could be easily resolved by the routine assignment of sponsorship undertakings by the federal government to the province of reception.' See Citizenship and Immigration Canada, *Report on the National Consultation on Family Class Immigration* (Toronto: Centre for Refugee Studies, and Ottawa: CIC, 1994), 6.

99 Yet another recommendation stated: 'The sponsor might be required to post a significant bond as a condition of the admission of a family member, which deposit would be forfeited in the event of sponsorship breakdown. If no mechanism can be devised to enforce sponsorship obligations, then social accountability might best be secured by limiting overall exposure by a numerical ceiling on the number of sponsorships which any one sponsor can make' (ibid. 6). One specific recommendation for such a sponsorship bond proposed that it be set at the rate of $20,000. See Don J. De Voretz, 'New Issues, New Evidence, and New Immigration Policies for the Twenty-first Century,' in Don J. Devoretz, ed., *Diminishing Returns: The Economics of Canada's Recent Immigration Policy* (Ottawa: C.D. Howe Institute, 1995), 8. See also, CIC, *The Report of Working Group #8*, 11.

100 CIC, *Immigration Consultations Report*, 28. This recommendation was made in the report of the working group mandated to specifically examine the family class.

101 CIC, *Report on the National Consutation on Family Class Immigration*, 2.

102 Ibid., 5.

103 The basis upon which this reassessment would take place was not specified in the report of the national consultation.

104 Amos and Parmer, 'Challenging Imperial Feminism'; Wilson, *Finding a Voice*; WING, *World's Apart*.

105 WING, *World's Apart*, 56.

106 CIC, *The Report of Working Group #8*, 11.

107 CIC, *Immigration Consultations Report*, 28.

108 Working Groups #6A and #6B were specifically mandated to address the integration of immigration policy with other areas of public policy. Both Groups underscored the importance of the family class by emphasizing its contributions; but I quote here from group #6A: 'Family members are admitted without being assessed on their labour market skills. But the group wished to emphasize that spouses and other family members who can work would likely enter the labour market shortly after their arrival. Immigrant families, like most other Canadian families, need at least two

incomes. Settlement, training and other immigration policies and programs should consider this reality of family life in Canada. Whether they come to Canada as sponsored family members, refugees or selected independents, immigrants want the chance to work, and to have meaningful work. They want to use the skills and knowledge which they have brought with them to Canada.' Citizenship and Immigration Canada, *The Report of Working Group #6A: 'How Do We Integrate Immigration Policy and Program Delivery within Such Areas as Housing, Health, Education and Training ... ?'* (Ottawa: CIC, 1994), 2–3.

109 Working Group #6B pointed out that the family class made the process of adjustment much easier for primary immigrants, thus reducing settlement costs and demonstrating the long-term commitment of immigrants to Canada: 'More emphasis should be placed on family reunification as this facilitates early adjustment and creates long term commitment to Canada. It should be recognized that the process of settlement and integration is made considerably easier for refugees, family or independent immigrants who have family members in Canada when they arrive or whose relatives join them at some point after arrival. As such, family reunification offers a considerable cost saving in terms of integration services.' See CIC, *The Report of Working Group #6B*, 6.

110 Citizenship and Immigration Canada, *The Report of Working Group #6A*, 1.

111 Citizenship and Immigration Canada, *The Report of Working Group #6B*, 4–5.

112 HRDC, *Agenda: Discussion Paper Summary*, 6.

113 State control of public finances was obscured in this discussion, as was the reality that the deficit 'crisis' had resulted from the not insignificant benefits to certain sectors of Canadian society in the form of reduced taxation for corporations and high interest payments to bondholders on the federal debt. See Shillington, 'The Tax System and Social Policy Reform,' and Ralph, 'How to Beat the Corporate Agenda.'

114 Department of Finance, *Creating a Healthy Fiscal Climate: A Presentation by The Honourable Paul Martin, P.C., M.P., to the House of Commons Standing Committee on Finance (October 18, 1994)* (Ottawa: Finance, Government of Canada, 1994), 4.

115 Finance, *A New Framework for Economic Policy*, 9.

116 Ibid., 3.

117 A number of theorists noted that the welfare state provided direct 'welfare' to the ruling elite in the form of tax relief, corporate grants, and tax loopholes, as well as indirect support in the form of the public sector, which provides the social infrastructure necessary for economic growth. The welfare programs that benefit capital have remained largely invisible in public

debates, while programs like social assistance, which benefit women and workers, have been given high visibility, stigmatizing the recipients during the 'welfare wars' of the 1990s. See Fraser and Gordon, 'Contract versus Charity'; Gordon, *Pitied But Not Entitled*; Ramesh Mishra, *The Welfare State in Capitalist Society* (Toronto: Harvester Wheatsheaf, 1990); and McQuaig, *The Wealthy Banker's Wife*.

118 HRDC, *A New Framework for Economic Policy*, 9.

119 The text stated: 'Reform of social security cannot be contemplated in isolation from the fiscal realities facing governments in Canada. Until the fiscal situation of governments improves, there will be no new money for new programs, including social programs. And existing expenditures must be brought under control and in some cases reduced' (HRDC, The Green Paper, 23).

120 The seriousness of the debt was repeatedly underscored: 'Let me be clear. What we seek is jobs and growth. To get there, we must stop the growth of the debt. Our ultimate goal is a balanced budget' (Finance, *Creating a Healthy Fiscal Climate*, 4).

121 National Anti-Poverty Organization, *An Action Guide for NAPO: 30 Million Good Reasons to Have National Standards for Welfare* (Ottawa: NAPO, 1995); Shillington, 'The Tax System and Social Policy Reform'; and McQuaig, *The Wealthy Banker's Wife*.

122 The benefit to 'foreigners' was thus described: 'There aren't enough savings in Canada to satisfy all the borrowing needs of government, the private sector and Canadians. So we go abroad – becoming more and more in debt to foreigners. In fact, 5 per cent of our national income is draining abroad each and every year to pay interest on our borrowing. Our level of foreign debt as a country is also the highest in the G-7. Therefore, we are subject to every whim, every sentiment of international markets. And our economic sovereignty is at risk' (Finance, *Creating a Healty Fiscal Climate*, 3).

123 The text stated the following about the debt: 'It is simply unsustainable and must be addressed. Facing up to the debt challenge is the keystone of responsible economic policy. If we fail at that, we will fail at everything else. It is not a question of focusing on jobs or the debt. It is a question of focusing on both. The debt stands in the way of the growth we seek; in a very real way, it limits our economy's ability to create jobs. The fact is that we will not get the quality of growth we need to generate the jobs we want until we gain control of the debt, until we have broken the back of the deficit' (ibid., 2).

124 HRDC, The Green Paper, 10. It went on to say, 'Too many young people leave school unprepared for the world of work. Too many people on social assistance or in low-wage jobs can't afford – or are not allowed by the sys-

tem – to upgrade their skills' (ibid., 22). Another report stated that 'more Canadians who lose their jobs find it hard to get new ones, because their skills are not up-to-date' (HRDC, *Agenda: Discussion Paper Summary*, 8).

125 Income assistance was identified as a particular concern: 'Many people spend years on social assistance – even though, with the right kind of employment and training support, they could find work. One problem is, CAP rules prevent the use of federal funding to provide the support they need. As a result, the system doesn't help people prepare for work. In many cases, it does just the opposite' (HRDC, *Agenda: Discussion Paper Summary*, 20). The Canada Assistance Plan (CAP) was a cost-sharing program between the federal and provincial governments for social assistance programs. Replacing the previous patchwork provision of social assistance by provincial governments, the CAP made federal funding conditional upon provinces agreeing to federal standards for social assistance programs. CAP funded programs included the provision of necessities such as 'food, shelter, clothing, fuel, utilities, household supplies and personal requirements' (Day and Brodsky, *Women and the Equality Deficit*, 15). The rights legislated under CAP included the right to an adequate amount of income assistance when in need; the right to appeal the decision if denied social assistance; the right not to be forced onto workfare as a condition of receiving assistance; and the prohibition of residency requirements (NAPO, *An Action Guide for NAPO*). The social assistance programs funded by CAP were especially important in providing income support to women as citizens (see also Scott, *Women and the CHST*).

126 In 1994, women represented 54 per cent of adult social assistance recipients (Scott, *Women and the CHST* 5). Bashevkin notes that single female-headed households were disproportionately represented among social assistance claimants (*Welfare Hot Buttons*).

127 HRDC, The Green Paper, 10–17.

128 Finance, *A New Framework for Economic Policy*, 4.

129 While the public discussion of social security certainly contributed to poor-bashing and, in particular, denigrated single mothers on social assistance, the SSR texts were careful to emphasize that even when Canadians made claims to social assistance, they were not personally at fault: 'In recent years, increasing numbers of Canadians who cannot find jobs have turned to social assistance' (HRDC, The Green Paper, 19). The SSR texts noted that social assistance claimants doubled from 1982 to 1993 to 3 million people (HRDC, *Agenda: Discussion Paper Summary*, 20). The Green Paper asked: 'Yet don't we as a society have a stake in doing more, in helping people who suddenly find their job skills inadequate and out-of-date to retool themselves

for the good jobs in today's economy?' (HRDC, The Green Paper, 8). Sylvia Bashevkin has argued that, although the Chrétien government stressed the notion that 'individual self-sufficiency was the sole aim of public spending on welfare,' Canadian political leaders largely refrained from resorting to the divisive and polarizing targeting of social assistance claimants (*Welfare Hot Buttons*, 67). She notes there were a number of exceptions, such as the Prime Minister's reference to welfare claimants as 'beer drinkers' and the reference of a Provincial Premier to fraudulent claimants as 'varmints' (21). Bashevkin acknowledges that the personal vilification of single mothers was rife in the United States and Britain, and that it sometimes 'spilled over in significant ways to Canada as well' (11).

Jean Swanson, then president of the National Anti-Poverty Organization, makes a different assessment. She has documented the poor-bashing rhetoric in the media that framed the restructuring of social security: 'About ten years ago the Canadian media launched a vicious attack on people who were poor. Two-inch headlines made criminals of people on welfare, without offering solid evidence. Gossip and lies in stories and columns reinforced false stereotypes and blamed people on welfare and unemployment for the deficit. When the media did deign to give people who were poor a voice, it was often in 'poornographic' articles as experts on suffering, while their understanding and analysis of social programs and the economy were ignored. The media onslaught made it acceptable for poor-bashing politicians to pass poor-bashing laws, chop welfare and UI even more, and force people to accept sub-poverty level jobs to survive.' See Jean Swanson, *Poor-Bashing: The Politics of Exclusion* (Toronto: Between the Lines, 2001), 90–1.

My point is that even when those living in poverty were stigmatized, they were also simultaneously exalted as nationals.

130 Finance, *A New Framework for Economic Policy*, 4.
131 Finance, *Creating a Healthy Fiscal Climate*, 7.
132 Ibid. The IPR likewise enabled the state to claim a partnership between nation and state on the basis of 'shared goals' and 'shared responsibilities' between 'government and its citizens' (CIC, *Immigration Consultations Report*, 1).
133 Finance, *Creating a Healthy Fiscal Climate*, 12.
134 Ibid., 11.
135 The government claimed that social assistance costs resulting from sponsorship breakdowns amounted to approximately $600 to $700 million annually. See CIC, *Into the Twenty-first Century: A Strategy for Immigration and Citizenship* (Ottawa: Minister of Supply and Services Canada, 1994), 39. This document also stated that 14 per cent of family class immigrants claimed

social assistance, which was a lower rate than the 16 per cent of Canadians who claimed social services. Any such claims for social assistance made by the family class, of course, relied upon the discretion of the provincial and municipal jurisdictions within which such claims were made. The sponsorship regulations, as I have discussed in chapter 3, required that sponsored immigrants were to be financially supported by their sponsor (EIC, *Canada's Immigration Law*).

136 See Sylvia Bashevkin for a fuller discussion of these measures. This is how she summarizes their effects: '[T]he very significant withdrawal of federal funds from social programs that was announced in the 1995 budget coincided with a loss of national policy guidelines or principles that has prevailed for three decades. The support for job training and child care that Liberals promised in their 1990 campaign platform failed to materialize, leaving poor women in Canada to face less generous, more punitive, and often more paternalistic welfare regimes at provincial and local levels' (*Welfare Hot Buttons*, 11).

137 Citizenship and Immigration Canada, *Statement: Speaking Notes for the Honourable Sergio Marchi, P.C., M.P. ...* (Ottawa: Governement of Canada, 1994), 2.

6 Nationality in the Age of Global Terror

* The research for this chapter has been funded by a Hampton Research Grant from the University of British Columbia.

1 Walter Benjamin, *Selected Writings*, vol. 4, *1983–1940*, ed. Howard Eiland and Michael W. Jennings, trans. Edmund Jephcott (Cambridge, MA: Harvard University Press, 2003), 392.

2 *Globe and Mail*, 27 March 2004, D6.

3 See Razack for a discussion of how the 'imperilled' Muslim woman is constructed in contemporary European discourses about arranged and forced marriages. 'Imperilled Muslim Women, Dangerous Muslim Men and Civilised Europeans: Legal and Social Responses to Forced Marriages,' *Feminist Legal Studies* (2004), 129–74.

4 See A. Coyne, 'We Are All Americans Now,' *National Post*, 3 October 2001, A7; C. Ford, 'Terrorism Makes Our Difference Irrelevant,' *Vancouver Sun*, 17 September 2001, A8; M. Wente, 'We're All Americans Now,' *Globe and Mail*, 13 September 2001, N3. The expression of this sentiment was certainly not confined to Canada. See also J. Colombani, *Le Monde*, 12 September 2001; A. Freeman, 'Today We Are All Americans – NATO Allies Pledge Support,' *Globe and Mail*, 13 September 2001, A6.

5 *The Province* (Vancouver), 13 September 2001, 1.

6 These measures included the strengthening of state powers of surveillance and detention; the imposition of greater restrictions on immigration and refugee policies; the increased scrutiny of immigrants and refugees (both at the borders and within the country) and a strengthening of the powers of deportation; a commitment to fighting the war against terrorism under the leadership of the Bush administration, most specifically to participate in the war on Afghanistan; and the intensification of intelligence, security, and military alliances with the United States. For discussion of the specific changes proposed in the anti-terrorism legislation, see R.J. Daniels, P. Macklem, and K. Roach, eds., *The Security of Freedom: Essays on Canada's Anti-Terrorism Bill* (Toronto: University of Toronto Press, 2002).

7 Stressing the 'common values' shared by Americans and Canadians, the next Liberal prime minister, Paul Martin Jr., stated that while he was committed to a 'distinctive' Canadian international stance, 'That certainly doesn't mean going along with the United States. What it means is doing what we think is right. And a lot of times that will be what the Americans think, because we do have a pretty common set of values.' M. Kennedy, 'Martin Sees Greater Military Cooperation with U.S.,' *Vancouver Sun*, 29 April 2003, A12.

8 Editorial, 'Harper's Ringing Words on the Afghan Mission,' *Globe and Mail*, 14 March 2006, A14.

9 'Canada Tarred Again as Haven for Terrorists,' read the headline of the *Globe and Mail* on 26 April 2002. The story by Colin Freeze reported the warnings of two former civil servants to Canadians about the 'serious problems in its immigration system,' which made it a 'haven for terrorists.' The intent of these warnings was clear: nationals needed to act quickly to toughen immigration policies if another catastrophe on the scale of the 9/11 attacks was to be averted.

On 28 February 2006, the Fraser Institute, a right-wing think tank with considerable influence and public presence, issued a news release with the headline, 'Canada [Was] Becoming a Haven for Terrorists Due to Lax Immigration and Refugee Policies According to New Study.'

10 Michael Hardt and Antonio Negri, *Empire* (Cambridge, MA: Harvard University Press, 2000).

11 T.Y. Ismael and J. Measor, 'Racism and the North American Media Following 11 September: The Canadian Setting,' *Arab Studies Quarterly* 25, nos. 1/2 (Winter/Spring 2003), 101–37.

12 Karim H. Karim, *Islamic Peril: Media and Global Violence* (Montreal: Black Rose Books, 2000), 175.

13 Edward Said, *Covering Islam* (New York: Pantheon Books, 1981).

14 This chapter is based on an examination of English-language national and provincial mainstream print media. It does not examine French-language media or the ethnic press. The recurring themes and patterns and the underlying assumptions in the reporting of the first phase of the war on terrorism and the war on Afghanistan are examined. I draw upon salient and representative examples in my discussion of this reporting.

15 The concept of the 'elite' was pioneered by the sociologist C. Wright Mills in his examination of the hegemonic role of dominant groups that exercise power across various sectors of society, including the state apparatus, the corporate sector, the military establishment, and the 'strategic command posts of the social structure' on the basis of their wealth and status. Analysing how power and knowledge remained largely concentrated in the hands of this elite, Mills argued that their decisions and actions had enormous impact on the lives of 'ordinary' people. He included the increasing prominence of the film industry in the consolidation of elite power. Mill's concept of the elite did not suggest a monolithic, homogenous group. Rather, it recognized that various sectors of the elite subscribe to different ideologies and discursive frames, that they are sometimes riven by internecine antagonisms, even as they simultaneously share similar interests vis-à-vis the larger population. See C. Wright Mills, *The Sociological Imagination* (London: Oxford University Press, 1959).

16 Appadurai, *Modernity at Large*.

17 Ibid., 28.

18 Ibid., 3.

19 See Robert Hackett and Yuezhi Zhao, *Sustaining Democracy? Journalism and the Politics of Objectivity* (Toronto: Garamond Press, 1998). See also Edward S. Herman and Noam Chomsky, *Manufacturing Consent: The Political Economy of the Mass Media* (New York: Pantheon, 1988); and R. Hackett et al., *The Missing News: Filters and Blind Spots in Canada's Press* (Ottawa: Canadian Centre for Policy Alternatives, and Toronto: Garamond Press, 2000), 55.

20 Hackett et al., *The Missing News*, 50. The Canadian Press, described as 'almost a central nervous system, for national and international news,' is owned by newspapers and its reports are regularly used in radio and television reporting (ibid., 51).

21 Ibid., 11–12.

22 Linda McQuaig, *Shooting the Hippo* (Toronto: Penguin, 1995); McQuaig, *The Wealthy Banker's Wife*; and Barlow and Campbell, *Straight through the Heart*.

23 The career of Israel Asper, the now deceased owner of CanWest Global Communications, provides yet another example of media concentration and the intersecting nature of elite interests across various sectors of society. CanWest

is one of the largest media conglomerates in the country and includes among its holdings television channels, radio stations, and Internet outlets. It is Canada's largest newspaper publisher, with both national and provincial newspapers among its holdings.

Mr Asper has been described as follows: 'movie house ticket clerk, lawyer, politician, pianist, media mogul, philanthropist ... He was a jazz-loving member of the cheeseburger set, a Liberal of distinctly bluish hue and a booster for Winnipeg with global ambitions and reach. An expert purveyor of popular American culture, he was also one of Canada's leading supporter of the fine arts and a host of other philanthropic causes.' See R. Boswell, 'The Many Lives of Israel Asper,' *Vancouver Sun*, 8 October 2003, A3. A past leader of the Manitoba provincial Liberal Party, Mr Asper was an astute businessman with decidedly strong opinions on many issues, including the Middle East, which he did not hesitate to popularize through his media empire. Under his stewardship, CanWest's chain of local newspapers came to regularly publish editorials written by the central office in Winnipeg, much to the consternation of some journalists and industry observers. With regard to the war on terrorism, CanWest was involved in a very vocal disagreement with the Reuters news agency and was found to have doctored news reports produced by the international agency. Whereas Reuters was reported to eschew the use of language such as 'terrorist' and 'terrorism' in favour of language with an 'absence of emotion in [its]vocabulary, so that events may be judged dispassionately,' CanWest's national newspaper, the *National Post*, attacked this policy in an editorial as 'a misleading gloss of political correctness.' See James Adams, 'CanWest, Reuters at Odds Over Use of "Terrorist,"' *Globe and Mail*, 21 September 2004, A13.

The owners of CanWest were certainly no exception in their hands-on control over their media/business empire. Mr Conrad Black, the media baron who controlled Hollinger Inc., was likewise not shy in expounding upon his opinions in his newspapers: 'In the world according to Conrad Black, trade unions, human rights legislation, Aboriginal self-government, social democracy, public institutions, feminism, the poor, and accommodation with Quebec nationalism are typically viewed as signs of stupidity, vested interest, or social and moral weakness. By contrast, topics such as free trade, the value of wealth, high-brow intellectualism, the American way of life, Margaret Thatcher, and Israel's hardliners are on the side of the angels,' argue Hackett et al., *The Missing News*, 55.

24 Quoted in ibid., 55. See also Ben Bagdikian, *The New Media Monopoly* (Boston: Beacon Press, 2004).

25 Hackett et al., *The Missing News*, 55.

26 Ibid., 51.

27 See Herman and Chomsky, *Manufacturing Consent.*

28 *Globe and Mail,* 18 October 2004, A1. A number of scholars have argued that notwithstanding the attacks of 9/11, the dangers of international terrorism actually declined during the last decades of the twentieth century. While the 'actual dangers from international terrorism have fallen substantially around the world, and indeed, fallen during the last decade,' perceptions of the threats of such attacks actually increased as a result of the shift in the media's news frame. See Pippa Norris, Montague Kern, and Marion R. Just, eds., *Framing Terrorism: The News Media, the Government and the Public* (New York: Routledge, 2003), 4.

29 M. Philp, 'Teaching a New Generation to Duck and Cover,' *Globe and Mail,* 18 October 2002, A8.

30 M. Hume, 'Terrorism High on Police Chief's List of Worries,' *Globe and Mail,* 8 April 2004, A9.

31 Sherene H. Razack, ed., *Race, Space, and the Law: Unmapping a White Settler Society* (Toronto: Between the Lines, 2002).

32 Remarks by the President to Business Leaders, 'President Calls on Senate to Act on Terrorism Insurance Legislation' (April 2002), retrieved 2 July 2002 from the White House website, www.whitehouse.gov/news/releases/2002/ 04/20020408-17.html.

33 President's State of the Union Address (29 January 2002), retrieved 2 July 2002 from the White House website, http://www.whitehouse.gov/news/ releases/2002/01/20020129-11.html.

34 For a discussion of the Enlightenment concept of history and its role in European colonialism, see Robert Young, *White Mythologies: Writing History and the West* (London: Routledge, 1990).

35 The representation of Islam and Muslims as uncivilized in the wake of 9/11 is hardly novel. In his study of representations of Islam in the mainstream western media, Edward Said identified a pattern that constituted such reporting as 'part fictional, part ideological': 'In many instances 'Islam' has licensed not only patent inaccuracy but also expressions of unrestrained ethnocentrism, cultural and even racial hatred, deep yet paradoxically freefloating hostility ... there is an unquestioned assumption that Islam can be characterized limitlessly by means of a handful of recklessly general and repeatedly deployed clichés.' See Said, *Covering Islam,* x–xi. In the particular case of Canada, Karim H. Karim has identified the widespread deployment of such clichés as 'Islamic terrorists,' 'Islamic extremism,' and 'Islamic fundamentalists,' such that 'Islam' becomes a 'synonym for fanaticism and senseless violence.' See Karim, *Islamic Peril,* v.

36 Stuart Hall, 'The West and the Rest: Discourse and Power,' in Stuart Hall et al., eds., *Modernity: An Introduction to Modern Societies* (Oxford: Blackwell Publishers, 1996), 184–228.

37 Ibid., 186.

38 Ibid., 187.

39 Said, *Orientalism*, 42.

40 Razack, *Looking White People in the Eye*; Narayan, *Dislocating Cultures*; and Chandra T. Mohanty, Ann Russo, and Lourdes Torres, eds., *Third World Women and the Politics of Feminism* (Bloomington: Indiana University Press, 1991).

41 See Ahmed, *Women and Gender in Islam*; Kumkum Sangari and Sudesh Vaid, eds., *Recasting Women: Essays in Colonial History* (New Delhi: Kali for Women, 1989); and Chandra T. Mohanty, 'Under Western Eyes: Feminist Scholarship and Colonial Discourses,' in Mohanty, Russo, and Torres, eds., *Third World Women and the Politics of Feminism*, 51–80.

42 Razack, *Looking White People in the Eye*; Narayan, *Dislocating Cultures*.

43 Ahmed, *Women and Gender in Islam*; and Sangari and Vaid, *Recasting Women*.

44 Chris Wattie, 'Detailed Training Needed for Attacks,' *National Post*, 14 September 2001, A13.

45 Sean M. Maloney, Michael A. Hennessy, and Scott Roberson, 'An Attack against Us All,' *National Post*, 12 September 2001, D7.

46 Stephen Hume, 'Calm in the Heart of Chaos: As Anger Grows in the Wake of Terrorism, Americans Should Temper the Momentum for Revenge,' *Vancouver Sun*, 12 September 2001, A23.

47 Even those who remained somewhat uneasy with the intensification of Canada's identification with U.S. imperial interests were not averse to this recasting of Canadian nationality. So, for instance, then Liberal prime minister, Jean Chrétien adopted a more careful, if somewhat critical, support for the war. However, even such careful distancing did not essentially challenge the dominant trope of western cultural supremacy.

In an interview with the Canadian Broadcasting Corporation on the first anniversary of 9/11, Prime Minister Chrétien commented that western 'greed' and 'arrogance' had to be addressed. His comments were immediately seized upon by his Conservative detractors as criticism of the United States and as placing the blame for the attacks of 9/11 on the United States. In response to these charges, the Prime Minister's Office swiftly issued a statement claiming his comments had been 'misreported': 'It is a gross misconstruction of his remarks to suggest that he was blaming the U.S. for the attacks.' See Allison Dunfield, 'PMO Says Media Misreported September 11 Remarks,' *Globe and Mail*, 12 September 2002.

Given the controversy created by the prime minister's comments, they merit a closer reading: 'You cannot exercise your powers to the point of humiliation for the others. That is what the Western world – not only the Americans, the Western world – has to realize. Because they are human beings too. There are long-term consequences ... And I do think that the Western world is getting too rich in relation to the poor world and necessarily will be looked upon as being arrogant and self-satisfied, greedy and with no limits. The 11th of September is an occasion for me to realize it even more.' See Sheldon Alberts, 'PM Links Attacks to "Arrogant" West,' *National Post*, 12 September 2002, A1.

Even as the prime minister expressed criticism of the west for being arrogant and greedy, he essentially upheld the discourse of the 'West and the rest,' arguing for a kindler, gentler version of the West. Rather than questioning this binary relationship, the prime minister's comments called for the adoption of a more humane approach by the west, and its recognition that 'they' too are 'human beings,' as a better option for protecting its long-term interests.

48 Wente, 'We're All Americans Now,' N3.
49 Numerous rallies, memorials, and other commemorative events organized to show solidarity with the United States were given ample coverage, while dissident voices attempting to stem the growing consensus for an immediate attack on Afghanistan were allowed little public space. I have discussed my own experience in attempting to challenge this consensus in 'War Frenzy,' *Atlantis: A Women's Studies Journal* 27, no. 1 (Fall 2002): 5–11.
50 For examples of this, see ibid.
51 For a discussion of this thesis, see Samuel P. Huntington, 'The Clash of Civilizations?' *Foreign Affairs* 72, no. 3 (Summer 1993), 22–49.
52 T. Modood, 'Muslims and the Politics of Multiculturalism in Britain,' in E. Hershberg and K.W. Moore, eds., *Critical Views of September 11: Analyses from Around the World* (New York: The New Press, 2002), 194.
53 A number of activists, scholars, writers, and journalists have argued that the war on terrorism is an imperialist project that the United States has undertaken in order to extend its reach over the vast oil and natural gas resources of Central Asia, as well as to protect its position as the world's hegemon. These include Noam Chomsky, Robert Fiske, and Arundhati Roy. See also my article, 'War Frenzy,' *Meridiens: Feminism, Race, Transnationalism* 2, no. 2 (2002), 289–97.
54 Mahmood Mamdani, 'Good Muslim, Bad Muslim: A Political Perspective on Culture and Terrorism,' in Hershberg and Moore, eds., *Critical Views of September 11*, 45.

55 Mahmood Mamdani, *Good Muslim, Bad Muslim: America, the Cold War and the Roots of Terror* (New York: Pantheon Books, 2004).

56 Two years after the attacks, and despite Canada's (overt) reluctance to endorse the invasion and occupation of Iraq, the country's oldest national newspaper could still express the earlier intensely emotional identification with the United States on its front page: '9/11/03: He Taunts Us Still' read the headline that accompanied the report of a bin Laden tape that had surfaced in the days preceding the second anniversary. Paul Koring, '9/11/03: He Taunts Us Still,' *Globe and Mail*, 11 September 2003, 1. The headline, which ran across the top of the entire front page in bold print, was notable for its use of the collective 'us,' thereby including Canadians in the 'taunts' alleged to emanate from Osama bin Ladin.

An editorial column in the *Calgary Herald* on the same day urged support for Canada's participation in the war: 'The technology of mass destruction, whether by nuclear or biochemical means, is widely dispersed. To suppose that terrorists, if left unchecked, will not attempt to use it in the West to further some end, at some time, is reckless complacency.' The editorial went on to state: 'And finally, we have hardly begun to bleed. U.S. and British casualties in the entire war on terror have yet to reach 1,000.' Editorial, 'The Enemy Within,' *Calgary Herald*, 11 September 2003. Here, U.S. and British casualties were claimed as 'ours' through the use of the collective 'we.'

Liberal Trade Minister Pierre Pettigrew commented in a speech to the Empire Club of Canada, 'Being next to the United States of America is a privilege. I mean there is no better place on the planet ... We represent for the rest of the planet a light in the world.' Steven Chase, 'Pettigrew Sings Praises of U.S.,' *Globe and Mail* (26 September 2003), A9. A Liberal senator tabled a private member's bill that sought to designate September 11 as 'America Day' in Canada. Tim Naumetz, 'Senator would like Canada to Honor the U.S. on Sept. 11,' *Vancouver Sun*, 24 September 2003, A3.

57 Marcus Gee, 'When It Comes to Osama, Canada Doesn't Get It,' *Globe and Mail*, 15 November 2002, A17.

58 The statement is credited to then deputy prime minister John Manley. Mike Trickey, 'Canada "Takes Terror Threat Seriously,"' *Vancouver Sun*, 14 November 2002, A8.

59 Wesley Wark, 'Learning to Live with Terror,' *Globe and Mail*, 15 November 2002, A17.

60 Brian Mulroney, 'A New World Order,' *Globe and Mail*, 21 October 2003, A25.

61 Brian Laghi, 'Harper's Surprise Afghan Visit,' *Globe and Mail*, 13 March 2006, A1, A4.

62 This is how Prime Minister Harper put it: 'The reality hit home with brutal

force on 9/11 when two dozen Canadians lost their lives, suddenly and senselessly, in the destruction of the World Trade Centre. These were ordinary people. People with families, partners, children, with hopes for the future.' Brian Laghi, 'We Won't Run Away, PM Vows,' *Globe and Mail*, 14 March 2006, A1, A6.

63 Editorial, 'Harper's Ringing Words on the Afghan Mission.'

64 Peter C. Newman, 'Terror Already Has Its Sea Legs,' *Globe and Mail*, 11 March 2006, F3. The column was written in the wake of a Dubai-based company's bid for a contract to manage harbours in the United States.

65 Ibid.

66 Indeed, Canada was mentioned specifically in a threat alleged to come from al Qaeda. Canada, Britain, and a number of other U.S. allies were identified as potential targets because of their participation in the war on Afghanistan and Iraq respectively. However, this threat was recast by the media as having been made because Canada is 'open' and democratic: 'Even if Canadians had not played such an active role in Afghanistan, our closeness to the U.S., as well as our openness as a society, would have made us an obvious target,' asserted one columnist. See Gee, 'When It Comes to Osama, Canada Doesn't Get It.' An editorial in the *Globe and Mail* supported this contention, arguing that because Canada stands for a host of values, such as 'an open society, democracy, religious tolerance and respect for diversity,' it was 'inevitable' that the country would become a target. Editorial, *Globe and Mail*, 14 November 2002.

67 Editorial, 'Harper's Ringing Words on the Afghan Mission,' A16.

68 For an excellent study of Canada's 'peacekeeping' missions and their impact on nationhood, see Sherene H. Razack, *Dark Threats and White Knights: The Somalia Affair, Peacekeeping, and the New Imperialism* (Toronto: University of Toronto Press, 2004).

69 Laghi, 'We Won't Run Away, PM Vows.'

70 Shohat and Stam, *Unthinking Eurocentrism*, 102.

71 President's State of the Union Address (29 January 2002).

72 President Bush, quoted in John Stackhouse, 'Afghans Run for Border,' *Globe and Mail*, 17 September 2001, A1. This language has been used by President Bush repeatedly in numerous television interviews and in his public speeches.

73 Hilary Mackenzie et al., 'U.S. Says 12 Hijackers Have Been Identified,' *Vancouver Sun*, 13 September 2001, A1.

74 R.W. Apple Jr., 'Home Front: Edgy Sunday,' *The New York Times*, 8 October 2001, A1.

75 Attributed to President Bush and reported in John Ibbitson, 'Prepared to

Attack Taliban, U.S. Says,' *Globe and Mail*, 17 September 2001, A4.

76 In one instance at least, President Bush's use of such language was credited to a Canadian author. The use of the term 'axis of evil' to describe the 'enemy' in the war on terrorism was apparently introduced into a presidential speech by a Canadian speechwriter employed by the White House, David Frum.

77 D. Leblanc and S. Richer, 'He's Armoured, But He's Not thick,' *Globe and Mail*, 30 July 2005, F1, F6.

78 Shohat and Stam, *Unthinking Eurocentrism*, 19.

79 Stewart Bell, 'Embrace Canadian Values or Leave, Fraser Institute Tells Immigrants,' *CanWest News Service*, 1 March 2006.

80 Ibid.

81 Mamdani, *Good Muslim, Bad Muslim*, 15.

82 Dua, 'The Hindu Woman Question.'

83 Narayan, *Dislocating Cultures*.

84 The Liberal Muslim senator who defended racial profiling was reported as having been the target of such profiling herself. See J. Aubry, 'I Understand Racial Profiling, Muslim Senator Says,' *Vancouver Sun*, 3 November 2001, A1.

85 Francis, *The Imaginary Indian*.

86 Agamben. *Homo Sacer*, 15. While racial profiling has being used by the police to target Black people in the United States since the launching of the War on Drugs in the 1980s, the practice was still largely considered to be illegal. The suspension of international law can also be witnessed with the United States (and its allies) bypassing the United Nations in the war on Iraq.

87 Ibid., 17–18.

88 John Ibbitson, 'Why Racial Profiling Is a Good Idea,' *Globe and Mail*, 3 June 2002, A15. See also S. Choudhry, 'Protecting Equality in the Face of Terror: Ethnic and Racial Profiling and S. 15 of the Charter,' in R.J. Daniels, P. Macklem, and K. Roach, eds., *The Security of Freedom: Essays on Canada's Anti-Terrorism Bill* (Toronto: University of Toronto Press, 2002), 367–82.

89 As a number of commentators have argued, the colonization of Aboriginal peoples and the enslavement of Black peoples are major underpinnings of the development of liberal-democracy in North America. See for example, Zinn, *A People's History of the United States*; and Wright, *Stolen Continents*.

90 Choudhry, 'Protecting Equality in the Face of Terror.'

91 The United States adopted an entry–exit registration system aimed at travellers with origins in thirty-five Muslim and Middle-Eastern countries. See John Ibbitson, 'U.S. Plans to Step Up Scrutiny of Visitors,' *Globe and Mail*, 6 June 2002, A1, A15. Although the new system targeted only those individuals 'whose background warrants suspicion' for photographing and finger

printing, by explicitly including all individuals from these thirty-five countries it cast suspicion on all these individuals. The mere fact that individuals came from a Muslim society made them potential threats to the national security of the United States. Included in such profiling were individuals whose national origins were not Canadian, even if their citizenship was.

92 The Department of Justice and the Secretary of Homeland Security were reported as planning to introduce a program called the Terrorism Information and Protection System (TIPS) in ten American cities in August 2002, and that they would recruit millions of 'American' workers to report suspicious activities. See John Ibbitson, 'U.S. Monitoring Plan Sparks Rights Fears,' *Globe and Mail*, 18 July 2002, A11. Discussed extensively in the media, this plan has since been placed on hold.

93 See Riad Saloojee, 'Why We Must Say No to Profiling,' *Globe and Mail*, 10 June 2002, A15.

94 M. Jimenez, 'Minister Targets Bogus Refugees,' *Globe and Mail*, 11 November 2004, A1.

95 Colin Freeze, 'Mistry Cancels U.S. Tour over Racial Profiling,' *Globe and Mail*, 2 November 2002, A1.

96 Choudhry, 'Protecting Equality in the Face of Terror,' 368.

97 Guidelines were issued to immigration officials in late September identifying particular groups for increased scrutiny. New Canadian and U.S. 'Integrated Cross-Border Enforcement Teams' were also set up. See Allison Dunfield, 'Canada, U.S. Beef Up Border Security Teams,' *Globe and Mail*, 23 July 2002, A4.

98 Aubry, 'I Understand Racial Profiling, Muslim Senator Says,' A1.

99 The public advocacy of racial profiling was certainly not unanimously defended among Canadian elites. A number of prominent Liberal politicians and media commentators voiced strong opposition to racial profiling, calling upon a multiculturalist sentiment in doing so. 'Canadians, regardless of their background, regardless of their religion, regardless of their colour, should be treated equally in this country and, as far as I am concerned anywhere in the world,' stated Ontario's Attorney General in opposing the measure. Ontario's Public Safety minister, however, had a different opinion in favour of the practice, 'I am not critical of the United States in this regard, and I think they recognize their vulnerabilities and are trying to address them.' CBC News Online, 'Islamic Group Slams U.S. Border Regulations' (1 November 2002), retrieved 5 November 2003 from http://ottawa.cbc.ca/template/servlet/view?filename=eckerosco0201030.

100 The U.S. Office of Homeland Security uses a 'colour-coded domestic security system' to issue warnings to alert Americans. For a fuller discussion of

this system, see John Ibbitson, 'New Colour-Coded System Puts Americans on Yellow Alert,' *Globe and Mail,* 13 March 2002, A5. Indeed, in the U.S., some patriots have even been reported to seek training from 'anti-terrorist tutors' in order to better prepare themselves for the task. M. Certenig, 'Patriot Games,' *Globe and Mail,* 13 April 2002, F1.

101 See Freeze, 'Canada Tarred Again as Haven for Terrorists.' See also Editorial, 'Canada Must Stop Being a Terrorist's Haven: Our Immigration Laws Are in Urgent Need of Reform,' *Vancouver Sun,* 14 April 2001; and David Bly, 'Canada "Second to U.S. for Terrorist Infiltration,"' *Vancouver Sun,* 27 May 2002, A5.

102 Rick Mofina, 'Canada's Asylum System "the Weakest Link," for U.S. Security,' *Vancouver Sun,* 21 August 2002, A6. The case of Ahmed Ressam, who sought entry into the United States from Canada during the millennium celebrations allegedly to plant a bomb at Los Angeles airport, had already generated intense speculation about whether Canada's immigration policies contributed to the vulnerability of the United States to terrorist attacks. The Ressam incident contributed much to extending the scale of the alleged 'terrorist' threat to the Canadian nation, so that it came to be seen as emanating not only from those who were outside the country's geographical borders and who might seek to enter the country but also from immigrants *already* in the country.

103 Dr M. Hatem, 'Democracy in Times of War' (paper presented at the Afghanistan and Beyond: Women's Activism in Times of War Conference, Five College Women's Studies Research Center, Mt. Holyoke, CT, 7–8 May, 2002).

104 G. Agamben, 'No to Bio-Political Tattooing,' *Le Monde,* 13 January 2004.

105 KOMO Staff and News Services, 'Here's A Twist: Canada Issues Travel Advisory Against U.S.,' 30 October 2002. See also 'TV Host Calls Canada a "Soviet Canukistan,"' *Globe and Mail,* 1 November 2002, A1, A6.

106 Michelle Shephard, 'Man Suing Ottawa for Jailing in Egypt,' *Toronto Star,* 13 February 2006, A1.

107 Ibid.

108 Jeff Sallot, 'RCMP Chief Muzzled, Friends Say,' *Globe and Mail,* 25 September 2006, A1, A4.

109 Jeff Sallot, "'Mr. Arar, I Wish to Take This Opportunity to Express Publicly to You, to Your Wife and to Your Children How Truly Sorry I Am," RCMP Commissioner Giullano Zaccardelli, Testifying before the House National Security Committee Yesterday,' *Globe and Mail,* 29 September 2006, A1, A4.

110 See Editorial, 'Arar and the Liberals,' *National Post,* 30 September 2006, A16; Editorial, 'How Zaccardeli Failed RCMP, Arar and Canada,' *Globe and Mail,* 29 September 2006, A12.

111 A. Woods, 'Charges Dropped against Indian National Suspected as Terrorist,' *Vancouver Sun*, 26 September 2003, A5. In a report in the *Globe and Mail*, journalist Marina Jimenez reported that being arrested as a suspected terrorist led to 'humiliation and social and professional disaster' for a young Pakistani doctor. The doctor lost his prospective bride after her family heard about the charges made against him. He also feared being deported from Canada, where he came to study for a Canadian medical degree. Marina Jimenez, 'All My Dreams Have Been Disturbed,' *Globe and Mail*, 15 September 2003, A1, A8.

Appendix

1 HRDC, The Green Paper, 5, 11.
2 Echoing the SSR texts, the economic framework stressed the partnership between the nation and state: 'a national dialogue lies ahead,' reiterating the state's commitment to working with Canadians. The state had 'made a commitment to Canadians to permanently open up the budget process' (Finance, *A New Framework for Economic Policy*, 1).
3 Pulkingham and Ternowetsky, *Remaking Canadian Social Policy*, 13.
4 Although The Green Paper was tabled in Parliament on 5 October 1994, the Liberal government had announced its intention to undertake a thorough restructuring of social security in the Speech from the Throne of 18 January 1994. See Jennissen, 'The Federal Social Security Review ...'; Pulkingham and Ternowetsky, *Remaking Canadian Social Policy*. Between October 1994 and January 1995, eight supplementary papers were released to provide more information on the specific issues to be covered by the SSR. These were: *Persons With Disabilities: A Supplementary Paper; From Unemployment Insurance to Employment Insurance: A Supplementary Paper; Income Security for Children: A Supplementary Paper; Child Care and Development: A Supplementary Paper; Reforming the Canada Assistance Plan: A Supplementary Paper; Employment Development Services: A Supplementary Paper; The Context of Reform: A Supplementary Paper;* and *Federal Support to Post-Secondary Education: A Supplementary Paper.* See Jennissen, 'The Federal Social Security Review ...'
5 Therese Jennissen has documented the various stages of the Social Security Review. See ibid.; Pulkingham and Ternowetsky, *Remaking Canadian Social Policy*; Battle and Torjman, 'Desperately Seeking Substance.'
6 Two texts by Finance, *A New Framework for Economic Policy* and *Creating a Healthy Fiscal Climate*, outlined this framework.
7 HRDC, The Green Paper, 82.
8 A number of non-governmental organizations and associations also orga-

nized consultations with their constituencies. The National Action Committee on the Status of Women organized a national consultation of women's organizations, and met with members of the Parliamentary Standing Committee on HRDC and the ministers of HRDC and finance to present their recommendations. Over eighty women's organizations sent representatives to this conference. Likewise, the Seventh Conference on Social Welfare Policy, representing 'academe, the public sector, First Nations, social workers, community groups and the voluntary sector,' was organized as an 'alternative venue to the 'official' consultation process' (Pulkingham and Ternowetsky, *Remaking Canadian Social Policy* 14). This conference solicited policy recommendations from participants to address the existing inequalities in social programs, and its organizers sought to feed these proposals into the Review process. The presentations and proposals made during the Seventh Conference on Social Welfare Policy are published in Pulkingham and Ternowetsky. The public consultations resulted in approximately 1,400 submissions from organizations and individuals. Two hundred Members of Parliament organized town-hall meetings within their constituencies and 25,000 individual workbooks were submitted. See Pulkingham and Ternowetsky (ibid., 3–4).

 9 HRDC, *Agenda: Discussion Paper Summary.*
10 The first topic, working, included programs such as Unemployment Insurance, job training programs, employment services and childcare. The second, 'learning', referred to education programs such as the Canada Student Loans and transfers to provinces for education. And the third, security, referred specifically to social assistance programs.
11 The Immigration Act 1976–77 stipulated the following: 'The Minister, after consultation with the provinces concerning regional demographic needs and labour market considerations and after consultation with such other persons, organizations and institutions as he deems appropriate, shall cause to be laid before Parliament, not later than the sixtieth day before the commencement of each calendar year or, if Parliament is not then sitting, not later than the fifteenth day next thereafter that either House of Parliament is sitting, a report specifying the number of immigrants that the Government of Canada deems it appropriate to admit during any specified period of time; and the manner in which demographic considerations have been taken into account in determining that number' (c. 52, s.7). This report is presented every year and is known as the Annual Plan.
12 The Consultation was organized to be the most extensive since The Green Paper on Canadian Immigration and Population Study of 1975, which had led to the creation of the Immigration Act of 1976–77.
13 CIC, *Canada 2005: Background Document,* 1. The consultation document

stated: 'As the world changes in very significant and complex ways, the challenges facing the effective management of Canada's immigration program are considerable. Thus, it was recognized that the effective management of the immigration program can only be achieved within the context of a long-term purpose and strategy. It was also recognized that there is tremendous public interest in immigration issues, and that Canadians need and want to participate in making the choices and decisions that impact their communities and their country.'

14 CIC, *Immigration Consultations Report*, 1–2.

15 Ibid., 2. The ten issues were supposedly identified at a meeting organized by the Public Policy Forum, which drew participants from the three levels of government, from 'international and social organizations, business, labour, academic institutions, and media representatives,' and from 'public safety and service agencies.' The minister and senior bureaucrats from the Department of Citizenship and Immigration were present at this meeting. No immigrants' rights organizations were recorded as having participated in this meeting. See CIC, *Canadian 2005: Background Document*, 2.

16 These groups were assigned issues #2 to #9 for consideration. Issue #6 was assigned to two groups: Working Group #6A was to address the integration of immigration policy with labour market policies; and Working Group # 6B was to address the integration of immigration policies with other public policies such as housing, policing, health, education, and municipal affairs. The working groups were each to decide upon their own structure and process, meeting between two to three times over a period of six weeks.

17 A kit was made available that included basic information on the immigration program, the ten issues for discussion, an organizer's guide to host meetings, a tabloid version of the discussion document, and a reporting form. A total of 13,000 kits were distributed, as were another 130,000 copies of the tabloid.

18 Public meetings were organized in Montreal, Halifax, Toronto, Vancouver, Winnipeg, Edmonton, and Hamilton between June and August 1994. The minister was present at four of these meetings and his parliamentary secretary participated in the other three.

19 A non-profit organization, the Democracy Education Network, organized study circles in six cities, with over 1,100 participants. Additionally, the minister met with several organizations, including the Canadian Council of Refugees, the Canadian Ethnocultural Council, the Canadian Bar Association, and the Canadian Association of Chiefs of Police, among others.

Bibliography

Books/Periodicals

Abdo, Nahla. '"Gender" is not a "Dummy": Research Methods in Immigration and Refugee Studies.' In R. Ng, ed., *Gendering Immigration: Integration Policy Research Workshop Proceedings and a Selective Review of Policy Research Literature 1987–1996*, 41–50. Ottawa: Status of Women Canada, 1998.

Abu-Laban, Yasmeen. 'Keeping 'em Out: Gender, Race and Class Biases in Canadian Immigration Policy.' In Joan Anderson, Avigail Eisenberg, Sherrill Grace, and Veronica Strong-Boag, eds., *Painting the Maple: Essays on Race, Gender, and the Construction of Canada*, 69–82. Vancouver: University of British Columbia Press, 1998.

Adamoski, Robert. 'The Child – the Citizen – the Nation: The Rhetoric and Experience of Wardship in Early Twentieth-Century British Columbia.' In R. Adamoksi, D.E. Chunn, and R. Menzies, eds., *Contesting Canadian Citizenship: Historical Readings*, 315–35. Peterborough, ON: Broadview Press, 2002.

Adamoski, R., D.E. Chunn, and R. Menzies, eds. *Contesting Canadian Citizenship: Historical Readings*. Peterborough, ON: Broadview Press, 2002.

Adhopia, Ajit. *The Hindus of Canada*. New Delhi: Inderlekh Publications, 1993.

Adilman, Tamara. 'A Preliminary Sketch of Chinese Women and Work in British Columbia 1858–1950.' In Barbara K. Latham and Roberta J. Pazdro, eds., *Not Just Pin Money: Selected Essays on the History of Women's Work in British Columbia*, 53–78. Victoria: Camosun College, 1984.

Agamben, Giorgio. *Homo Sacer: Sovereign Power and Bare Life*. Translated by Daniel Heller-Roazen. Stanford: Stanford University Press, 1997.

Ahmad, Waqar I., and Charles Husband. 'Religious Identity, Citizenship, and Welfare: The Case of Muslims in Britain.' *The American Journal of Islamic Social Sciences* 10, no. 2 (1993): 217–33.

Ahmed, Leila. *Women and Gender in Islam: Historical Roots of a Modern Debate.* New Haven: Yale University Press, 1992.

Ahmed, Sara. *Strange Encounters: Embodied Others in Post-Coloniality.* London: Routledge, 2000.

Amos, Valerie, and Pratibha Parmar. 'Challenging Imperial Feminism.' *Feminist Review,* no. 17 (1984): 3–20.

Anderson, Benedict. *Imagined Communities.* London: Verso, 1991.

Anderson, Claud. *Black Labor, White Wealth: The Search for Power and Economic Justice.* Edgewood, MD: Duncan and Duncan, 1994.

Anghie, Anthony. 'Francisco de Vitoria and the Colonial Origins of International Law.' In E. Darian-Smith and P. Fitzpatrick, eds., *Laws of the Post Colonial,* 89–107. Ann Arbor: The University of Michigan Press, 1999.

Appadurai, A. *Modernity at Large: Cultural Dimensions of Globalization.* Minneapolis: University of Minnesota Press, 1996.

Arat-Koc, Sedef. 'Immigration Policies, Migrant Domestic Workers and the Definition of Citizenship in Canada.' In Vic Satzewich, ed., *Deconstructing a Nation: Immigration, Multiculturalism and Racism in '90s Canada,* 229–42. Halifax: Fernwood, 1992.

Arnup, Katherine. 'Education for Motherhood: Creating Modern Mothers and Model Citizens.' In R. Adamoski, D. Chunn, and R. Menzies, eds., *Contesting Canadian Citizenship: Historical Readings,* 247–71. Peterborough, ON: Broadview Press, 2002.

Axworthy, Lloyd. *Navigating a New World: Canada's Global Future.* Toronto: Alfred A. Knopf, 2003.

Backhouse, Constance. *Colour-Coded: A Legal History of Racism in Canada, 1900–1950.* Toronto: University of Toronto Press, 1999.

Bagdikian, Ben. *The New Media Monopoly.* Boston: Beacon Press, 2004.

Baines, C., P. Evans, and S. Neysmith, eds. *Women's Caring: Feminist Perspectives on Social Welfare.* Toronto: McClelland and Stewart, 1991.

Bakan, Abigail. 'The International Market for Female Labour and Individual Deskilling: West Indian Women Workers in Toronto.' *Canadian Journal of Latin American and Caribbean Studies* 12, no. 24 (1987): 69–85.

Balibar, Etienne, and Immanuel Wallerstein. *Race, Nation, Class: Ambiguous Identities.* London: Verso, 1991.

Bannerji, Himani. *The Dark Side of the Nation: Essays on Multiculturalism, Nationalism and Gender.* Toronto: Women's Press, 2000.

– *Thinking Through: Essays on Feminism, Marxism, and Anti-Racism.* Toronto: Women's Press, 1995.

– ed. *Returning the Gaze: Essays on Racism, Feminism and Politics.* Toronto: Sister Vision Press, 1993.

Barbee, E., and Little, M. 'Health, Social Class and African-American Women.'
In S. James et al., eds., *Theorizing Black Feminisms: The Visionary Pragmatism of
Black Women*, 182–99. London: Routledge, 1994.

Barker, Martin. *The New Racism*. London: Junction Books, 1981.

Barlow, Maude, and Bruce Campbell. *Straight through the Heart*. Toronto: Harper-
Collins, 1993.

Barman, Jèan. 'Taming Aboriginal Sexuality: Gender, Power, and Race in British
Columbia, 1850–1900.' *BC Studies: The British Columbian Quarterly*. Special
Issue, Numbers 115/116 (Autumn/Winter 1997/98): 237–66.

Barroso, Carmen, and Cristina Bruschini. 'Building Politics from Personal Lives:
Discussions on Sexuality among Poor Women in Brazil.' In Chandra Mohanty,
Ann Russo, and Lourdes Torres, eds., *Third World Women and the Politics of Fem-
inism*, 153–72. Bloomington: Indiana University Press, 1991.

Basran, G.S. 'Indo-Canadian Families: Historical Constraints and Contemporary Contradictions.' *Journal of Comparative Family Studies* 24, no. 3 (1993):
339–51.

Bashevkin, Sylvia. *Welfare Hot Buttons: Women, Work, and Social Policy Reform*. Toronto: University of Toronto Press, 2002.

Bateman, R. 'Comparative Thoughts on the Politics of Aboriginal Assimilation.'
BC Studies: The British Columbian Quarterly, no. 114 (Summer 1997): 59–83.

Battle, Ken, and Sheri Torjman. 'Desperately Seeking Substance: A Commentary
on the Social Security Review.' In Jane Pulkingham and Gordon Ternowetsky,
eds., *Remaking Canadian Social Policy*, 52–66. Halifax: Fernwood, 1996.

Behdad, Ali. 'Eroticism, Colonialism and Violence.' In Hent de Vries and S.
Weber, eds., *Voilence, Identity, and Self-Determination*. Stanford: Stanford University Press, 1997.

Bellah, R.N. 'The Ritual Roots of Society and Culture.' In M. Dillon, ed., *Handbook of the Sociology of Religion*, 31–44. Cambridge: Cambridge University Press,
2003.

Benhabib, Seyla. *The Rights of Others: Aliens, Residents and Citizens*. Cambridge:
Cambridge University Press, 2004.

Benjamin, Walter. *Selected Writings*. Vol. 1, *1913–1926*. Edited by M. Bullock and
M. Jennings. Cambridge, MA: Harvard University Press, 1996.

– *Selected Writings*. Vol. 4, *1938–1940*. Edited by Howard Eiland and Michael W.
Jennings. Cambridge, MA: Harvard University Press, 2003.

Bernasconi, R., and S. Cook, eds. *Race and Racism in Continental Philosophy*.
Bloomington: Indiana University Press, 2003.

Bhabha, Homi. *The Location of Culture*. London: Routledge, 1994.

Bolaria, B. Singh. 'From Immigrant Settlers to Migrant Transients: Foreign Professionals in Canada.' In Vic Satzewich, ed., *Deconstructing a Nation: Immigra-*

tion, Multiculturalism and Racism in '90s Canada, 211–28. Halifax: Fernwood, 1992.

Bolaria, B. Singh, and Peter S. Li. *Racial Oppression in Canada*. Toronto: Garamond Press, 1985.

Bottomore, Tom. 'Citizenship and Social Class, Forty Years On.' In T.H. Marshall and Tom Bottomore, *Citizenship and Social Class*, 55–93. London: Pluto Press, 1992.

Bottomore, T. et al. *A Dictionary of Marxist Thought*. Cambridge, MA: Harvard University Press, 1983.

Boyd, Monica. 'Foreign-Born, Female, Old and Poor.' *Canadian Woman Studies* 12, no. 4 (1992): 50–2.

– *Gender, Visible Minority and Immigrant Earnings Inequality: Reassessing an Employment Equity Premise*. Ottawa: Carleton University Press, 1991.

– 'Immigration and Income Security Policies in Canada: Implications for Elderly Immigrant Women.' *Population Research and Policy Review* 8, no. 1 (1989): 5–24.

– *Migrant Women in Canada: Profiles and Policies*. Ottawa: Employment and Immigration Canada, 1987.

Brah, A. *Cartographies of Diaspora: Contesting Identities*. London: Routledge, 1996.

Brodie, Janine. 'Three Stories of Canadian Citizenship.' In R. Adamoski, D. Chunn, and R. Menzies, eds., *Contesting Canadian Citizenship: Historical Readings*, 43–65. Peterborough, ON: Broadview Press, 2002.

– 'Canadian Women, Changing State Forms, and Public Policy.' In Janine Brodie, ed., *Women and Canadian Public Policy*, 1–30. Toronto: Harcourt Brace, 1996.

– *Politics on the Margins*. Halifax: Fernwood, 1995.

Buchignani, Norman, and Doreen Indra, with Ram Srivastava. *Continuous Journey*. Toronto: McClelland and Stewart, 1985.

Calliste, Agnes. 'Race, Gender and Canadian Immigration Policy: Blacks from the Caribbean, 1900–1932.' In Joy Parr and Mark Rosenfeld, eds., *Gender and History in Canada*, 70–87. Toronto: Copp Clark, 1996.

Calliste, Agnes, and George Dei, eds. *Anti-Racist Feminism: Critical Race and Gender Studies*. Halifax: Fernwood, 2000.

Cannadine, David. *Ornamentalism: How the British Saw Their Empire*. Oxford: Oxford University Press, 2001.

Cardozo, A., and M. Louis, eds. *The Battle over Multiculturalism: Does It Help or Hinder Canadian Unity?* Vol. 1. Ottawa: Pearson Shonoma Institute, 1997.

Carrothers, W.A. *Emigration from the British Isles*. London: P.S. King and Son, 1929.

Carter, Sarah. 'Categories and Terrains of Exclusion: Constructing the "Indian Woman" in the Early Settlement Era in Western Canada.' In Joy Parr and Mark Rosenfeld, eds., *Gender and History in Canada*, 30–49. Toronto: Copp Clark, 1996.

Carty, Linda, and Dionne Brand. '"Visible Minority Women": A Creation of the Canadian State.' In Himani Bannerji, ed., *Returning the Gaze: Essays on Racism, Feminism and Politics*, 207–22. Toronto: Sister Vision Press, 1993.

Carty, R.K., and P. Ward. 'The Making of a Canadian Political Citizenship.' In R.K. Carty and P. Ward, eds., *National Politics and Community in Canada*, 65–79. Vancouver: University of British Columbia Press, 1986.

Chatterjee, Partha. *The Partha Chatterjee Omnibus*. New Delhi: Oxford University Press, 1999.

– *The Nation and Its Fragments: Colonial and Postcolonial Histories*. New Delhi: Oxford University Press, 1995.

Chinese Canadian National Council (CCNC). *Jin Guo: Voices of Chinese Canadian Women*. Toronto: The Women's Book Committee, CCNC, 1992.

Choudhry, S. 'Protecting Equality in the Face of Terror: Ethnic and Racial Profiling and S. 15 of the Charter.' R.J. Daniels, P. Macklem, and K. Roach, eds., *The Security of Freedom: Essays on Canada's Anti-Terrorism Bill*, 367–82. Toronto: University of Toronto Press, 2002.

Chrisjohn, Ronald, and Sherri Young, with Michael Maraun. *The Circle Game: Shadows and Substance in the Indian Residential School Experience in Canada*. Penticton, BC: Theytus Books, 1997.

Chua, A. *World on Fire: How Exploring Free Market Democracy Breeds Ethnic Hatred and Global Instability*. New York: Anchor Books, 2004.

Churchill, Ward. *Kill the Indian, Save the Man: The Genocidal Impact of American Indian Residential Schools*. San Francisco: City Light Books, 2004.

– *Fantasies of the Master Race*. San Francisco: City Light Books, 1998.

– *A Little Matter of Genocide: Holocaust and Denial in the Americas 1492 to the Present*. San Francisco: City Light Books, 1997.

Clarke, John, Allan Cochrane, and Carol Smart. *Ideologies of Welfare: From Dreams to Disillusion*. London: Routledge, 1992.

Cohen, Marjorie. *Women and Economic Structures*. Ottawa: The Canadian Centre for Policy Alternatives, 1991.

– 'The Razor's Edge: Feminism's Effect on Economics.' *International Journal of Women's Studies* 8, no. 3 (1985): 286–98.

Correa, Sonia. *Population and Reproductive Rights: Feminist Perspectives from the South*. London: Zed Books, 1994.

Cowan, Helen I. *British Immigration before Confederation*. Ottawa: The Canadian Historical Association, 1968.

368   Bibliography

Culhane, Dara. *The Pleasure of the Crown: Anthropology, Law and First Nations.* Burnaby, BC: Talonbooks, 1998.

Daniels, R.J., P. Macklem, and K. Roach, eds. *The Security of Freedom: Essays on Canada's Anti-Terrorism Bill.* Toronto: University of Toronto Press, 2002.

Das Gupta, Tania. 'Families of Native People, Immigrants, and People of Colour.' In B. Crow and L. Gotell, eds., *Open Boundaries: A Canadian Women's Studies Reader,* 199–216. Toronto: Prentice Hall, 2005.

– 'The Politics of Multiculturalism: 'Immigrant Women' and the Canadian State.' In Enakshi Dua and Angela Robertson, eds., *Scratching the Surface: Canadian Anti-Racist Feminist Thought,* 187–206. Toronto: Women's Press, 1999.

– *Racism and Paid Work.* Toronto: Garamond Press, 1996.

– 'Families of Native Peoples, Immigrants, and People of Colour.' In Nancy Mandell and Anne Duffy, eds., *Canadian Families: Diversity, Conflict and Change,* 141–74. Toronto: Harcourt Brace, 1995.

Davies, Megan. '"Services Rendered, Rearing Children for the State": Mothers' Pensions in British Columbia 1919–1931.' In Barbara K. Latham and Roberta J. Pazdro, eds., *Not Just Pin Money: Selected Essays on the History of Women's Work in British Columbia,* 249–64. Victoria: Camosun College, 1984.

Davis, Angela. *Women, Race and Class.* New York: Vintage Books, 1983.

Davis, Morris, and Joseph F. Krauter. *The Other Canadians: Profiles of Six Minorities.* Toronto: Metheun, 1971.

Day, Shelagh, and Gwen Brodsky. *Women and the Equality Deficit: The Impact of Restructuring Canada's Social Programs.* Ottawa: Status of Women Canada, 1998.

Demirjian, Annie, Douglas Gray, and David Wright. *The 1947 Canadian Citizenship Act: Issues and Significance.* Prepared for Citizenship and Immigration Canada. Ottawa: Consulting and Audit Canada, 1996.

DeVoretz, Don J. 'New Issues, New Evidence, and New Immigration Policies for the Twenty-First Century.' In Don J. DeVoretz, ed., *Diminishing Returns: The Economics of Canada's Recent Immigration Policy,* 1–30. Ottawa: C.D. Howe Institute, 1995.

Dobash, R. Emerson, and Russell Dobash, eds. *Rethinking Violence against Women.* Thousand Oaks, CA: Sage, 1998.

Doman, Mahinder Kaur. 'A Note on Asian Indian Women in British Columbia 1900–1935.' In Barbara K. Latham and Roberta J. Pazdro, eds., *Not Just Pin Money: Selected Essays on the History of Women's Work in British Columbia,* 99–104. Victoria: Camosun College, 1984.

Donald, James, and Ali Rattansi, eds. *'Race,' Culture and Difference.* London: Sage and Open University Press, 1992.

Dua, Enakshi. '"The Hindu Woman's Question": Canadian Nation Building and the Social Construction of Gender for South-Asian Canadian Women.' In

Agnes Calliste and George Dei, eds., *Anti-Racist Feminism*, 55–72. Halifax: Fernwood, 2000.

– 'Beyond Diversity: Exploring the Ways in which the Discourse of Race Has Shaped the Institution of the Nuclear Family.' In Enakshi Dua and Angela Robertson, eds., *Scratching the Surface: Canadian Anti-Racist Feminist Thought*, 237–59. Toronto: Women's Press, 1999.

Dua, Enakshi, and Angela Robertson, eds. *Scratching the Surface: Canadian Anti-Racist Feminist Thought*. Toronto: Women's Press, 1999.

Du Bois, W.E.B. *The World and Africa: An Inquiry into the Part which Africa Has Played in World History*. New York: International Publishers, 1965.

– *The Souls of Black Folk*. New York: Signet Classics, 1969.

Dyck, Noel. *What Is the Indian 'Problem': Tutelage and Resistance in Canadian Indian Administration*. St John's, NL: Institute of Social and Economic Research, 1991.

Eley, G., and R.G. Suny, eds. *Becoming National: A Reader*. New York: Oxford University Press, 1996.

Esses, V., and R.C. Gardiner. 'Multiculturalism in Canada: Context and Current Status.' Special Issue: Ethnic Relations in a Multicultural Society. *Canadian Journal of Behavioural Science* 28 (1996). Retrieved 3 March 2004 from www.cpa.ca/cjbsnew/1996/vol28-3.html.

Estable, Alma. *Immigrant Women in Canada – Current Issues*. Ottawa: The Canadian Advisory Council on the Status of Women, 1986.

Evans, M., and Wekerle, G.R., eds. *Women and the Welfare State: Challenges and Change*. Toronto: University of Toronto Press, 1997.

Fanon, Frantz. *Black Skin, White Masks*. London: Pluto Press, 1986.

– *A Dying Colonialism*. New York: Grove Press, 1965.

– *The Wretched of the Earth*. New York: Grove Press, 1963.

Faubion, J.D., ed. *Michel Foucault: Power*. New York: New Press, 1994.

Finkel, Alvin. 'The Origins of the Welfare State in Canada.' In Leo Panitch, ed., *The Canadian State: Political Economy and Political Power*, 433–70. Toronto: University of Toronto Press, 1977.

Fiske, Jo-Anne. 'The Womb Is to the Nation as the Heart Is to the Body: Ethnopolitical Discourses of the Canadian Indigenous Women's Movement.' *Studies in Political Economy* 51 (Fall 1996): 65–96.

– 'Political Status of Native Indian Women: Contradictory Implications of Canadian State Policy.' *American Indian Culture and Research Journal* 19, no. 2 (1995): 1–30.

Fitzpatrick, Peter, ed. *Nationalism, Racism and the Rule of Law*. Aldershot, UK: Dartmouth Publishing, 1995.

Foucault, Michel. *The History of Sexuality: Introduction*. Vol. 1. New York: Vintage, 1990.

Fournier, Suzanne, and David Crey. *Stolen from Our Embrace: The Abduction of First Nations Children and the Restoration of Aboriginal Communities.* Vancouver: Douglas and McIntyre, 1997.

Francis, Daniel. *The Imaginary Indian: The Image of the Indian in Canadian Culture.* Vancouver: Arsenal Pulp Press, 1992.

Fraser, Nancy. *Unruly Practices.* Minneapolis: University of Minnesota Press, 1989.

Fraser, Nancy, and Linda Gordon. 'Contract versus Charity.' *Socialist Review* 22, no. 3 (1992): 45–65.

Frideres, James S. *Native People in Canada: Contemporary Conflicts.* Scarborough, ON: Prentice-Hall, 1983.

Galeano, Eduardo. *Open Veins of Latin America: Five Centuries of the Pillage of a Continent.* New York: Monthly Review Press, 1973.

Geller, Gloria, and Jan Joel. 'Struggling for Citizenship in the Global Economy: Bond Raters Versus Women and Children.' In Jane Pulkingham and Gordon Ternowetsky, eds., *Remaking Canadian Social Policy,* 303–16. Halifax: Fernwood, 1996.

George, Usha. 'Toward Anti-Racism in Social Work in the Canadian Context.' In Agnes Calliste and George Dei, eds., *Anti-Racist Feminism: Critical Race and Gender Studies,* 111–22. Halifax: Fernwood, 2000.

Gibson, N. 'Losing Sight of the Real.' In R. Bernasconi and S. Cook, eds., *Race and Racism in Continental Philosophy,* 129–50. Bloomington: Indiana University Press, 2003.

Gilroy, Paul. *The Black Atlantic: Modernity and Double Consciousness.* Cambridge, MA: Harvard University Press, 1993.

– *There Ain't No Black in the Union Jack.* Chicago: University of Chicago Press, 1991.

Ginsburg, Norman. *Divisions of Welfare: A Critical Introduction to Comparative Social Policy.* London: Sage, 1992.

Goldberg, David Theo. *The Racial State.* Malden, MA: Blackwell, 2002.

Goodleaf, Donna K. '"Under Military Occupation": Indigenous Women, State Violence and Community Resistance.' In Linda Carty, ed., *And Still We Rise: Feminist Political Mobilizing in Contemporary Canada,* 225–42. Toronto: Women's Press, 1993.

Gordon, Lewis P., T. Denean Sharpley-Whiting, and Renee T. White, eds. *Fanon: A Critical Reader.* Cambridge, MA: Blackwell Publishers, 1996.

Gordon, Linda. *Pitied But Not Entitled: Single Mothers and the History of Welfare.* Cambridge, MA: Harvard University Press, 1994.

Gordon, Paul. *Policing Immigration: Britain's Internal Controls.* London: Pluto Press, 1985.

Green, Alan G., and Green, David A. 'The Economic Goals of Canada's Immigration Policy, Past and Present.' Paper Presented at the British Columbia Centre for Excellence on Immigration, Vancouver, 1997.

Green, Joyce A. 'Towards a Détente with History: Confronting Canada's Colonial Legacy.' *International Journal of Canadian Studies* 12 (Fall 1995): 85–105.

Hackett, Robert et al. *The Missing News: Filters and Blind Spots in Canada's Press.* Ottawa: Canadian Centre for Policy Alternatives, and Toronto: Garamond Press, 2000.

Hackett, Robert, and Yuezhi Zhao. *Sustaining Democracy? Journalism and the Politics of Objectivity.* Toronto: Garamond Press, 1998.

Hage, Ghassan. *White Nation: Fantasies of White Supremacy in a Multicultural Society.* London: Routledge, 2000.

Hall, Stuart. 'Who Needs Identity?' In S. Hall and P. du Gay, eds., *Questions of Cultural Identity*, 1–17. London: Sage, 1996.

– 'The West and the Rest: Discourse and Power.' In Stuart Hall et al., eds., *Modernity: An Introduction to Modern Societies*, 184–228. Oxford: Blackwell Publishers, 1996.

Harding, Jennifer, and E. Deidre Pribham. 'Losing Our Cool? Following Williams and Grossberg on Emotions.' *Cultural Studies* 18, no. 6 (2004): 863–83.

Hardt, Michael, and Negri, Antonio. *Empire.* Cambridge, MA: Harvard University Press, 2000.

Harris, Cole. *Making Native Space: Colonialism, Resistance, and Reserves in British Columbia.* Vancouver: University of British Columbia Press, 2002.

Hartmann, Heidi. 'The Unhappy Marriage of Marxism and Feminism: Towards a More Progressive Union.' In Lydia Sargent, ed., *Women and Revolution*, 1–42. Montreal: Black Rose Books, 1981.

Hatem, Mervat. 'Democracies in Times of War.' Paper presented at the Afghanistan and Beyond: Women's Activism in Times of War Conference, Five College Women's Studies Research Center, Mt. Holyoke, CT, 7–8 May 2002.

Hawkins, Freda. *Critical Years in Immigration: Canada and Australia Compared.* Montreal: McGill-Queen's University Press, 1989.

Hayter, Teresa. *Open Borders: The Case against Immigration Controls.* London: Pluto Press, 2000.

Herman, Edward S., and Noam Chomsky. *Manufacturing Consent: The Political Economy of the Mass Media.* New York: Pantheon, 1988.

Hess, Melanie. 'Major Directions and Proposals for Reform from the Federal Government: A Listing.' In Jane Pulkingham and Gordon Ternowetsky, eds., *Remaking Canadian Social Policy*, 33–50. Halifax: Fernwood, 1996.

Hester, Marianne, Liz Kelly, and Jill Radford. *Women, Violence, and Male Power: Feminist Activism, Research, and Practice.* Philadelphia: Open University Press, 1996.

Hill Collins, Patricia. 'It's All in the Family: Intersections of Gender, Race, and Nation.' In Uma Narayan and Sandra Harding, eds., *Decentering the Center: Philosophy for a Multicultural, Postcolonial and Feminist World*, 156–76. Bloomington: Indiana University Press, 2000.

– *Black Feminist Thought: Knowledge, Consciousness and the Politics of Empowerment.* New York: Routledge, 1991.

hooks, bell. *Talking Back: Thinking Feminist, Thinking Black.* Toronto: Between the Lines, 1988.

– *Yearning: Race, Gender, and Cultural Politics.* Boston: South End Press, 1990.

– *Ain't I a Woman.* Boston: South End Press, 1981.

Huntington, Samuel P. 'The Clash of Civilizations?' *Foreign Affairs* 72, no. 3 (Summer 1993): 22–49.

Huttenback, Robert A. *Racism and Empire: White Settlers and Colored Immigrants in the British Self-Governing Colonies 1830–1910.* Ithaca, NY: Cornell University Press, 1976.

Hymer, Stephen Herbert. *The Multinational Corporation: A Radical Approach.* Cambridge: Press Syndicate of the University of Cambridge, 1979.

Iacovetta, Franca. 'Making "New Canadians": Social Workers, Women, and the Reshaping of Immigrant Families.' In Franca Iacovetta and Marianna Valverde, eds., *Gender Conflicts: New Essays in Women's History*, 261–303. Toronto: University of Toronto Press, 1992.

Iacovetta, Franca, and Marianna Valverde, eds. *Gender Conflicts: New Essays in Women's History.* Toronto: University of Toronto Press, 1992.

India Mahila Association. *Spousal Abuse: Experiences of 15 Canadian South Asian Women.* Vancouver: IMA and Feminist Research Education Development and Action, 1994.

Ismael, T.Y., and Measor, J. 'Racism and the North American Media Following 11 September: The Canadian Setting.' *Arab Studies Quarterly* 25, nos. 1/2 (Winter/Spring 2003): 101–37.

Jakubowski, Lisa Marie. *Immigration and the Legalization of Racism.* Halifax: Fernwood, 1997.

Jennissen, Therese. 'The Federal Social Security Review, Process and Related Events (December 1993–June1995): A Chronology.' In Jane Pulkingham and Gordon Ternowetsky, eds., *Remaking Canadian Social Policy*, 30–2. Halifax: Fernwood, 1996.

Jesuit Refugee Service (JRS). 'Racism and Xenophobia against Refugees and Immigrants in Canada.' Occasional Paper No.1. Toronto: JRS, 1995.

Jiwani, Yasmin. 'On the Outskirts of Empire: Race and Gender in Canadian TV News.' In Sherrill E. Grace et al., eds, *Painting the Maple: Essays on Race, Gender and the Construction of Canada*, 53–68. Vancouver: University of British Columbia Press, 1998.

Johnson, Andrew, Stephen McBride, and Patrick Smith, eds. *Continuities and Discontinuities: The Political Economy of Social Welfare and Labour Market Policies in Canada.* Toronto: University of Toronto Press, 1994.

Kalbach, Warren E. 'A Demographic Overview of Racial and Ethnic Groups in Canada.' In Peter Li, ed., *Race and Ethnic Relations in Canada*, 18–47. Toronto: Oxford University Press, 1990.

Karim, Karim H. *Islamic Peril: Media and Global Violence.* Montreal: Black Rose Books, 2000.

Khosla, Punam. *Review of the Situation of Women Canada, 1993.* Toronto: The National Action Committee on the Status of Women, 1993.

Kilian, Crawford. *Go Do Something Beautiful: The Black Pioneers of British Columbia.* Vancouver: Douglas and McIntyre, 1978.

Kline, Marlee. 'Complicating the Ideology of Motherhood: Child Welfare Law and First Nation Women.' In B. Crow and L. Gotell, eds., *Open Boundaries: A Canadian Women's Studies Reader*, 189–99. Toronto: Prentice Hall, 2005.

Klug, Francesca. '"Oh to be in England": The British Case Study.' In Nira Yuval-Davis and Floya Anthias, eds., *Women-Nation-State*, 16–35. New York: St. Martin's Press, 1989.

Kratochwil, Friedrich. 'Citizenship: On the Border of Order.' *Alternatives* 19 (1994): 485–506.

Kunin, Roslyn, Robert Trempe, and Susan Davis. *Not Just Numbers: A Canadian Framework for Future Immigration.* Ottawa: Minister of Public Works and Government Services Canada, 1997.

Kymlicka, Will, and Wayne Norman. 'Return of the Citizen: A Survey of Recent Work on Citizenship Theory.' *Ethics* 104 (January 1994): 352–81.

Law, Ian. *Racism, Ethnicity and Social Policy.* London: Prentice Hall, 1996.

Lawrence, Bonita. *'Real' Indians and Others: Mixed Blood Urban Native Peoples and Indigenous Nationhood.* Vancouver: UBC Press, 2004.

– 'Rewriting Histories of the Land: Colonization and Indigenous Resistance in Eastern Canada.' In Sherene H. Razack, ed., *Race, Space, and the Law: Unmapping a White Settler Society*, 21–46. Toronto: Between the Lines, 2002.

Lewis, G. *'Race,' Gender, Social Welfare: Encounters in a Postcolonial Society.* Oxford: Polity Press, 2000.

Lewis, Jane. 'The Working-Class Wife and Mother and State Intervention, 1870–1918.' In Jane Lewis, ed., *Labour and Love: Women's Experience of Home and Family, 1850–1940*, 99–122. Oxford: Basil Blackwell, 1986.

Li, Peter. *The Chinese in Canada.* Toronto: Oxford University Press, 1998.
– 'The Economics of Brain Drain: Recruitment of Skilled Labour to Canada, 1954–1986.' In Vic Satzewich, ed., *Deconstructing a Nation: Immigra-tion, Multiculturalism and Racism in '90s Canada,* 145–62. Halifax: Fernwood, 1992.
– ed. *Race and Ethnic Relations in Canada.* Toronto: Oxford University Press, 1991.
Lieberman, Robert, C. 'Race and Limits of Solidarity.' In Sanford F. Schram, Joe Soss, and Richard C. Fording, eds., *Race and the Politics of Welfare Reform,* 23–46. Ann Arbor: University of Michigan Press, 2003.
Lister, Ruth. 'Dilemmas in Engendering Citizenship.' *Economy and Society* 24, no. 1 (1995): 1–40.
– 'Tracing the Contours of Women's Citizenship.' *Policy and Politics* 21, no. 1 (1993): 3–16.
– 'Citizenship Engendered.' *Critical Social Policy* 11, no. 2(32) (1991): 65–71.
Lorde, Audre. (1984) *Sister Outsider: Essays and Speeches by Audre Lorde.* Trumansburg, NY: The Crossing Press, 1984.
Lowe, L. *Immigrant Acts: On Asian American Cultural Politics.* Durham, NC: Duke University Press, 1998.
Lui-Gurr, Susanna. 'The British Columbia Experience with Immigrants and Welfare Dependency, 1989.' In Don J. DeVoretz, ed., *Diminishing Returns: The Economics of Canada's Recent Immigration Policy,* 128–65. Ottawa: C.D. Howe Institute, 1995.
MacDonald, Martha. 'What is Feminist Economics?' *Beyond Law* 5, no. 14 (1996): 11–36.
Mackey, Eva. *The House of Difference: Cultural Politics and National Identity in Canada.* Toronto: University of Toronto Press, 2002.
Mama, Amina. *The Hidden Struggle: Statutory and Voluntary Sector Responses to Violence against Black Women in the Home.* London: London Race and Housing Research Unit, 1989.
– 'Black Women, the Economic Crises and the British State.' *Feminist Review,* no. 17 (1984): 21–36.
Mamdani, Mahmood. *Good Muslim, Bad Muslim: America, the Cold War and the Roots of Terror.* New York: Pantheon Books, 2004.
– 'Good Muslim, Bad Muslim: A Political Perspective on Culture and Terrorism.' In E. Hershberg and K.W. Moore, eds., *Critical Views of September 11: Analyses from Around the World,* 44–60. New York: The New Press, 2002.
– *When Victims Become Killers: Colonialism, Nativism, and the Genocide in Rwanda.* Princeton, NJ: Princeton University Press, 2001.
Mandell, Nancy. 'Women, Families and Intimate Relations.' In Nancy Mandell,

ed., *Feminist Issues: Race, Class, and Sexuality*, 193–218. Toronto: Prentice Hall, 2001.

Mann, Michael. 'Ruling Class Strategies and Citizenship.' *Sociology* 21, no. 3 (1987): 339–54.

Maracle, Lee. 'Racism, Sexism and Patriarchy.' In Himani Bannerji, ed., *Returning the Gaze: Essays on Racism, Feminism and Politics*, 148–58. Toronto: Sister Vision Press, 1993.

Marshall, T.H. 'Citizenship and Social Class.' In T.H. Marshall and Tom Bottomore. *Citizenship and Social Class*, 3–51. London: Pluto Press, 1992.

Marx, Karl. *A Contribution to the Critique of Political Economy*. London: Lawrence and Wishart, 1981.

– 'The Eighteenth Brumaire of Louis Bonaparte.' In Robert C. Tucker, ed., *The Marx-Engels Reader*, 594–617. New York: W.W. Norton, 1978.

– *The Economic and Philosophic Manuscripts of 1844*. Edited by Dirk J. Struik. New York: International Publishers, 1964.

Marx, Karl, and Friedrich Engels. 'The Communist Manifesto.' In Robert C. Tucker, ed., *The Marx-Engels Reader*, 469–500. London: W.W. Norton, 1978.

Mazumdar, Sucheta. 'Colonial Impact and Punjabi Emigration to the United States.' In Lucie Cheng and Edna Bonacich, eds., *Labor Immigration under Capitalism: Asian Workers in the United States before World War II*, 316–36. Berkeley: University of California Press, 1984.

Mbembe, Achille. 'Necropolitics.' *Public Culture: Violence and Redemption* 15, no. 1 (Winter 2003): 11–40.

– *On the Postcolony*. Berkeley: University of California Press, 2001.

McBride, Stephen, and John Shields. *Dismantling a Nation*. Halifax: Fernwood, 1993.

McClintock, Anne. *Imperial Leather*. New York: Routledge, 1995.

McIvor, Sharon. 'A Social Policy Agenda for First Nations Women.' In Frank Tester, Chris McNiven, and Robert Case, eds., *Critical Choices, Turbulent Times*, 100–7. Vancouver: The School of Social Work, University of British Columbia, 1996.

McLaren, Angus. *Our Own Master Race: Eugenics in Canada, 1885–1945*. Toronto: McClelland and Stewart, 1990.

McLaren, Margaret A. *Feminism, Foucault, and Embodied Subjectivity*. Albany: State University of New York Press, 2002.

McQuaig, Linda. *Shooting the Hippo*. Toronto: Penguin, 1995.

– *The Wealthy Banker's Wife: The Assault on Equality in Canada*. Toronto: Penguin, 1993.

Memmi, Albert. *The Colonizer and the Colonized*. Boston: Beacon Press, 1965.

Menzies, R., R. Adamoski, and D. Chunn. 'Rethinking the Citizen in Canadian

Social History.' In R. Adamoski, D. Chunn, and R. Menzies, eds., *Contesting Canadian Citizenship: Historical Readings,* 11–42. Peterborough, ON: Broadview Press, 2002.

Mies, Maria. *Patriarchy and Accumulation on a World Scale.* London: Zed Books, 1986.

Mihn-ha, Trinh T. *Woman Native Other.* Bloomington: Indiana University Press, 1989.

Miki, Roy, and C. Kobayashi. *Justice in Our Time: The Japanese Canadian Redress Settlement.* Vancouver: National Association of Japanese Canadians, 1991.

Miles, Angela, and Geraldine Finn, eds. *Feminism from Pressure to Politics.* Montreal: Black Rose Books, 1989.

Miles, Robert. *Racism after 'Race Relations.'* London: Routledge, 1993.

Mills, C. Wright. *The Sociological Imagination.* London: Oxford University Press, 1959.

Mills, Sara. *Discourse.* London: Routledge, 1997.

Mintzes, B., A. Hardon, and J. Hanhart, eds. *Norplant: Under Her Skin.* Delft, The Netherlands: Eburon, 1993.

Mishra, Ramesh. *The Welfare State in Capitalist Society.* Toronto: Harvester Wheatsheaf, 1990.

– *Society and Social Policy: Theoretical Perspectives on Welfare.* London: Macmillan Press, 1977.

Mitchell, Marjorie, and Anna Franklin. 'When You Don't Know the Language, Listen to the Silence: An Historical Overview of Native Indian Women in BC.' In Barbara K. Latham and Roberta J. Pazdro, eds., *Not Just Pin Money: Selected Essays in the History of Women's Work in British Columbia,* 17–36. Victoria: Camosun College, 1984.

Mitter, Swasti. *Common Bond, Common Fate: Women in the Global Economy.* London: Pluto Press, 1986.

Modood, T. 'Muslims and the Politics of Multiculturalism in Britain.' In E. Hershberg and K.W. Moore, eds., *Critical Views of September 11: Analyses from Around the World,* 193–208. New York: The New Press, 2002.

Mohanty, Chandra T., Ann Russo, and Lourdes Torres, eds. *Third World Women and the Politics of Feminism.* Bloomington: Indiana University Press, 1991.

Mohanty, Chandra T. 'Under Western Eyes: Feminist Scholarship and Colonial Discourses.' In Chandra T. Mohanty, Ann Russo, and Lourdes Torres, eds., *Third World Women and the Politics of Feminism,* 51–80. Bloomington: Indiana University Press, 1991.

Monture-Angus, Patricia. *Thunder in My Soul: A Mohawk Woman Speaks.* Halifax: Fernwood, 1995.

Moreau, Bernice. 'Black Nova Scotian Women's Schooling and Citizenship: An

Education of Violence.' In R. Adamoski, D.E. Chunn, and R. Menzies, eds., *Contesting Canadian Citizenship: Historical Readings*, 293–311. Peterborough, ON: Broadview Press, 2002.

Morton, Stephen. *Gayatri Chakravorty Spivak.* New York: Routledge, 2003.

Moscovitch, Allan, and Glenn Drover, eds. *Inequality: Essays on the Political Economy of Social Welfare.* Toronto: University of Toronto Press, 1981.

Napolean, Val. 'Extinction by Number: Colonialism Made Easy.' *Canadian Journal of Law and Society* 16, no. 1 (2001): 113–45.

Narayan, Uma. 'Contesting Cultures: "Westernization," Respect for Cultures, and Third World Feminists.' In L. Nicholson, ed., *The Second Wave: A Reader in Feminist Theory*, 396–414. New York: Routledge, 1997.

– *Dislocating Cultures: Identities, Traditions, and Third World Feminism.* New York: Routledge, 1997.

Nasir, S. '"Race," Gender and Social Policy.' In C. Hallett, ed., *Women and Social Policy*, 15–30. London: Prentice Hall, 1996.

National Anti-Poverty Organization. *An Action Guide from NAPO: 30 Million Good Reasons to Have National Standards for Welfare.* Ottawa: NAPO, 1995.

Neu, Dean, and Richard Therrien. *Accounting for Genocide: Canada's Bureaucratic Assault on Aboriginal People.* Halifax: Fernwood, 2003.

Ng, Roxana. 'Gendering Policy Research on Immigration.' In Roxana Ng, ed., *Gendering Immigration: Integration Policy Research Workshop Proceedings and a Selective Review of Policy Research Literature 1987–1996*, 13–22. Ottawa: Status of Women Canada, 1998.

– 'Multiculturalism as Ideology: A Textual Analysis.' In Marie Campbell and Ann Manicom, eds., *Knowledge, Experience, and Ruling Relations: Studies in the Social Organization of Knowledge*, 35–48. Toronto: University of Toronto Press, 1995.

– 'Sexism, Racism, Canadian Nationalism.' In Himani Bannerji, ed., *Returning the Gaze: Essays on Racism, Feminism and Politics*, 223–41. Toronto: Sister Vision Press, 1993.

– *The Politics of Community Services.* Toronto: Garamond Press, 1988.

Ng, Roxana, and Janet Strout. *Services for Immigrant Women: Report and Evaluation of a Series of Four Workshops Conducted in the Summer, 1977.* Vancouver: Women's Research Centre, 1977.

Ng, Roxana, and Alma Estable. 'Immigrant Women in the Labour Force: An Overview of Present Knowledge and Research Gaps.' *Resources for Feminist Research* 30 (1987): 29–33.

Ng, Winnie Wun Wun. 'In the Margins: Challenging Racism in the Labour Movement.' MA thesis, University of Toronto, 1995.

Norris, Pippa, Montague Kern, and Marion R. Just, eds. *Framing Terrorism: The News Media, the Government and the Public.* New York: Routledge, 2003.

O'Connor, Julia S. 'Gender, Class and Citizenship in the Comparative Analysis of Welfare State Regimes: Theoretical and Methodological Issues.' *British Journal of Sociology* 44, no. 3 (1993): 501–18.

Okin, Susan Moller. 'Women, Equality, and Citizenship.' *Queen's Quarterly* 99, no. 1 (1992): 57–71.

Omi, Michael, and Howard Winant. *Racial Formation in the United States: From the 1960s to the 1990s.* New York: Routledge, 1994.

Ong, A. *Flexible Citizenship: The Cultural Logics of Transnationality.* Durham, NC: Duke University Press, 1999.

Palmer, Howard, ed. *Immigration and the Rise of Multiculturalism.* Toronto: Copp Clark, 1975.

Panitch, Leo. 'Changing Gears: Democratizing the Welfare State.' In Andrew Johnson, Stephen McBride, and Patrick Smith, eds., *Continuities and Discontinuities: The Political Economy of Social Welfare and Labour Market Policy in Canada,* 36–43. Toronto: University of Toronto Press, 1994.

– 'The Role and Nature of the Canadian State.' In Leo Panitch, *The Canadian State: Political Economy and Political Power,* 3–27. Toronto: University of Toronto Press, 1977.

Parekh, Bhikhu, ed. *Colour, Culture and Consciousness: Immigrant Intellectuals in Britain.* London: George Allen and Unwin, 1974.

Parmer, Prathiba. 'Gender, Race and Class: Asian Women in Resistance.' In Centre for Contemporary Cultural Studies, ed., *The Empire Strikes Back: Race and Racism in 70s Britain,* 236–75. London: Centre for Contemporary Cultural Studies, 1982.

Parr, Joy. 'Gender History and Historical Practice.' In Joy Parr and Mark Rosenfeld, eds., *Gender and History in Canada,* 8–28. Toronto: Copp Clark, 1996.

– 'The Skilled Emigrant and Her Kin: Gender, Culture, and Labour Recruitment.' *Canadian Historical Review* 68, no. 4 (1987): 529–51.

Pateman, Carol. *The Sexual Contract.* Cambridge: Polity Press, 1988.

Peterson, William. 'Canada's Immigration: The Ideological Background.' In Howard Palmer, ed., *Immigration and the Rise of Multiculturalism,* 22–33. Toronto: Copp Clark, 1975.

Pettman, Jan Jindy. 'Border Crossings/Shifting Identities: Minorities, Gender, and the State in International Perspective.' In Michael J. Shapiro and Hayward R. Alker, eds., *Challenging Boundaries: Global Flows, Territorial Identities,* 261–84. Minneapolis: University of Minnesota Press, 1996.

Phizacklea, Annie. 'In the Front Line.' In Annie Phizacklea, ed., *One Way Ticket: Migration and Female Labour,* 95–112. London: Routledge and Kegan Paul, 1983.

Porter, John. *The Vertical Mosaic.* Toronto: University of Toronto Press, 1966.

Potts, Lydia. *The World Labour Market: A History of Migration*. London: Zed Books, 1990.

Poz, J.M. 'Invisible Women, Crossing Borders.' *Chicago Review* 39, nos. 3/4 (1993): 44–9.

Prado, C.G. *Starting with Foucault: An Introduction to Genealogy*. Boulder, CO: Westview Press, 2000.

Praeger, Jeffrey. 'American Political Culture and the Shifting Meaning of Race.' *Ethnic and Racial Studies* 10, no. 1 (1987): 62–81.

– 'White Racial Privilege and Social Change: An Examination of Theories of Racism.' *Berkeley Journal of Sociology* 17 (1972/73): 117–50.

Pulkingham, Jane, and Gordon Ternowetsky, eds. *Remaking Canadian Social Policy*. Halifax: Fernwood, 1996.

Rafiq, Fauzia. *Towards Equal Access: A Handbook for Service Providers*. Ottawa: Immigrant and Visible Minority Women Against Abuse, 1991.

Ralph, Diana. 'How to Beat the Corporate Agenda: Strategies for Social Justice.' In Jane Pulkingham and Gordon Ternowetsky, eds., *Remaking Canadian Social Policy*, 288–302. Halifax: Fernwood, 1996.

Ransby, Barbara. 'US: The Black Poor and the Politics of Expendability.' *Race & Class* 38, no. 2 (1996): 1–12.

Rattansi, Ali, and Sallie Westwood, eds. *Racism, Modernity and Identity on the Western Front*. Cambridge: Polity Press, 1994.

Razack, Sherene H. *Dark Threats and White Knights: The Somalia Affair, Peacekeeping, and the New Imperialism*. Toronto: University of Toronto Press, 2004.

– 'Imperiled Muslim Women, Dangerous Muslim Men and Civilised Europeans: Legal and Social Responses to Forced Marriages.' *Feminist Legal Studies* (2004): 129–74.

– ed., *Race, Space, and the Law: Unmapping a White Settler Society*. Toronto: Between the Lines, 2002.

– *Looking White People in the Eye: Gender, Race, and Culture in Courtrooms and Classrooms*. Toronto: University of Toronto Press, 1998.

Resnick, Phil. 'Neo-Conservatism and Beyond.' In Andrew Johnson, Stephen McBride, and Patrick Smith, eds., *Continuities and Discontinuities: The Political Economy of Social Welfare and Labour Market Policy in Canada*, 25–35. Toronto: University of Toronto Press, 1994.

Retamar, Roberto Fernández. *Caliban and Other Essays*. Minneapolis: University of Minnesota Press, 1989.

Richardson, Boyce. *Peoples of Terra Nullius: Betrayal and Rebirth in Aboriginal Canada*. Vancouver: Douglas and McIntyre, 1993.

Roberts, Barbara. *Whence They Came: Deportation from Canada 1900–1935*. Ottawa: University of Ottawa Press, 1988.

Rodney. Walter. *How Europe Underdeveloped Africa.* London: Bogle-L'Ouverture Publications, 1972.

Roger, Kerstin. "'Making" White Women through the Privatization of Education on Health and Well-Being in the Context of Psychotherapy.' In Agnes Calliste and George Dei, eds., *Anti-Racist Feminism: Critical Race and Gender Studies,* 123–42. Halifax: Fernwood, 2000.

Rose, Eliot Joseph B., et al. *Colour and Citizenship: A Report on British Race Relations.* London: Oxford University Press, 1969.

Royal Commission on the Status of Women (RCSW). *The Status of Women in Canada.* Ottawa: RCSW, 1973.

Said, Edward. *Covering Islam.* New York: Pantheon Books, 1981.

– *Orientalism: Western Conceptions of the Orient.* London: Penguin, 1978.

Sampat-Mehta, Ramdeo. *International Barriers.* Ottawa: Harpell's Press, 1973.

Samuel, T. John. *Family Class Immigrants to Canada, 1981–1984: Labour Force Activity Aspects.* Ottawa: Employment and Immigration Canada, 1986.

Sangari, Kumkum, and Sudesh Vaid, eds. *Recasting Women: Essays in Colonial History.* New Delhi: Kali for Women, 1989.

Sargent, Lydia, ed. *Women and Revolution.* Montreal: Black Rose Books, 1981.

Sassen, Saskia. *Losing Control? Sovereignty in the Age of Globalization.* New York: Columbia University Press, 1996.

– *The Mobility of Labor and Capital: A Study in International Investment and Labor Flow.* New York: Cambridge University Press, 1988.

Satzewich, Vic. 'The Political Economy of Race and Ethnicity.' In Peter Li, ed. *Race and Ethnic Relations in Canada,* 251–68. Toronto: Oxford University Press, 1990.

Sayad, A. *The Suffering of the Immigrant.* Cambridge: Polity Press, 2004.

Schick, Carol. 'Keeping the Ivory Tower White: Discourses of Racial Domination.' In Sherene H. Razack, ed., *Race, Space, and the Law: Unmapping a White Settler Society,* 99–119. Toronto: Between the Lines, 2002.

Scott, Katherine. *Women and the CHST: A Profile of Women Receiving Social Assistance in 1994.* Ottawa: Status of Women Canada, 1998.

Segal, Gary L. *Immigrating to Canada.* Vancouver: International Self-Counsel Press, 1986.

Seward, Shirley B., and Kathryn McDade. *Immigrant Women in Canada: A Policy Perspective.* Ottawa: Canadian Advisory Council on the Status of Women, 1988.

Sharma, Nandita. 'Cheap Myths and Bonded Lives: Freedom and Citizenship in Canadian Society.' *Beyond Law* 6, Issue 17 (1997): 35–62.

Shillington, Richard. 'The Tax System and Social Policy Reform.' In Jane Pulkingham and Gordon Ternowetsky, eds., *Remaking Canadian Social Policy,* 100–111. Halifax: Fernwood, 1996.

Shiva, Vandana. *Biopiracy: The Plunder of Nature and Knowledge.* Toronto: Between the Lines, 1997.

Shohat, E., and R. Stam. *Unthinking Eurocentrism: Multiculturalism and the Media.* London: Routledge, 1994.

Sifton, Clifford. 'Only Farmers Need Apply.' In Howard Palmer, ed., *Immigration and the Rise of Multiculturalism,* 34–8. Toronto: Copp Clark, 1975. Originally published in *Maclean's,* 1 April 1992, 16.

Silvera, Makeda. 'Speaking of Women's Lives and Imperialist Economics: Two Introductions from *Silenced.*' In Himani Bannerji, ed., *Returning the Gaze: Essays on Racism, Feminism and Politics,* 242–69. Toronto: Sister Vision Press, 1993.

Silverstein, Paul A. *Algeria in France: Transpolitics, Race and Nation.* Bloomington: Indiana University Press, 2004.

Sivanandan, A. *Communities of Resistance: Writings on Black Struggles for Socialism.* London: Verso, 1990.

Skeggs, Beverley. *Class, Self and Culture.* London: Routledge, 2004.

Solomos, John, and Les Back. *Racism and Society.* New York: St. Martin's Press, 1996.

Solomos, John, and John Wrench, eds. *Racism and Migration in Western Europe.* Oxford: Berg Publishers, 1993.

SOPEMI. *Trends in International Migration: Continuous Reporting System on Migration.* Annual Report 1994. Paris: Organization for Economic Co-Operation and Development, 1995.

Stafford, James. 'The Impact of the New Immigration Policy on Racism in Canada.' In Vic Satzewich, ed., *Deconstructing a Nation: Immigration, Multiculturalism and Racism in '90s Canada,* 69–92. Halifax: Fernwood, 1992.

Stasiulis, Daiva. 'The Political Economy of Race, Ethnicity and Migration.' In Wallace Clement, ed., *Understanding Canada: Building the New Political Economy,* 141–71. Montreal: McGill-Queen's University Press, 1997.

Stasiulis, Daiva, and Nira Yuval-Davis, eds. *Unsettling Settler Societies: Articulations of Gender, Race, Ethnicity and Class.* London: Sage, 1995.

Stasiulis, Daiva, and Radha Jhappan. 'The Fractious Politics of a Settler Society: Canada.' In Daiva Stasiulis and Nira Yuval-Davis, eds., *Unsettling Settler Societies:* 95–131. London: Sage, 1995.

Stoffman, Daniel. *Who Gets In: What's Wrong with Canada's Immigration Program, and How to Fix it.* Toronto: Macfarlane Walter and Ross, 2002.

Stoler, Laura Ann. *Race and the Education of Desire.* Durham, NC: Duke University Press, 1995.

Stout, M.D., and G.D. Kipling. *Aboriginal Women in Canada: Strategic Research Directions for Policy Development.* Ottawa: Status of Women Canada, 1998.

Strikwerda, Carl, and Camille Guerin-Gonzales, eds. 'Labor, Migration, and Pol-
itics.' In Camille Guerin-Gonzales and Carl Strikwerda, eds., *The Politics of
Immigrant Workers: Labor Activism and Migration in the World Economy Since 1830.*
New York: Holmes and Meier, 1993.
Strong-Boag, Veronica. 'The Citizenship Debates: The 1885 *Franchise Act.*' In R.
Adamoski, D. Chunn, and R. Menzies, eds., *Contesting Canadian Citizenship:
Historical Readings,* 69–94. Peterborough, ON: Broadview Press, 2002.
– '"Setting the Stage": National Organization and the Women's Movement in
the Late Nineteenth Century.' In Susan Mann Trofimenkoff and Alison Pren-
tice, eds., *The Neglected Majority: Essays in Canadian Women's History,* 87–103.
Toronto: McClelland and Stewart, 1977.
Strong-Boag, Veronica, Sherrill Grace, Avigail Ginsberg, and Joan Anderson,
eds. *Painting the Maple: Essays on Race, Gender and the Construction of Canada.*
Vancouver: University of British Columbia Press, 1998.
Swanson, Jean. *Poor-Bashing: The Politics of Exclusion.* Toronto: Between the Lines,
2001.
– 'The Poverty of Progress.' In Frank Tester, Chris McNiven, and Robert Case,
eds., *Critical Choices, Turbulent Times,* 73–82. University of British Columbia:
School of Social Work, 1996.
Swift, Jamie, and Brian Tomlinson, eds. *Canada and the Third World.* Toronto:
Between the Lines, 1991.
Taylor, Charles. 'Modern Social Imaginaries.' *Public Culture* 14, no.1 (Winter
2002): 91–124.
Taylor, D. 'Citizenship and Social Power.' *Critical Social Policy* 9, no. 2, Issue 26
(1989): 19–31.
Taylor, D.M., K.M. Ruggiero, and W.R. Louis. 'Personal/Group Discrimination
Discrepancy: Towards a Two-Factor Explanation.' Special Issue: Ethnic Rela-
tions in a Multicultural Society. *Canadian Journal of Behavioural Science* 28
(1996). Retrieved 3 March 2004 from www.cpa.ca/cjbsnew/1996/
ful_taylor.html.
Thobani, Sunera. 'War Frenzy.' *Atlantis: A Women's Studies Journal* 27 no. 1 (Fall
2002): 5–11.
– 'War Frenzy.' *Meridiens: Feminism, Race, Transnationalism* 2, no. 2 (2002): 289–97.
– 'Racism, Women's Equality and Social Policy Reform.' In Luciana Ricciutelli
et al., eds., *Confronting the Cuts: A Sourcebook for Women in Ontario,* 23–8.
Toronto: Inanna Publications, 1998.
– 'Racism, Women's Equality and Social Policy Reform.' In Frank Tester, Chris
McNiven, and Robert Case, eds., *Critical Choices, Turbulent Times,* 92–100. Uni-
versity of British Columbia, School of Social Work, 1996.
Thornhill, Esmeralda. 'Focus on Black Women!' In Jesse Vorst et al., eds., *Race,*

Class, Gender: Bonds and Barriers, 26–36. Toronto: Between the Lines and Society for Socialist Studies, 1989.

Thornton-Dill, Bonnie. 'The Dialectics of Black Womanhood.' In Sandra Harding, ed., *Feminism and Methodology,* 97–108. Bloomington: Indiana University Press and Open University Press, 1987.

Trofimenkoff, Susan Mann, and Alison Prentice, eds. *The Neglected Majority: Essays in Canadian Women's History,* 7–13. Toronto: McClelland and Stewart, 1977.

Troper, H. 'American Immigration to Canada, 1896–1914.' In Howard Palmer, ed., *Immigration and the Rise of Multiculturalism,* 38–43. Toronto: Copp Clark, 1975.

Turner, Bryan S. 'Outline of a Theory of Citizenship.' *Sociology* 24, no. 2 (1990): 189–217.

– *Citizenship and Capitalism: The Debate over Reformism.* London: Allen and Unwin, 1986.

Ty, Eleanor. *The Politics of the Visible in Asian North American Narratives.* Toronto: University of Toronto Press, 2004.

Ujimoto, K. Victor. 'Multiculturalism and the Global Information Society.' In Vic Satzewich, ed., *Deconstructing a Nation: Immigration, Multiculturalism and Racism in '90s Canada,* 351–8. Halifax: Fernwood, 1985.

Ujimoto, K. Victor, and Gordon Hirayabashi, with P.A. Saram. *Visible Minorities and Multiculturalism: Asians in Canada.* Toronto: Butterworth, 1980.

Ungerleider, Charles. 'Immigration, Multiculturalism, and Citizenship: The Development of the Canadian Social Justice Infrastructure.' *Canadian Ethnic Studies* 24, no. 3 (1992): 7–22.

Ursel, Jane. *Private Lives, Public Policy: 100 Years of State Intervention in the Family.* Toronto: Women's Press, 1992.

Valverde, Marianna. 'When the Mother of the Race Is Free.' In F. Iacovetta and M. Valverde, eds., *Gender Conflicts: New Essays in Women's History,* 3–26. Toronto: University of Toronto Press, 1992.

Van Dieren, Karen. 'The Response of the WMS to the Immigration of Asian Women 1888–1942.' In Barbara K. Latham and Roberta J. Pazdro, eds., *Not Just Pin Money: Selected Essays on the History of Women's Work in British Columbia,* 79–98. Victoria: Camosun College, 1984.

Van Kirk, Sylvia. 'The Impact of White Women on Fur Trade Society.' In S. Trofimenkoff and A. Prentice, eds., *The Neglected Majority: Essays in Canadian Women's History,* 27–48. Toronto: McClelland and Stewart, 1977.

– *'Many Tender Ties': Women in Fur-Trade Society.* Winnipeg: Watson Dwyer, 1980.

Vibert, Elizabeth. 'Real Men Hunt Buffalo: Masculinity, Race and Class in British

Fur Trader's Narratives.' In Joy Parr and Mark Rosenfeld, eds., *Gender and History in Canada*, 50–68. Toronto: Copp Clark, 1996.

Vizenor, Gerald Robert. *Fugitive Poses: Native American Indian Scenes of Absence and Presence*. Lincoln: University of Nebraska Press, 1998.

Vosko, Leah. '*Irregular* Workers: *New* Involuntary Social Exiles: Women and U.I. Reform.' In Jane Pulkingham and Gordon Ternowetsky, eds., *Remaking Canadian Social Policy*, 256–72. Halifax: Fernwood, 1996.

Walcott, Rinaldo. 'Lament for a Nation: The Racial Geography of the "Oh! Canada Project."' *Fuse* 19, no. 4 (1996): 15–23.

Walby, Sylvia. 'Is Citizenship Gendered?' *Sociology* 28, no. 2 (1994): 379–95.

– 'Gender Politics and Social Theory.' *Sociology* 22, no. 2 (1988): 215–32.

Warburton, Rennie. 'Neglected Aspects of the Political Economy of Asian Racialization in British Columbia.' In Vic Satzewich, ed., *Deconstructing a Nation: Immigration, Multiculturalism and Racism in '90s Canada*, 343–50. Halifax: Fernwood, 1992.

Ward, Peter. *White Canada Forever: Popular Attitudes and Public Policy Toward Orientals in British Columbia*. Montreal: McGill-Queen's University Press, 2002.

Weintraub, Sidney, and Stanley R. Ross. *'Temporary' Alien Workers in the United States*. Boulder, CO: Westview Press, 1982.

Williams, Rhonda. 'Race, Deconstruction and the Emergent Agenda of Feminist Economic Theory.' In Marianne A. Ferber and Julie A. Nelson, eds., *Beyond Economic Man: Feminist Theory and Economics*, 144–53. Chicago: University of Chicago Press, 1993.

Wilson, Amrit. *Finding a Voice: Asian Women in Britain*. London: Virago, 1978.

Winant, Howard. *Racial Conditions*. Minneapolis: University of Minnesota Press, 1994.

Wiseman, John. 'National Social Policy in an Age of "Global Power": Lessons from Canada and Australia.' In Jane Pulkingham and Gordon Ternowetsky, eds., *Remaking Canadian Social Policy*, 130–50. Halifax: Fernwood, 1996.

Women, Immigration and Nationality Group (WING). *World's Apart: Women Under Immigration and Nationality Law*. London: Pluto Press, 1985.

Women's Migration and Overseas Appointments Society (WMOAS). *New Horizons: A Hundred Years of Women's Migration*. London: Her Majesty's Stationery Office, 1963.

Wong, Lloyd L., and Nancy S. Netting. 'Business Immigration to Canada: Social Impact and Racism.' In Vic Satzewich, ed., *Deconstructing a Nation: Immigration, Multiculturalism and Racism in '90s Canada*, 93–122. Halifax: Fernwood, 1992.

Wong, R. 'Willows Bend but Don't Break: Review of Dora Nipp's *Under the Willow Tree*.' *Kinesis* (July/August 1997), 21.

Woodsworth, J.S. *Strangers within Our Gates: Or Coming Canadians*. Toronto: University of Toronto Press, 1972.

Wright, Ronald. *Stolen Continents: The 'New World' Through Indian Eyes*. Toronto: Penguin, 1993.

Yalnizyan, Armine. 'The Dismantling of a Nation: Public Perceptions of Debt, Deficit and Social Policy.' In Luciana Ricciutelli et al., eds., *Confronting the Cuts: A Sourcebook for Women in Ontario*, 15–22. Toronto: Inanna Publications, 1998.

Yee, May. 'Finding the Way Home through Issues of Gender, Race and Class.' In Himani Bannerji, ed., *Returning the Gaze: Racism, Feminism and Politics*, 3–44. Toronto: Sister Vision Press, 1993.

Young, Iris Marion. *Justice and the Politics of Difference*. Princeton, NJ: Princeton University Press, 1990.

Young, Robert. *White Mythologies: Writing History and the West*. London: Routledge, 1990.

Zinn, Howard. *A People's History of the United States*. New York: Harper Collins, 1980.

Zlotnik, Hania. 'The South-to-North Migration of Women.' *International Migration Review* 29, no. 1 (1995): 229–54.

– 'Conference Report: International Migration Policies and the Status of Female Migrants.' *International Migration Review* 24, no. 2 (1990): 372–81.

Government Documents

Canadian Citizenship Act, 1947, An Act Respecting Citizenship, Nationality, Naturalization and Status of Aliens. Retrieved 6 February 2000 from www.cic.gc.ca/english/department/legacy/chap-5.html#chap5-2.

Citizenship and Immigration Canada (CIC). *Facts and Figures: Overview of Immigration*. Ottawa: Minister of Supply and Services, 1994.

– *Canada and Immigration: Facts and Issues*. Ottawa: CIC, 1994.

– *Public Meetings: Summaries of Discussions*. Ottawa: CIC, 1994.

– *The Report of Working Group #2: 'What Criteria Should We Set to Achieve Our Social and Economic Objectives in Determining Who Will Come to Canada?'* Ottawa: CIC, 1994.

– *The Report of Working Group #3: 'How Do We Meet Our Humanitarian Obligations Including the 1951 Convention Relating to the Status of Refugees?'* Ottawa: CIC, 1994.

– *The Report of Working Group #4: 'How Do We Achieve a Coherent Strategy within Canada and among Nations to Deal with International Migration Pressures?'* Ottawa: CIC, 1994.

– *The Report of Working Group #5: 'What Are the Key Elements of a Strategy for Integrating Newcomers into Canadian Society?'* Ottawa: CIC, 1994.

- *The Report of Working Group #6A:* '*How Do We Integrate Immigration Policy and Program Delivery within Such Areas as Housing, Health, Education and Training in order to Better Integrate Immigrants into Canada and Improve Overall Effectiveness of Public Programs?*' Ottawa: CIC, 1994.
- *The Report of Working Group #6B:* '*How Do We Integrate Immigration Policy and Program Delivery with Areas such as Housing, Health, Education and Training in order to Better Integrate Immigrants into Canada and Improve Overall Effectiveness of Public and Programs?*' Ottawa: CIC, 1994.
- *The Report of Working Group #7:* '*How Do We Establish a Framework for Enforcement in the Immigration/Refugee Systems that Meets Public Expectations and Respects the Integrity of the Program?*' Ottawa: CIC, 1994.
- *The Report of Working Group #8:* '*How Do We Realize the Benefits of Immigration to Canada in Areas Such as Regional Impact, Workforce Skills, Job Creation and International Competitiveness?*' Ottawa: CIC, 1994.
- *The Report of Working Group #9:* '*How Do We Build More Effective Partnerships with Other Levels of Government in Addressing a Broad Range of Immigration Issues?*' Ottawa: CIC, 1994.
- *The Report of Working Group #10:* '*How Do We Build a Common Data Base on Immigration to Serve Public Policy and Programme Goals?*' Ottawa: CIC, 1994.
- *Report on the National Consultation on Family Class Immigration.* Toronto: Centre for Refugee Studies, and Ottawa: CIC, 1994.
- *Canada 2005: A Strategy for Citizenship and Immigration: Background Document.* Ottawa: CIC, 1994.
- *Canada 2005: A Strategy for Citizenship and Immigration, Conference Proceedings.* Ottawa: CIC, 1994.
- *Immigration Consultations Report.* Ottawa: Minister of Supply and Services Canada, 1994.
- *Statement: Speaking Notes for the Honorable Sergio Marchi, P.C., M.P., Minister of Citizenship and Immigration, Tabling of the Strategy and the Immigration and Citizenship Plan, House of Commons (Nov. 1, 1994).* Ottawa: Government of Canada, 1994.
- News Release. *Minister Marchi Tables Long-term Immigration and Citizenship Strategy, and 1995–2000 Immigration and Citizenship Plan.* Ottawa: CIC, 1994.
- *A Broader Vision: Immigration and Citizenship Plan 1995–2000, Annual Report to Parliament.* Ottawa: Minister of Supply and Services Canada.
- *Into the Twenty-first Century: A Strategy for Immigration and Citizenship.* Ottawa: Minister of Supply and Services Canada, 1994.
- *Employee Consultation Report.* Ottawa: CIC, 1994.
- *Strengthening Family Sponsorship.* Ottawa: Minister of Supply and Services Canada, 1995.

Department of Canadian Heritage. *Annual Report on the Operation of the Canadian Multiculturalism Act, 2003–04.* Ottawa: Department of Canadian Heritage, 2004.

Department of Finance. *Budget Speech.* Ottawa: Finance Canada, 1995.

– *Reforming the Canada Assistance Plan: A Supplementary Paper.* Ottawa: Government of Canada, 1994.

– *A New Framework for Economic Policy: A Presentation by The Honourable Paul Martin, P.C., M.P. (October 17, 1994).* Ottawa: Finance, Government of Canada, 1994.

– *Creating a Healthy Fiscal Climate: A Presentation by The Honourable Paul Martin, P.C., M.P., To the House of Commons Standing Committee on Finance (October 18, 1994).* Ottawa: Finance, Government of Canada, 1994.

Employment and Immigration Canada (EIC). *Canada's Immigration Law: An Overview.* Ottawa: Minister of Supply and Services Canada, 1983.

'Federal Response, The.' Appendix to Hansard, 8 October 1971. Retrieved 22 October 2004 from http://www.canadahistory.com/sections/documents/trudeau_-_on_multiculturalism.htm.

House of Commons. *Canadian Citizenship: A Sense of Belonging.* Ottawa: Report of the Standing Committee on Citizenship and Immigration, June 1994.

Human Resources Development Canada (HRDC). *Agenda: Jobs and Growth: Improving Social Security in Canada, A Discussion Paper* (The Green Paper). Ottawa: Minister of Supply and Services Canada, 1994.

– *Agenda: Jobs and Growth: Improving Social Security in Canada, Discussion Paper Summary.* Ottawa: HRDC, 1994.

Immigration Act, 1976–77. Ottawa: Queen's Printer for Canada, 1977.

Immigration Regulations (1978). Consolidated Regulations of Canada. Ottawa: Queen's Printer for Canada, 1978.

Ministry of Immigration and Colonization. *The Houseworker in Canada: Opportunities for Success, Work and Wages, Where to Go and What to Take.* Ottawa: MIC, 1928.

Newspapers/Media Refrences

Agamben, G. 'No to Bio-Political Tattooing.' *Le Monde,* 13 January 2004.

Adams, James. 'CanWest, Reuters at Odds Over Use of "Terrorist."' *Globe and Mail,* 21 September 2004, A13.

Alberts, Sheldon. 'PM Links Attacks to "Arrogant" West.' *National Post,* 12 September 2002, A1.

Apple Jr., R.W. 'Home Front: Edgy Sunday.' *The New York Times,* 8 October 2001, A1.

Aubry, J. 'I Understand Racial Profiling, Muslim Senator Says.' *Vancouver Sun*, 3 November 2001, A1.

Bell, Stewart. 'Embrace Canadian Values or Leave, Fraser Insitute Tells Immigrants.' *CanWest News Service*, 1 March 2006.

Bly, David. 'Canada "Second to U.S. for Terrorist Infiltration."' *Vancouver Sun*, 27 May 2002, A5.

Boswell, R. 'The Many Lives of Israel Asper.' *Vancouver Sun*, 8 October 2003, A16.

Bronskill, Jim. 'I.D. Proposals Spark Concern.' *Toronto Star*, 6 September 2004, A1.

Canadian Broadcasting Corporation. *CBC News*, 'Smelly Eateries Face Fines in West Vancouver,' 24 November, 2004. Retrieved 5 January 2005 from www.cbc.ca/story/canada/national/2004/11/23/smell-restaurant-041123.

Certenig Miro. 'Patriot Games.' *Globe and Mail*, 13 April 2002, F1.

Chase, Steven. 'Pettigrew Sings Praises of U.S.' *Globe and Mail*, 26 September 2003, A9.

Coyne, A. 'We Are All Americans Now.' *National Post*, 3 October 2001, A7.

Curry, B. 'Natives Make Up 30–40 per cent of Kids in the State's Care.' *Vancouver Sun*, 5 January 2005, A4.

Dunfield, Allison. 'PMO Says Media Misreported Sept. 11 Remarks.' *Globe and Mail*, 12 September 2002.

– 'Canada, U.S. Beef Up Border Security Teams.' *Globe and Mail*, 23 July 2002, A4.

Ford, C. *'Terrorism Makes Our Difference Irrelevant.'* *Vancouver Sun*, 9 September 2001, A8.

Freeman, A. 'Today We Are All Americans – NATO Allies Pledge Support.' *Globe and Mail*, 13 September 2001, A6.

Freeze, Colin. 'Canada Tarred Again as Haven for Terrorists.' *Globe and Mail*, 26 April 2002, A1.

– 'Mistry Cancels U.S. Tour over Racial Profiling.' *Globe and Mail*, 2 November 2002, A1.

Gee, Marcus. 'When It Comes to Osama, Canada Doesn't Get It.' *Globe and Mail*, 15 November 2002, A17.

Hume, M. 'Terrorism High on Police Chief's List of Worries.' *Globe and Mail*, 8 April 2004, A9.

Hume, Stephen. 'Calm in the Heart of Chaos: As Anger Grows in the Wake of Terrorism, Americans Should Temper the Momentum for Revenge.' *Vancouver Sun*, 2 September 2001, A23.

Ibbitson, John. 'Canada's Immigrant Challenge.' *Globe and Mail*, 11 March 2005, A4.

– 'Canada's Vanishing Peoples.' *Globe and Mail*, 21 September 2004, A4.

– 'New Colour-Coded System Puts Americans on Yellow Alert.' *Globe and Mail*, 13 March 2002, A5.
– 'Why Racial Profiling Is a Good Idea.' *Globe and Mail*, 3 June 2002, A15.
– 'U.S. Plans to Step Up Scrutiny of Visitors.' *Globe and Mail*, 6 June 2002, A1, A15.
– 'U.S. Monitoring Plan Sparks Rights Fears.' *Globe and Mail*, 18 July 2002, A11.
– 'Prepared to Attack Taliban, U.S. Says.' *Globe and Mail*, 17 September 2001, A4.
Jimenez, Marina. 'All My Dreams Have Been Disturbed.' *Globe and Mail*, 15 September 2003, A1, A8.
– 'Minister Targets Bogus Refugees.' *Globe and Mail*, 11 November 2004, A1.
Kennedy, Mark. 'Martin Sees Greater Military Cooperation with U.S.' *Vancouver Sun*, 29 April 2003, A12.
Koring, Paul. '9/11/03: He Taunts Us Still.' *Globe and Mail*, 11 September 2003, 1.
Laghi, Brian. 'Harper's Surprise Afghan Visit.' *Globe and Mail*, 13 March 2006, A1, A4.
– 'We Won't Run Away, PM Vows.' *Globe and Mail*, 14 March 2006, A1, A6.
Luba, Frank. 'Report: Keep Immigrants Out of the Big Three Cities.' *The Province*, 24 September 2002, A6.
Mackenzie, Hilary et al. 'U.S. Says 12 Hijackers Have Been Identified.' *Vancouver Sun*, 13 September 2001, A1.
Makin, Kirk. 'Implications Huge for Other Organizations.' *Globe and Mail*, 26 March 2004, A4.
– 'Landmark Claims Rulings Made.' *Globe and Mail*, 19 November 2004, A7.
Maloney, Sean M., Michael A. Hennessy, and Scott Robertson. 'An Attack against Us All.' *National Post*, 12 September 2001, D7.
Mofina, Rick. 'Canada's Asylum System "the Weakest Link," for U.S. Security.' *Vancouver Sun*, 21 August 2002, A6.
Mulroney, Brian. 'A New World Order.' *Globe and Mail*, 21 October 2003, A25.
Naumetz, Tim. 'Senator Would like Canada to honor the U.S. on Sept. 11.' *Vancouver Sun*, 24 September 2003, A3.
Newman, Peter C. 'Terror Already Has Its Sea Legs.' *Globe and Mail*, 11 March 2006, F3.
O'Neil, Peter. 'Vancouver Could See Race Riots: Study Says.' *Vancouver Sun*, 23 September 2002, A1.
Philp, M. 'Teaching a New Generation to Duck and Cover.' *Globe and Mail*, 18 October 2002, A8.
Saloojee, Riad. 'Why We Must Say No to Profiling.' *Globe and Mail*, 10 June 2002, A15.

Shephard, Michelle. 'Man Suing Ottawa for Jailing in Egypt.' *Toronto Star*, 13 February 2006, A1.

Stackhouse, John. 'Afghans Run for Borders.' *Globe and Mail*, 17 September 2001, A1.

Trickey, Mike. 'Canada "Takes Terror Threat Seriously."' *Vancouver Sun*, 14 November 2002, A8.

Wark, Wesley. 'Learning to Live with Terror.' *Globe and Mail*, 15 November 2002, A17.

Wattie, Chris. 'Detailed Training Needed for Attacks.' *National Post*, 14 September 2001, A13.

Wente, M. 'We're All Americans Now.' *Globe and Mail*, 13 September 2001, N3.

Woods, A. 'Charges Dropped against Indian National Suspected as Terrorist.' *Vancouver Sun*, 26 September 2003, A5.

Speeches

Bush, President George W. State of the Union Address. 29 January 2002. Retrieved 2 July 2002 from www.whitehouse.gov/news/releases/2002/01/20020129-11.html.

– Remarks by the President to Business Leaders. 'President Calls on Senate to Act on Terrorism Insurance Legislation,' April 2002. Retrieved 2 July 2002 from www.whitehouse.gov/news/releases/2002/04/20020408-17.html.

King, Mackenzie. 'Text of the Prime Minister's Speech.' *Ottawa Citizen*, 4 January 1947.

Trudeau, Pierre Eliott. Prime Minister Trudeau's Speech to the House of Commons, 8 October 1971. Retrieved 3 February 2004 from www.pch.gc.ca/progs/pubs/Speeches/08osb_e.cfm.

Index

Aboriginal people: access to citizenship, 74, 82, 98–9; access to education, 97, 172–3, 277n85; access to social security, 188; and Canadian national subject, 9; categorization of, 39–40, 50–1, 58–9, 61–2, 119, 267n14; denied outside nationalism, 248; dictatorship of, 25; the economy and, 184; effect of liberalization on, 97; ejected from nation, 249; elements of social welfare by, 110; erasure of, 16–17, 144; family as threat to nation, 118–19; genocide of, 42–3, 268–70nn26–32, 325n24; individual land ownership, 82; land claims of, 53–5; lands as empty, 47, 63; marginalized by multiculturalism, 162; marginalized by settler society, 95–6; in media, 225; in racial hierarchy, 28; racial values imposed on, 127, 312n97; romanticization of, 58–60, 238, 279n99, 280–1nn107–10; under rule of law, 35; self determination, 150; societies of, 47, 50–1, 55, 272nn51–3, 276n76, 278n90, 281n113; sovereignty and, 40, 55–6,

62, 267–8n17; treated as authentic, 14, 261n30; violence against, 151; as wards of Canada, 45, 81; welfare state and, 108–10, 140. *See also* child welfare system; residential schools

Aboriginal women, 275n61; in Aboriginal societies, 273n52; access to citizenship of, 82; colonial stereotypes of, 123; enfranchisement, 287n42; loss of agency, 120; rape of, 42; and residential schools, 121–2, 310n78, 311n80; rights under the Indian Act, 49–51, 58–9, 89, 119, 274–5n59, 275n61, 275n67; as service-deliverers, 127, 312n97. *See also* women

Abu Ghraib, 245

Adamoski, Robert, 312n98

adoption, 51, 82, 109, 124, 311n72, 311n82

affirmative action, 180–1

Afghanistan, war on, 355n66; as Canada's, 234; Canadian troops in, 219–21, 348n6; explanations for, 231; in media, 349n14; racializing the enemy, 235; as rescuing

gender: in defining good and bad
Muslims, 237; division of labour,
115, 117, 191, 305n34; equality,
118; in immigration, 134–6; in
issue of overpopulation, 199; racialized roles under multiculturalism,
167–8; in Social Security Review,
337n46; in view of history, 228;
within welfare state, 106–8, 300n6
Geneva Convention on the Status of
Refugees, 283n5
George, Usha, 139
Gilroy, Paul, 158, 164
Ginsburg, Norman, 319–20n132
Girls Friendly Society, 306n40
Gitskan-West'suwet'en, 63
globalism: and Age of Empire, 220;
citizenship and, 3, 70; cultural capital of professionals, 162, 328n49;
democracy, 227–8; intellectual
property rights in, 287n39; media
and governance, 222–4; multiculturalism in, 153–4, 325–6nn28–9;
'our competitors,' 337n41; threat
to Canada from, 188–9; and U.S.
sovereignty, 220–1
Globe and Mail, 217, 219, 225, 232,
264n49, 351n28, 359n111
Goldberg, David T., 24, 75, 91,
265n55
Gordon, Linda, 106, 110, 118, 128,
140, 301n9
government, use of term, 23–4. See
also Liberal government
Gradual Civilization Act (1857),
287n41
Gradual Enfranchisement Act
(1867), 48
Gramsci, 23
Great Depression, 111, 146

Green, Joyce, 274n58
Green Paper, The (HRDC), 105, 253–
5, 335n28
Grotius, Hugo, 271n40
Group of Seven, 60, 280n108
Gruneau, R., 223
Guantanamo Bay, 245
gurdwaras, 314n115

Hackett, Robert, 223
Hage, Ghassan, 26, 153–4, 169,
330n67, 331n77
Hall, Stuart, 227
Hamas, 235
Hardt, Michael, 220
Harper, Stephen, 219, 232, 354–5n62
Harris, Cole, 56–8
Hawkins, Freda, 86–7, 146–7, 332n8,
335n28, 339n73
head taxes, 90, 92, 294nn85–6,
295n88, 295n92, 313n107,
314n109, 314–15n115
health care of immigrants, 341n94
Hegel, 5, 12, 15, 227, 262n33
hegemony, 23
Henry VII, 42
Hezbollah, 235
hierarchies, racial, 162–3. See also rac-
ism
hijab, 170. See also clothing of Muslim
women
Hill Collins, Patricia, 113, 301n9
Hobbes, Thomas, 279n99, 282n115
Hollinger Inc., 224
House of Commons Public Safety
Committee, 245
housing, 79, 314–15n115
Hudson Bay Company, 278n93
Human Resources Development Canada (HRDC), 105, 253–5

human rights and rights of a state, 68–9
Huntington, Samuel, 230
Husband, Charles, 101

Iacovetta, Franca, 133, 312n102
Ibbitson, John, 67
identity: of Aboriginal people, 124; Canada's racial, 75; citizenship as racialized, 100; created by law, 61; cultural, 323n10; development of Canadian political, 88–90; immigrants as threat to national, 194–5; multiculturalism and, 153, 162, 323n8; national, 20–1, 24–5, 279–80nn103–5; national as bilingual and bicultural, 145; national crisis of, 181; in new global climate, 169; racialized national, 24, 93, 101, 266n57; redefinition of national, 144; social security and national, 187–8; values as part of, 193–4, 338n54; of women in caring professions, 126–7
ideological state apparatus, 23
ideology: of community, 324n21; of free trade, 182; of immigration class system, 135, 137, 185–6; of Immigration Policy Review, 186–7, 210; in law over Aboriginal people, 48; of motherhood, 310n74; of multiculturalism, 145–6; social evolution, 281n113; of social security review, 188, 210; of welfare state, 300n3
imagined communities, 222–3, 302n13
immigrant communities: funding of settlement services, 203–8; response to multiculturalism, 161–2; welfare systems, 132–3

immigrants, 25; as always foreign, 136, 190; Canada's need for, 183; and Canadian national subject, 9; categorization of, 90–1, 158, 263n36, 316–17nn122–5; as citizens, 88; effect of liberalization on, 152–3; effect of welfare state on, 109–10; government management of, 332n8; knowledge of immigration system, 196; limits to tolerance of, 171–2; marginalized by war on terror, 251–2; national encounters with, 22–3; in national imaginary, 4, 6; as the new racists, 155; non-European, 14–15, 261n31; population levels of, 199; post-9/11, 236, 247; in public opinion, 22–3, 26–7, 264n49; qualified inclusion of, 15–16; racialization of, 72–3; racialized category of, 76–7, 97, 147–8, 201; recruitment of, 200, 286n31, 298–9n105, 324n12 (*see also* nation building); referred to as 'newcomers,' 327n38; as scapegoats, 181–3; seen as connected to tradition, 163–4; as strangers, 258n6; use of social services, 207–8, 211–12. *See also* immigrant women
immigrant women: as blamed for overpopulation, 199–200, 340n79; as dependents, 109, 130–4, 139, 316–21nn123–35; employment for, 136–7; from Japan, 295n95; nationality of, 313–14nn108–9; in nation-building project, 84–5, 92, 116–18, 289–90nn51–3, 303n19, 306–7nn38–40; South Asian, 329n57; statistics on, 314n113; as threat to national interests, 117. *See also* women